Essential Writings of

Meredith G. Kline

BOOKS BY MEREDITH G. KLINE

Treaty of the Great King: The Covenant Structure of Deuteronomy, Studies and Commentary

By Oath Consigned: A Reinterpretation of the Covenant Signs of Circumcision and Baptism

The Structure of Biblical Authority

Images of the Spirit

Kingdom Prologue: Genesis Foundations for a Covenantal Worldview

Glory in Our Midst: A Biblical-Theological Reading of Zechariah's Night Visions

God, Heaven and Har Magedon: A Covenantal Tale of Cosmos and Telos

Genesis: A New Commentary

Essential Writings of
Meredith G. Kline

HENDRICKSON
PUBLISHERS

Essential Writings of Meredith G. Kline

P. O. Box 3473
Peabody, Massachusetts 01961-3473
www.hendrickson.com

ISBN 978-1-61970-853-2

Printed in the United States of America

First Printing—August 2017

Cover texture ©iStock.com/Baretsky.
Jacket and case cover design by Karol Bailey.

Library of Congress Cataloging-in-Publication Data

A catalog record for this title is available from the Library of Congress
Hendrickson Publishers Marketing, LLC ISBN 978-1-61970-853-2

Contents

Part Four: Redemption

Part Five: Resurrection and Consummation

Foreword

When I learned that Hendrickson Publishers planned on publishing a collection of essays by my former professor Meredith G. Kline, I could not have been happier. Professor Kline has had and continues to have a tremendous influence on many biblical scholars, theologians, and church leaders, but the republication of these seminal studies will spread his work even further with a new generation of readers.

I, of course, read most of these articles when they first appeared, but reading them again reminded me just how much Professor Kline's thinking shaped my own approach to the biblical text. At the time I was an MDiv student at Westminster Theological Seminary (1974–1977), he was traveling down to teach occasional intensive courses from Boston, where he was professor at Gordon-Conwell Theological Seminary. I was privileged to take two such courses from him, but his thinking also reached me and my fellow students through our regular professors, including especially Raymond Dillard.

Professor Kline impressed upon us the importance of studying the Old Testament in its ancient Near Eastern context. Perhaps most significantly, he was among the first to draw out the importance of the connection between biblical covenant, so important particularly to the Reformed church community he was a part of, and ancient Hittite treaties (in the present collection, see in particular "The Two Tables of the Covenant"). Such study deepened and sharpened our understanding of biblical covenants. It also impressed on many in the next generation of his students how important it is to read the Old Testament, borrowing a phrase from John Walton, in its original "cognitive environment."

Perhaps most importantly, Professor Kline impressed upon us the need to explore the interconnections between biblical texts and to use our exegetical imaginations to see the organic unity of Scripture. On occasion he could be criticized for reading too much into a biblical passage or metaphor based on other passages, but he encouraged us to go beyond a kind of arid historical-grammatical exegesis and to take into account the resonances of a biblical text within the canon. In a way, he anticipated the interest in intertextuality and canonical criticism that many of us find so helpful today.

Professor Kline's work on the opening two chapters of Genesis has also been of major import for the study of these texts, which has once again grown intense among evangelical Protestants in the aftermath of the sequencing of the human genome. His studies going back to the late '50s (see in this volume "Because It Had Not Rained") and beyond ("Space and Time in the Genesis Cosmogony") demonstrated to many of us how wrong-minded it was to take these chapters as a straightforward depiction of how God created creation.

Professor Kline wrote during a time when evangelical Old Testament scholarship was at a low. Evangelical scholars were more marginalized than they are now. Fewer evangelicals had doctorates and wrote studies derived from their academic research than at the present. Meredith Kline was a beacon of light in that rather dark period. His work encouraged the students of the next generation, including myself, who were part of a kind of evangelical renaissance in church and academy, to follow in his footsteps. Having been produced predominantly in this period of marginalization, Professor Kline's writings deserve a broader reading beyond the Reformed and evangelical audience that will continue to benefit from his work. With great pleasure, I invite you to read these incredibly stimulating and important studies that take us from the creation to the consummation.

Tremper Longman III, PhD
Robert H. Gundry Professor of Biblical Studies, Westmont College

Acknowledgments

Original Publication Information

"Oracular Origin of the State" was originally published as pp. 132–41 in *Biblical and Near Eastern Studies: Essays in Honor of William Sanford LaSor*, ed. G. A. Tuttle (Grand Rapids: Eerdmans, 1978). Reprinted by permission of the publisher; all rights reserved.

"Death, Leviathan, and the Martyrs: Isaiah 24:1–27:1" was originally published as pp. 229–49 in *A Tribute to Gleason Archer*, ed. Walter C. Kaiser Jr. and Ronald R. Youngblood (Chicago: Moody Press, 1986). Reprinted by permission of the publisher.

"Trial by Ordeal" was originally published as pp. 81–93 in *Through Christ's Word: A Festschrift for Dr. Philip E. Hughes*, ed. W. Robert Godfrey and Jesse L. Boyd III (Phillipsburg, NJ: P&R, 1985). Used with permission from P&R Publishing Co., P. O. Box 817, Phillipsburg, NJ 08865. www.prpbooks.com.

"Space and Time in the Genesis Cosmogony" was originally published in *Perspectives on Science and the Christian Faith* 48.1 (Mar. 1996): 2–15. Used by permission. http://network.asa3.org/?page=PSCF.

The following articles are used by permission of Wipf and Stock Publishers. www.wipfandstock.com.

> "The Two Tables of the Covenant." Pp. 113–30 in Meredith G. Kline, *The Structure of Biblical Authority* (Eugene, OR: Wipf & Stock, 1997). Originally published in *WTJ* 22 (1960): 133–46. (The original page numbers for this article, which are set off in double brackets in the present book, are the page numbers from *The Structure of Biblical Authority*.)

> "The Old Testament Origins of the Gospel Genre." Pp. 172–203 in Meredith G. Kline, *The Structure of Biblical Authority* (Eugene, OR: Wipf &

Stock, 1997). Originally published in *WTJ* 38 (1975): 1–27. (The original page numbers for this article, which are set off in double brackets in the present book, are the page numbers from *The Structure of Biblical Authority*.)

"The Rider of the Red Horse." Pp. 1–30 in Meredith G. Kline, *Glory in Our Midst: A Biblical-Theological Reading of Zechariah's Night Visions* (Eugene, OR: Wipf & Stock, 2001). Originally published in two parts in *Kerux* 5.2 (Sept. 1990): 2–20 and *Kerux* 5.3 (Dec. 1990): 9–28. (The original page numbers for this article, which are set off in double brackets in the present book, are the page numbers from *Glory in Our Midst*.)

The following articles were originally published in the *Journal of the Evangelical Theological Society* and are reprinted here by permission:

"*Lex Talionis* and the Human Fetus." *JETS* 20 (1977): 193–201.

"Double Trouble." *JETS* 32 (1989): 171–79.

"The Feast of Cover-over." *JETS* 37 (1994): 497–510.

"Har Magedon: The End of the Millennium." *JETS* 39 (1996): 207–22.

The following articles were originally published in *The Westminster Theological Journal*, which retains the copyrights, and are reprinted here by permission:

"Because It Had Not Rained." *WTJ* 20 (1958): 146–57.

"Divine Kingship and Genesis 6:1–4." *WTJ* 24 (1962): 187–204.

"Abram's Amen." *WTJ* 31 (1968): 1–11.

"The First Resurrection." *WTJ* 37 (1975): 366–75.

"The First Resurrection: A Reaffirmation." *WTJ* 39 (1976): 110–19.

Bible Translations

The articles that are included in this book were produced over the span of four decades, from 1957 to 1996, and (as indicated above) they originally appeared in a variety of journals and books. For these reasons, the articles employ a number of different Bible translations, only some of which are explicitly marked. In many cases the author used either the KJV or produced his own translations, but he also sometimes quoted the following translations (occasionally, though not usually, marking them): AV, ASV, RSV, NIV.

Verse Numbers

In biblical citations, when an English (or, in the case of a Septuagint reference, a Greek) verse number differs from the Hebrew verse number, the former is listed first, then the latter (in brackets).

Indexes

The publisher gratefully acknowledges the generous work of John Muether of Reformed Theological Seminary in compiling the indexes for this volume.

Abbreviations

General

1QH	Hodayot (Thanksgiving Hymns)
ASV	American Standard Version
AV	Authorized Version
cf.	see (by way of comparison)
ch(s).	chapter(s)
e.g.	for example
esp.	especially
ff.	and the following verses/pages
ibid.	the same
i.e.	that is
in loc.	in the place (cited)
KJV	King James Version
LXX	Septuagint
n.	note
NIV	New International Version
obv.	obverse
rev.	reverse, revised
RSV	Revised Standard Version
sec.	section
sing.	singular
v(v).	verse(s)

Journals, Series, and Reference Works

AB	Anchor Bible
ANET	*Ancient Near Eastern Texts Relating to the Old Testament.* Edited by James B. Pritchard. 3rd ed. Princeton: Princeton University Press, 1969

AnOr	Analecta Orientalia
ARM	Archives royales de Mari
BA	*Biblical Archaeologist*
BAR	*Biblical Archaeology Review*
BASOR	*Bulletin of the American Schools of Oriental Research*
BibOr	Biblica et Orientalia
CBQ	*Catholic Biblical Quarterly*
CT	*Christianity Today*
EA	El-Amarna tablets. According to the edition of Jørgen A. Knudtzon. *Die el-Amarna-Tafeln*. Leipzig: Hinrichs, 1908–1915. Repr., Aalen: Zeller, 1964
GKC	*Gesenius' Hebrew Grammar*. Edited by Emil Kautzsch. Translated by Arthur E. Cowley. 2nd ed. Oxford: Clarendon, 1910
HTR	*Harvard Theological Review*
HUCA	*Hebrew Union College Annual*
IB	*Interpreter's Bible*. Edited by George A. Buttrick et al. 12 vols. New York, 1951–1957
Int	*Interpretation*
JANESCU	*Journal of the Ancient Near Eastern Society of Columbia University*
JBL	*Journal of Biblical Literature*
JCS	*Journal of Cuneiform Studies*
JETS	*Journal of the Evangelical Theological Society*
JJS	*Journal of Jewish Studies*
JNES	*Journal of Near Eastern Studies*
JTS	*Journal of Theological Studies*
KAI	*Kanaanäische und aramäische Inschriften*. Herbert Donner and Wolfgang Röllig. 2nd ed. Wiesbaden: Harrassowitz, 1966–1969
NIGTC	New International Greek Testament Commentary
OtSt	*Oudtestamentische Studiën*
PRR	*Presbyterian and Reformed Review*
RB	*Revue biblique*
ResQ	*Restoration Quarterly*
SHR	Studies in the History of Religions
TDNT	*Theological Dictionary of the New Testament*. Edited by Gerhard Kittel and Gerhard Friedrich. Translated by Geoffrey W. Bromiley. 10 vols. Grand Rapids: Eerdmans, 1964–1976

TDOT	*Theological Dictionary of the Old Testament.* Edited by G. Johannes Botterweck and Helmer Ringgren. Translated by John T. Willis et al. 8 vols. Grand Rapids: Eerdmans, 1974–2006
TWNT	*Theologische Wörterbuch zum Neuen Testament.* Edited by Gerhard Kittel and Gerhard Friedrich. Stuttgart: Kohlhammer, 1932–1979
TynBul	*Tyndale Bulletin*
UF	*Ugarit-Forschungen*
UT	*Ugaritic Textbook.* Cyrus H. Gordon. AnOr 38. Rome: Pontifical Biblical Institute, 1965
VT	*Vetus Testamentum*
VTSup	Supplements to Vetus Testamentum
WBC	Word Biblical Commentary
WMANT	Wissenschaftliche Monographien zum Alten und Neuen Testament
WTJ	*Westminster Theological Journal*
ZAW	*Zeitschrift für die alttestamentliche Wissenschaft*

Books by Meredith G. Kline Cited in This Volume

BOC	*By Oath Consigned: A Reinterpretation of the Covenant Signs of Circumcision and Baptism.* Grand Rapids: Eerdmans, 1968
IOS	*Images of the Spirit.* Grand Rapids: Baker, 1980
KP	*Kingdom Prologue: Genesis Foundations for a Covenantal Worldview.* Eugene, OR: Wipf & Stock, 2006
SBA	*The Structure of Biblical Authority.* 2nd, rev. ed. Grand Rapids: Eerdmans, 1975
TGK	*Treaty of the Great King: The Covenant Structure of Deuteronomy, Studies and Commentary.* Grand Rapids: Eerdmans, 1963

Meredith G. Kline: A Biographical Sketch

My father, Meredith George Kline (December 15, 1922–April 14, 2007), was a covenant theologian. Providentially, my dad's academic career began as scholars started to compare the recently discovered Hittite diplomatic treaties to biblical covenants. Because of his training at Westminster Theological Seminary in Philadelphia (WTS), my dad recognized that the concept of covenant is a core component in Reformed theology. The task of developing the implications of the correlations between these ancient Near Eastern texts and the Bible set the trajectory for the next half a century of my dad's scholarly research. What follows is a sketch of his vocational and research paths.

Vocational Path

The ability to steer his artistic and analytic skills in a specific direction was evident in the path my dad's vocational activity took. After he graduated from Boston Latin School in 1940, he wondered whether he should be a dentist, a schoolteacher, or a commercial artist. He contemplated what he might accomplish after fifty years of one of these endeavors and realized that he wanted a lifework that would produce fruit found in eternity as well as on earth. As a result, he withdrew his registration at Harvard University and enrolled at Gordon College of Theology and Missions (later named simply Gordon College), in order to prepare for the ministry of the gospel.

Vocationally, my father functioned as a preacher, pastor, presbyter, and professor. From 1947 to 1950 he actually was engaged in all four activities, while simultaneously pursuing doctoral studies and helping to raise a growing family.[1] Over the course of the next two decades, he ended his involvement in the first three areas so he could concentrate on being an academic

1. I was born in June 1945 and my brother Sterling in June 1947, while Dad was a student at WTS. Calvin was born in June 1950, as Dad finished his tenure as pastor at the Orthodox Presbyterian church in Ringoes, New Jersey.

research scholar. He felt most at home in the study[2] and the classroom, not at the pulpit or in administrative meetings.

Preacher

Already at the age of eighteen, during his first semester of college, my dad, who had acquired the nickname "Rev" (i.e., "Reverend"), was studying homiletics and, as a member of the college "Gospel Team," was going to various venues to play violin solos and engage in evangelism. He also preached a couple evening sermons at his boyhood church, Central Congregational in Dorchester, Massachusetts,[3] which at the time was led by a theologically conservative pastor, Norman King. Throughout college Dad continued to preach at chapels, including a Six Principle Baptist congregation in Rhode Island, which belonged to the denomination in which his fiancée's father had been ordained in London, England, and for which he subsequently pastored in Rhode Island.

During his student days at WTS, my dad also preached frequently at Orthodox Presbyterian Church (OPC) congregations in the Philadelphia area. After graduating from seminary, he preached twice on Sundays and monthly at a jail service as part of his pastoral responsibilities at an OPC congregation in Ringoes, New Jersey.

During his years of full-time teaching at WTS (1950–1965), he occasionally preached for Reformed churches within a couple hours' drive of Philadelphia, as well as at the OPC's Boardwalk Chapel in Wildwood, New Jersey, at French Creek (Pennsylvania) Bible Conference, and at Deerwander Bible Conference in Maine (part of the youth ministry of the OPC New York and New England Presbytery).[4] After moving to Massachusetts to teach at Gordon Divinity School (GDS; later named Gordon-Conwell Theological

2. Imitating his Jewish paternal grandfather, Jacob Klein, who immigrated to America at the turn of the twentieth century and, according to family report, spent his days studying Torah. Jacob's son Harry, my dad's father, did not carry on in this tradition, abandoning Jewish culture and changing the spelling of his last name.

3. Dad had been born in Coplay, Pennsylvania, but grew up in Dorchester, Massachusetts.

4. Dad was the speaker/preacher at Deerwander in August 1957. Subsequently, he functioned as Deerwander's waterfront director (during college summers he had been a counselor with waterfront duties at Camp Waldron on Lake Winnipesaukee in New Hampshire, and for one year during seminary days he had swimming responsibilities at the Abington, Pennsylvania, YMCA). He also was the staff class teacher at Deerwander for over forty years.

Seminary), he preached only sporadically at non-Presbyterian churches, and he stopped doing this altogether in early 1968. Even though preaching by seminary professors is sometimes viewed by their institutions as a partial job responsibility with public relations benefits, Dad subsequently did not preach even when he again taught at WTS in Philadelphia and at the WTS campus in Escondido, California. He never participated as a minister in any of his sons' or grandkids' weddings or at the baptisms of three generations of Klines.

The only biblical book my father preached a series on was Philippians. He did, however, have groups of sermons on topics, such as the five points of Calvinism, the Ten Commandments, and the Beatitudes. His sermons were exegetical and doctrinal in the tradition of his homiletics professor, R. B. Kuiper, whom he admired, but were not biblical-theological in the style of Ed Clowney, a subsequent WTS colleague of his with whom he discussed biblical theology in car rides to the seminary or to presbytery meetings. His later sermons were often related to subjects he was working on for books, so they tended to be more academic. Yet he was always oriented to the heart as well as the head. Richard Barker, clerk of the OPC New Jersey Presbytery, once wrote to my dad to say that he considered the devotional my dad had given at a presbytery meeting to have been the best he had heard in his twenty years of attendance.[5]

Presbyter

My father was ordained in the New Jersey Presbytery of the OPC in 1948. During his Ringoes pastorate and WTS teaching days, he participated in presbytery and general assembly activities. He took part in ordination services, served on candidate credentialing[6] and congregational visiting committees, and was even moderator of the presbytery from 1960 to 1961. He also served on general assembly committees dealing with doctrinal issues. By the time he left Westminster in 1965, he had written minority reports, whose ideas were not followed by the denomination, on the

---

5. Similarly, graduates of Gordon-Conwell who told me my dad's lectures had profoundly influenced their thinking would also comment that they greatly appreciated his prayers before class.

6. After moving to Massachusetts, he sometimes agreed to administer Hebrew qualifying exams for ordination candidates of the New York and New England Presbytery.

doctrine of divine guidance and on the concept of medical missions. When it came to church-cultural relations, he was an "old school," Reformed-wing rather than a "new school," evangelical-wing Presbyterian, believing that the church's duty is to proclaim the gospel and nurture its members, who would appropriately attempt to steer the culture in biblical directions through involvement in parachurch and secular institutions. Thus in 1963 he wrote a minority report for the OPC committee investigating whether the denomination should build a hospital in Eritrea. He argued that an ecclesiastical institution should not construct and operate medical facilities; he thought this was the responsibility and an appropriate function of the nonecclesiastical architectural and medical professions and corporations. According to my dad, the distinction was subtle but crucial for the biblical use of church funds.[7]

After he moved to Massachusetts to teach at Gordon Divinity School, my dad did not participate in ecclesiastical life as pastor or presbyter, since he felt the best use of his gifts was in the academic arena. He did agree, however, to engage in discussions about the doctrine of justification at Westminster Theological Seminary in the late 1970s at the request of Ed Clowney, who was then the seminary's president; this was a controversy that also involved OPC actions. As he told me at the time, he only agreed to invest the time, energy, and emotional stress in the matter because he thought the gospel was at stake.

Professor

Starting in the fall of 1948, my dad taught for two years as an instructor at WTS, while pastoring in Ringoes. From 1950 to 1965 he taught at WTS full time, and in the fall of 1965 he left WTS for Gordon Divinity School. Dad had been invited to Gordon earlier, in 1958, but had declined that invitation.[8] Although he was frustrated at WTS over meetings that had occurred about his differences with Old Testament colleague E. J. (Joe) Young over

---

7. Interestingly, at the same time, when the family of one of my high school classmates took the Abington, Pennsylvania, school system to the U.S. Supreme Court because the protocol at the beginning of the school day included recitation by students and faculty of the Lord's Prayer along with the Pledge of Allegiance, my dad would go to meetings of Christians to explain why the atheists were correct that such a required religious practice has no place in a secular institution.

8. My dad also declined invitations in 1958 and 1959 to teach at Calvin Theological Seminary, and an invitation in 1965 to teach at Trinity Evangelical Divinity School.

the interpretation of Gen 1, my dad's main reasons for leaving WTS lay elsewhere: these included his unhappiness with his teaching load and course assignments, his desire to be the head of an Old Testament department, his financial hardships, and the fact that at the time his two oldest sons were college students in Boston. Another factor involved in the move was that he loved New England and its evergreen trees (he made sure to plant some around the house he purchased in South Hamilton, Massachusetts); when he drove his family from Philadelphia to Boston to visit his parents and his sister's family, he always let out a shout of joy when we crossed the state line into Massachusetts.

An additional significant reason for his returning to Boston, where he and my mom had grown up, and his maintaining it as his base, even during his later involvement with both Westminster seminaries, was my mom's emotional health. Muriel Grace had spent months on multiple occasions in the 1950s in a psychiatric hospital for bouts of depression and was later diagnosed as paranoid schizophrenic. According to a note she wrote for the family, this was reflected in the fact that she signed her paintings as Muriel and used that name with doctors but went by Grace at home, church, and the assisted-living facility where she resided the last ten years of her life. After moving back to Massachusetts, her condition was moderated by medicine, but it remained a struggle the rest of her life. As a consequence of my mom's health, in 1957 Dad canceled a projected sabbatical in Basel; in fact, he never ended up traveling abroad. In the 1950s, while teaching at WTS and writing his PhD dissertation at Dropsie College, Dad spent extended periods during Grace's hospitalizations as a single parent of three young boys, surviving with generous assistance from our neighbors, Joe Young's family, and other friends from the WTS and Glenside, Pennsylvania, OPC communities. In order to adequately perform his academic responsibilities, my dad maintained tight control over family activities and restricted his professional engagements beyond the classroom.

My dad taught at Gordon Divinity School from 1965 to 1993. But his heart remained with Westminster Theological Seminary, first with the Philadelphia campus and later with the one in Escondido, California (now Westminster Seminary California). After Joe Young died unexpectedly in February 1968, the WTS faculty voted to bring Dad back, but after protracted negotiations a compromise was worked out according to which my dad would teach in Philadelphia only during Januarys, which he did most years through 1977. Dad then arranged to teach during Januarys at Reformed Theological Seminary in Jackson, Mississippi, which he did through 1982. In

February 1982, he began to teach during spring semesters at the Escondido, California, campus of Westminster Theological Seminary, a practice he continued through 2001 (while continuing, through 1993, to teach during the fall semesters at GCTS). At this point, Dad confided to me that he no longer had the stamina to maintain a weekly schedule of classes and manage daily life away from home. He was happy that he had finished his teaching career at WSC, since he identified with its theological convictions most strongly and since it was continuing to pass on his ideas.

From 1999 to 2002 my father also taught classes, one evening a week in the fall, at the Granite State School of Theology and Missions, which was sponsored by his friend Greg Reynolds, who pastored Amoskeag Presbyterian Church (OPC) in Manchester, New Hampshire, where the classes were held.

My dad maintained high academic standards for five decades and did not board the grade-inflation train. He had a reputation as a tough grader, and students would take his courses pass-fail. He would use blackboards or whiteboards to scribble words during his lectures. The board might start out with a semblance of order, but by the end of class it resembled a Jackson Pollock painting. That may be the reason a student once complained that he was lost trying to follow the day's lecture—to which my dad responded, "Let me share the gospel with you!" While an indication of my dad's sense of humor, the retort reflects his constant concern that the Christian's pastoral, apologetic, teaching, or counseling responsibility is to clearly present the good news of how Christ's death and resurrection delivered us from the divine wrath to which we were subject based on our union with Adam and our personal transgressions of covenant requirements. It was also the reason he regularly assigned Isa 52:13–53:12 as the passage for the paper in his Prophets course.

Research Path

Major Influences

Training at Westminster Theological Seminary from 1944 to 1947 provided my father with a solid foundation in Reformed theology. My dad respected his teachers. Joe Young, his Old Testament professor, was a model as a strong proponent of the inerrancy of the Bible and a defender of conservative positions on matters of Old Testament introduction; but he also guided Dad into preaching opportunities, a pastoral job, a doctoral program, and a teaching position. In addition, Joe Young sold my parents some of his property, on which our Willow Grove house ended up being built, and his family supported us through difficult times. Ned Stonehouse, supervisor of Dad's ThM thesis on the structure of the Apocalypse, passed on his love for Geerhardus Vos, as did John Murray, though my dad later disagreed with Murray's views on covenant theology. My dad learned much about Presbyterian polity from Westminster's church historian, Paul Woolley.

Of all his WTS professors, however, Cornelius Van Til had the greatest impact on my dad's thinking and methodology. Van Til sought an apologetic method that was consistent with biblical truth, which he believed was most accurately represented by Reformed theology.[9] Central to Van Til's position is the antithesis between the believer's and the unbeliever's systems of belief, insofar as these systems are consistent with one's epistemological foundations. Like Van Til, my dad applied this concept of system coherence to differing theological perspectives. When one discusses a particular theological issue, it may be possible to arrange competing positions on a spectrum; nevertheless, when theological systems are compared in their totality, they are incompatible in significant respects. For example, dispensationalism, theonomy, and various versions of covenant theology might be plotted on a scale representing the amount of continuity or discontinuity they perceive between the old and new covenants. My dad, however, was most interested in the congruence of each interpretive paradigm with the sum of biblical truth, with the goal of arriving at a unified "field theory" of covenant theology.

My dad's other significant educational mentor was his PhD advisor, Cyrus Gordon, who confidently followed into uncharted waters the conclusions that he thought facts pointed to, even against vociferous naysayers. Gordon's confidence in this pursuit stemmed from his thorough knowledge of ancient texts in their original languages and from his integrated understanding of how cultural phenomena functioned. My dad had to be well prepared for his doctoral classes, especially the one in which Gordon (who reportedly could identify any biblical text by seeing only the vowels) was the professor and Nahum Sarna (who supposedly had memorized *Gesenius' Hebrew Grammar*!) was the other student. In later years, after my dad had moved back to Massachusetts to teach at GDS, Gordon permitted him to sit

9. Since covenant theology is the core of Reformed doctrine, my dad would have approved Scott Oliphint's change in nomenclature for Van Til's apologetics from "presuppositional" to "covenantal" in *Covenantal Apologetics: Principles and Practice in Defense of Our Faith* (Wheaton, IL: Crossway, 2013).

in on his lectures at Brandeis University. My dad imitated Gordon's tenacity in defending unpopular positions and not acquiescing to academic or administrative opposition.

In addition to his skill at thinking analytically, my dad applied artistic talent to his work. Dad was an amateur artist. In his high school days he created cartoons for Boston Latin School publications, and in his student days at Gordon College of Theology and Missions he served for a year as art editor of the school yearbook. Also while in college, he joined my mother, Muriel Grace, in taking classes at the Museum of Fine Arts in Boston. During the 1950s, while sitting in Saturday morning faculty meetings at WTS concerning administrative matters, he drew plans for our house in Willow Grove, Pennsylvania, and sketched his colleagues. After returning to teach at GDS in 1965, he and my mother both became members of the Beverly (Massachusetts) Guild of Artists.

Dad combined the strategies he derived from Cornelius Van Til and Cyrus Gordon with rigorous scholarship and artistic capabilities in a way that allowed him to move comfortably between exegetical detail and canonical unity.

Reputation

My father was a creative but controversial scholar. His readers—not only his Presbyterian brethren but also Baptists who differed on their understanding of the church-membership sacrament, or those who recoiled at his conservative views of Scripture—could appreciate the depth of his research while disagreeing with his conclusions.

My dad's WSC colleague John Frame, while acknowledging methodological and conceptual differences between them, wrote, "I regard him as the most impressive biblical theologian of my lifetime. . . . His work is orthodox, yet often original, and it always provides us with rich analysis of Scripture."[10]

In a review of *Images of the Spirit*, Liberty Baptist Seminary professor James Borland commented that

> anyone familiar with the writings of Meredith G. Kline has probably come to expect clarity and precision in expression, penetrating analysis of pertinent viewpoints, meticulous documentation, complete familiarity with ancient

10. *The Doctrine of the Christian Life* (Phillipsburg, NJ: P&R, 2008), 520.

> Near Eastern religious laws and customs, and a careful use of the Biblical languages, all brought to focus on elucidating some scriptural text or idea.

Yet Borland also realized that

> dispensational pretribulationists will dispute Kline's identification of the lampstands in Revelation 11 with the Church. This involves a substitution of symbolical, typological interpretation for normal, literal, hermeneutical principles and selectively ignores details not in accord with the symbolic understanding.[11]

Horace Hummel, a Lutheran reviewer of *Images of the Spirit*, commented that

> not only Lutherans, but many conservatives, will often find Kline hard going, however.[12] This is true not only because of his very compact style and close attention to details of the Biblical text, but precisely because he uses exegetical or Biblico-theological categories, not systematic or dogmatic ones.

He added that

> throughout, of course, Kline proceeds Christologically and typologically. In fact, the unity of Scripture and the material content of "verbal inspiration" are worked out so beautifully that one wonders how higher-critics will be able to tune into Kline's labors at all.[13] He excels at demonstrating how the highly variegated Biblical imagery (so often the despair of the more systematically oriented) can and must ultimately be unified.

Hummel finished by stating:

> Inevitably, one will not be equally convinced about all the exegetical judgments, but it is hard to see how anyone could read—or preach on—the Bible in the same way after "inwardly digesting" the contents of this exceedingly rich and stimulating work.[14]

---

11. Review of *Images of the Spirit* in *JETS* 24 (1981): 275–76.

12. Students often reported that they had to read *Kingdom Prologue* two or three times before understanding it.

13. As illustrated by Brevard Childs's comments in his *Introduction to the Old Testament as Scripture* (Philadelphia: Fortress, 1979), 56, on *The Structure of Biblical Authority*: "Kline's basically dogmatic formulation of the history of the canon in terms of divine inspiration which assured an inerrant transmission of the Word of God reflects completely the pre-Semler, seventeenth-century understanding which has not even seen the historical problem. These issues are far too complex simply to circumscribe by a strictly theological definition. Therefore, in spite of some excellent insights, the total impact of the book misses its intended goal."

14. Review of *Images of the Spirit* in *Concordia Journal* 8.1 (1982): 34–35.

These readers of my dad's writings recognized that he applied his artistic and analytical abilities to his literary analysis of Scripture and ancient Near Eastern texts in the original languages for semantic precision, structural symmetries, and thematic continuities. He had skills as a linguist, a literary critic, and a systematic thinker. He was equally comfortable and proficient in demonstrating the thematic unity of Scripture and in defining its concepts.

Linguist

Since he was proficient in multiple languages, my dad could have had a capable career as a Bible translator. One of his sisters-in-law, Joan Law, who was a Gordon College classmate and later a Wycliffe translator, envied the ease with which he learned Spanish.[15] He had studied Latin and Greek at Boston Latin School and Greek and Hebrew in college. At Dropsie he studied multiple ancient Near Eastern languages as part of his doctoral program, and he even taught courses on Egyptian at WTS. Part of his doctoral dissertation under Cyrus Gordon on the Ḫabiru[16] involved linguistic analysis of the name of the group.[17] Later he was one of the translators for the NIV version of the Old Testament. He and his GCTS colleague Elmer Smick did the original work on the difficult poetry of Job and Psalms.

Several of my dad's articles hinged on linguistic points—"Abram's Amen" on the function of a verb form; "The Feast of Cover-over" on the Egyptian origin of the word traditionally translated as "Passover"; and "Har Magedon" on the derivation of "Magedon" from the Hebrew word for "assembly" rather than from the name of a Canaanite town. Dad was also a word-coiner. Examples of his kennings include the "endoxation" of the Holy Spirit (to parallel the "incarnation" of the Son); "metaworld," for the invisible heaven; and many hyphenated words involving "glory," such as "Glory-cloud" (for the Old Testament Shekinah that filled the Israelite tabernacle and temple).

---

15. My dad must have assumed his students would have comparable proficiency in mastering languages since he expected them to learn Aramaic as part of a month-long exegesis course on the biblical book of Daniel!

16. In 1955 he completed his doctoral dissertation entitled *The Ḫa-BI-ru: Kin or Foe of Israel?*, which he later published as articles in the *Westminster Theological Journal*.

17. While I was studying with Cyrus Gordon from 1972 to 1973, he commented to me that my dad had been the best linguist of his students to that time.

Literature Analyst

Dad looked at Scripture as an artist, analyzing how the parts fit into the whole. Underlying his textual analysis was the visualization of literary patterns, whether at the level of the parallelism of the lines of poetic verse, of topical repetitions in a pericope (as in Gen 1), or of the organization of a whole book (as seen in his presentations of the structures of Genesis, Zechariah, and Revelation). He also was skilled at seeing comparisons, whether of genres (such as when comparing the organization of Deuteronomy with that of ancient Near Eastern diplomatic treaties), of cultural phenomena (such as God's questioning of Job, which he considered to be modeled after ancient Near Eastern belt-wrestling contests), or of typological relations between various forms of the covenant community or between different biblical characters.

Systematician

Dad's most significant influence for his covenant theology was Geerhardus Vos. Dad's teaching responsibilities at WTS included a course on Old Testament Biblical Theology. That course of subsequent myriad names taught at multiple seminaries ultimately blossomed as *Kingdom Prologue*, a covenant theology in the tradition of Vos, whose *Biblical Theology* was always a required text for the course. Dad received the Vos influence from his WTS professors (particularly Stonehouse, and also Murray and Van Til, as mentioned above), who championed Vos's presentation of Reformed covenant theology. But my dad was also sympathetic with his WTS colleague Ed Clowney's development of biblical-theological preaching, since, like my dad, Clowney had artistic talents and could perceive beautiful relationships among biblical passages.

Dad also utilized his artistic ability to perceive parallels among various biblical data. For example, he correlated Eden and Israelite territory as holy lands where a theocracy was regulated by a works covenant. Likewise, he viewed the conflicts of our first parents versus the serpent, incarnated deity versus a fallen angel, and the Lamb's army versus draconic forces as all taking place on the heavenly Mount of Assembly.

In addition to these creative literary comparisons, Dad also developed rigorous arguments for theological conceptions—preeminently, his understanding of covenant theology, but also concepts such as the image of God, biblical canon, justification, and the Sabbath.

Research Trajectory

In the four centuries prior to my dad's beginning his teaching career at WTS in 1950, ideas about covenant theology had been based solely on biblical data. But that changed with the publication, just before World War II, of second-millennium BC Hittite diplomatic treaties. After the war, biblical scholars began to integrate ancient Near Eastern treaty material with biblical covenants, and Dad quickly realized the significance of the new evidence for elaborating the distinctive ideas of Reformed theology. As I mentioned at the beginning of this biographical sketch, that project oriented his scholarly output for the next five decades as he creatively, and controversially, applied the recent archaeological findings in new directions. He was in the forefront of those comparing the treaties with the texts of the Decalogue and Deuteronomy, which resulted in *Treaty of the Great King*, published in 1963. In this book he demonstrated the formal unity of Deuteronomy and supported a second-millennium date for the book, to the pleasure of conservatives and the consternation and contempt of critical scholars, whose documentary hypothesis it undermined.

After applying information derived from ancient Near Eastern treaties to biblical form criticism and the dating of Old Testament texts, Dad related treaty ratification methods to the sacraments in *By Oath Consigned* (1968). This book treated both circumcision and baptism as symbols of the curse sanctions of their respective covenants and as rites establishing their recipients, whether adult or infant, as members of the covenant community, which made previous Presbyterian arguments for the doctrine more concrete. Some Baptists still feel obligated to interact with Dad's arguments.[18]

Next, in *The Structure of Biblical Authority* (1972), Dad related the Deuteronomic document clause to the topic of biblical canon. Here he attempted to demonstrate the covenantal nature of all of Scripture, and used the administrative functions performed by historical and prophetic books in directing the covenant community to argue for the traditional dating of biblical books. Critical scholars were not convinced, because of the lack of extrabiblical documentation of significant portions of biblical texts before the Qumran material. Because my dad changed the definition of canon from a completed list of authoritative texts (the definition that had dominated

18. See Duane Garrett, "Meredith Kline on Suzerainty, Circumcision, and Baptism," in *Believer's Baptism: Sign of the New Covenant in Christ*, ed. Thomas Schreiner and Shawn Wright (Nashville: B&H Academic, 2006), 257–84.

the debate between conservatives and liberals) to texts that functioned in the administration of the covenant community, he proposed that since the form of the covenant community changed from a theocracy for the Old Testament to the church for the New Testament, the Old Testament was no longer canon for the church (in his redefined sense of the term "canon"), a concept that conservatives consider controversial.

At about the same time in his career, Dad's focus on the form of the covenant community also was central in his opposition to theonomy, because of the latter's manner of applying some Israelite theocratic laws and sanctions to non-theocratic geopolitical institutions. Likewise, he distinguished ecclesiastical (cultic or kingdom of heaven) activity from cultural (kingdom of earth) endeavors, a distinction that currently has his followers engaged with neo-Kuyperians in the two-kingdoms debate.[19]

My dad's core course on covenant theology culminated, as mentioned above, in *Kingdom Prologue* (written over the course of the 1980s), which considers Genesis as the historical background to the forming of the Israelite kingdom by means of the Sinai covenant and its renewal on the Plains of Moab. The book demonstrates the existence of a Covenant of Works in Eden and explores how the principles of works and grace function in the accomplishment and application of redemption.

The other major course my dad taught at WSC was on the Old Testament prophetical books. In it he tackled the exegesis of passages that were central to dispensational or various millennial interpretations, arguing for an amillennial position.[20] His eschatological views and an argument for his controversial view on the Sabbath appeared in his final book, *God, Heaven and Har Magedon* (2006). This book, which deals with universal history from the "Alpha Radiation" to the "Omega Apocalypse," evidences the way in which my dad analyzed the Bible as a literary whole, as do his articles on Genesis and Job in one-volume Bible commentaries[21] and his posthumously published Genesis commentary.[22]

---

19. For an entry into the discussion, see David VanDrunen, *Living in God's Two Kingdoms: A Biblical Vision for Christianity and Culture* (Wheaton, IL: Crossway, 2010).

20. Some in the OPC thought his arguments so cogent that they talked about making adherence to amillennialism a requirement for ordination in the denomination!

21. "Genesis," in *The New Bible Commentary Revised*, ed. D. Guthrie and J. Motyer (Grand Rapids: Eerdmans, 1970), and "Job," in *The Wycliffe Bible Commentary*, ed. Charles Pfeiffer and Everett Harrison (Chicago: Moody, 1962).

22. *Genesis: A New Commentary* (Peabody, MA: Hendrickson, 2016).

An example of how my dad followed biblical imagery where it took him was his development of the concept of the image of God in *Images of the Spirit* (1980). The book illustrates how the glory of God was replicated in human royal, priestly, and prophetic functions. These evidences of the majestic divine beauty pointed to their fulfillment in the incarnation of the Second Person of the Trinity, whose splendor was prophesied in the book of Zechariah, an idea my dad developed in *Glory in Our Midst* (2001).

My father felt confident in his ability to fathom the intricacies and complexities of biblical texts and theological conceptualizations. At first, he naively thought that what in his mind were undisputable scholarly results would convert honest researchers to conform deviant and diverse theories to hard data. The evidence from second-millennium suzerainty treaties would, he thought, surely convince critics to abandon a first-millennium dating of Deuteronomy in favor of the traditional belief in Mosaic authorship. Or surely Baptists would all become Presbyterians because of the clear implications of ancient diplomatic treaty-ratification rituals. Alas, the failure of his optimistic hope that fellow fighters of theological battles would follow his lead ultimately led to his final academic productions being intellectual tours de force devoid of documentation, leaving readers to ferret out the identity of even his theologically closest interlocutors.

As a professor training predominantly pastors along with a few future seminary professors, Dad attempted to convey the reliability and organic unity of Scripture, with its focus on the glory of our divine covenant Lord, the Creator, Redeemer, and Consummator. The articles collected in this volume evidence different aspects of my father's creativity and reveal stimulating, if sometimes controversial, interpretational perspectives.

Meredith M. Kline, ThD
Retired Director of Goddard Library and Ranked Adjunct Assistant
Professor of Oriental Languages, Gordon-Conwell Theological Seminary

Introduction

For years I have wanted to put together a collection of my grandfather's writings that showcased what I consider to be the "best of" his thinking and scholarship. Of the approximately seventy articles my grandfather wrote during his half-century-long career, I have chosen the sixteen included in this volume because they seem to me to manifest most clearly his primary strengths and his main ideas. In addition, and as is reflected in the section headings of this book, these articles represent the breadth of his interests, which ranged, according to the familiar phrase, from creation to consummation.

As I reflect in more detail on what led me to select these articles as the most compelling pieces my grandfather wrote, the word to which I keep returning is *creativity*. My grandfather was, of course, thoroughly Reformed and evangelical in his theology; his view of Scripture and his interpretations of both individual biblical passages and of the Bible as a whole were always shaped by his particular interpretive grid, which circumscribed his beliefs and set the ideological limits for his intellectual activity. Within the particular hermeneutical framework in which he operated, however, he exercised—in what ended up being a kind of counterforce to his traditionalism—a great deal of ingenuity in his approach to the Bible. The result was a unique and interesting blend of classical Reformed theology and innovative ideas. For this reason, despite the fact that some of his writings have a dated feel (they were nearly all produced in the second half of the twentieth century), they continue to be fascinating and thought-provoking works that are worth rereading and pondering.

One example of my grandfather's creative approach to the Bible is found in the fresh interpretations he offered for the Hebrew and Greek texts of particular passages, especially ones that historically have proven difficult to understand or that have been used to support traditional dogmas that in his view are misguided. This kind of approach can be seen, for example, in "Oracular Origin of the State" (pp. 49–61), "Abram's Amen" (pp. 105–13), and "Double Trouble" (pp. 139–48). My grandfather's innovative philological discussions were often coupled with enlightening and sometimes novel interpretations of ancient Near Eastern material (mostly textual, but occasionally pictorial as well) that he thought had a direct bearing on biblical interpretation. For example, his identification in "Divine Kingship and Genesis 6:1–4" (pp. 63–78) of the characters in this passage not as celestial beings (the common view) but as self-deifying human kings draws on his understanding of the concept of divine kingship in the ancient Near East. And in "The Two Tables of the Covenant" (pp. 79–92) he used the evidence of ancient diplomatic treaties to provide a novel interpretation of the nature of the Ten Commandments. Even if in certain cases one is not convinced by my grandfather's arguments in these or others of his articles, his analyses are undeniably interesting and provocative. As the best biblical scholarship tends to do, these treatments force us to take the text seriously and to wrestle with and try to make sense of its difficult parts.

Another way in which my grandfather approached the Bible creatively was by reading it in the light of modern discoveries, specifically those from the realm of natural science. In "Because It Had Not Rained" (pp. 9–19) and "Space and Time in the Genesis Cosmogony" (pp. 21–45), he tried to deal with apparent contradictions between the biblical text and the currently accepted scientific conclusion that the earth is very much older than a literal reading of the beginning of Genesis allows. My grandfather's main goal in these pieces was to demonstrate that "general revelation" (natural science) and "special revelation" (the Bible) are in harmony with one another, since God is the source of them both. He believed that if these two modes of revelation appear to contradict each other, then our interpretation of one or the other (or perhaps both) must be faulty or incomplete. Although he always considered the Bible to have the ultimate authority, he did allow current scientific hypotheses to prompt him to ask whether certain traditional interpretations of the Bible are perhaps incorrect or unnecessary.

A final way in which my grandfather exercised creativity in his approach to biblical interpretation can be seen in the fact that he was often on the lookout for new, surprising, or overlooked elements in the text. Often this search resulted in his identification of unexpected redemptive reversals. One example of this is found in "Trial by Ordeal" (pp. 169–82), in which he argues that Satan is the one who is really on trial in the book of Job. This startling interpretation, according to which the accuser ultimately turns out to be the accused, reflects my grandfather's view that, despite circumstances and appearances, God always advocates and fights for his people, especially in their trials. Similarly, in a trio of articles he wrote on the theme of resurrection—"Death, Leviathan, and the Martyrs" (pp. 217–37), "The First Resurrection" (pp. 239–47), and "The First Resurrection: A Reaffirmation" (pp. 249–57)—my grandfather argued that for Christian believers death should actually be viewed as a resurrection (the "first" resurrection), since this experience ushers them, redeemed and vindicated on account of Christ's death and resurrection on their behalf, into God's presence.

My grandfather's novel interpretations sometimes grew—as I alluded to above—out of his frustration over traditional interpretations that in his view have distracted people from what he considered to be the Bible's primary message, particularly its emphasis on the justifying work of Christ on behalf of his people. He lamented that Christians expend so much time, energy, and thought defending ideas such as a literal, twenty-four-hour-day interpretation of Gen 1 (see "Because It Had Not Rained" and "Space and Time in the Genesis Cosmogony") and a literal interpretation of the millennium in the book of Revelation (see "Har Magedon: The End of the Millennium"; pp. 259–77). He viewed these and similar interpretations as harmful, self-imposed stumbling blocks that discredit the Christian witness and that distract believers from Scripture's positive and encouraging messages about God's power and kingship (the point of Gen 1) and God's abiding presence with his people in the midst of their tribulations throughout the entire church age (the point of "the millennium").

Although like many writers of his time my grandfather did not shy away from a theological fight—he engaged in vociferous argumentation especially (and ironically) with those who ideologically were most like him—he was, in person, a sweet and humble man. His awareness of the fact that his penchant toward polemic needed to be tempered by his efforts to love his neighbor as himself comes out in a humorous way in his opening statement in "The First Resurrection: A Reaffirmation," which he wrote as a rejoinder to one of his seminary colleagues:

> The characteristic courtesy of Ramsey Michaels in discussion, even when the discussion is a disagreement, is amply evidenced again in his Response to my earlier article. I admire the virtue and appreciate this particular instance of it, but as one notably deficient in irenic grace I could almost wish he had set a less noble example! Despairing of matching it, I tender my apologies beforehand, ere the ardor of offensive defensiveness has quite carried me away.

Folks who knew my grandfather, or knew of him, often remark when they meet me that I am the third-generation Old Testament scholar in our family. (My father, who wrote the biographical sketch for this volume, is also a scholar in the field.) This is true, but the story goes back even further. My grandfather had Jewish heritage; his own grandfather, who immigrated to the United States from Latvia around the turn of the twentieth century, was reportedly devoted to studying Torah. I don't know much more about this part of our heritage, unfortunately, and I wonder how far back the tradition of biblical study in our family goes. Since the time I learned about this aspect of our history, I have come to appreciate how my grandfather's way of interpreting the Bible bears some resemblance—and perhaps may be directly indebted—to the way in which his forebears likely read the text. I began my remarks above by saying that in light of my grandfather's theological traditionalism, it is interesting to consider the degree to which he exercised creativity and ingenuity in his interpretations of the biblical text. However, in light of our family history, this may make more sense: it seems that it is not too much to say that my grandfather's interpretations are often "midrashic." This term is notoriously difficult to define, of course, and I am not using it here in any technical sense; I simply mean to invoke the brilliantly creative way in which many traditional Jewish exegetes have interpreted the Bible's individual words and phrases by connecting them in fascinating and sometimes counterintuitive ways with other parts of Scripture. I see my grandfather as following very much in this tradition—even though he combined his activity in this regard with careful attention to modern philological and historical research, and even though the broad conclusions to which he came (especially given his intensely christological focus) differed markedly with those his ancestors would have espoused.

I would like to mention one final aspect of our family history in connection with my grandfather's creativity. His wife, Grace—my grandmother—was a painter, primarily a watercolorist. One of her oil paintings adorns the cover of my grandfather's last book, *God, Heaven and Har Magedon*, and over the years I have met a number of my grandfather's students who (like me and most of his and Grace's other descendants) have some of my grandmother's paintings hanging in their home. My grandfather loved and supported my grandmother's artwork, and he himself enjoyed sketching and painting, especially in his younger days. It seems to me that, in addition to his Jewish heritage, this artistic inclination was another element of my grandfather's personality that influenced his biblical interpretation. In a way, he saw the Bible as a grand painting—a vast, panoramic masterwork whose individual parts all contribute to the beauty of the whole, and (correlatively) whose whole provides meaning, context, and significance to the individual parts.

The creative tension that lies at the heart of my grandfather's work—his unique blend of tradition and innovation—has elicited strong reactions from readers. Some have considered his work too Reformed, while others have considered it not Reformed enough or too novel for their taste. But other readers and students—and this seems to be the attitude of most people I have met who took a class from him or who have read something he wrote—have deeply appreciated his blend of classical theology and creative exegesis; in their view, this rare mixture has produced a brilliant, paradigm-changing way of understanding the Bible that is both intellectually and spiritually satisfying. It is my hope that the collection of "essential writings" found in this book—which my family, colleagues, and I offer in love and respect for the memory of my grandfather and in friendship to the book's readers—will be welcomed not only by those who have already come to appreciate his work but also by new audiences who desire to further explore the beauty and wonder of God's word and his continued work in the world.

* * * * *

My editorial touch on the articles in this book has been relatively light, but I have made some minor changes in order to make the reader's experience as smooth and consistent as possible. Abbreviations for all biblical book names have been made consistent, for example, as have (inasmuch as was practicable) the capitalization and spelling of words that were treated differently in the original articles. I have transliterated everything that was originally in either Hebrew or Greek script in the articles in order to make this consistent throughout the volume and in order to ensure that the argumentation will be fully accessible to readers who do not know these languages.

Despite my efforts to make everything in this book as consistent as possible, the fact remains that my grandfather produced the articles found here in a variety of journals (or, occasionally, books) over a period of forty years. It is inevitable, therefore, that some minor inconsistencies of style remain, and it seemed neither practical nor desirable to try to smooth all of these out. In any case, I hope that such inconsistencies as may remain will create little if any distraction for the reader.

In order to help the reader locate the original page numbers for the articles in this volume (in case the reader finds these cited in another work by my grandfather, for example), I have included all the original page numbers in a small font and in double brackets (e.g., [[184]]).

All citations of *Kingdom Prologue* in this volume have been updated to reflect the page numbers of the most recent edition, which was published in 2006 by Wipf & Stock.

Jonathan G. Kline, PhD
Associate Editor, Hendrickson Publishers

PART ONE

Creation

CHAPTER ONE

Because It Had Not Rained

(1958)

There are no signs that the debate over the chronological data of Gen 1 is abating. Among those who hold biblical views of the inspiration of the Scriptures certain interpretations of that chronology have, indeed, long been traditional. These may disagree as to the duration of the "days" of Gen 1 but they have in common the opinion that the order of narration in that chapter coincides with the actual sequence of creation history. Although these traditional interpretations continue to be dominant in orthodox circles there also continues to be debate and its flames have recently been vigorously fanned by the bellows of the dissenters.[1]

At the heart of the issue, though its crucial character appears to be generally overlooked, is the question of whether the *modus operandi* of divine providence was the same during the creation era as that of ordinary providence now. This is not to raise the question of whether Gen 1 leaves the door open for some sort of evolutionary reconstruction. On the contrary, it is assumed here that Gen 1 contradicts the idea that an undifferentiated worldstuff evolved into the present variegated universe by dint of intrinsic potentialities whether divinely "triggered" or otherwise. According to Gen 1, the divine act of absolute beginning—or creation *in nihilum*—was followed by a succession of divine acts of origination, both *ex nihilo* and *intra aliquid*.[2] The present [[147]] world with the fulness thereof is the net result of

1. Two discussions in particular have evoked animated reactions among evangelicals in this country: B. Ramm, *The Christian View of Science and Scripture* (Grand Rapids: Eerdmans, 1954), 173ff. and N. H. Ridderbos, *Is There a Conflict Between Genesis 1 and Natural Science?* (Grand Rapids: Eerdmans, 1957).

2. *In nihilum* serves to distinguish the initial creative act as alone having had no setting of prior created reality. *Intra aliquid* has the advantage over *ex materia* (for productions like that of Adam's body out of existent dust) that it does not obscure the pure creativeness of the divine act. There should be no hesitation in classifying such works as creation in the strict sense. The opinion that Calvin refused to do so

this succession of discrete creation acts of God completed within the era of the "six days" (Gen 2:1–3).[3]

Though this closed era of the "six days" was characteristically the era of creation, it was not exclusively so. That is, the works of creation were interlaced with the work of providence in a manner analogous to the mingling of natural and supernatural providence in the structure of subsequent history.[4] As a matter of fact, one aspect of the creative acts themselves (excepting the act of absolute beginning) may properly be subsumed under the rubric of providence. They were works of providence in that they were part of the divine government of the world in so far as that world was already existent before each new creative act occurred. In the discussion which follows, however, predications made concerning the *modus* [[148]] *operandi* of divine providence during the creation era will have in view only the work of God other than his acts of creation.

---

is mistaken. (Cf. the criticism of B. B. Warfield on this point by J. Murray in "Calvin's Doctrine of Creation," *WTJ* 17 [1954]: 29ff.) Calvin does on occasion insist that the word "create" be restricted to *ex nihilo* fiat. Thus, in commenting on the use of the word "create" in Gen 1:21 for the origin of creatures of sea and air, which Calvin interprets (mistakenly) as having involved the use of existent water, he accounts for this usage solely on the ground that the material employed belonged to the universal matter created *ex nihilo* on the first "day." However, in such a passage it must be observed that Calvin is exclusively concerned with the precise meaning of the *Hebrew* word *bārāʾ*, not at all with the general theological use of the word "create."

3. There have been acts of creation since the creation of man which terminated the era of the "six days"; cf., e.g., the origin of souls and such miracles as the multiplying of the loaves and fishes. None of these, however, has added to the "kinds" originated within the "six days."

4. Cf. B. B. Warfield, "Christian Supernaturalism," in *Studies in Theology* (New York: Oxford University Press, 1932), 37ff. The likeness of creation acts to subsequent supernatural acts is profound. They are alike highways to consummation. It is by the road of his successive creation acts that God has betaken himself to the Sabbath of the seventh "day." In the sequel, it is by the way of supernaturalism that God directs his image-bearer to union with him in his consummation rest. Adam wakes to the supernatural voice and it is to him from the very beginning a voice that speaks to him out of God's Sabbath, challenging him with the invitation, "Come up hither"—to consummation. And every supernatural word thereafter issues from and beckons covenant-man unto that same Sabbath dwelling-place of God, while every supernatural work propels him towards it. The redemptive principle becomes necessary by the supernaturalism that conducts *fallen* man to consummation rest and it is, therefore, prominent in biblical revelation; but it is nevertheless subordinate to the eschatological thrust that marks all supernaturalism.

The traditionalist interpreter, as he pursues his strictly chronological way through the data of Gen 1, will be compelled at one point or another to assume that God in his providential preservation of the world during the "six days" era did not operate through secondary means in the manner which men now daily observe and analyze as natural law. The question, therefore, is whether the Scriptures justify this traditional assumption of supernatural providence for the creation era or whether they contradict it—or whether possibly they leave it an open question. It will be the central contention of this article that a clear answer to that question is available in Gen 2:5 and that that answer constitutes a decisive word against the traditional interpretation.

Genesis 2:5ff.

The major English versions exhibit marked divergence in the way they translate Gen 2:5 and relate it grammatically to verses 4 and 6–7.

Authorized	*American Standard*	*Revised Standard*
(4) These *are* the generations of the heavens and of the earth when they were created, in the day that the LORD God made the earth and the heavens, (5) and every plant of the field before it was in the earth, and every herb of the field before it grew: for the LORD God had not caused it to rain upon the earth, and *there was* not a man to till the ground. (6) But there went up a mist from the earth, and watered the whole face of the ground. (7) And the LORD God formed man *of* the dust of the ground . . .	(4) These are the generations of the heavens and of the earth when they were created, in the day that Jehovah God made earth and heaven. (5) And no plant of the field was yet in the earth, and no herb of the field had yet sprung up; for Jehovah God had not caused it to rain upon the earth: and there was not a man to till the ground; (6) but there went up a mist from the earth, and watered the whole face of the ground. (7) And Jehovah God formed man of the dust of the ground . . .	(4) These are the generations of the heavens and the earth when they were created. In the day that the LORD God made the earth and the heavens, (5) when no plant of the field was yet in the earth and no herb of the field had yet sprung up—for the LORD God had not caused it to rain upon the earth, and there was no man to till the ground; (6) but a mist went up from the earth and watered the whole face of the ground—(7) then the LORD God formed man of dust from the ground . . .

[[149]] Of these versions the treatment of verse 5 in the ASV is alone acceptable. A Hebrew idiom for expressing an emphatic negative found in the original of this verse has been muffed by the AV with the result that it is obscured at best. The RSV like the ASV correctly renders the negative element but has other serious defects. It treats verse 5 as though it were part of an involved temporal section extending from 4b through 6, all subordinated to the action of verse 7. This is an old interpretation which Delitzsch properly rejects because it required "a clumsy interpolated period" such as is "not to be expected in this simple narrative style."[5] The RSV rendering would also compel Gen 2 to teach that man was created before vegetation, whereas the ASV permits the exegete to regard the arrangement of its contents as topical rather than chronological. If the arrangement of Gen 2 were not topical it would contradict the teaching of Gen 1 (not to mention that of natural revelation) that vegetation preceded man on the earth.[6]

Set against the vast background of creation history, these verses serve to bring together man and the vegetable world in the foreground of attention. This prepares for the central role of certain objects of the vegetable kingdom, i.e., the garden of God and especially the trees in the midst of it, in the earliest history of man as recorded in the immediately following verses (cf. 2:8ff. and 3:1ff.).

Verse 5 itself describes a time when the earth was without vegetation. And the significant fact is a very simple one. It is the fact that an explanation—a perfectly natural explanation—is given for the absence of vegetation at that time: "for the LORD God had not caused it to rain upon the earth." The Creator did not originate plant life on earth before he had prepared an environment in which he might preserve it without by-passing secondary means and without having recourse to extraordinary means such as marvelous methods of fertilization. The unargued presupposition of Gen 2:5 is clearly that the divine providence was operating during the [[150]] creation period through processes which any reader would recognize as normal in the natural world of his day.

The last clause of verse 5 cites as a second reason for the lack of vegetation the absence of men. Though there be no rainfall, if man is present "to till the ground" and, in particular, to construct a system of artificial ir-

---

5. *New Commentary on Genesis* (Edinburgh: T&T Clark, 1888), 1:115. Cf. W. H. Green, *The Unity of the Book of Genesis* (New York: Scribner's, 1910), 25.

6. That much is deducible from Gen 1:26–30 whatever one's view of the chronological character of the order of narration in Gen 1 as a whole.

rigation, he can make the desert blossom as the rose.[7] The effect of this last clause of Gen 2:5 is to confirm and strengthen the principle that normal providential procedure characterized the creation era.[8]

Verses 6 and 7 then correspond respectively to the two clauses in verse 5b and relate how the environmental deficiencies there cited were remedied. First, "flooding waters[9] [[151]] began to rise from the earth and watered all the face of the ground" (v. 6). Here was a source of natural irrigation to compensate for the want of rain. The first verb is a Hebrew imperfect and the inceptive nuance—"began to"—is legitimate for that form and is required in this case if verse 6 is not to neutralize the first clause in verse 5b. The English versions of verse 6 convey the impression that there was an ample watering

7. This verse reflects conditions in the East where irrigation is of the essence of farming and distinct terms are found to distinguish land that is naturally irrigated from land that is artificially irrigated. Cf. T. H. Gaster, *Thespis: Ritual, Myth, and Drama in the Ancient Near East* (New York: Schuman, 1950), 123, 126.

8. If the view of some exegetes were adopted that the sphere of Gen 2:5 is limited to such cultivated plants as were found in the garden of Eden, the concept of providential operations involved would remain the same. The text would still affirm that at a point prior to the creation of man and, therefore, within the creation era the absence of certain natural products was attributable to the absence of the natural means for their providential preservation. It may here be added that this avoidance of unnecessary supernaturalism in providence during the "six days" accords well with the analogy of subsequent divine providence for the latter too is characterized by a remarkable economy in its resort to the supernatural.

9. The meaning of the Hebrew word *ʾēd* is uncertain. It probably denotes subterranean waters which rise to the surface and thence as gushing springs or flooding rivers inundate the land. The watering of the garden of Eden by a river in the immediate sequel (v. 10) may be intended as a specific localized instance of the *ʾēd* phenomena (v. 6). Note the similar advance in the case of man, viewed in verse 5b as the artificial irrigator, from the general statement of verse 7 to the specific assignment in the garden (vv. 8, 15). The word *ʾēd* appears elsewhere in the Old Testament only in Job 36:27. That passage is also difficult; but *lĕʾēdô* there seems to denote the underground ore, as it were, from which the raindrops are extracted and refined, i.e., by the process of evaporation in the cycle of cloud formation and precipitation. (For the translation of the preposition *lĕ* as "from" see C. H. Gordon, *Ugaritic Manual* [Rome: Pontifical Biblical Institute, 1955], 75.) The Hebrew *ʾēd* is probably to be derived from the Akkadian *edû*, a Sumerian loanword which denotes overflowing waters. (Cf. E. Speiser, "*ʾed* in the Story of Creation," *BASOR* 140 [1955]: 9–11.) Other views are that it comes from Akkadian *id*, "river," also a Sumerian loanword (used in the Mari texts as the name of the river god) or from *Îda*, the name of a high mountain in central Crete (a tentative suggestion of C. H. Gordon in "Homer and Bible," *HUCA* 26 [1955]: 62–63).

of the earth during the very time which verse 5 describes. If that were so, the explanatory statement of verse 5, "for the Lord God had not caused it to rain upon the earth," would be stranded as an irrelevance. Actually, verse 6 reports the emergence of a new natural phenomenon, the necessary preliminary to the creation of the florae described in verse 5a.

Verse 7 then records the creation of man. With adequate natural irrigation already available, the mere preservation of vegetation does not require man's husbandry. But its full horticultural exploitation does. Besides, the mention of man at this point need not be accounted for solely in terms of his services to the vegetable kingdom for he was not made for it but it for him.

Genesis 2:5ff. and the Interpretation of Genesis 1

Embedded in Gen 2:5ff. is the principle that the *modus operandi* of the divine providence was the same during the creation period as that of ordinary providence at the present time. It is now to be demonstrated that those who adopt the traditional approaches cannot successfully integrate this revelation with Gen 1 as they interpret it.

In contradiction to Gen 2:5, the twenty-four-hour day theory must presuppose that God employed other than the ordinary secondary means in executing his works of providence. To take just one example, it was the work of the "third day" that the waters should be gathered together into [[152]] seas and that the dry land should appear and be covered with vegetation (Gen 1:9–13). All this according to the theory in question transpired within twenty-four hours. But continents just emerged from under the seas do not become thirsty land as fast as that by the ordinary process of evaporation. And yet according to the principle revealed in Gen 2:5 the process of evaporation in operation at that time was the ordinary one.

The results, indeed, approach the ludicrous when it is attempted to synchronize Gen 2:5 with Gen 1 interpreted in terms of a week of twenty-four-hour days. On that interpretation, vegetation was created on what we may call "Tuesday." Therefore, the vegetationless situation described in Gen 2:5 cannot be located later than "Tuesday" morning. Neither can it be located earlier than that for Gen 2:5 assumes the existence of dry land which does not appear until the "third day." Besides, would it not have been droll to attribute the lack of vegetation to the lack of water either on "Sunday" when the earth itself was quite unfashioned or on "Monday" when there was nothing but water to be seen? Hence the twenty-four-hour day theorist must think of the Almighty as hesitant to put in the plants on "Tuesday" morning because it would not rain until later in the day! (It must of course be supposed that it did rain, or at least that some supply of water was provided, before "Tuesday" was over, for by the end of the day the earth was abounding with that vegetation which according to Gen 2:5 had hitherto been lacking for want of water.)

How can a serious exegete fail to see that such a reconstruction of a "Tuesday morning" in a literal creation week is completely foreign to the historical perspectives of Gen 2:5? It is a strange blindness that questions the orthodoxy of all who reject the traditional twenty-four-hour day theory when the truth is that endorsement of that theory is incompatible with belief in the self-consistency of the Scriptures.

But any strictly chronological interpretation of Gen 1, even if the "days" are regarded as ages, forces the exegete inescapably into conflict with the principle disclosed in Gen 2:5. The traditional day-age theorist must, for example, imagine that during the creation era plants and trees flourished on the face of an earth spinning alone through a sunless, [[153]] moonless, starless void. Now it will be recognized that that is not ordinary botanical procedure—and yet Gen 2:5 takes for granted ordinary botanical procedure.

In the vain attempt to avoid such a reconstruction, according to which vegetation (product of the "third day") thrives without benefit of the sun (product of the "fourth day"), the most unwarranted notions of the work of the "fourth day" have been substituted for the straightforward statements of the text. Genesis 1:14–19 declares that the heavenly bodies were on the "fourth day" created and set in their familiar positions. Moses is certainly not suggesting merely that hitherto hidden heavenly bodies now become visible on earth. He knew how to express such an idea in Hebrew if that had been his intent (cf. his account of the appearance of the continents from under the seas, v. 9). The very least that transpired on the "day" in question is that the sun was brought into a radically new relationship to the earth wherein it began to govern earth's times and seasons and in general to affect life on earth as men now observe it to do. But the strictly chronological view of Gen 1, even with such a minimizing exegesis of the "fourth day," must still suppose that prior to this reordering of the universe on the "fourth day," plant life had flourished on the earth contrary to present natural law.

On this traditional reconstruction it is impossible to make sense of Gen 2:5. Surely if vegetation could have flourished without the sun it could have survived without rain. Laws quite unlike any we know would then have prevailed. For that matter, God could have preserved forests in space without so much as roots in a dry earth. It would then, however, be completely irrelevant for Gen 2:5 to assign natural reasons for the absence of vegetation. Indeed, the very fact that it offered a perfectly natural explanation would bring Gen 2:5 into principial contradiction to Gen 1.

To the divisive higher critic this might mean only that there is another item to add to this list of alleged contradictions between the two variant creation accounts he supposes he has discovered in Gen 1 and 2. But the orthodox exegete, having been confronted with the evidence of ordinary providential procedure in Gen 2:5 will be bound to reject the rigidly chronological interpretations of Gen 1 for the reason [[154]] that they necessarily presuppose radically different providential operations for the creation period.

If Gen 2:5 obviates certain traditional interpretations of Gen 1, by the same token it validates the not so traditional interpretation which regards the chronological framework of Gen 1 as a figurative representation of the time span of creation and judges that within that figurative framework the data of creation history have been arranged according to other than strictly chronological considerations.

To be sure, certain features are found in their proper relative positions chronologically. But where that is so it must be determined by factors other than the order of narration. It is perfectly obvious, for example, that the rest of the "seventh day," expressive of the divine joy in creation consummated, must follow chronologically the creation labors themselves. Again, the implications of man's position as lord of creation, the scope of the cultural mandate, and other considerations require that the creation of man concluded the creative acts of God in the actual historical sequence as well as in the order of narration.

Nevertheless, Gen 2:5 forbids the conclusion that the order of narration is exclusively chronological. The rationale of the arrangement involves other factors. To some extent a topical approach informs the account. As has been frequently observed, a succession of correspondences emerges when the contents of "days" one to three are laid alongside the contents of "days" four to six. Another literary interest at work within this parallelism is that of achieving climax, as is done, for example, in introducing men after all other creatures as their king.

Of greater significance for the life of man than these merely literary devices is the Sabbathic pattern of the overall structure of Gen 1:1–2:3. For the Creator's way in the day that he made the earth and the heavens must be the way of his image-bearer also. The precise ratio of man's work to his rest is a matter of following the chronological structure of the revelation in which God was pleased to record his creation triumph. The aeons of creation history could have been divided into other than six periods. For temporally the "days" are not of equal length (cf., e.g., the seventh "day" [[155]] which is everlasting), and logically the infinitely diversified creative works were susceptible of analysis into other than six divisions. But the Creator in his wisdom, adapting the proportions of the ordinance, it would seem, to the constitutional needs of man, chose to reveal his creative acts in terms of six "days" of work followed by a seventh "day" of rest.

The divine demand for human imitation inherent in the Sabbathic pattern of that revelation becomes articulate in the fourth word of the Decalogue. The comparison there drawn between the divine original and the human copy is fully satisfied by the facts that in each case there is the Sabbathic principle and the six-one ratio. The argument that Gen 1 must be strictly chronological because man's six days of labor follow one another in chronological succession forces the analogy unnecessarily. The logic of such argument would not allow one to stop short of the conclusion that the creation "days" must all have been of equal duration and twenty-four hours at that.

The Literary Genre of Genesis 1

Quite apart from the evidence of Gen 2:5 the figurative framework interpretation of Gen 1 which it demands would commend itself to us above the traditional interpretations. Only brief mention will be made here of other lines of evidence since it is the main burden of this article to center attention on Gen 2:5 whose decisive import for the Gen 1 problem has (to the writer's knowledge) been hitherto unappreciated.

The literary character of Gen 1:1–2:5 prepares the exegete for the presence there of a stronger figurative element than might be expected were it ordinary prose. This passage is not, of course, full-fledged Semitic poetry. But neither is it ordinary prose. Its structure is strophic and throughout the strophes many refrains echo and re-echo. Instances occur of other poetic features like parallelism (1:27; 2:2) and alliteration (1:1). In general then the literary treatment of the creation in Gen 1 is in the epic tradition.

Having made such an observation concerning the literary [[156]] genre of the creation record, it is imperative (especially in the present theological scene) that one convinced of the genuinely historical nature of the events recorded in the opening chapters of Genesis promptly add that the disregard for historical truth associated with the usual epic is not imported along with the formal literary aspects of the epic style into the divine revelation. Such importation was no more inevitable than that the polytheism of pre-biblical psalmody, for example, must have been carried over with the religious lyric form into the biblical Psalter. Though Gen 1 be epic in literary style, its contents are not legendary or mythical in either a Liberal or Barthian sense. The semi-poetic style, however, should lead the exegete to anticipate the figurative strand in this genuinely historical record of the origins of the universe.

It also needs considerable emphasis, even among orthodox exegetes, that specific evidence is required for identifying particular elements in the early chapters of Genesis as literary figures. The semi-poetic form of Gen 1 does not make it an exception. Exegesis which disregards this degenerates into allegorizing and these chapters are not allegories.

The specific exegetical evidence for the figurative character of the several chronological terms in Gen 1 has been repeatedly cited. The word "day" must be figurative because it is used for the eternity during which God rests from his creative labors. The "day's" subordinate elements, "evening" and "morning," must be figurative for they are mentioned as features of the three "days" before the text records the creation of those lights in the firmament of heaven which were to divide the day from the night. (From the position taken in this article the last argument is, of course, only *ad hominem*. But on the other hand, if the validity of the interpretation advocated here is recognized, the figurative nature of the "evenings" and "mornings" follows with equal necessity.)

Purely exegetical considerations, therefore, compel the conclusion that the divine author has employed the imagery of an ordinary week to provide a figurative chronological framework for the account of his creative acts. And if it is a figurative week then it is not a literal week of twenty-four-hour days. Furthermore, once the figurative nature of the chronological pattern is appreciated the literalness of the sequence is [[157]] no more sacrosanct than the literalness of the duration of the days in this figurative week.

Whether the events narrated occurred in the order of their narration would, as far as the chronological framework of Gen 1 is concerned, be an open exegetical question. The question is actually closed in favor of the non-chronological interpretation by the exegetical evidence of Gen 2:5. But if the exegete did not have the light of Gen 2:5, he would certainly be justified in turning to natural revelation for possible illumination of the question left open by special revelation. And surely natural revelation concerning the sequence of developments in the universe as a whole and the sequence of the appearance of the various orders of life on our planet (unless that revelation has been completely misinterpreted) would require the exegete to incline to a not exclusively chronological interpretation of the creation week.

The exegete could then find confirmation of this view in the evidence of a topical interest in the arrangement of Gen 1 and in the non-chronological mode of representing history which is certainly common enough elsewhere in Scripture. He might also well observe the likeness between Moses' record of the creation "week" and certain visions of John, the seer of the Apocalypse, which are heptad in structure with successively numbered divisions and yet are not strictly chronological in sequence. It appears that the God of revelation chose to reveal the primeval ages of creation and the eschatological ages of re-creation in similar literary form.

CHAPTER TWO

Space and Time in the Genesis Cosmogony

(1996)

To rebut the literalist interpretation of the Genesis creation "week" propounded by the young-earth theorists is a central concern of this article. At the same time, the exegetical evidence adduced also refutes the harmonistic day-age view. The conclusion is that as far as the time frame is concerned, with respect to both the duration and sequence of events, the scientist is left free of biblical constraints in hypothesizing about cosmic origins.

The opening section gives a biblico-theological sketch of the two-register nature of cosmology as presented in Scripture. The second major section shows how two-register cosmology informs and shapes the treatment of both the space and time dimensions in the Genesis prologue. It is found that a metaphorical relationship obtains between the two levels, the heavenly level (upper register) being described in figures drawn from the earthly level (lower register). As for the seven-day scheme, it belongs to the upper register and is, therefore, to be understood figuratively, not literally. The point of the concluding section is that Gen 1, on any view that identifies the narrative order with the temporal sequence, would contradict the teaching of Gen 2:5 concerning the natural mode of providence during the creation process.

* * * * *

An *apologia* is needed for addressing again the question of the chronological data in the Genesis creation account. Simply put—the editor made me do it. Over thirty years ago, I made an exegetical case for a non-literal interpretation of the chronological framework.[1] In the interval, that approach has found increasing acceptance. Its most distinctive

1. "Because It Had Not Rained," *WTJ* 20 (1958): 146–57 [= pp. 9–19 in the present volume].

argument, derived from Gen 2:5, has occasionally been incorporated in studies with similar views of the chronological issue.[2] Advocacy of the literalist tradition, however, is as clamant as ever, and it was thought that a more accessible statement of my exegetical arguments could prove useful at this date.

In preparing the restatement another line of exegetical evidence has come to the fore in my thinking. It concerns a two-register cosmological concept that structures the whole biblical cosmogony. This matter developed into the main point and has become in this essay the umbrella under which the other, restated arguments are accorded an ancillary place here and there. My *apologia* concludes then with a claim of adding something somewhat fresh to the old debate.

Two-Register Cosmology

Central in biblical revelation is the relationship of God, whose dwelling place is heaven's glory (Ps 115:16), to man on earth. A two-register cosmos is thus the scene of the biblical drama, which features constant interaction between the upper and lower registers.[3]

From the perspective of man (more precisely, of man in his pre-consummation state), the heavenly [[3]] register is an invisible realm. However, heaven is not to be thought of as occupying a separate place off at a distance from the earth or even outside the cosmos. Heaven and earth relate to each other spatially more after the manner of (speculated) dark matter and visible matter. When earthlings experience a proleptic opening of their eyes, they see that the very spot where they are is the gate of heaven (Gen 28:16, 17), filled with heavenly chariots of fire (2 Kgs 6:17).

Reference to the invisible realm as "above" is simply a spatial figure based on a natural analogy between what is physically higher and what is more exalted in dignity and honor. This same analogy accounts for the designating of the invisible sphere by the name of the upper level within the visible world. Visible space is itself divided into heaven and earth (and,

2. Cf. H. Blocher, *In the Beginning* (Downers Grove, IL: InterVarsity Press, 1984); C. E. Hummel, *The Galileo Connection* (Downers Grove, IL: InterVarsity Press, 1986); R. Maatman, *The Impact of Evolutionary Theory: A Christian View* (Sioux Center: Dordt College Press, 1993).

3. Theological differences aside, the cosmology of mythology is analogous. Indeed, mythology may be defined formally precisely as a portrayal of human affairs in terms of a dynamic interrelating of divine and human realms.

in tripartite formulations, the waters under the earth). The visible heaven consists of the star-studded canopy of the sky overhead, with the clouds, the waters that are above the earth. Taking its name from this above-section of visible space, supernal space (the above-section of the two-register cosmos) is then called "heaven."[4] Further, when the heavenly Glory is revealed in visible theophany, it is a manifestation in clouds and related phenomena. So close is the association of God's dwelling and actions with the visible heaven (cf., e.g., Ps 104:2–4) that it may be difficult to determine in given cases whether "heaven" refers to the visible or invisible heaven, or both at once.[5]

The two-register character of biblical cosmology, relative as it is to man's preglorification status, is not permanent. It belongs only to the first stage of an eschatological movement that was integral to creation from the beginning and leads to a final stage of consummation. As we trace this eschatological development, an important feature that emerges is the archetype-replica (original-likeness) relationship between the upper and lower registers.

From the beginning, God's presence was peculiarly and preeminently associated with the invisible heaven. That was where he dwelt, the site of his enthronement (cf., e.g., Deut 26:15; 1 Kgs 8:39, 43, 49; Pss 11:4; 102:20 [19]; 103:19; Isa 66:1; Matt 5:45; 7:21). It was there that he manifested his Glory to the angels, the Glory that fills invisible space and makes it a temple, the Glory-epiphany that is itself God's temple. But though the invisible, upper register heaven was God's true sanctuary, the earth also was at the first the scene of a special visible divine presence.[6] Invisible space was the holy of holies; and visible space (visible heaven and earth) was a holy place. Creation was sanctified in all its spatial dimensions, with lower register space a replica of the upper register archetypal temple.

Eden was the sacred center of the earthly reproduction of the heavenly reality. Here in the garden of the Lord, the Spirit-Glory that fills the heavenly temple was visibly manifested on the mountain of God (cf. Isa 51:3; Ezek 28:13ff.; 31:8–9), the vertical cosmic axis linking heaven and earth. The revealed presence of the King of Glory crowning this sacred mountain marked the earth as a holy theocratic domain. Reflecting the identity of

---

4. Similarly, the depths of the sea or subsurface earth metaphorically signify the infernal realm.

5. "Heaven of heavens" (cf. Deut 10:14; 1 Kgs 8:27; Neh 9:6; Pss 115:16; 148:4) apparently distinguishes a "higher" heaven, possibly the clouds of heaven (the water "above the heavens," cf. Ps 148:4) or the invisible heavens.

6. For elaboration of this theme see *KP*, 47–49.

Eden as a sanctuary was the priestly responsibility assigned to man to guard the garden from profanation (Gen 2:15). The sequel underscores this. When man forfeited his priestly role, guardianship of the holy site was transferred to the cherubim (Gen 3:24). They were guardians of the heavenly temple throne and the extension of that function to Eden accents the identity of this earthly spot as a visible reproduction of the temple above.[7]

Man's fall radically altered the way the replication of holy heaven on earth was to unfold. As a consequence of the breaking of the creation covenant, the Glory-theophany was presently withdrawn and the earth, though still under the sovereign control of the King of heaven, was left an unsanctified place. Only by way of redemptive intrusion does theophany-centered holy place reappear in the otherwise non-holy, post-fall world—most prominently in the cultus of Israel's typological theocratic kingdom.

[[4]] Where sanctuary does emerge again on earth, its nature as a copy of the heavenly archetype is emphasized. The tabernacle and temple, restorations of Eden's sanctuary with cherubim-guarded throne of God, are made after the pattern of the upper register temple revealed to Moses and Solomon.[8] They point ahead typologically to the apocalypse of the heavenly temple at the end of the ages. At that consummation of redemptive history, presaged by the Sabbath ordinance, the visible-invisible differentiation of space comes to an end as the heavenly Glory is unveiled to the eyes of redeemed earthlings, their perceptive capabilities transformed now by glorification. The boundary of heaven and earth disappears. All becomes one cosmic holy of holies. God himself is the Glory-temple, the true temple, archetype and antitype of prototypical temples and provisional theophanies.

Redemption is a way of achieving the original telos of creation despite the fall. A successful probation by the first Adam would have let through a cosmologically two-register history to an eschatological climax at which Eden's Glory would have been absorbed into the surpassing heavenly Glory. At the dawning of the eternal Sabbath for humanity, all space, without distinction any longer of upper and lower cosmological levels, would have become a consummate revelation of the Glory of heaven's King. Because of the fall, that eschatological omega-point had to be won by the second Adam.

---

7. Ibid.

8. The tabernacle and temple were so designed that both in their horizontal and vertical sectioning they also portrayed the visible register of the cosmic temple with its corresponding partitioning. Cf. *IOS*, 39–42.

Two-register cosmologies left their imprint on the form of ancient graphic and literary materials in a variety of ways. A quite literal case of the two-register format is seen in graphic representations like the Assyrian reliefs that picture the king in a lower register, whether driving forward in battle or returning triumphantly, and in a higher register the god in a matching stance.[9] The book of Job offers a clear instance of the shaping of a piece of literature by the two-layer cosmology. In the prologue, heavenly scenes (Job 1:6–12; 2:1–6) alternate with closely related earthly scenes (Job 1:1–5, 13–22; 2:7–10). A similar movement from the upper to the lower register is found throughout the book of Revelation. Each series of visions of happenings on earth is introduced by a disclosure of the heavenly control center of the universe, where the earthly judgments are decreed and whence their executive agents descend. With its characteristic opening of the heavens, the apocalyptic genre is a place we naturally expect to find the formative impact of two-register cosmology on literature. Another such place is a cosmogony like the Genesis prologue.

Cosmology of the Genesis Prologue

The creation prologue (Gen 1:1–2:3) presents a theological mapping of the cosmos with space and time coordinates. Both these dimensions exhibit the biblical two-register cosmology, a construct that functions as an infrastructure of the entire account. And this, we discover, has a decisive bearing on the interpretation of the chronological data.

The Space Coordinate

Two-Register Space

Genesis 1:1. What this opening verse states is that God, in the beginning,[10] created both the upper and lower spatial spheres. "The heavens and the earth" is not just a merismus, a pair of antonyms which as a set signifies totality. The

9. This example thus contains the additional feature of the likeness of the lower to the upper phenomenon. Comparison of these reliefs with literary accounts of warfare as a two-level affair involving earthly conflict of nations below and divine or angelic contention in the heavens (cf. Dan 10:12, 13, 20, 21; Zech 9:13, 14) illustrates how these cultural media can be mutually illuminating.

10. For a discussion of *bĕrēʾšît*, see below.

phrase rather denotes concretely the actual two components that together comprehend all of creation. That does indeed amount to everything, but in translating, the separate, specific identity of each of these two components must be preserved. One thing demanding this is that verse 2, resuming "the earth" of verse 1, treats it by itself as a distinct, individual sphere.[11]

More precisely, what Gen 1:1 affirms is that God created not just the spatial dimensions immediately accessible to man, but the heavens too, that is, the invisible realm of the divine Glory and angelic beings. This interpretation is reflected in the apostle Paul's Christological exposition of Gen 1:1, declaring that the Son created "all things that are in heaven and that are in earth, visible and invisible, whether they be thrones, or dominions, or principalities, or powers" (Col 1:16; cf. John 1:1–3). Similarly Nehemiah, reflecting on the Genesis creation account, finds a reference there to the invisible heaven of the angels (Neh 9:6), and the only possible referent is "the heavens" of Gen 1:1 (and the reference to that in Gen 2:1, if the latter summation does in fact include Gen 1:1, not just 1:2–31).[12]

Moreover, in the context of Gen 1 itself, the visible "heaven" or "firmament" (v. 8) is derived from what is called "earth" in verses 1 and 2. Hence, [[5]] the "heavens" that are distinguished from that "earth" in verse 1 must be the invisible heavens. This would not necessarily be the case if verse 1 were a summary heading for the entire account. But what Gen 1:1 says about "the beginning" cannot be summing up the entire process of creation, for the allusions to the *bĕrēʾšît* of Gen 1:1 in Prov 8:22, 23 identify that "beginning" as prior to (not coextensive with) the developments traced in Gen 1:2ff. Though it is an independent statement, Gen 1:1 is, therefore, not a heading but a declaration concerning the initial phase of creation history.

Some oppose construing Gen 1:1–2 as I have because, they insist, the phrase "the heavens and the earth" always signifies the finished product, the well-ordered, occupied universe, and hence "the earth" that appears in that phrase in verse 1 cannot be the unfinished, uninhabitable place called "earth" in verse 2.[13] But contrary to this often repeated claim, in other appearances of the phrase "(the) heavens and (the) earth" in Scripture, the idea

11. See further W. P. Brown, *Structure, Role, and Ideology in the Hebrew and Greek Texts of Genesis 1:1–2:3* (Atlanta: Scholars Press, 1993), 102 n. 12.

12. The same question arises in Exod 20:11. On this, see the discussion of the phrase "the heavens and the earth" below.

13. If one does so insist, then recognition of what Prov 8 reveals about *bĕrēʾšît* in Gen 1:1 would compel adoption of some variety of the discredited gap theory to account for the earth in Gen 1:2.

that these realms were finished and inhabited is not what is signified by this phrase itself but would have to be supplied by the context. And even if all references after Gen 1:1 happened to be to a heaven and earth in such a finished state, that would not be determinative for the Gen 1:1 context, which deals with the very process of developing the product from an empty to a furnished condition.[14] In fact, it may well be that in all the appearances of "(the) heavens and (the) earth" (over half of which are allusions to the creation account, acknowledging the Lord as the maker of heaven and earth), the phrase signifies precisely the invisible and the visible realms, and thus the whole two-register world.

There is, therefore, no reason to resist the clear direction of Prov 8:22–23 for the interpretation of Gen 1:1 as referring to an earlier juncture, not to a later stage when the earth had become habitable for man. In point of fact, though the visible realm, the "earth," was not completed until the end of the creation "week," completion of the invisible heavenly realm (with its angelic hosts) had evidently been accomplished "in the beginning." Job 38:7 indicates that the celestial sons of God existed at the point in earth's development described in Gen 1:2ff. Thus, in view of the close allusive relationship of Job 38 to Gen 1, Job 38:7 also furnishes independent support for the interpretation of "the heavens" in Gen 1:1 as the invisible sphere of the angels of God.

Genesis 1:1, therefore, states—and how eminently fitting is this affirmation for the opening of the canonical Scriptures—that God in the beginning made the whole world, both its upper and lower spatial registers, both its invisible and visible dimensions, heaven and earth, all.

Genesis 1:2. Both invisible and visible space, introduced in Gen 1:1 as "the heavens" and "the earth" respectively, appear again in verse 2. Focusing on the lower register, this verse describes the earth at an early inchoate stage (v. 2a and b). But it also prepares for the following account of how this uninhabitable world was transformed into a paradisiacal home for man by pointing to the God of the invisible heaven, present above the darkness-enshrouded waters of the earth below (v. 2c). This creative Spirit-Presence is depicted in avian metaphor[15] as hovering in fostering fashion above the

14. Cf. the observations of A. Heidel, *The Babylonian Genesis* (Chicago: University of Chicago Press, 1963), 91.

15. On the common use of avian imagery for deity in the ancient Near East see my "The Feast of Cover-over," *JETS* 37 (1994): 497–98 (hereafter, "Cover-over") [= pp. 151–52 in the present volume]. Cf., e.g., in pharaonic nomenclature the Horus (or *serekh*) name.

world. As shown (for one thing) by the striking echo of Gen 1:2 in Deut 32:10, 11, the "Spirit" here refers to that heavenly epiphany which is known in its manifestation within the visible world as the Shekinah, the theophanic cloud of glory.[16] Including as it does then the Spirit-Glory of the temple in heaven along with the earth below, Gen 1:2 carries forward the two-register cosmology contained in verse 1.

Genesis 1:3–2:3. The several creative fiats by which visible space gets fashioned into a habitable world in the course of the six days (Gen 1:3ff.) are sovereign decrees. They clearly evoke the throne of the King of Glory, the King invisible, the only God, dwelling in light unapproachable (1 Tim 1:17; 6:16). Each such fiat, therefore, signals the continuing presence of the upper register sphere in the panoramic scenario of the creation narrative. That these fiats emanate from the invisible heavens is indicated with particular clarity in the account of man's creation in God's image. For there (Gen 1:26) the divine fiat takes the consultative "let us" form that reveals the setting to be the angelic council,[17] the judicial assembly which is a regular feature in disclosures of the heavenly reality denoted "Spirit" in Gen 1:2.

Another index of the continued inclusion of the heavenly register in the scene is the motif of the divine surveillance and judgment found in the refrain: "and God saw that it was good" (Gen 1:4, 10, 12, 18, 21, 25, 31). For repeatedly conjoined with statements that the invisible heaven is the site of [[6]] God's temple-throne is the declaration that from there he engages in a judicial scrutiny of the world. From that throne "his eyes behold, his pupils try the sons of men" (Ps 11:4c). It was from his throne in heaven that the divine Masterbuilder looked down, saw the unfolding work of his hands, and pronounced it "good," that is, in perfect accord with his architectonic plan (cf. Prov 8:30, 31).

Further, the full two-register cosmology comes to expression in the fiat-fulfillment format, which is the basic structure of each of the six day-stanzas. While the "let there be" is uttered at the upper register, the "and it was so" transpires at the lower register. The fiat of the Logos-Word above is executed by the Spirit in the earth below.[18]

16. For an extensive treatment of this see *IOS*.

17. Cf. ibid., 22–23.

18. This alternating sequence of heavenly and earthly scenes is similar to the pattern of the prologue to Job. The similarity is not just formal, for in each case what takes place in the lower register is determined by the sovereign word of God revealed in the heavenly council.

Once again and quite directly God's throne in the upper section of the two-register cosmos is alluded to in statements about the Creator's seventh day rest, which is his heavenly enthronement (Gen 2:2b, 3b). The earthly register is also included in the day seven section, for along with the Creator's Sabbath of royal resting above, it also contains the appointment of the Sabbath ordinance for human observance on earth below (Gen 2:3).[19]

Table 1. Two-Register Space in Genesis Prologue

	Verse 1	**Verse 2**	**Days 1–6**	**Day 7**
Upper Register	heaven	Spirit	fiats	God's Sabbath
Lower Register	earth	deep	fulfillments	Sabbath Ordinance

The summary chart of the space dimension theme in the Genesis prologue (Table 1) shows that two-register cosmology is present not only as a concept but as a pervasive factor in the organization of the composition. Additional evidence of its influence on the literary structure of the passage will be noted below.

Replication Relationship of the Two Registers

The lower register relates to the upper as replica to archetype. Before seeing how that comes to expression in the creation account, we must call attention to how the six days fall naturally into two triads, one dealing with creation kingdoms and the other with the creature kings given dominion over them. As frequently noticed, the two triads run in parallel with obvious correlation of their successive members.[20]

The earthly products of the first three days mirror one or another characteristic of the invisible heaven, the above realm, the realm of light

19. Space and time are conceptually correlative in the Sabbath. In our analysis of the time coordinate of this cosmological charting the Sabbath will be given closer consideration.

20. This will be spelled out in our discussion of the replication relationship of the two registers. Evidence will appear there for preferring the kingdom-king analysis of the themes of the two triads over something more general, like regions and their occupants or habitations and inhabitants.

and overarching Glory (Gen 1:2). The day-light called forth on day one was a replica of that Glory-light. The bright firmament-vault of day two was so much the likeness of its archetype that they shared the same name, "heaven" (Gen 1:8). The lofty trees, the climactic fruit of day three, are used in Scripture as an apt figure for the cosmos (cf. Dan 4:10–12). With their high spreading branches a realm for the birds of the heaven, they are comparable to the firmament-heaven in which the birds fly (Gen 1:20), a towering image pointing to the overarching Spirit-heaven above.

Moving on from copies of the heavenly kingdom to images of the heavenly King, the second triad of days presents creature kings whose roles in the hierarchy of creation are earthly reflections of the royal rule of the Creator enthroned above. Royal terminology is explicitly used for the luminaries of day four. In that they regulate the cycle of light and darkness, they are said to "rule over" the kingdom of day and night produced on day one (Gen 1:16; cf. Ps 136:8, 9). God's blessing-mandate to the creatures of day five closely resembles the dominion mandate afterwards given to man. In each case royal occupation of the assigned domain is to be accomplished by being fruitful, multiplying, and filling (Gen 1:22, 28). So the birds and fish would exercise their rule over the sky and sea, the kingdom realms of day two. Incidentally, the birds of day five and the luminaries of day four—both associated with the "firmament of heaven" (Gen 1:14, 15, 17, 20)—are like the King of heaven in other ways besides their ruling function. The birds' overshadowing of their nests (Deut 32:11) and the luminosity of the sun and moon become biblical figures for the Glory-Spirit as a protective covering, the heavenly Sun and Shield (cf. Ps 84:12 [11]).[21] Culminating the series of earthly replicas of the Creator-King is the final creature of day six, man, the image of God and his holy angels (Gen 1:26). In this earthling, made like unto the Glory-Spirit with respect to the threefold glory of royal dominion, moral excellence, and (in eschatological prospect) visual luminosity,[22] [[7]] creaturely reproduction of the heavenly King of kings is perfected.

The replication motif emerges distinctly on day seven in the Sabbath ordinance, designed to call man to the imitation of the divine sabbatical pattern. Discussion of this will be deferred, however, until we are dealing with the time coordinate of the Genesis cosmology.

As a final illustration of replication in the spatial dimension, we turn to the way the two-register pattern of the total cosmos, visible and invisible, is

21. Cf. my "Cover-over" [= pp. 151–67 in the present volume].

22. Cf. *IOS*.

repeated within the visible, lower register by itself in its subdivision into an upper realm (heaven) and a lower realm (earth). This secondary, replicated two-register structure is highlighted by the arrangement of the contents of the two parallel triads of days according to their upper or lower location.

The first members of each triad are related to the upper level, the heaven: the light of the sky on day one and the heavenly luminaries on day four. The third members belong to the lower level, the earth: the land and its vegetation on day three and the land animals and man on day six. And the second members are strikingly designed to serve as links between the first and third members. For these middle units of the two triads each combines both upper and lower levels: the sky and the sea in day two and the birds of the air and fish of the sea in day five.

Table 2. Location of Triads' Productions

First Triad		Level		Second Triad
day one	—	upper	—	day four
day two	{	upper lower	}	day five
day three	—	lower	—	day six

Here again we see that the two-register cosmology construct was a decisive factor in determining the literary shape of the Genesis prologue.[23]

The Time Coordinate

Space and time, the cosmological coordinates, are correlative. Interlocking of the two is pronounced in God's seventh day rest, a temporal concept that connotes the spatial reality of the holy site of God's enthronement. Also indicative of their correlation is the giving of the temporal names "day" and "night" to the spatial phenomena of light and darkness (Gen 1:5). It is inevitable then that the two-register structuring of the spatial dimension will

23. These data also attest further to the parallelism between the successive members of the two triads of days.

also be found in the temporal dimension, and with it the archetype-replica relationship between the two registers. We have seen that by reason of this replication relationship earthly things are a rich source of metaphor for the realities of the invisible heaven. God is portrayed as hovering like an eagle over its nest and as resting like a man after his work is done (cf. Exod 31:17); upper register space is designated "heaven" after the upper level of visible space; etc. We naturally expect then that in the case of time, as of space, the upper register will draw upon the lower register for its figurative depiction. Hence, when we find that God's upper level activity of issuing creative fiats from his heavenly throne is pictured as transpiring in a week of earthly days, we readily recognize that, in keeping with the pervasive contextual pattern, this is a literary figure, an earthly, lower register time metaphor for an upper register, heavenly reality.[24]

Lower Register Time

Twin Record. Earthly Time is articulated in the astronomical phenomena that measure off and structure its flow. It is the astral-solar-lunar relationships of the earth that define the units, the years and the days, in which man experiences (lower register) time. They produce the sequence of light and darkness that marks the days. They arrange the signs in the sky that announce the seasonal round of the years. Time is named, its meaning is expressed, in this system of calibration. The establishing of this regulatory order by which lower register time is defined and in which it has its being is recorded in the creation account. Twice in fact: once at the beginning of the first triad of days (Gen 1:3–5) and a second time at the beginning of the second triad (Gen 1:14–19).

Temporal Recapitulation. The non-sequential nature of the creation narrative, and thus the non-literal nature of the creation "week," is evident from the recording of the institution of lower register time in both the

24. Following nineteenth-century theologian W. G. T. Shedd, C. J. Collins identifies the creation days as an anthropomorphism, part of an extended anthropomorphic portrayal of the Creator as the worker-craftsman; cf. "How Old Is the Earth? Anthropomorphic Days in Genesis 1:1–2:3," *Presbyterion* 20 (1994): esp. 117–18 (hereafter, "How Old"). As over against the literalists, this is moving in the right direction. But the explanation needs adjustment, for not all the metaphors used of God are anthropomorphic (cf., e.g., the avian image in Gen 1:2) and some of them refer to heavenly realities other than God. It is rather a matter of two-register cosmology and an archetype-ectype relationship between the entire two registers in both their spatial and temporal dimensions.

first and fourth day-sections. This point must be developed here because of its importance as an independent argument against the solar-day and day-age views and because the exegesis involved is preparatory to other arguments below.

The forming and stationing of the sun, moon, and stars are attributed to day four. Their functions [[8]] with respect to the earth are also stated here, first in the fiat section (Gen 1:14, 15) and again (in reverse order) in the fulfillment section (Gen 1:16–18). They are to give light on the earth and to rule by bounding light/day and darkness/night, as well as by demarcating the passage of years and succession of seasons. These effects which are said to result from the production and positioning of the luminaries on day four are the same effects that are already attributed to the creative activity of day one (Gen 1:3–5). There too daylight is produced on the earth and the cycle of light/day and darkness/night is established. In terms of chronology, day four thus brings us back to where we were in day one, and in fact takes us behind the effects described there to the astral apparatus that accounts for them. The literary sequence is then not the same as the temporal sequence of events.

To avoid this consequence, alternative interpretations of day four have been sought. According to one proposal, the luminaries (though unmentioned previously) were in existence before the point in time dealt with in day four and were indeed present at day one as the source of light spoken of there.[25] Day four describes simply their coming into sight, not their creation. Any such view is falsified by the language of the text, which is plainly that of actual production: "Let there be . . . and God made . . . and God set (lit., gave)." The attempt[26] to override this language cannot be passed off as just another instance of phenomenological description. The proposed evasive tactic involves a very different notion—not just the general denominating of objects according to their everyday observed appearance at any and all times, but the relating of a specific event at a particular juncture in the creation process as though witnessed by an observer of the course of events, someone who at the moment reached on day four is supposed to catch sight of the luminaries, hitherto somehow hidden, perhaps by clouds. Disclaimers notwithstanding, this proposal is guilty of foisting an unwarranted meaning on the language affirming God's making and positioning of the luminaries. In the accounts of the other days, everybody rightly recognizes

25. I would agree that this is in fact a correct view of the day one situation, but not that that situation was before day four.

26. For a recent example, cf. Collins, "How Old," 123 n. 55.

that the same language of divine fiat and creative fulfillment signifies the bringing into existence of something new, not just a visual detecting of something that was there all the while. And there is no more excuse for reducing divine acts of production into human acts of perception in day four than there would be elsewhere.

Some advocates of the controverted approach to day four acknowledge more forthrightly its distinctiveness and develop more fully its peculiar feature of the seer figure.[27] An attempt is made to explain the precise sequence of the entire creation narrative by the exigencies of the visual experience of the hypothesized human spectator, as he is conducted through all the successive scenes. Besides the basic objection that it is belied by the language of origination used for the day four event, this form of the observer hypothesis is beset with a special problem of its own. Its suggested guided-tour perspective is a feature of apocalyptic visions and there the presence of the seer figure is plainly mentioned. He is in fact the one who narrates the visions unfolding before him. No such figure is introduced in the creation account; the alleged human spectator is a fiction imposed on the text contrary to its non-visionary genre.

Recognizing that the actual making of the luminaries is related in day four, but still trying to avoid the conclusion that the narrative order is thematic rather than sequential, some would subordinate the statement about the making of the luminaries (vv. 16, 17a) to the statement about their purpose or functions (vv. 17b, 18a), alleging that the only distinctive new development of day four is that these functions then become operational. But the primary declaration that the luminaries were made cannot be eliminated as a day four event in that way—no more so than the statement in the day two account that God made the firmament may be reduced to the idea that a previously existing firmament began to perform its stated purpose of dividing between the waters above and below (Gen 1:6, 7). Moreover, this minimalist view of day four would share the fatal flaw of all views that eliminate the forming of the luminaries from the happenings of day four: it would leave day four with no new contribution, for all the functions mentioned there are already said to be operative in day one.[28]

---

27. A recent case is D. L. Roth, "Genesis and the Real World," *Kerux* 9 (1994): 30–54.

28. The role of ruling cannot be isolated as a new function distinct from those mentioned in day one. In Gen 1:18 ruling the day and night is explicated as dividing the light from the darkness (equivalent to dividing the day from the night, v. 14).

Also entailed in the minimalist interpretation of day four is the pluperfect rendering of the verbs expressing the making of the luminaries in the fulfillment section (vv. 16, 17), introduced by "and it [[9]] was so" (v. 15b). If adopted, the pluperfect could not be restricted to these verbs. For consistently in Gen 1, what immediately follows the fiat and the "and it was so" formula that answers to the fiat is a detailing of what God proceeded to bring into being in execution of the fiat. In day four then the verbs of fulfillment in verses 16, 17 cannot be pluperfect with respect to the fiat of verses 14, 15a. Temporally they follow the fiat, which means the fiat would have to be put in the same pluperfect tense as its subsequent fulfillment, yielding the translated "And God had said." That is, day four as a whole would have to be cast in the pluperfect, and that with reference to the time of the events in the preceding days. Ironically, such a translation would make explicit the non-chronological sequence of the narrative, the very thing the pluperfect proposal was trying to avoid.[29]

Understandably dissatisfied with the contrived nature of these attempts to avoid acknowledging that the act of making the luminaries was a day four event, other opponents of the non-sequential view of the creation narrative have been driven to seek a solution in a reinterpretation of day one. They would account for the presence of light and the cycle of day and night in day one by positing for this point in time some light source other than the one whose origin they admit is assigned to day four and which (according to their commitment to the temporally sequential order of the narrative) did not, therefore, exist until three days (or ages) after day one.

Some speculate about a supernatural light source, a manifestation of divine glory in space. But that distorts the eschatological design of creation's history, according to which the advent of God's Glory as the source of illumination that does away with the need for the sun awaits the consummation.[30] Indeed, the assumption of such a supernatural mode of ongoing

29. A pluperfect rendering of the *wayyiqtol*-form introducing this section is grammatically defensible, precisely because it begins a paragraph, and that would bring out the true temporal relationship of Gen 1:14ff. to what immediately precedes. But though this would establish my thesis without more ado, I would retain the translation, "And God said (v. 14) . . . and God made" (v. 16) in order to preserve the picture of seven successive days, leaving it to the other available evidence to demonstrate the figurative nature of this picture and the dischronologized sequence of the contents of the days.

30. Note also that the presence of this divine Luminary puts an end to the cycle of day and night instituted on day one (Rev 22:5).

providence during the creation week is contradicted by the assumptions that inform Gen 2:5ff.[31]

No more satisfactory is the suggestion that the hypothetical lighting system was some natural arrangement. That would raise questions about the wisdom of the divine procedure. Why would God create such a vast cosmic order only to discard it three days (or ages) later? Why create a replacement cosmos to perform the very same functions already being performed perfectly well by the original system?[32] Like the gap theory of Gen 1:2, this scenario, with its mid-course cosmic upheaval and starting over, would introduce a jarring, discordant note into the simple, stately symphony of the cosmic house-building—planned, performed, and perfected by the all wise master builder.

Any such approach that disconnects the luminaries of day four from the light of day one, denying the cause-effect relationship of the two, violates the overall thematic scheme of the creation narrative. As we have seen, the successive members of the first triad of days correspond to the successive days of the second triad, the relationship of each matching pair being that of creation kingdom (theme of the first triad) to creature king (theme of the second triad). The correspondence is especially close in the day one–day four pair. It is clearly the light phenomena (kingdom) of day one over which the luminaries (kings) of day four rule, producing and regulating it. Temporal recapitulation most certainly occurs at day four and hence there is no escaping the conclusion that the narrative sequence is not intended to be the chronological sequence.

Upper Register Time

The Beginning. As observed above, the allusions in Prov 8:22, 23 to the *bĕrēʾšît* of Gen 1:1 show that this "beginning" precedes the situation surveyed in Gen 1:2ff. It stands at the head of the creation days. While belonging to the creation week,[33] it marks the interface of precreation and the space-time continuum, pointing back to what is signified by "was" in the identification

31. On this, see below.

32. Indeed, in line with the anthropic principle, the original system would necessarily have been virtually the same as its replacement. Cf. R. Maatman, *The Bible, Natural Science, and Evolution* (Sioux Center: Dordt College Press, 1970), 111; A. Lightman, *Ancient Light* (Cambridge: Harvard University Press, 1991), 117–21.

33. This conclusion is required by Exod 20:11, particularly if the "heaven" it refers to as being made during the "six days" includes the invisible heavens, whose formation, unlike that of the earth, was exclusively within "the beginning."

of God as the one "who is, and who was, and who is to come" (Rev 1:8). In Gen 1:1 the "beginning" is peculiarly associated with God himself. Similarly, echoes of *bĕrēʾšît* in the Scriptures focus on divine acts and intratrinitarian relationships back of creation. Equating the beginning with a stage "before the earth was," Prov 8:23 asserts that the personified divine Wisdom was present with God at the beginning (cf. Col 1:17). The prologue of John's gospel identifies "the beginning" in terms of the relationship between God and the Logos, who was God and made all things (John 1:1–3), the one who identifies himself as "the beginning of the creation of God" (Rev 3:14; cf. Rev
[[10]] 21:6; 22:13; Col 1:15–18) and speaks of the glory he had with the Father "before the world was" (John 17:5).

All indicators tell us that "in the beginning" belongs to the upper register, where Father, Son, and Spirit act together in sovereign purpose, word, and power to create the world. "In the beginning" is a time coordinate of invisible space. Entry into the six days that it is, "the beginning" serves to identify them as also belonging to the invisible cosmological register.

The Seventh Day. God is present at the beginning of creation; he *is* "the beginning." He is also "the end," for he appears at the completion of creation as the Sabbath Lord. The seventh day has to do altogether with God, with the upper register. The divine rest which characterizes the seventh day is the reign of the finisher of creation, enthroned in the invisible heavens in the midst of the angels.[34] It is precisely the (temporary) exclusion of man from this heavenly Sabbath of God that gives rise to the two-register cosmological order. At the consummation, God's people will enter his royal rest, the seventh day of creation (Heb 4:4, 9, 10), but until then that seventh creation day does not belong to the lower register world of human solar-day experience. It is heaven time, not earth time, not time measured by astronomical signs.

Not only the identification of the Sabbath rest with God's royal session on high, but the unending nature of that seventh day of creation differentiates it from earthly, solar days. Consisting as it does in God's status as the one who has occupied the completed cosmic temple as the King of Glory—a status without the possibility of any interruption or limitation—the seventh day is in the nature of the case unending. This is confirmed by the treatment of the theme of God's "rest" in Heb 4. That rest is identified in verses 3 and 4 as God's seventh day of Gen 2:2 (which is quoted). The passage then expounds God's rest as an ongoing reality, entrance into which is the eschatological hope of God's people (see esp. vv. 10, 11; cf. John 5:17). If the seventh

34. Cf. *KP*, 33–38.

day were not an unending Sabbath rest for God but a literal day, would the next day be another work day, introducing another week of work and rest for him, to be followed by an indefinite repetition of this pattern? Are we to replace the Sabbath-consummation doctrine of biblical eschatology with a mythological concept of cyclic time?[35] In the Genesis prologue the unending nature of God's Sabbath is signalized by the absence of the evening-morning formula from the account of the seventh day.

The Six Days. Under consideration here is the series of six numbered days plus the accompanying evening-morning refrain. This refrain is not to be connected with the solar time phenomena of days one and four, for it is not confined to those two contexts but is included in all six day-sections and in every case is immediately conjoined to the numbered day. The imagery of the evening and morning is simply a detail in the creation-week picture. This refrain thus functions as part of the formulaic framework of the account.

The question whether the references to the six days (with their evenings and mornings) describe lower register time phenomena or whether they belong to the upper register is answered in favor of the latter by the interlocking of the six days on both sides with upper register temporal features. Certainly the six days are part of the same strand as the seventh day, and the "beginning," as suggested above, is to be taken as the threshold of the creation week. Psalm 104 reflects this by similarly bracketing its treatment of the works of the six creation days (vv. 5–26 or 30) with upper register scenes of God in heaven, before (vv. 1–4) and after (vv. 27 or 31–35).

The six evening-morning days do not then mark the passage of time in the lower register sphere. They are not identifiable in terms of solar days, but rather relate to the history of creation at the upper register of the cosmos. The creation "week" is to be understood figuratively, not literally—that is the conclusion demanded by the biblical evidence.

Replication: The Sabbath Ordinance

Rounding out the series of acts of spatial and temporal replication in the Genesis prologue is the reproduction of the pattern of the Creator's time in the instituting of the Sabbath ordinance.[36] This ordinance superimposed a special

35. The issue of creation-consummation eschatology is theologically crucial, for bound up with it is the Bible's doctrine of the covenant with its decisive probationary crisis and the principle of federal representation.

36. For a discussion of the Sabbath as a creation ordinance, see *KP*, 79–80.

temporal grid on [[11]] the calendar of days and seasons marked by astronomical sequences. The Sabbath was designed for symbolic purposes within the covenant community, as a sign calling to consecration and the imitation of God and as a seal promising consummation of the kingdom to the covenant keepers.[37] By this promise the Sabbath reminds us that lower register history as a whole is patterned after upper register time in that it is a consummation-directed eschatological movement. The weekly scheme of the Sabbath ordinance portrays this overall seventh-day-bound design of lower register time, while it also symbolically mirrors the archetypal heavenly creation week itself.

Exodus 20:11 brings out explicitly that the continuing earthly pattern of sabbatical weeks is a human copy of a divine original. Within the two-register cosmology of the creation account with all its replications of upper register realities in the lower register world, all of them reproductions with a difference, there can be no doubt about the figurative nature of the relationship of the Sabbath ordinance to God's upper register creation week. The gratuitous insistence of literalists that the terms of the Sabbath ordinance in Exod 20:11 demand that the creation week be one of literal solar days is contradicted by the metaphorical character of the whole series of creation replications to which the original Sabbath ordinance (Gen 2:3) belongs. Like man's nature as image of God, man's walk in imitation of God's sabbatical way is not a matter of one-to-one equivalence but of analogy, of similarity with a difference. Like all the other lower register replicas, the sabbatical week of the ordinance is a likeness of its original, not exactly the same; it is an earthly metaphor for the heavenly archetype.

The Genesis prologue thus concludes with the record of the instituting of the lower register phenomena that provides the figurative chronological framework on which this literary composition has itself been constructed, the seven-day metaphor employed for the time dimension of God's creating the heavens and the earth.

Cosmogony and Providence

Our argument for the metaphorical nature of the creation week has included evidence that the narrative sequence of Gen 1 is determined by thematic factors and is not intended to correspond to the actual temporal sequence, as maintained by both the solar-age and day-age views. For further light on this issue we now turn to Gen 2:5–7.

37. Ibid., 80–82.

The Genesis 2 Context

After the prologue, Genesis divides into ten sections with a refrain formula ("these are the generations of N." [lit.]) serving as the heading for each.[38] In keeping with the uniform meaning of this formula, Gen 2:4 signifies that what follows recounts not the origins but the subsequent history of the heavens and the earth. Genesis 2:5ff. is thus identified as a record of the sequel to the world's creation, not as a second account of creation. This section does, however, pick up the story within the creation period (as does the next section at Gen 5:1ff.). In doing so it incidentally reveals something about the nature of divine providence during the creation week, something that cannot be accommodated by strictly sequential interpretations of Gen 1.

Genesis 2 fixes attention on the lower register and, more precisely, on Eden as it sets the stage for the covenant crisis of Gen 3. Here again the arrangement of the narrative is thematic rather than strictly chronological. At the beginning (vv. 5–7) and end (vv. 18–25) the man and woman, the human principals in the probationary crisis, are reintroduced (cf. Gen 1:27). The middle of the chapter describes the site of the dramatic event (vv. 8–14), calling attention to the two critical trees in the midst of the garden (v. 9), and it reports the covenant stipulations on which the decisive testing was based (vv. 15–17), here too emphasizing the probation tree (vv. 16, 17). Genesis 2 having thus set the scene with its major features (the man, the woman, and the judgment tree), Gen 3 proceeds to relate the fateful action.

From this overview of Gen 2 it is evident why, in the narrative of man's creation (vv. 5–7), the origin of vegetation (and thus of trees) is intertwined with his. Also, looking back at Gen 1, we can now appreciate the artful designing that brought the first triad of days to a climax in trees and the second triad in man, so anticipating the crucial connection of the two unfolded in Gen 2 and 3.

Exegesis of Genesis 2:5–7

[[12]] To bring out the sovereign lordship of Yahweh-Elohim in establishing the covenantal order of man in the garden, under probation with its demands and promises, both represented by trees, the account takes us back to a time before there was a man or a garden and trees in order then

38. Cf. ibid., 6–7.

to tell us how the Lord proceeded to form the man, plant the garden, and make its trees grow.

Genesis 2:5a says that at a certain time and place within the creation process vegetation did not yet exist. The language allows that the earth as a whole is referred to but the area particularly in view might be the Eden region, on which the following narrative focuses. Absent at this point in time were all plants, whether belonging to the unpeopled wilderness or to cultivated areas.

Genesis 2:5b explains why Yahweh-Elohim had not yet produced the vegetation. Rain is needed for the preservation and growth of plants, and God had not yet initiated the rain cycle. Of course, man can compensate for the local lack of rainfall by constructing an irrigation system, but man was not on the scene either. It is the assumption underlying this explanation for the timing of the creation of vegetation that confirms the conclusion that the Gen 1 narrative is not chronologically sequential. To this we shall presently return.

Genesis 2:6 tells of the provision of a supply of water, the absence of which had previously delayed the appearance of vegetation. Whatever the meaning of the Hebrew *ʾēd* (traditionally "mist"), this verse cannot be describing another circumstance adverse to plant life (like chaotic flood waters), for the effect of the *ʾēd* was a beneficial watering, such being the consistent meaning of the verb *šāqâ*.[39] Verse 6 must then be relating a new development, not something concurrent with the situation described in verse 5. For otherwise verse 6 would be affirming the presence of the supply of water necessary for the survival of vegetation at the very time when verse 5b says the absence of vegetation was due to the lack of such a water supply. The context thus demands the translation: "but an *ʾēd* began to rise," an inceptive meaning that is agreeable to the usage of the imperfect form of the verb employed here.[40]

---

39. Ancient Near Eastern cosmogonies contain the motif of an absence of water that is subsequently remedied, with fruitful fields resulting. Examples are the Sumerian myth of *Enki and the World Order* and the Akkadian *Myth of Anzu*. For discussion see R. J. Clifford, *Creation Accounts in the Ancient Near East and in the Bible* (Washington, DC: Catholic Biblical Association of America, 1994), 34–35, 84.

40. See the discussions of preterital *yiqtol* in P. Joüon and T. Muraoka, *A Grammar of Biblical Hebrew* (Rome: Pontifical Biblical Institute, 1993), 368–69 and of incipient past non-perfective in B. K. Waltke and M. O'Connor, *An Introduction to Biblical Hebrew Syntax* (Winona Lake, IN: Eisenbrauns, 1990), 503–4. Cf. S. R. Driver, *A Treatise on the Use of the Tenses in Hebrew*, 2nd ed. (Oxford: Clarendon,

The *ʾēd* in verse 6 answered to the previous lack of rain in verse 5b. If the *ʾēd* does not refer to rain but to some satisfactory alternative, the previous absence of that alternative should have been included in verse 5b in the listing of the missing sources of water. Indeed, if the *ʾēd* solution is not equatable with the rain whose absence was the problem, the citing of the absence of rain in verse 5b would itself be stranded as an irrelevance. These considerations argue in support of the identification of the Hebrew *ʾēd* with the Eblaite *ì-du*, "rain-cloud."[41] Also, the one other context where *ʾēd* is found is all about rain-clouds. That passage, Job 36, extols the greatness of God, who spreads the clouds abroad and sends down showers on man, so giving food in abundance (vv. 26–33). Verse 27a speaks of God's drawing forth the drops of water and then, repeating the image, the parallel clause in verse 27b adds the source from which the rain is distilled, namely the *ʾēd*, apparently the rain-clouds. Similarly in Gen 2 the originating of the *ʾēd* as a watering system (v. 6) is implicitly attributed to Yahweh-Elohim by virtue of the previous tracing of the absence of that provision to his determination (v. 5b). Another Joban echo of this is heard in Job 38:25–30. Challenging Job's knowledge of storm phenomena, the Lord illustrates his own creation-wide sovereignty by the example of his provision of rain and vegetation, not just in agricultural areas but in the wilderness where no man is.

The springing forth of plants (at least the wild plants that need only the rain, not man the cultivator) is taken for granted in Gen 2:6 as a consequence of the provision of the prerequisite water, a consequence occurring before the creation of man (v. 7). Even the Lord's planting of the garden with its trees (v. 8) is not to be located after the creation of man, since the form of the verb for planting can express the pluperfect.[42] In the absence of rainfall, man can dig irrigation ditches to bring the necessary water to his cultivated land,[43] and therefore, to round out the explanation of the absence

---

1881), 27, 36ff. Suggested examples, besides cases involving stative verbs, include Gen 37:7; Exod 15:5, 12, 14; 2 Sam 15:37 (cf. 16:15); 1 Kgs 7:7, 8; Jer 6:14.

41. Cf. M. Dahood, "Eblaite *ì-du* and Hebrew *ʾēd*, 'Rain Cloud,'" *CBQ* 43 (1981): 534–38. Other suggested etymologies for *ʾēd* produce meanings like flood or subterranean rivers, which break through and water the surface. On such interpretations (and on the rain-cloud view too) the *ʾereṣ* from which the *ʾēd* ascends could be the deeps beneath the earth (cf. Exod 15:12).

42. Compare the similar grammatical-compositional situation in Gen 2:19, which surely does not intend to suggest that the animals were made after the creation of Adam and his experience in the garden described in verses 7–18.

43. This is a function of mankind featured in the ancient cosmogonies.

of vegetation in Gen 2:5b, the absence of man was added to the absence of rain. But once God had caused it to rain, the Eden-garden could be planted without man being yet present.

When, therefore, the creation of man is narrated in Gen 2:7, this act is not subordinated to the theme of the production of vegetation. However symbiotic [[13]] the relationship of man and the cultivated plants, man was not made for the plants but the plants for man. The report of man's creation (v. 7) stands apart as an independent statement announcing the presence of the main party in the upcoming probationary crisis to take place in connection with the trees of the garden—the theme of the following narrative.

Genesis 2:5 and the Creation "Week"

What was the nature of divine providence during the creation "week"? More specifically, by what means did God preserve such things as he had brought into existence? Embedded in Gen 2:5 is an answer to that question that has decisive implications for the interpretation of the chronological framework of the creation account.

Whatever uncertainty may perplex the exegesis of various details in Gen 2:5–7, the point I am now making does not depend on the adoption of a particular interpretation of any of these details. It rests on—indeed, consists in—the simple, incontestable fact that Gen 2:5 gives an explanation, a perfectly natural explanation, for the absence of vegetation somewhere within the creation "week."[44] Genesis 2:5 tells us that God did not produce the plants of the field before he had established an environment with a watering system, the natural, normal precondition for plant life. The assumption underlying Gen 2:5 is clearly that a natural mode of divine providence was in operation during the creation "days."

Acts of supernatural origination did initiate and punctuate the creation process. And had God so pleased, his providential oversight of what he had created might also have been by supernatural means during that process. Genesis 2:5, however, takes it for granted that providential operations were not of a supernatural kind, but that God ordered the sequence of creation acts so that the continuance and development of the earth and its creatures

44. One thing showing that the situation described is within the six-day era is that man was not yet present. My essential contention is not affected whether the lack of vegetation mentioned be earth-wide or local (the Eden area) and no matter to which "day" the vegetationless situation pertains.

could proceed by natural means. This unargued assumption of Gen 2:5 contradicts the reconstructions of the creation days proposed by the more traditional views.

The scenario conjured by the literalists' solar-day interpretation is, in fact, utterly alien to the climate and tenor of Gen 2:5. Within the flurry of stupendous events which their view entails, each new cosmic happening coming hard on the heels of the last and all transpiring within a few hours or days, the absence of vegetation or anything else at any given point would not last long enough to occasion special consideration of the reasons for it. Within that time-frame such a question would be practically irrelevant. Genesis 2:5 reflects an environmental situation that has obviously lasted for a while; it assumes a far more leisurely pace on the part of the Creator, for whom a thousand years are as one day. The tempo of the literalists' reconstructed cosmogony leaves no room for the era-perspective of Gen 2:5.[45]

And in specific contradiction of the disclosure of Gen 2:5, both the solar-day and day-age theories must assume that God used other than the ordinary secondary means in the providential sustaining and further shaping of what his creative word had called into being.

We have already seen that any view that insists day four presents events chronologically later than those in day one must posit some means other than the sun, moon, and stars of day four, something extraordinary or even supernatural, to account for the effects of light and the day-night cycle mentioned in day one. It would also have to be by some such means that the vegetation whose production is described in day three was sustained apart from the presence of the normally prerequisite sun of day four. Likewise, on any strictly sequential interpretation of the narrative, the existence of all flora (day three) before any fauna (days five and six) would include extraordinary means of preservation in those symbiotic situations where the survival of a particular kind of vegetation is dependent on the activity of animal life. And of course the existence of the earth itself on day one confronts the traditional approaches with a gigantic exception to normal providential procedure. For according to them the earth would have come into existence by itself as a solitary sphere, not as part of the cosmological process by which stars and their satellites originate, and it would have continued alone, suspended in the spatial void (if we may so speak) for the

45. Endorsing my argument as originally published, H. Blocher examines the criticism of it by E. J. Young (*Studies in Genesis One* [Philadelphia: P&R, 1964], 58–65) and concludes that Young "misses the main point" (*In the Beginning*, 56 n. 56).

first three "days" of creation. All the vast universe whose origin is narrated on day four would then be younger (even billions of years younger) than the speck in space called earth. So much for the claimed harmony of the narrative sequence of Gen 1 with scientific cosmology.[46]

[[14]] In short, if the narrative sequence were intended to represent the chronological sequence, Gen 1 would bristle with contradictions of what is revealed in Gen 2:5. Our conclusion is then that the more traditional interpretations of the creation account are guilty not only of creating a conflict between the Bible and science but, in effect, of pitting Scripture against Scripture. The true harmony of Gen 1 and Gen 2:5 appears, however, and the false conflict between the Bible and science disappears, when we recognize that the creation "week" is a lower register metaphor for God's upper register creation-time and that the sequence of the "days" is ordered not chronologically but thematically.[47]

---

46. Some of these problems of sequence (but not the major one involving days one and four) would be resolved by a variation on the day-age view which allows that the days may overlap. The idea is that while what is described as happening on a given day must have begun to happen before the next day's developments began, the completing of the earlier day's creative work would have overlapped the activity of subsequent days. This contrived interpretation not only fails to salvage the chronological sequence, but it actually amounts to a virtual acknowledgment that chronological sequence yields to thematic interests in the ordering of the days.

47. In this article I have advocated an interpretation of biblical cosmogony according to which Scripture is open to the current scientific view of a very old universe and, in that respect, does not discountenance the theory of the evolutionary origin of man. But while I regard the widespread insistence on a young earth to be a deplorable disservice to the cause of biblical truth, I at the same time deem commitment to the authority of scriptural teaching to involve the acceptance of Adam as a historical individual, the covenantal head and ancestral fount of the rest of mankind, and the recognition that it was the one and same divine act that constituted him the first man, Adam the son of God (Luke 3:38), that also imparted to him life (Gen 2:7).

PART TWO

Covenant, Law, and the State

CHAPTER THREE

Oracular Origin of the State

(1978)

Because of an overall misreading of Gen 4:15 and a misleading fascination with the supposed "mark of Cain" in particular, the import of this verse as an inceptive divine disclosure concerning the institution of the state has escaped attention. It is set in a judicial context. Form-critical analysis has led to the observation that Gen 4 exhibits a legal-court pattern closely paralleling the judgment pattern in Gen 3.[1] Within the judicial process, Gen 4:15 is a response of the judge to a complaint against his judgment. Direction in the quest for the meaning of the response may be expected from a study of the appeal (Gen 4:13, 14).

Cain's Appeal

Cain's complaint-appeal is expressed in the quantitative terms common in negotiations of various kinds:[2] "My punishment is greater than I can bear" (4:13). The alternative interpretation of verse 13 as an acknowledgment by Cain that his sin was beyond forgiveness is not favored by the active form of the infinitive or by Cain's concern, as he continues his complaint (4:14), with the severity of the punishment—not with the enormity of his sin.

Banishment from the face of the ground (v. 14a) and from the face of God (v. 14b)—so Cain saw his punishment. In the second half of verse 14 the significance of each aspect of the punishment mentioned in the first

1. In a recent reexamination of the matter, W. M. Clark finds nine elements in this pattern, covering the entire episode from the initial imposition of divine obligation to the execution of judgment ("The Flood and the Structure of the Pre-Patriarchal History," *ZAW* 83 [1971]: 195–203). Narrative development, style and specific vocabulary all come under the influence of the judicial form.

2. Cf. expressions like "is it too small," "it is enough," "too much," "how long," "speedily." This is a point of contact between Cain's lament and Psalter laments. On this, see further below.

half of the verse is traced in turn, so that the verse as a whole assumes an A:B::A′:B′ form. To be driven from the death-defiled ground, forced to leave by its refusal to yield him its life, was to be doomed to an unsettled, wandering exile existence (v. 14c). To be denied access to the face of God was to be abandoned to the mortal perils of a lawless world (v. 14d). Cain laments that the ground will not respond to his labor and, far more intolerable, God will not respond to his cry.

It is this second (or B) element in Cain's description of his fate to which God's response (v. 15) is addressed, and what needs to be perceived if we are to understand verse 15 is the juridical nature of the situation referred to in verse 14b and d. [[133]] "I will be hidden from your face" (v. 14b). The point of Cain's complaint is that he will be denied God's judicial oversight. The N-stem of the verb is not to be taken here as reflexive, but passive.[3] Cain does not bemoan the fact that he must henceforth ever be trying to conceal himself from God's judicial scrutiny. Quite the contrary, it is the absence of such scrutiny that worries him—not, to be sure, the absence of scrutiny of his own actions but of the violence that threatens him.

The judicial connotation is regularly present when it is said that God hides his face.[4] The expression is common in the lament genre in the Psalms, which is a form of legal (covenantal) appeal. In Ps 27, for example, where the writer describes himself as seeking God's face (v. 8)[5] and pleads with God not to hide his face (v. 9a), the judicial significance of that plea becomes evident as the psalmist goes on to request that he not be abandoned to the hostility of false witnesses who are testifying against him (v. 12). Constantly, where the image is found in the Psalter, the concern is for divine judicial intervention. How long will God hide his face? Let God hear the cry of the psalmist and see the evil done against him; let God speedily exercise judgment, delivering the afflicted and requiting his enemy (Pss 10:11; 13:2; 22:25; 30:8; 44:25; 69:18;

3. In other instances of the phrase with the verb in the N-stem (see below), the reflexive meaning is not suitable because of the impersonal nature of the subject of the action. If, with M. Dahood (*Psalms I*, AB 16 [Garden City, NY: Doubleday, 1966], 64), we regard the verb as an infixed-t formation of *sûr* ("turn aside"), the reflexive meaning would be awkward even in Gen 4:14.

4. If Dahood's parsing of the verb is correct (see note 3), an adjustment in the translation is necessary, but this would not affect our discussion of the judicial force of the idiom.

5. The use of this idiom by the vassals of the pharaoh (EA 165:5ff.) shows that it has been adopted from the secular judicial field to express the religious-covenantal relationship.

88:15; 102:3; 143:7). Job asks why God hides his face as he pleads—in vain it seems—for a legal hearing for his mysterious case (Job 13:24; cf. 18ff.). In the covenant administration defined in Deuteronomy, the hiding of God's face from Israel means his absence from their midst (Deut 31:17, 18), not entering into judgment in their behalf to avenge their blood (Deut 32:20; cf. 35–36, 41ff.). A similar usage is found in the prophets (Isa 8:17; Mic 3:4).

The passive formulation, which is used in Gen 4:14b (Cain will be hidden from God's face), has the same judicial connotation as the active.[6] Thus, in Isa 40:27, Israel's complaint that its way is hidden from God has as its parallel the thought that God disregards Israel's plea for vindicating judgment. In Jer 16:17, the fact that the offenders' ways are not hidden from God's face means that his eyes are upon their iniquity to recompense it (cf. Ps 10:11).[7] See also Ps 38:10; Job 3:23; and Isa 65:16.

In view of Gen 4:16a (lit., "Cain went away from the face of Yahweh"), it may be that the similar terminology of Cain's complaint intends to suggest that his hiddenness from God will be attributable to the distance that will be put between him in his exile east of Eden and the presence of God in the garden. Of course, that would be to misconstrue the significance of the Creator's special theophanic identification with his garden-sanctuary. But one need not expect Cain to be orthodox. In fact, for Cain to suggest that his problem was a matter of geography is precisely the kind of obscurantism that is to be expected here. The theme of the obscuration of man's ethical responsibility by metaphysical theories of existential predicament begins with the satanic version of man's probationary decision. Ignoring the issue of sovereign, divine command and human obedience, Satan reduced the matter to a question of metaphysical evolution towards godhood (Gen 3:5). Subsequently, Adam explained his hiding from God's presence as due to his nakedness, a physical problem for which it had seemed [[134]] reasonable to seek a geographical solution—behind the trees (Gen 3:8–10).[8] That

6. On Dahood's parsing (see note 3 above), the passive form would mean that something had been turned aside or removed from God's presence or attention. In Gen 4:14b, an excellent parallelism with the image of being driven away in verse 14a then results.

7. Relevant here is the evidence, biblical and extrabiblical, for the use of this eye-terminology in connection with the royal office of surveillance and investigation.

8. This hiding in Gen 3 is a case of the offenders hiding themselves from judicial exposure and punishment. The verb (*niphal* and *hithpael* of *ḥābāʾ*) is not the one used in Gen 4:14. But this close parallel to our Gen 4 passage does lead us to expect that the hiding from the face of God in the latter will also have a judicial orientation.

is the theological tradition in which Cain stood. Moreover, avoidance of confession of blame and guilt would be consistent with Cain's own previous behavior. But though Cain's statement would thus involve the idea of physical separation from God, that idea would still figure only as the (false) rationale for the problem of judicial hiddenness which constitutes the essential point of the complaint: in his accursed exile from Eden he will be beyond the range of God's judicial oversight.

Apparently, Cain once again feels aggrieved by the difference in God's treatment of him and his brother. God's rejection of Cain's offering had prompted the jealous hatred that led to the murder of the favored Abel (Gen 4:4ff.). Now Cain sees another instance of discrimination in the fact that God hears and heeds the legal plea[9] of Abel's blood calling for vengeance (Gen 4:10ff.),[10] whereas, as Cain supposes, his own cry for judicial assistance will not reach the ears of God over the distance put between them.

The consequences of the judicial dereliction Cain anticipates (Gen 4:14b) will be, he laments, that everyone in the family of mankind, kinsmen all of his innocent victim, Abel, will be let loose in a mindless blood feud to take vengeance on him (v. 14d): "Everyone who finds me will kill me."[11] Hidden from God's face, he will have no judge to appeal to. Society east of Eden will be devoid of God's judicial ordering. Cain will be exposed to lawless men bent on vengeance. He will be *ex lex* on a God-forsaken earth.

What Cain dreaded as his fate was that unbearable forsakenness depicted as overtaking the one who speaks in the lament of Ps 22. In his suffering he complains that he is abandoned to the malice of the encompassing wicked: "Everyone that sees me laughs me to scorn (v. 8). . . . My God, why have you forsaken me. . . . I cry . . . you do not hear" (vv. 2, 3; cf. Matt 27:46; Mark 15:34). Thus he suffers until God heeds his cry and ceases to hide his face from him (v. 25).

---

9. Cf. Gen 18:20; Deut 22:24, 27; 2 Kgs 8:3; Job 16:18.

10. See Ps 18:7 for an expansion of the idea of the "voice" coming before the divine judge.

11. In a discussion of this passage commendable for its perception of what some of the real issues are, R. Rushdoony (*The Institutes of Biblical Law* [Nutley, NJ: Craig Press, 1973], 358ff.) presents an interpretation of Cain's fear quite the reverse of that offered above. He suggests that Cain fears not the absence of a judicial authority structure but the existence of one, namely, the already existing law-order of the family. Then, according to Rushdoony, God acts to protect Cain from execution by the family because God's design for the family's role in law enforcement excludes the execution of the death penalty, that being reserved for the state when it should emerge.

God's Response

That Cain's world was not now totally severed from God's judicial interest, as he complained, was made at once evident by the fact that this complaint received a hearing and a response (Gen 4:15). Agreeably, the content of the response was to the effect that there would be a divinely sanctioned law structure in man's fallen exile-world. The response contains no direct reflection on the first element in this complaint; man was indeed to be an outcast, a creature driven across the face of the cursed earth. But the second element of the complaint is dealt with explicitly in the response. God does not mitigate his announced judgment, but he does clarify it, correcting Cain's misconception.[12] God's face will not be hidden; there will be an exercise of the divine *imperium* among men (v. 15a; cf. v. 14b). Hence, the situation will not be such that Cain will be a prey to anarchical terrorism (v. 15b; cf. v. 14d).

[[135]] The introductory *lākēn* gives the response the formal character of a solemn affirmation. This word, usually mistranslated "therefore," signalizes a vow, binding asseveration or oath.[13] It is often found introducing divine declarations, either by itself or with formulae of oracular pronouncement like "thus says Yahweh," "utterance of Yahweh," and the oath formula "as I live."[14] It is used in statements sealing agreements or providing guarantees of commitments (cf. Gen 30:15; Exod 6:6; Num 25:12; Judg 11:8; 1 Sam 28:2; 2 Kgs 19:32; 22:20; Isa 7:14; 61:7). Of particular interest for the interpretation of Gen 4:15 is the usage of *lākēn* in conjunction with *ʾôt* (Isa 7:14; cf. Isa 37:30, 33; 2 Kgs 19:29, 32).

"If anyone kills Cain, he shall be avenged sevenfold." This asseveration of Gen 4:15a is in the form of a law, the formulation being of an infrequent type in which the offense is expressed by a participle[15] and the penalty by a

12. W. M. Clark ("Pre-Patriarchal History," 197) interprets Gen 4:15 as a mitigation of the sentence and sees it as corresponding in this respect to verse 21 in the parallel Gen 3 pattern.

13. Cf. F. C. Goldbaum, "Two Hebrew Quasi-Adverbs: לכן and אכן," *JNES* 23 (1964): 132–34. Is it composed of emphatic *lamed* and *kēn*, "yes," a compact "verily, verily"? "Agreed!" would be a suitable translation in many cases; it is an equivalent of *ʾāmēn*.

14. See Ezek 5:11; 35:6, 11; Zeph 2:9; cf. Jer 5:2 (where the *lākēn* is possibly to be taken as a quotation of the false swearers); 1 Kgs 22:16, 19; Isa 5:13, 14, 24 (where *lākēn* is an alternate for *ʾim lôʾ*).

15. The reinforcing of the participle of the protasis by *kōl* is found elsewhere in legal, decretive, and imprecatory genres. See J. G. Williams, "Concerning One of the Apodictic Formulas," *VT* 14 (1964): 486–88. Cf. Exod 22:18.

third-person imperfect (usually preceded by an infinitive absolute).[16] God's response to Cain is then to be seen as the promulgation of a law—a law that envisaged the establishment of an entire law-order.

In the laws with participial protasis the subject of the verb in the penalty clause (usually *môt yûmat*, "he shall be put to death") is the offender denoted by the participle. But in the apodosis in Gen 4:15a a different verb (*yuqqām*) is used, and the reference made by Lamech to this divine pronouncement later in the same chapter (v. 24) indicates that the object, not the subject, of the participial action is the subject in this penalty clause. However, even though the law says that Cain is to be avenged rather than that vengeance is to be taken on the one who kills him, the avenging of Cain is to be accomplished through the punishment of his slayer. Either way, therefore, this divine legal provision calls for the punishment of the murderer and thereby institutes a structure for the administration of justice—a structure that was to be more precisely defined by subsequent revelation.[17]

This judicial order is characterized by the prescription in Gen 4:15 as an administration of *divine* justice. For the adverbial *šibᶜātayim* "sevenfold," which serves instead of the infinitive absolute usually used in laws of this type to strengthen the verb in the penalty clause, describes the stipulated vindication as divine in its ultimate authority. In support of that, it will suffice here to mention only some of the more pertinent data. The brief selection does, however, represent a variety of literary traditions and the passages individually are reflective of Gen 4:15 in various ways.

From the revelatory form of the divine work of creation (Gen 1:1–2:3) seven emerges as a sign of divine action in its perfection. This Sabbath-seven sign in the heightened form of the Jubilee symbol is connected with

16. See Exod 21:15, 17; 22:17, 19; 31:14; Lev 24:16; cf. Lev 20:2, 9–13, 15, 16, 27. Alt's classification of the participial formulation as apodictic does not commend itself. The participial protasis is simply a variation of the usual "if" clause in casuistic law. Cf. G. J. Wenham, "Legal Forms in the Book of the Covenant," *TynBul* 22 (1971): 102; M. Weinfeld, *Deuteronomy and the Deuteronomic School* (Oxford: Clarendon, 1972), 239.

17. In Exod 21:20, a law dealing with the killing of a slave, *nāqôm yinnāqēm* appears in the penalty clause. G. E. Mendenhall, commenting on the ambiguity of the subject, whether master or slave, observes that neither one is the logical subject of the passive verb. "Rather, it is a command that the sovereign authority of Yahweh should be placed in action in order to punish/redress an action that is incompatible with the sovereignty of that same ultimate authority" (*The Tenth Generation: The Origins of the Biblical Tradition* [Baltimore: Johns Hopkins University Press, 1973], 91).

divine vindication when the final Jubilee, the messianic *mīšarum* act, finds exposition as "the day of vindication (*nāqām*) of our God" (Isa 61:2b). In Lev 26, the curse with which God threatens Israel for breach of his covenant, the covenant whose sign is the Sabbath, is called a "vindication of the covenant" (v. 25), and it consists in his punishing them sevenfold for their sin (v. 24).[18] From the historical records of the monarchy comes the account of the sevenfold avenging of the Gibeonites for Saul's blood-guilt with reference to them (2 Sam 21:1ff.). That it is a matter of [[136]] divine vindication is evident from several factors: the episode unfolds from a judicial response of the Lord to David, who has sought God's face; the offense was a violation of an oath in God's name; and the punishment takes place "before Yahweh." Turning to the Psalms, the lament of Ps 79 appeals to God to avenge the blood of his people and vindicate his name (vv. 9, 10) by returning the taunts of the enemy sevenfold into their bosom (v. 12). The same motif appears in the New Testament apocalyptic tradition in the judicial appeal of the martyrs to the Lord to avenge their blood (Rev 6:10). This appeal is set within the framework of the book with the seven seals, and, more significantly, the sevenfold judgment series of the seven trumpets and the seven vials of divine wrath are both presented as responses to these appeals of God's people for vindication (Rev 8:3, 4 and 15:7; cf. 5:8).[19] It is then a common conception throughout biblical literature that sevenfold vindication is divine vindication.[20]

Mendenhall, in his illuminating study of the root *nqm*, shows that in its biblical usage, as elsewhere, the taking of vengeance into one's own hands in blood feud in a situation devoid of orderly legal procedure is not what is in view. "Instead of representing merely a primitive custom incompatible with any stable peaceful society, the root *NQM* has to do with the very foundations of political legitimacy and authority long before the time of

---

18. The sevenfold covenant curse appears in the extrabiblical treaties too. See, e.g., *Sefîre* I.A.27ff. and II.A.6ff. (*KAI* 222, 223).

19. Judicial appeal, constituting, as it thus does, the setting for the major structural heptads of the book, emerges as a fundamental perspective in the Apocalypse. The book revolves around the appeal of the martyr-church for covenantal vindication—"Come, Lord Jesus"—and his response as Lord of the covenant and Judge of the nations, giving assurance of timely judicial intervention—"I come quickly." Such is the closing summation in Rev 22:20.

20. Cf. also Gen 7:2, 3; 21:28ff.; Lev 4:6, 17; 8:11; Isa 30:26; Ps 12:7; Prov 6:31. The association of seven with oaths is to be noted in view of the combination of the seven motif and *lākēn*, itself an introduction to oaths, in Gen 4:15.

Moses."[21] The "vengeance of Yahweh" is an exercise of the legitimate divine sovereignty, or *imperium*, whether for defensive or punitive vindication. As for Gen 4, Mendenhall feels the two occurrences of *nqm* there are probably survivals of an old usage in which it had associations with the blood feud, but he qualifies that with the observation that the custom is attributed in Gen 4 to the intervention and authority of Yahweh.[22] And that, he suggests, strongly implies that God is to be understood as the logical subject of the action denoted there by *nqm*.

It would appear that the Gen 4 usage of *nqm* is actually quite consistent with the normal usage as Mendenhall has analyzed it. In the case of Gen 4:15, what is authorized by Yahweh is not the custom of blood feud, but precisely the kind of political-judicial order whose legitimate acts of vindication are normally denoted by the root *nqm*, and, indeed, one that is ultimately an administration of God's own *imperium*. Quite apart from the presence of the root *nqm* in this verse, we have seen that the divine response is a correction of Cain's false assumption that he was being driven into a situation of lawless vengeance. The fact that *nqm* is used in the penalty clause of this divine prescription is, in the light of Mendenhall's study, highly significant as a further confirmation that Gen 4:15 contemplates the establishment of an institutional structure for a legitimate judicial office in man's fallen world.

Understood as a foundational revelation of the judicial order of the state, Gen 4:15 fits coherently into the thematic development of the early chapters of Genesis. The Lord's earlier judicial pronouncements concerning fallen mankind (Gen 3:16ff.) revealed that history was to be informed by the principle of common grace-common curse, with the institution of the family continuing as a societal framework for man's cultural occupation. The Gen 4:15 disclosure [[137]] supplemented that with its intimation of the emergence of the authority-structure of the state as a further provision of the common grace of God. It is with precisely this theme of the city of man that the narrative continues in Gen 4:17ff.,[23] and the second occurrence of *nqm* in Gen 4 is in the declaration of one who stands in the dynastic succession of the city. Lamech's boast (Gen 4:23, 24) cites the tradition about the

21. Mendenhall, *Tenth Generation*, 75.

22. Ibid., 74, 88.

23. As this narrative shows, the curse of exile was tempered by a measure of stability and community. And it was this city community that was invested with the judicial function referred to in God's response to Cain. Genesis 4:15 does then speak indirectly to Cain's complaint about his exile-existence (Gen 4:14a and c) but without having to correct his understanding of this aspect of his judgment.

divine avenging of Cain, but Lamech repudiates the divine authorization of his office. Absolutizing the judicial authority in himself, he regards himself incomparably more competent for vengeance than any deity who might have promised Cain sevenfold vengeance. The seventy-sevenfold vengeance Lamech threatens is not an escalation of the blood feud but an idolatrous perverting of the divine institution of the state.[24] When the city of man theme resumes in Gen 6:1ff., this ideology of divine kingship becomes explicit in the self-identification of the royal tyrants as sons of the gods.[25] The judgment of God overtook the world of Gen 6, but immediately after the record of the deluge the narrative returns to the theme of the city of man. And in the postdiluvian covenant by which God renewed the earth-order of common grace, the stipulation concerning the state's avenging function is presented in terms drawn from Gen 4. The murder to be avenged is a Cain-like act of fratricide (Gen 9:5). The authorization of blood-vindication is formulated in the participial style of Gen 4:15 (Gen 9:6), and this interrelationship furnishes additional support of the present thesis.[26]

God's legally formulated response to Cain's complaint (Gen 4:15a) gave solemn assurance that his face would not be hidden (cf. v. 14b), for he would establish in his common grace the political order of the state as an authority ordained of God, a minister of God to execute his vengeance in this world. Cain was not provided with a divine guarantee that he would never be a murderer's victim. Verse 15a assumes the possibility of Cain's being killed and simply tells him that in that event there will be divine vindication.[27] Cain had not complained that he had no guarantee of absolute inviolability but that he would be exposed to absolute anarchy. The divine response announces that, on the contrary, controls will be instituted. Just as the curse addressed to Adam and Eve (Gen 3:16ff.)—the curse with the implicit disclosure of common-grace provisions—had in view all men and women, so this supplementary disclosure of the common-grace order, though directed to Cain, had to do with all mankind. After all, why should Cain have been

---

24. Lamech's conjoined claims of seventy-sevenfold vengeance and divine status are another indication of the significance of seven as a divine emblem in the sevenfold avenging of Gen 4:15.

25. Cf. my "Divine Kingship and Genesis 6:1–4," *WTJ* 24 (1962): 187–204 [= pp. 63–78 in the present volume].

26. Clark ("Pre-Patriarchal History," 196) sees in this stylistic comparison evidence of a possible "legal background" for Gen 4:15.

27. For posthumous vindication compare the case of the slain slave in Exod 21:20.

singled out for a unique individual protection from lawless violence?[28] Cain would participate in the benefit that would be afforded by the promised law-order, but that was just incidental to the common provision for all.

Genesis 4:15a answers to verse 14b, and verse 15b corresponds to verse 14d. Thus, in Gen 4:15b the language of Cain's complaint in verse 14d is repeated in order to negate its point: since the world would not be a lawless chaos, but judicially structured, it would not really be the case that anyone and everyone who came upon Cain would be bent on killing him.

The present interpretation differs from the usual views as to the general structure of Gen 4:15. According to most interpreters the first part of the verse [[138]] quotes God's response and the second part relates an additional action. But on the view taken here, verse 15b does not refer to some distinct divine act but is rather a recapitulation of God's response.[29] Grammatically, this clause with *waw*-consecutive plus imperfect is of the narrative summation type where the *waw* may be translated "thus."[30] The word *ʾôt*, on this view, refers to the divine response quoted in verse 15a. We must return to the question of the meaning of *ʾôt*, but may first observe that the infinitive clause following *ʾôt* is not a negative final clause but a restatement of the substance of God's response. A similar use of the infinitive after *ʾôt* to express the substance of the "sign" is found in Ezek 20: "[the Sabbath] will be a sign between me and you, an acknowledgment that I, Yahweh, am your God" (v. 20; cf. v. 12). Genesis 19:21 offers an interesting grammatical and situational parallel to Gen 4:15. Here too it is a matter of response to an appeal in the midst of judgment. Lot bargains with the Lord of the angels for a small concession (vv. 19, 20). The response assures him that his request is granted and the content of that grant (which is one with the content of the appeal[31]) is expressed, as in Gen 4:15b, by *lĕbiltî* and the infinitive: "I grant

---

28. God's judgment on Cain's act of murder was, indeed, distinctive in its sentence of exile rather than the death penalty subsequently prescribed for that crime; but that is another matter.

29. B. Jacob (*Das erste Buch der Tora—Genesis* [Berlin: Schocken, 1934], 146) adopts a similar view of the structure, but in other respects his exegesis differs widely from that given here. According to Jacob, Cain is told that he will be punished (not avenged) and yet he himself will not be killed because the punishment will descend only after a sevenfold delay. Jacob's handling of the participial phrase in verse 15a is particularly awkward; taking it as a broken quotation of verse 14d, he detaches it from the following clause.

30. Cf., e.g., Gen 21:32a and Josh 24:25.

31. In the responses to both Cain and Lot, their positive statements are recast in negative form.

you this request that I should not overthrow the city." Translating Gen 4:15b accordingly, it reads (freely): "Thus Yahweh gave Cain an *ʾôt* to the effect that everyone who came upon him would not be out to kill him."

As for the word *ʾôt*, it is first to be noted that it may have a verbal rather than visual character.[32] It is used for prophecies delivered without any visual accompaniment then and there (cf. Isa 7:14; 37:30; Deut 13:2). In the encounter of Isaiah with Ahaz the verbal *ʾôt* that God gives is in definite contrast to the visible kind of sign that Ahaz had refused. A prediction embodied in a name is designated an *ʾôt*. Isaiah and his children are "signs" (Isa 8:18) by virtue of their prophetic names (cf. Isa 7:3; 8:3; 12:2); in effect, it is their names that constitute the sign.[33] In Exod 3:12, God gives as an *ʾôt* that he has sent Moses a verbal assurance that after the exodus Israel will serve God on this mountain where he was now speaking to Moses. A similar usage is found in Josh 2:12. The *ʾôt* Rahab requests is usually identified as the scarlet cord (cf. vv. 18, 21), but it seems rather to be a reference to the oath that has just been mentioned. Rahab asks the spies to swear by Yahweh (v. 12a) and specifies that their oath be one of fidelity (*ḥesed*) to her father's house (v. 12b). Then, repeating her request, she asks that they give an *ʾôt* of truth or faithfulness (*ʾĕmet*) to her (v. 12c), again specifying that they show mercy to her family (v. 13). In complying, the spies unite the doubled request, committing themselves to deal with her in both *ḥesed* and *ʾĕmet* (v. 14). Apparently, commentators have missed what seems to be the obvious identification of this *ʾôt* with the oath[34] precisely because they have been under the domination of the notion that an *ʾôt* must be something visible.

An *ʾôt* may then consist simply of words. We must, however, try to identify the special characteristics of statements that may be so designated. It would appear from the above examples that within the sphere of religious relationship at least, *ʾôt* is applicable to affirmations of intention, assurances of commitment, prophetic guarantees. Moreover, all these instances involve divine authentication [[139]] of the trustworthiness of what is affirmed. The

32. The discussion of *ʾôt* by K. H. Rengstorf ("σημεῖον," *TDNT* 7:209ff., esp. 211–12) does not do justice to the evidence for the nonvisual usage. The argument drawn from the association of *ʾôt* with *rāʾâ* is pressed too far, particularly in view of the range of meaning of *rāʾâ* (cf., e.g., Isa 13:1).

33. Note the contrast between the *ʾôt* function of Isaiah and his sons (Isa 8:18) and the hiding of Yahweh's face from the house of Jacob (v. 17).

34. In Isa 19:20 *ʾôt* is a synonym of *ʿēd*, "witness," in a context of judicial appeal and response.

ʾôt-statement is directly spoken by God, inspired by God or sanctioned by his name.[35]

It is in the light of this usage that *ʾôt* is to be understood in Gen 4:15b. Verse 15a, the referent of *ʾôt*, is a direct divine revelation, a self-authenticating divine word, prophetically decretive, affirming God's intention to institute a judicial order. Enhancing the *ʾôt*-character of this oracular pronouncement and affording it an oath quality[36] is the inclusion in it of the symbolic seven, sign of divine presence and sanction.

There is then no reference in Gen 4:15 to an unspecified wonder-sign that God performed for Cain's personal assurance, with the reader left to speculate about what it might have been. And certainly the language does not suggest a "mark of Cain" imprinted on his body. Such interpretations assume that Cain was being given a special individual guarantee, but that, as we have seen, is not the point of the passage. It is rather concerned with a general world-order that would condition the life of all men. The meaning of the passage will therefore be brought out if we translate, not "And Yahweh gave a sign to Cain," but "Thus Yahweh signified to Cain that . . ."

---

35. Foundational to the general semantic development of *ʾôt* is its formal function of pointing or identifying. It is used as a synonym for the identifying name (Isa 55:13; Exod 13:9; cf. 3:15) and as a designation of the name-bearing standard (Num 2:2; cf. Isa 19:19, 20). Also, "signs" are given so that people might know God's name, Yahweh. It was natural then that in theological usage *ʾôt* should designate what identified or named God as author, whether the self-authenticating word spoken or inspired by God, or the event—supernatural happening or fulfillment of prediction—that pointed in attestation to the divine identity of such a word.

It is beyond the scope of this article to attempt a broad lexical survey of *ʾôt*, but it should be observed that the relation of *ʾôt* to Akkadian *ittu* ("sign") has been dismissed too lightly in the treatments of *ʾôt* in the theological dictionaries (cf. K. H. Rengstorf, "σημεῖον," 209, and F. J. Helfmeyer, "אוֹת," *TDOT* 1:167). The semantic range of the two is remarkably similar and this makes it difficult not to accept an etymological relationship (cf. especially the *idat*- base of *ittu*). The common duplication of *ittu* written Á.MEŠ GISKIM.MEŠ, "signs and wonders," is an interesting parallel to the frequent biblical combination of *ʾōtôt* and *môpĕtîm*. Of particular importance among the meanings of *ittu* are: "characteristic, nature (as in the divine name written [d]*Man-nu-i-da-at-su-i-di*, 'Who-understands-his-nature'; cf. Judg 13:18), signal, password, inside (i.e., authentic) information, (due advance) notice (used with *riksu*, 'contract'), acknowledgment, proof, omen." The aspects of verbal, legal confirmation and oracular disclosure are especially significant for the meaning of *ʾôt* in Gen 4:15.

36. See note 20 above.

The author's concern with the subject of God's judicial relation to men is attested once again in Gen 4 when he turns from the Cainite succession to the line of Seth (vv. 25, 26). For he capsulates the nature of this community in their act of confessing (naming) Yahweh as covenant Lord to whom their judicial appeal was directed. There is, of course, a radical difference between the exercise of God's *imperium* that is in view in Gen 4:15, and his vindication of the blood of Abel and the martyr-seed of the woman restored in the line of Seth and continuing to the last judgment (cf. Rev 6:10, 11). To Cain, God signified that for mankind in general he would provide in his common grace an institutional agent to bear the sword of his wrath in the temporal course of world history (cf. Rom 13:4). For the people of his covenant, God's judicial vindication is an act of his saving grace, a coming in personal immediacy as their eschatological, redemptive Avenger.

CHAPTER FOUR

Divine Kingship and Genesis 6:1–4

(1962)

Critique of Prevailing Interpretations

Genesis 6:1–4 is, according to the prevailing opinion of the day, a piece of raw mythology. In fact, the claim is repeatedly made that it is the most blatant instance of that sort of thing anywhere in the sacred canon. It is supposed to relate how certain divine beings, enticed by the beauty of earthly women, entered into unholy wedlock with them and so gave rise to a race of gigantic heroes of antiquity.[1] The current fashion is to credit the editor responsible for incorporating the mythical fragment into the biblical narrative with the intention of using it simply as a symbolic vehicle to convey the sense of man's demonic potentialities for good or evil on a heroic scale.[2] But even this demythologizing old Israelite existentialist will have transmitted the primitive pagan tale startlingly undisguised.

The decisive difficulties, both exegetical and theological, which beset the interpretation of Gen 6:1–4 in terms of non-terrestrial beings have been presented long since and need not all be repeated here.[3] Advocates of this divine, or demonic, [[188]] invasion view have themselves been most disturbed

1. For a recent discussion of the passage from this very ancient viewpoint see Emil G. Kraeling, "The Significance and Origin of Gen. 6:1–4," *JNES* 6 (1947): 193–208; cf. G. von Rad, *Genesis* (Philadelphia: Westminster, 1961; translation of *Das erste Buch Mose, Genesis* [Göttingen: Vandenhoeck & Ruprecht, 1956]).

2. Cf. A. Richardson, *Genesis I–XI* (London: SCM, 1953), 93–94; R. H. Elliott, *The Message of Genesis* (Nashville: Broadman, 1961), 62–63.

3. Cf. John Murray, *Principles of Conduct* (London: Tyndale, 1957), 243–49; W. H. Green, "The Sons of God and the Daughters of Men," *PRR* 5 (1894): 654–60 and *The Unity of the Book of Genesis* (New York: Scribner's: 1910), 51–61. It must be conceded that the force of some (but only some) of the criticisms is escaped by a view such as that of Franz Delitzsch, who interpreted "the sons of God" as angels who acted through the instrumentality of demoniacs; cf. his *New Commentary on Genesis*, vol. 1 (Edinburgh: T&T Clark, 1888).

by the exclusive attention paid to "man" and to him as a creature of "flesh" in the verdict of God pronounced against the sin of "the sons of God" (v. 3). The obvious awkwardness of this for the view that the chief offenders under judgment were non-human, incorporeal beings has encouraged doubts as to the propriety of the present location of verse 3. It has been conjectured, for example, that verse 4 ought to follow immediately upon verse 2; then the condemnation of "man" (v. 3) might be related to the Nephilim-Gibborim (v. 4), who were the at least half-human and quite corporeal offspring of "the sons of God."[4] But for all who are concerned with interpreting the meaning of the author of the narrative in its canonical form (and there is no objective evidence that the Masoretic Text differs significantly from the original) it is apparent that the verdict of verse 3 refers primarily to the activity of "the sons of God" (v. 2), and that precludes all likelihood that the author regarded the latter as preternatural spirits.[5]

Except perhaps for the fact that "sons of God" often denotes angels in the Old Testament[6] and practically equivalent terminology is used for minor deities in extrabiblical literature,[7] what has contributed most to the continuing dominance [[189]] of the mythical (or at least angelic) interpretation of the passage has been the absence of a satisfactory alternative.[8] On the orthodox side, the view apparently generally held today is that which has long been

4. Cf. Kraeling, "Significance and Origin"; von Rad, *Genesis*. Other textual rearrangements have been suggested. For example, only verses 1 and 2 are original (J^1) and these were first located in Gen 11 before verse 4, but then moved by J^2 to a position after verse 8. Later they were relocated by the priestly redactor in their present position and supplemented with the groundwork of verses 3 and 4. Cf. C. Simpson, "The Book of Genesis," *IB* 1:533.

5. Even on the interpretation that possessed men were the instruments of demons (cf. note 3), it would not be the possessed humans but the demons who were the agents with primary responsibility and the chief objects of the divine displeasure, as one may judge from the encounters of our Lord with demoniacs as related in the gospels. K. Rabast, recognizing the difficulty, would salvage the angel interpretation by the implausible suggestion that verses 1 and 2a describe a sin of angels, but verse 2b (assuming an abrupt change of subject) describes a corresponding sin of men. It would then be the punishment of the latter only which is mentioned in verse 3. Cf. his *Die Genesis* (Berlin: Evangelische Verlagsanstalt, 1950), 130ff.

6. See Job 1:6; 2:1; 38:7; cf. Pss 29:1; 89:7.

7. Cf. the *bn ilm* of the Ugaritic texts, the *bn ʾlm* of the Azitawadd inscription, and the *bn ʾlm* of the Incantation of Arslan Tash.

8. Although Rabast (*Die Genesis*) suggests what he deems a possible solution, he declares after his survey of the standard interpretations that the passage remains an unsolved enigma.

popular in the church and among some Jewish interpreters, namely, that "the sons of God" and "the daughters of men" represent respectively the Sethite and Cainite lines which are set in contrast to one another as the godly and the ungodly in Gen 4 and 5. The sin of "the sons of God" was then their failure to marry within the covenant.[9] Therein is said to lie the explanation of the otherwise unexplained development that degeneracy prevailed universally outside the family of Noah, the Sethite line being scarcely able to preserve its specific covenantal identity in the face of the advancing tide of Cainite ungodliness.

This view has the advantage of doing justice to the terms of the verdict of verse 3 by understanding all parties to the sinful marriages as human beings. Against it, however, the serious objection has been directed that it takes *hāʾādām* in two different senses in verses 1 and 2. In verse 1 it understands *hāʾādām* as mankind generically; in verse 2, as the Cainite line specifically. That such a shift in meaning is certainly not intended becomes apparent as soon as one observes that the "men" of both verses are identified as the fathers of the "daughters" of the two verses and surely the "daughters" of the two verses are identical.

This difficulty can, however, be overcome in such a way that an interpretation of at least the same general tenor remains as a plausible possibility. It is necessary simply to regard *hāʾādām* as generic in verse 2 as well as in verse 1 where it is certainly so. There would then be no specific reference to Cainite women. But the sin of the Sethite men, "the sons of God," would on this modified approach still be their failure to show covenantal discrimination in their selection of marriage partners inasmuch as they made their choice out of the generality of women according to their own unrestricted pleasure. The emphasis would now fall on *mikkōl ʾăšer bāḥārû,* [[190]] the *min* being partitive, i.e., they selected mates out of the category "any that they chose," or possibly explicative, i.e., "even all that they chose." Their choice would of course often be a Cainite woman, but even when they chanced to select a Sethite woman they only chanced to select a covenant woman and so did not act in conscious fidelity to the covenant but in careless independence of its holy requirements.

But a yet more serious problem is posed for any variety of the prevalent orthodox view by verse 4 if the Nephilim-Gibborim there referred to are the offspring of the marriages of "the sons of God" and "the daughters of men." For it is not at all clear why the offspring of religiously mixed marriages

9. Cf. Gen 24:3, 4; 26:34, 35; 27:46; 28:1, 2, 6–8; 34.

should be Nephilim-Gibborim, however these be understood within the range of feasible interpretation. Now it is unwarranted to suppose as some have that our passage was designed to serve primarily as an aetiological story accounting for the origin of the Nephilim. But on the other hand, difficult though the verse is, we must agree with the judgment expressed by Dillmann: "That the Nephilim were the fruits of those marriages is certainly the meaning, and is also clearly evident from אֲשֶׁר יָבֹאוּ וג' [*ʾăšer yābōʾû* etc.]."[10] For if the author's intention had been to say nothing more than that the Nephilim-Gibborim were contemporary with the marriages mentioned, he would have simply referred to those marriages in language similar to or even identical with that in verse 2. But his reference to the conjugal act and to childbearing finds justification only if he is describing the origin of the Nephilim-Gibborim.[11] Unless the difficulty which follows from this conclusion can be overcome, the religiously mixed marriage interpretation of the passage ought to be definitely abandoned.[12]

The traditional ecclesiastical view has also been criticized for interpreting "the sons of God" in a spiritual sense, i.e., [[191]] godly men. For one thing, a specific part of the genus is thus set in contrast to the genus itself, i.e., godly men over against men. Other examples of that sort of thing can, however, be cited.[13] There is also the question of whether a reference to spiritual sonship would not be anachronistic in Gen 6. But it cannot be demonstrated that the concept of man as a spiritual son of God was unknown in the antediluvian period. Moreover, the terminology in Gen 6:2 need not reflect the thought or language of any earlier stage in revelation than the time when this inspired interpretation of the antediluvian history was produced in its Pentateuchal form, and the idea of spiritual sonship is found elsewhere in the Pentateuch.[14] Nevertheless, the use of the designation "sons of God" for

---

10. *Genesis* (Edinburgh: T&T Clark, 1897), 1:241.

11. It is not necessary to the above interpretation but *hannĕpīlîm hāyû bāʾāreṣ* . . . may be translated: "The Nephilim arose [rather than 'were'] in the earth in those days . . . when, etc." For such a rendering in sentences of similar construction, cf., e.g., Gen 7:6, 10; 15:17.

12. Cf. Rabast, *Die Genesis*.

13. Cf., e.g., Gen 14:16; Ps 73:5; Isa 43:4; Jer 32:20. "The explanation lies in the circumstance that in such cases the whole is thought of as having only the generic characteristics and nothing more, whereas to the part a certain distinction is attributed which raises it above the genus, to which nevertheless logically it belongs" (G. Vos, *Biblical Theology* [Grand Rapids: Eerdmans, 1954], 60).

14. Cf. Deut 14:1; 32:5, 6. On Exod 4:22 see below.

members of the covenant community would be isolated in the context of the book of Genesis and would moreover be so remarkable as to demand a more plausible explanation for its appearance there than can be readily discovered. One is constrained to seek for some other interpretation of the *bĕnê-hāʾĕlōhîm*.

Divine Kingship

Is not the key to the identity of the *bĕnê-hāʾĕlōhîm* provided by the sacral kings who are so much in the center of interest in current studies of ancient Near Eastern life and culture? From the several great kingdoms which formed the setting of Old Testament history the evidence has been amassed, showing that kings were often regarded as in one sense or another divine and that they were indeed called sons of the various [[192]] gods.[15] An especially interesting example comes from the Ugaritic epics where king Krt is called *krt bn il*.[16]

From the titulary of this pagan ideology of divine kingship the term *bĕnê-hāʾĕlōhîm* was appropriated in Gen 6:1–4 as a designation for the antediluvian kings. It is accordingly to be translated, "the sons of the gods."[17] By

15. For the evidence see such standard treatments as I. Engnell, *Studies in Divine Kingship in the Ancient Near East* (Uppsala: Almqvist & Wiksell, 1943); H. Frankfort, *Kingship and the Gods* (Chicago: University of Chicago Press, 1948); J. de Fraine, *L'Aspect religieux de la royauté israélite* (Rome: Pontifical Biblical Institute, 1954); A. R. Johnson, *Sacral Kingship in Ancient Israel* (Cardiff: University of Wales Press, 1955); S. H. Hooke, ed., *Myth, Ritual, and Kingship* (Oxford: Clarendon, 1958); and International Congress for the History of Religions, *La Regalità Sacra—The Sacral Kingship*, SHR 4 (Leiden: Brill, 1959).

16. C. H. Gordon, *Ugaritic Handbook* (Rome: Pontifical Biblical Institute, 1948), 125:20. In this passage, which describes the mourning over the sick king, there is voiced the question raised by the prospect of the death of a divine being. "How can it be said, 'Krt is a son of El, the offspring of Lṭpn and Qdš?' Or do gods die, the offspring of Lṭpn not live?" (lines 20–23).

17. There is no more theological difficulty in this than there is in the *ad hominem* objectification of the gods of the nations which is common in the Old Testament. Another biblical instance of such usage is probably found in Ps 138:1. "Before the gods [*ʾĕlōhîm*] I will sing praise unto thee." The context indicates that these *ʾĕlōhîm* are the gentile rulers; see verse 4 and compare Ps 119:46. The addition of *bĕnê* in Gen 6 does not alter the sense radically, if at all. It could be a case of *bēn* used to denote an individual of a particular class. Cf. the parallelism of *ʾĕlōhîm* and *bĕnê ʿelyôn* in Ps 82:6. Or the use of *bēn* in Gen 6 might be to reflect the claim of

this simple literary stroke the author at once caught the spirit of ancient paganism and suggested darkly the satanic shapes that formed the background of the human revolt against the King of kings. For these "sons of the gods" were of all the seed of the serpent most like unto their father. One brief title thus serves to epitomize the climactic developments in the history of man's covenant breaking during those generations when the judgment of God was impending by which the world that then was perished. It has been a merit of some who have thought that they found in this passage a preternatural intrusion into earthly history, a sort of pseudo-messianic embodiment of demonic spirits in human flesh, that they have sensed more [[193]] fully than the advocates of the traditional exegesis, the titanic, one might almost say the eschatological, character of this ancient crisis.

Still interpreting the *bĕnê-hāʾĕlōhîm* as kings, it is also possible to regard that designation not as a direct appropriation from the pagan titulary but as a genuinely theistic expression honoring these potentates in their office as "the sons of God."[18] The kings' own self-designation as the son of this or that god will still have supplied the inspiration for our author's use of *bĕnê-hāʾĕlōhîm*, but as it stands in Gen 6 the expression will be an adaptation, reinterpreting the kingly dignity for what it is in truth. "For they are God's ministers," Paul could say even in the days of the *bĕnê-hāʾĕlōhîm* who ruled from Rome (Rom 13:6).

Support for the interpretation of the *bĕnê-hāʾĕlōhîm* as kings is found in the use of similar titles for theocratic rulers in Israel. In the Book of the Covenant those who administer justice as the representatives of God are called *ʾĕlōhîm*.[19] Particularly important is the evidence of Ps 82. There the Israelite magistrates, because of their God-like dignity and authority, and in spite even of their malfeasance (vv. 2ff.) which brings upon them a

---

the heathen kings to divine paternity rather than their claim to divinity as such. In either case, the addition of *bĕnê* in Gen 6 would also achieve a better verbal balance and a more complete conceptual contrast with the *bĕnôt hāʾādām*, "the daughters of men."

18. Cf. Rom 13:7.

19. See Exod 21:6; 22:8, 9, 28 [7, 8, 27]. Particularly significant is the parallelism in 22:28 between *ʾĕlōhîm* and *nāśîʾ bĕʿammĕkā*, "the ruler of thy people." (Cf. Acts 23:5.) This contradicts the suggestion that *ʾĕlōhîm* in these passages denotes sacred images such as were used in court ordeals elsewhere; cf. C. H. Gordon, "אלהים in Its Reputed Meaning of *Rulers, Judges*," *JBL* 54 (1935): 139–44. The same perspective is found in the Deuteronomic stipulations (19:17) where to stand for judgment "before the Lord" is explained by the appositional "before the priests and the judges."

divine warning of their mortality (v. 7), are called *ʾĕlōhîm* (vv. 1, 6) and in synonymous parallelism with that in verse 6, *bĕnê ʿelyôn* "sons of the Most High."[20] Similarly, the scion of David is heir to the divine promise: "I will be his father and he shall be my son."[21] [[194]] And that covenant is fulfilled uniquely in him whom the Father sanctified and sent into the world, the messianic Son of God.[22]

On the basis of such biblical usage the view anciently arose among the Jews that the *bĕnê-hāʾĕlōhîm* of Gen 6 were men of the aristocracy, princes and nobles, in contrast to the socially inferior "daughters of men." This interpretation came to expression, for example, in the Aramaic Targums[23] and in the Greek translation of Symmachus[24] and it has been followed by many Jewish authorities down to the present.[25] Always lightly dismissed in critical surveys of the long debate over the exegesis of Gen 6:1–4, this Jewish view was indeed deficient as a total assessment of the Gen 6 crisis. In particular, it failed to recognize the precise nature of the transgression of the *bĕnê-hāʾĕlōhîm*. Nevertheless, it alone of all the views was on the right track, only wanting the necessary substantiation and a correct orientation. That the clue to a similar but more precise and comprehensive solution of the ancient mystery of the *bĕnê-hāʾĕlōhîm* has now been made available by the studies in divine kingship would have been more readily recognized had not the mythical view of Gen 6:1–4 become in the meantime so unquestioned a tenet of critical Old Testament scholarship.

Dynasty of Tyrants

It is the genealogical nature of the treatment of the antediluvian history that accounts for the focusing of attention on the marriages of the royal *bĕnê-hāʾĕlōhîm*. The precise character of these marriages and especially of

---

20. Cf. John 10:34, 35.

21. 2 Sam 7:14. Cf. Exod 4:22–23, where God's identification of Israel as "my son" seems to signify Israel's royal status as heir of the kingdom of God. That is suggested by the contrast drawn between Israel, God's firstborn son, and pharaoh's firstborn, who was of divine birth according to Egyptian king ideology and so one of "the sons of the gods."

22. Cf. Pss 2:6, 7; 45:6; 110:1.

23. The Targum of Onkelos renders *bny rbrbyʾ*.

24. *Hoi huioi tōn dynasteuontōn.*

25. Cf., e.g., A. Cohen, ed., *The Soncino Chumash: The Five Books of Moses, with Haphtaroth* (London: Soncino, 1956), *in loc.*

the sin involved in them can best be seen if Gen 6:1–4 is viewed in relation to the preceding context. The beginnings of the genealogical history of the *bĕnê-hāʾĕlōhîm* are found in the genealogy of Cain (4:16–24).

Significantly, at the very outset of Cain's genealogy the [[195]] origin of city organization is noted (Gen 4:17). It was precisely in the urban political unit that the stage was set for the emergence of kingship.[26] What, therefore, begins as the genealogy of Cain becomes in the course of its development the dynasty of Cain.

In Cain's dedication of his city to the name of his heir there was foreshadowed the lust for a name that was increasingly to mark these city rulers until, when the city-states began to be theocratically conceived, they esteemed themselves veritable sons of the gods, and so "men of name" (Gen 6:4) indeed. Outstanding representative of the Cainite dynasty was Lamech. Concerning his court life it is recorded that he practiced bigamy (Gen 4:19) and of his royal enforcement of law it is witnessed out of his own mouth that his policy was one of tyranny, a tyranny that reckoned itself through the power of the sword of Tubal-cain more competent for vengeance than God himself (Gen 4:23, 24).

With this portrait of the kingship of Cainite Lamech the dynastic genealogy of Cain breaks off so that the genealogy of Seth may be given (Gen 4:25–5:32). But then Gen 6:1–4 resumes the thread of the history where it was dropped at Gen 4:24. Structurally, the accounts of Lamech (Gen 4:19–24) and of the *bĕnê-hāʾĕlōhîm* (Gen 6:1ff.) are much alike. In each case there are the taking of wives, the bearing of children, and the dynastic exploits. The one passage closes with the boast of Lamech concerning his judgment of those who offend him; the other issues in the Lord's announcement of the judgment he purposes to visit on the earth which has become offensive to him. Genesis 6:1ff. simply summarizes and concludes the course of dynastic development which had already been presented in the individual histories of the several rulers, indicating how the evil potential of Cainite kingship, betrayed even in its earliest beginnings, was given such full vent in its final stages as to produce a state of tyranny and corruption intolerable to the God of heaven.

Accordingly, the sinfulness of the marriages described in Gen 6:1, 2 was not that they were mixed—whether the [[196]] mixture be regarded as a mixture of two worlds (as on the angel view) or of two religious communities (as

26. For the conjunction of the origins of kingship and cities in the Sumero-Babylonian sources see below.

on the Sethite view) or of two social classes (as on the old Jewish view).[27] The sin was that of Cainite Lamech, the sin of polygamy, particularly as it came to expression in the harem, characteristic institution of the ancient oriental despot's court.[28] In this transgression the *bĕnê-hāʾĕlōhîm* flagrantly violated the sacred trust of their office as guardians of the general ordinances of God for human conduct.[29]

The princes born into these royal houses of the *bĕnê-hāʾĕlōhîm* were the Nephilim-Gibborim (v. 4), the mighty tyrants who Lamech-like esteemed their might to be their right. So as man abounded on the face of the earth (v. 1) God saw that the wickedness of man abounded in the earth (v. 5). By reason of the polygamy and tyranny practiced by the dynasty of the *bĕnê-hāʾĕlōhîm* in the name of divine-royal prerogative and justice, the earth became corrupt before God and filled with violence (vv. 5–7, 11–13) and so hasted to destruction.

The validity of this interpretation of Gen 6:1–4 as the culmination of the antediluvian kings' outrage against God may be tested by a comparison of the biblical narrative with the Sumero-Babylonian flood tradition. Such a comparison will also be found to have relevance for the question of whether this passage is an integral part of the history leading to the flood or whether, as popular critical opinion has it, it was originally a postdiluvian tradition.[30]

---

27. There was, of course, nothing inherently improper in a mixed marriage of the type involved on the old Jewish view.

28. Cf. Kraeling's comment on verse 2b: "A polygamous situation is implied in these words" ("Significance and Origin," 197). Cf. Rabast, *Die Genesis*, 132. Translate *mikkōl ʾăšer bāḥārû*, "even all that they chose," the *min* being explicative; cf. Gen 7:22; 9:10; Lev 11:32. Verse 1a, "when man began to abound on the earth," is a more apt introduction to verse 2 if the sin there is polygamy than if it is some sort of mixed marriage.

29. The description of their self-indulgence in defiance of the divine appointment (cf. Gen 2:21–24) recalls that of beguiled Eve (cf. Gen 3:6 and 6:2).

30. Kraeling, who grants that from its original inclusion in what he analyzes as the source J^1 Gen 6:1–4 was an episode preparatory to the flood, states that in this judgment he finds himself "running counter to the almost unanimous opinion of Old Testament scholarship" ("Significance and Origin," 195). The majority, following Wellhausen and Budde, has regarded Gen 6:1–4 as an aetiological legend purporting to account for the Nephilim of Num 13:33; and they have, therefore, concluded that originally it was a story dealing with postdiluvian times, since if antediluvian the Nephilim would have been wiped out in the deluge. (The ingenuity of some Jewish exegetes would overcome such a problem by the assumption that the Nephilim strain was preserved through the deluge in the persons of Noah's daughters-in-law. Cf. Cohen, *Soncino Chumash, in loc.*)

[[197]] The flood story as narrated by Utnapishtim to Gilgamesh (in Tablet XI of the Gilgamesh Epic) begins with a reference to the flood hero's city of Shurippak, of which it is affirmed that it was old "and the gods were in its midst."[31] But no explanation is given of what led the great gods to send the flood. Something on this subject is, however, found in the Old Babylonian flood epic commonly called after the hero, The Atraḫasis Epic. The first fragment, containing part of the introduction to the flood, begins:

> The land became wide, the peop[le became nu]merous, the land *bellowed* like wild oxen. The god was disturbed by their uproar. [Enlil] heard their clamor (and) said to the great gods: "Oppressive has become the clamor of mankind. By their uproar they prevent sleep."[32]

Alexander Heidel's observation is correct that the manner in which this epic begins with a reference to the population increase is "a point in favor of treating Gen 6:1–4 not as a separate fragment but as the introduction to the story of the deluge, regardless of whether the biblical account is dependent on the Babylonian or whether both have a common origin."[33] A further point of similarity to Gen 6:1–4 in the Atrah˘asis Epic is that a period of grace is given to man, during which men are visited with a series of monitory plagues.[34]

[[198]] A valuable contribution to our knowledge of the principal themes, particularly the introductory themes, of the ancient flood traditions is made by the Sumerian Deluge account, found on a fragmentary tablet at Nippur. The preserved portion of the first column deals with the creation. Then after a break the second column relates that kingship was lowered from heaven and that five cities were founded and apportioned to particular gods.[35] When the text continues on the third column after another lacuna, the subject is the flood itself.

---

31. Line 13. On Shurippak as the last center of kingship and cult before the flood see below.

32. Column 1, lines 2–8. Translation of E. A. Speiser in *ANET*, 104.

33. *The Gilgamesh Epic and Old Testament Parallels* (Chicago: University of Chicago Press, 1949), 226 n. 2.

34. Cf. Gen 6:3; 1 Pet 3:19, 20. The reference to the one hundred and twenty years in Gen 6:3 is, of course, one of the clearest marks of the passage as a prelude to the flood judgment, if the verse is recognized as original and it is interpreted as setting a temporal limit to the divine forbearance with men.

35. The cities are Eridu, Bad-tibira, Larak, Sippar, and Shurippak.

Further light is shed on the contents of the important second column by the closely related antediluvian preamble of the Sumerian King List.[36] That list begins, "When kingship was lowered from heaven," and it goes on to state that kingship was successively at five cities, the same as those mentioned in the Sumerian Deluge text. The kings who ruled at each of these royal centers are named and the phenomenal lengths of their reigns given. Thus, for example: "(In) Bad-tibira, En-men-lu-Anna ruled 43,200 years; En-men-gal-Anna ruled 28,800 years; the god Dumu-zi, a shepherd, ruled 36,000 years. Three kings (thus) ruled it for 108,000 years."[37] This section of the king list concludes: "These are five cities, eight kings ruled them for 241,000 years. (Then) the Flood swept over (the earth)."[38]

[[199]] It appears then that the theme of antediluvian kingship centering in cities under the hegemony of various gods constituted the main introductory motif in the Sumero-Babylonian flood traditions. This kingship was of heavenly origin and significantly it numbered a god among its representatives.[39] Now it is evident that our interpretation of the *běnê-hāʾĕlōhîm* of Gen 6:1–4 as sacral kings in a dynasty reaching back into the Cainite genealogy of Gen 4 provides a theme which parallels this major motif in the Sumero-Babylonian antediluvian traditions. For all who are familiar with the way in which Genesis repeatedly is found to share the formal thematic interests of other ancient literature the parallelism just noted should be persuasive evidence that our interpretation is in its basic orientation sound. Or, to

36. See Thorkild Jacobsen, *The Sumerian King List* (Chicago: University of Chicago Press, 1939), 58–61.

37. Translation that of A. Leo Oppenheim in *ANET*, 265.

38. Ibid. In this connection, the conclusion of Kraeling may be noted that the Gibborim of Gen 6:4 "are a Western adaptation of the Babylonian tradition of the antediluvian kings" ("Significance and Origin," 200). We do not agree with the way he reconstructs the literary relationship and do not accept the exegesis of his supporting argument, i.e., that Gen 6:3 is the Yahwistic contradiction of the immensely long lives attributed to the kings by the polytheistic source. But Kraeling is correct in detecting a historical parallel in the two passages. Incidentally, the longevity theme is in the Bible explicitly associated with the Sethite line and we suspect that this genealogy too is, or at least becomes in its later stages, dynastic. The Sumerian Noah, Ziusudra, appears as a king in the Sumerian Deluge account. As kings the Sethites would also be *běnê-hāʾĕlōhîm*, in the sense of "sons of God." They could not, however, be identified with the dynasty of corruption and oppression described in Gen 6:1ff.

39. The god Dumu-zi (i.e., Tammuz) is listed; cf. column I, line 15. Dumu-zi reappears as one of the postdiluvian kings, along with other divine or partly divine beings like "the god Lugal-banda" and "the divine Gilgamesh" (cf. column III, lines 12–20).

state the corollary, the fact that a historical theme so prominently treated in the Sumero-Babylonian epic tradition finds no counterpart in Gen 3–6 according to the standard interpretations is itself good reason to suspect that these interpretations have been missing the point.[40] And in addition to corroborating the interpretation of Gen 6:1–4 in terms of divine kingship, the thematic parallelism which is thus discovered between the biblical and extrabiblical antediluvian accounts offers, in contradiction to the subjective surmisings of the documentary theorists, convincing confirmation of the integrity of the passage within the antediluvian context.

Kingship from Adam to Abraham

It may be useful to observe the kingship theme of Gen 6:1–4 in the perspective of its broader development in the early chapters of Genesis.

[[200]] To the God-like one among his creatures the Creator assigned the dignity of kingly dominion over all other creatures and commissioned him with the royal mandate to subjugate and cultivate the earth (Gen 1 and 2). This kingdom program was to be executed through the basic institutions of marriage and labor. Through these the earth was to be filled with a race of gifted rulers who would exercise their stewardship of talent and dominion in the perfecting of the consecration of all sub-human creation to the interests of man, as the royal representative and priest of God. This program was reinstituted after the fall with the intimation given that it would be realized as a soteric accomplishment of the Lord (Gen 3).

At the flood, which terminated the first great historical epoch, the royal mandate may be seen fulfilled after a figure. For within the ark there was found the paradisaical kingdom of God renewed in miniature, with regal Noah, scion of Seth's faithful dynasty, together with his princely heirs established in dominion over the representatives of all the sub-human creation and triumphant over the natural elements. And from the ark the loyal covenant servant emerged as the redeemed king into the new world, cult-centered and rainbow-crowned (Gen 5, 7, and 8).

---

40. Attempts have been made to equate many of the names in the antediluvian genealogies of the Bible with those in the extrabiblical king lists. But even if this effort is in a measure successful, it comes short of finding an explicit reference to kingship in these biblical passages, much less of finding in kingship the dominant theme preparatory to the flood. In particular, the climactic introductory episode of the *bĕnê-hāʾĕlōhîm* is still left standing unrelated to the kingship motif.

Over against this realization of the royal ideal by means of the soteric intervention of God, there is set the failure of the royal enterprise as conducted by the dynasty of Cain. Within this succession of the *bĕnê-hāʾĕlōhîm*, the marriage ordinance was desecrated and the extension of dominion was sought by violence rather than through godly labor. But though they exalted themselves against the heavenly King, their breath was in their nostrils and their regal aspirations to divinity perished in the same waters of divine vengeance which bore the righteous king into his new world (Gen 4, 6, and 7).

The history of kingship from the flood to Abraham as described in Gen 9–12 repeats the antediluvian pattern found in Gen 3–8. Man was again commissioned to the kingdom program and enthroned as lord over all the lower orders (Gen 9:1ff.). Even the special office of king was specifically provided for in that the human community was invested with the power of the sword for the punishment of [[201]] all who shed man's blood, whether the man-slayer be "any kind of beast" or a fellow man, and so a "brother" of the slain (Gen 9:5, 6; cf. 4:15, 24).[41]

Once more too the mystery of iniquity developed in this new aeon towards a climactic episode of defiance against the God of heaven. The author begins to trace this theme in Gen 9:20ff., as he had in Gen 4:3ff., with the record of a transgression by a son of the covenant patriarch which issued in an echo of the primeval curse (Gen 9:25; cf. 4:11; 3:14). He continues, as he had in Gen 4:16ff., with a survey, within a genealogical framework, of the cultural-political advance of mankind outside the covenant community (Gen 10:1ff.). It presently appears that kingship was again "lowered from heaven" in the postdiluvian period. In the midst of the Gen 10 survey there looms the figure of Nimrod in whom the climactic Babel episode is anticipated and possibly even individualized (v. 8), so providing a parallel

41. "His brother" (*ʾāḥîw*) in Gen 9:5 does not denote the kinsman avenger as though responsibility were here being laid upon him to overtake the murderer. Each instance of *ʾedrōš min* in this verse must have the same force and, as the case of "every kind of beast" clearly indicates, its force is to hold the slayer liable to punishment. The *ʾāḥîw* declares that every murder is like the first murder a case of fratricide. The *šōpēk dam hāʾādām* of verse 6 then summarizes all the manslayers of verse 5, both men and beasts, as this verse goes on to assign to man in his kingly capacity the responsibility for putting all manslayers to death. In view of our thesis that the *bĕnê-hāʾĕlōhîm* are kings it is tempting to interpret verse 6b (*kî bĕṣelem ʾĕlōhîm ʿāśâ ʾet-hāʾādām*) as an appeal to the God-like nature of man as the justification for his executing the divine judgment. But it seems at least as plausible to refer this description to the victim and so find in it a measure of the enormity of the crime of murder.

to the relationship which obtains between the figure of Lamech (Gen 4:19ff.) and the irreligious dynasty of Gen 6:1–4.

The account of Nimrod is of particular interest for the interpretation of Gen 6:4 because he is described as one belonging to the category of the Gibborim (Gen 10:8). That Nimrod was a king is clear from Gen 10:10 (which locates his dominion in the land of Shinar, cf. Gen 11:2), and this supports the interpretation of the Gibborim of Gen 6:4 and their fathers, the *běnê-hāʾĕlōhîm*, as a royal dynasty. If one bears in mind the divine ordinance of Gen 9:5, 6, by which the civil [[202]] power was authorized to destroy man-slaying beasts as well as human murderers, it will be seen that Gen 10:9 need not be judged an interpolation which breaks the thematic unity of verses 8 and 10, simply because it specifies that Nimrod was *gibbōr-ṣayid*. Nimrod's hunting exploits were not mere sport but a function properly pertaining to his royal office and quite necessary in his historical situation.

The ungodly dynasty of human kingship challenged the ordinances of the Creator until at Babel it was ripe for judgment. Genesis 11:1ff. parallels Gen 6:1ff. The spirit of the two is the same; the kingdom builders of Shinar, like the ancient Gibborim, were bent on a name (11:4; cf. 6:4). And of course each episode leads directly to the divine reckoning and intervention.

But while there was this rebellious development of human kingship that led on to the judgment of God, the era of Gen 9–12 like that of Gen 3–8 moved towards an outstanding realization of a kingship of man which was after God's own heart and towards a significant portrayal of the kingdom of God among men. The earlier age led to Noah and the kingdom in the ark; the following age led to Abraham and the kingdom in the promises.[42] The fall of the dynasty of the *běnê-hāʾĕlōhîm* was the foil to Noah's triumph. So in contrast to the debacle at Babel there is set the establishment of God's covenant with Abraham as the crowning fruit of the Noahic era, the fruit in which there was in turn the seed of the future of God's kingdom and of a righteous kingship on earth.

In opposition to the world center which rose from the accursed ground of Shinar, destined to desolation, there appears in the covenant promises

42. Noah was introduced in a genealogy of the covenant generations which was recorded between the accounts of Lamech and the *běnê-hāʾĕlōhîm* (Gen 4:25–5:32) and was resumed after the latter (Gen 6:9, 10). Similarly, the genealogy that introduces Abraham intervenes between the genealogy in which Nimrod appears and the Babel episode (Gen 10:21–31) and is resumed after the latter (Gen 11:10ff.), although there is minor structural variation at this point.

given to Abraham the city of God, which descends from heaven and endures forever. In [[203]] those promises Abraham possessed a kingdom which was the fulfillment, first in a pre-messianic symbol and afterwards in messianic reality, of the kingdom mandate given to Adam in the garden of God. Fill the earth and subdue it, was the divine commission given to Adam; thy descendants shall be as the stars of the heaven and they shall conquer and inherit a new paradise land of milk and honey, was the corresponding divine promise given to Abraham.

It was in that kingdom of God that true human kingship was to prosper and be perfected. It would produce a kingship not bent on its own name but consecrated to the glory of God. For the covenant by which it was administered was a vassal covenant—a declaration of the lordship of the God who gave it and an establishment of the dynasty of the faithful who received it as servant-kings, vicegerents of the Almighty.

In the unfolding of that covenant the ideal of true kingship was ever more clearly delineated. The true theocratic king must not like the *běnê-hāʾĕlōhîm* "multiply wives to himself" (Deut 17:17). He must not like the Gibborim fill the earth with violence by committing injustice against the weak but rather judge the people with righteousness, break in pieces the oppressor, and redeem the soul of the needy from deceit and violence (cf. Ps 72).

None, however, among the *běnê-hāʾĕlōhîm* of ancient Israel actually reigned in perfect righteousness. Some so far fell short that the conditions of Gen 6 returned in Israel (cf. Ps 82:1–5) and these "sons of the Most High" had to be warned in words which seem to allude to the verdict and judgment against the prediluvian dynasty of the *běnê-hāʾĕlōhîm*: "Ye shall die like men, and fall like one of the princes" (Ps 82:7; cf. Gen 6:3ff.).

But it is the confession of the church that the king-ideal has found embodiment in the seed of David whom David called "my Lord" (Ps 110:1; cf. Matt 22:43ff.; Mark 12:36–37; Luke 20:42ff.; Acts 2:33ff.); to whom God declared, "Thou art my Son; this day have I begotten thee" (Ps 2:7); who was a priest-king after the order of Melchizedek, "without father, without mother";[43] the righteous Servant who was the King of [[204]] kings and the

43. Cf. Heb 7:3a. This disclaimer of human parentage was made by ancient kings like Gudea and Assurbanipal. For a discussion see, e.g., Frankfort, *Kingship and the Gods*, 300; Engnell, *Studies in Divine Kingship*, 16, 78. The formula was apparently a negative way of claiming divine appointment for the dynasty. It was associated with a positive claim to divine "parentage." Melchizedek is thus portrayed by the author of Hebrews as one appointed to his kingship by his God, *ʾēl ʿelyôn*,

Gibbor of Gibborim, for he was *ʾēl gibbôr*, the mighty One who is God (Isa 9:6); who lusted not after a name but humbled himself in obedience unto the death of the cross, and therefore has been given a name which is above every name, that at his name every knee should bow and every tongue confess that Jesus Christ is Lord, to the glory of God the Father (Phil 2:9–11).

---

and so as one of the *bĕnê ʿelyôn* (cf. Ps 82:6; Gen 14:18ff.), a godly counterpart to the Lamech-Nimrod type of *bĕnê-hāʾĕlōhîm*. Thus, too, was he "made like unto the Son of God" (Heb 7:3b).

CHAPTER FIVE

The Two Tables of the Covenant

(1960, rev. 1975)

"And he declared unto you his covenant, which he commanded you to perform, even ten commandments; and he wrote them upon two tables of stone" (Deut 4:13).

It has been commonly assumed that each of the stone tables contained but a part of the total revelation proclaimed by the voice of God out of the fiery theophany on Sinai. Only the subordinate question of the dividing point between the "first" and "second tables" has occasioned disagreement.[1] A reexamination of the biblical data, however, particularly in the light of extrabiblical parallels, suggests a radically new interpretation of the formal nature of the two stone tables, the importance of which will be found to lie primarily in the fresh perspective it lends to our understanding of the divine oracle engraved upon them.

[[114]] Attention in recent years is being directed more and more to the remarkable resemblance between God's covenant with Israel and the suzerainty (also called vassal) type of international treaty found in the ancient Near East.[2] Similarities have been discovered in the areas of the documents,

1. The dominant opinion has been that the "second table" opens with the fifth commandment, but Jews usually count the fifth commandment as the last in the "first table," filial reverence being regarded as a religious duty. (Here and elsewhere in this chapter the designation of specific commandments is based on the common Protestant enumeration.) For a different ancient Jewish opinion anticipating the conclusion of the present study, see *Midrash Rabbah* 47.6.

2. See G. E. Mendenhall, "Covenant Forms in Israelite Tradition," *BA* 17.3 (1954): 50–76; this was republished in *Law and Covenant in Israel and the Ancient Near East* (Pittsburgh: Biblical Colloquium, 1955). D. J. Wiseman had previously read a paper on some of the parallels to the Society for Old Testament Studies (Jan. 1948). Cf. K. Baltzer, *Das Bundesformular: Seine Ursprung und seine Verwendung im Alten Testament*, WMANT 4 (Neukirchen: Neukirchener Verlag, 1960).

There are references to such international treaties in the third millennium BC. Actual treaty texts of the New Hittite Empire in the full classic form of the

the ceremonies of ratification, the modes of administration, and, most basically, of course, the suzerain-servant relationship itself. On the biblical side, the resemblance is most apparent in the accounts of the theocratic covenant as instituted through the mediatorship of Moses at Sinai and as later renewed under both Moses and Joshua. Of most interest for the subject of this chapter is the fact that the pattern of the suzerainty treaty can be traced in miniature in the revelation written on the two tables by the finger of God.

"I am the Lord thy God," the opening words of the Sinaitic proclamation (Exod 20:2a), correspond to the preamble of the suzerainty treaties, which identified the suzerain or "great king" and that in terms calculated to inspire awe and fear. For example, the treaty of Mursilis with his vassal Duppi-Teshub of Amurru begins: "These are the words of the Sun Mursilis, the great king, the king [[115]] of the Hatti land, the valiant, the favorite of the Storm-god, the son of Suppiluliumas, etc."[3]

Such treaties continued in an "I-thou" style with a historical prologue surveying the great king's previous relations with, and especially his benefactions to, the vassal king. In the treaty just referred to, Mursilis reminds Duppi-Teshub of the vassal status of his father and grandfather, of their loyalty and enjoyment of Mursilis' just oversight, and climactically it is narrated how Mursilis, true to his promise to Duppi-Teshub's father, secured the dynastic succession for Duppi-Teshub, sick and ailing though he was. In the Decalogue the historical prologue is found in the further words of the Lord: "which have brought thee out of the land of Egypt, out of the house of bondage" (Exod 20:2b). This element in the covenant document was clearly designed to inspire confidence and gratitude in the vassal and thereby dispose him to attend to the covenant obligations, which constitute the third element in both Exod 20 and the international treaties.

There are many interesting parallels to specific biblical requirements among the treaty stipulations; but, to mention only the most prominent, the fundamental demand is always for thorough commitment to the suzerain to

mid-second millennium BC were discovered some fifty years ago in the archives of ancient Hattusa. The evidence for this period has been supplemented by a few treaty fragments found at Ugarit. Other recent finds bring the evidence for vassal treaties down into the first half of the first millennium BC. Most significant are the three Aramaic inscriptions from Sefireh and the Assyrian treaties of Esarhaddon found at Nimrud.

3. Translation of A. Goetze in *ANET*, 203. Cf. V. Korošec, *Hethitische Staatsverträge* (Leipzig: Hinrichs, 1931), 36ff.

the exclusion of all alien alliances.[4] Thus, Mursilis insists: "But you, Duppi-Tessub, remain loyal toward the king of the Hatti land, the Hatti land, my sons (and) my grandsons forever. . . . Do not turn your eyes to anyone else!"[5] And Yahweh commands his servant: "Thou shalt have no other gods before me" (Exod 20:3; cf. vv. 4, 5).

Stylistically, the apodictic form of the Decalogue apparently finds its only parallel in the treaties, which [[116]] contain categorical imperatives and prohibitions and a conditional type of formulation equivalent to the apodictic curse (cf. Deut 27:15–26), both being directly oriented to covenant oaths and sanctions. The legislation in the extant legal "codes," on the other hand, is uniformly of the casuistic type.

Two other standard features of the classic suzerainty treaty were the invocation of the gods of the suzerain and (in the Hittite sphere) the gods of the vassal as witnesses of the oath and the pronouncing of imprecations and benedictions, which the oath deities were to execute according to the vassal's deserts.

Obviously, in the case of God's covenant with Israel there could be no thought of a realistic invocation of a third party as divine witness.[6] Indeed, it is implicit in the third word of the Decalogue that all Israel's oaths must be sworn by the name of Yahweh (Exod 20:7). The immediate contextual application of this commandment is that the Israelite must remain true to the oath he was about to take at Sinai in accordance with the standard procedure in ceremonies of covenant ratification (cf. Exod 24).

Mendenhall[7] finds no reference to an oath as the foundation of the Sinaitic Covenant; he does, however, allow that the oath may have taken the form of a symbolic act rather than a verbal formula. But surely a solemn affirmation of consecration to God made in the presence of God to his mediator-representative and in response to divine demand, sanctioned by divine threats against the rebellious, is tantamount to an oath. Moreover,

4. Cf. further, Korošec, *Hethitische Staatsverträge*, 66ff.; D. J. Wiseman, *The Vassal-Treaties of Esarhaddon* (London: British School of Archaeology in Iraq, 1958), 23ff.; Mendenhall, "Covenant Forms," 59.

5. *ANET*, 204.

6. There is a formal literary approximation to the invocation of the oath witnesses in Deut 4:26; 30:19; and 31:28, where, by the rhetorical device of apostrophe, God calls heaven and earth to be witnesses of his covenant with Israel. Heaven and earth are also invoked along with the mountains and rivers, etc., at the close of this section in the treaties. Cf. Matt 5:34, 35; 23:16–22.

7. "Covenant Forms," 66.

Israel's eating and drinking in the persons of her [[117]] representatives on the mount of God (Exod 24:11) was a recognized symbolic method by which people swore treaties.[8]

The curses and blessings are present in Exod 20, though not as a separate section. They are, rather, interspersed among the stipulations (see vv. 5, 6, 7, 11, 12). Moreover, an adaptation of the customary form of the curses and blessings to the divine nature of the Suzerain who here pronounced them was necessary. Thus, the usual invocative form has yielded to the declarative, and that in the style of the motive clause, which is characteristic of Old Testament legislation and illustrative of what may be called the reasonableness of Israel's Lord.[9]

There is one final point of material correspondence between Exod 20 and the secular treaties. It provides the key to the nature of the two tables of stone, and to this we shall presently return. The parallelism already noted, however, is sufficient to demonstrate that the revelation committed to the two tables was rather a suzerainty treaty or covenant than a legal code. The customary exclusive use of "Decalogue" to designate this revelation, biblical terminology though it is (cf. "the ten words,"[10] Exod 34:28; Deut 4:13; 10:4), has unfortunately served to obscure the whole truth of the matter. That this designation is intended as only *pars pro toto* is [[118]] confirmed by the fact that "covenant" (*bĕrît*; Deut 4:13) and "the words of the covenant" (Exod 34:28) are alternate biblical terminology. So, too, is "testimony" (*ʿēdût*; Exod 25:16, 21; 40:20; cf. 2 Kgs 17:15), which characterizes the stipulations as oath-bound obligations or as a covenant order of life.[11] Consequently, the two tables are called "the tables of the covenant" (Deut 9:9, 11, 15) and "the tables of the testimony" (Exod 31:18; 32:15; 34:29); the ark, as the depository of the tables,

8. Cf. Wiseman, *Vassal-Treaties*, 84, and lines 154–156 of the Ramataia text.

9. Cf. B. Gemser, "The Importance of the Motive-Clause in Old Testament Law," in *Congress Volume: Copenhagen, 1953*, ed. G. W. Anderson et al., VTSup 1 (Leiden: Brill, 1953), 50–66. It must be borne in mind that the Decalogue does not stand alone as the total revelation of the covenant at Sinai. For curses and blessings, see also the conclusion of the Book of the Covenant (Exod 23:20–33); and cf. Deut 27–30.

10. The contents of the treaties are also called the "words" of the suzerain.

11. *ʿēdût* is related to the Akkadian *adē*, which is used as a general appellation for the contents of suzerainty treaties. Wiseman (*Vassal-Treaties*, 81) defines *adū* (sing.) as "a law or commandment solemnly imposed in the presence of divine witnesses by a suzerain upon an individual or people who have no option but acceptance of the terms. It implies a 'solemn charge or undertaking on oath' (according to the view of the suzerain or vassal)."

"the ark of the covenant" or "the ark of the testimony"; and the tabernacle, where the ark was located, "the tabernacle of the testimony."

The two stone tables are not, therefore, to be likened to a stele containing one of the half-dozen or so known legal "codes" earlier than or roughly contemporary with Moses, as though God had engraved on these tables a corpus of law.[12] The revelation they contain is nothing [[119]] less than an epitome of the covenant granted by Yahweh, the sovereign Lord of heaven and earth, to his elect and redeemed servant, Israel.

Not law, but covenant—that must be affirmed when we are seeking a category comprehensive enough to do justice to this revelation in its totality. At the same time, the prominence of the stipulations, reflected in the fact that "the ten words" are the element used as *pars pro toto*, signalizes the centrality of law in this type of covenant. There is probably no clearer direction afforded the biblical theologian for defining with biblical emphasis the type of covenant God adopted to formalize his relationship to his people than that given in the covenant he gave Israel to perform, even "the ten commandments." Such a covenant is a declaration of God's lordship, consecrating a people to himself in a sovereignly dictated order of life.

But what, now, is the significance of the fact that the covenant was recorded not on one but on two stone tables?

Apart from the dubious symbolic propriety of bisecting a treaty for distribution over two separate documents, all the traditional suggestions as to how the division should be made are liable to the objection that they do violence to the formal and logical structure of this treaty. The results of the traditional type of cleavage are not two reasonably balanced sets of laws but one table containing almost all of three of the four treaty elements plus a part of the fourth, i.e., the stipulations, and a second table with only

---

12. There does appear to be some literary relationship between the legal "codes" and the suzerainty treaties. J. Muilenburg ("The Form and Structure of the Covenantal Formulations," *VT* 9 [1959]: 347ff.) classifies both under "the royal message." Hammurapi in his "code," which is still the most complete of the extant ancient Oriental "codes," introduces himself in the prologue with a recital of his incomparable qualifications for the promulgation of laws, then presents the laws, and in the epilogue pronounces curses and blessings on future kings as they ignore or honor his "code." The identity of the Decalogue with the suzerainty treaties over against such law "codes" is evidenced by features like the covenant terminology, the *adē* character of the stipulations, the "I-thou" formulation, and the purpose of the whole as manifested in both the contents and the historical occasion, i.e., the establishment of a covenant relationship between two parties.

a fraction of the stipulations plus possibly a blessing formula. The preamble and historical prologue must be neither minimized nor ignored because of their brevity, for this is a covenant in miniature. In comparison with the full-scale version, the stipulations are proportionately as greatly reduced as are the preamble and the historical prologue. That would be even clearer if the additional strand of the curses and blessings were not interwoven with the commandments. Certainly, too, there was no physical necessity for distributing the material [[120]] over two stones. One table of such a size that Moses could carry, and the ark contain, a pair of them, would offer no problem of spatial limitations to prevent engraving the entire text upon it, especially since the writing covered both obverse and reverse (Exod 32:15). In fact, it seems unreasonable, judging from the appearance of comparable stone inscriptions from antiquity, to suppose that all the area of both sides of two tables would be devoted to so few words.

There is, moreover, the comparative evidence of the extrabiblical treaties. Covenants such as Exod 20:2–17 has been shown to be are found written in their entirety on one table, and, indeed, like the Sinaitic tables, on both its sides.[13] As a further detail in the parallelism of external appearance it is tempting to see in the Sabbath sign presented in the midst of the ten words the equivalent of the suzerain's dynastic seal found in the midst of the obverse of the international treaty documents.[14] Since in the case of the Decalogue the suzerain is Yahweh, there will be no representation of him on his seal; but the Sabbath is declared to be his "sign of the covenant" (Exod 31:13–17). By means of his Sabbath-keeping, the image-bearer of God images the pattern of that divine act of creation which proclaims God's absolute sovereignty over man, and thereby he pledges his covenant consecration to his Maker. The Creator has stamped on world history the sign of the Sabbath as his seal of ownership and authority. That is precisely what the pictures on the dynastic seals symbolize and their captions claim in behalf of the treaty gods and their representative, the suzerain.

[[121]] These considerations point to the conclusion that each stone was complete in itself. The two tables were duplicate copies of the covenant. And

---

13. Cf., e.g., Wiseman, *Vassal-Treaties*, plates I and IX.

14. The closing paragraph of the Egyptian text of the parity treaty of Hattusilis III and Ramses II is a description of the seal, called "What is in the middle of the tablet of silver" (*ANET*, 201). For the Mitannian practice of placing the seal on the reverse, cf. D. J. Wiseman, *The Alalakh Tablets* (London: British Institute of Archaeology at Ankara, 1953), plates VII and VIII, texts 13 and 14.

the correctness of this interpretation is decisively confirmed by the fact that it was normal procedure in establishing suzerainty covenants to prepare duplicate copies of the treaty text.

Five of the six standard sections of the classic suzerainty treaty were mentioned above. The sixth section contained directions for the depositing of one copy of the treaty document in the sanctuary of the vassal and another in a sanctuary of the suzerain.[15] For example, the treaty made by Suppiluliuma with Mattiwaza states: "A duplicate of this tablet has been deposited before the Sun-goddess of Arinna. . . . In the Mitanni land (a duplicate) has been deposited before Tessub. . . . At regular *intervals* shall they read it in the presence of the king of the Mitanni land and in the presence of the sons of the Hurri country."[16] Enshrinement of the treaty before the gods was expressive of their role as witnesses and avengers of the oath. Even the vassal's gods were thereby enlisted in the foreign service of the suzerain.[17]

Similar instructions were given Moses at Sinai concerning the two tables. They were to be deposited in the ark, which in turn was to be placed in the tabernacle (Exod 25:16, 21; 40:20; Deut 10:2). Because Yahweh was at once Israel's covenant Suzerain and God of Israel and of Israel's oath, there was but one sanctuary for the depositing [[122]] of both treaty duplicates. The specified location of the documents as given in Hittite treaties can be rendered "under (the feet of)" the god, which would then correspond strikingly to the arrangements in the Israelite holy of holies (see Exod 25:22).[18] The two tables themselves do not contain instructions concerning their deposition, for the legislation regarding the ark and sanctuary had not yet been given. The same is true of the Book of the Covenant (Exod 20:22–23:33). However, it is significant that when such legislation was given after the ceremony of covenant ratification (Exod 24), the ark was the first object described in detail and directions for depositing the two tables in it were included (Exod 25:10–22).

As for the further custom of periodic public reading of treaty documents, the contents of the two tables were, of course, declared in the hearing

---

15. Cf. Korošec, *Hethitische Staatsverträge*, 100–101. On a stele from Ras Shamra an oath-taking ceremony is depicted with the two parties raising their hands over two copies of the treaty (*Ugaritica* III, plate VI).

16. Translation of A. Goetze, *ANET*, 205. In various treaties the public reading requirement specifies from one to three times annually.

17. Cf. 2 Kgs 18:25 and the observations of M. Tsevat, "The Neo-Assyrian and Neo-Babylonian Vassal Oaths and the Prophet Ezekiel," *JBL* 78 (1959): 199.

18. Cf. Korošec, *Hethitische Staatsverträge*, 100.

of all Israel and the Book of the Covenant was read to the people as part of the ratification ceremony (Exod 24:7); but the practice of periodic proclamation was first formulated some forty years later in the book of Deuteronomy when God was renewing the covenant unto the second generation. When suzerainty covenants were renewed, new documents were prepared in which the stipulations were brought up to date. Deuteronomy is such a covenant renewal document; hence its repetition with modernizing modifications of the earlier legislation, as found, for example, in its treatment of the Decalogue (5:6–21) or of the Passover (16:5ff.; cf. Exod 12:7, 46).[19] Another case in point is Deuteronomy's addition of this requirement for the regular public reading of the covenant law at the Feast of Tabernacles in the seventh year of release (31:9–13), a [[123]] requirement that became relevant and applicable with the arrival of the Israelites at the threshold of their inheritance in Canaan. The document which was to be brought forth and read was not one of the stone tables but the "book of the law" which Moses wrote and had placed by the side of the ark (31:9, 26). However, even if "this book of the law" is identified with Deuteronomy alone, reading it would have included a reproclamation of the contents of the tables.

The relevance of the foregoing for higher critical conclusions concerning the Decalogue may be noted in passing. Along with a decreasing reluctance in negative critical studies to accept the Mosaic origin of the Decalogue,[20] the judgment continues that the present form of the Sinaitic Decalogue is an expansion of the original, which is then reduced to an abridged version of the ten words, without preamble, historical prologue,

19. Taking Pentateuchal history at its face value, we discover that the book of Deuteronomy exhibits precisely the legal form which contemporary second-millennium-BC evidence indicates a suzerain would employ in his rule of a vassal nation like Israel at such a historical juncture. It will no longer suffice for negative critics to grant only that certain individual ancient laws and cultic patterns are preserved in Deuteronomy; for the fact is that its total structure conforms to the classic structure of suzerainty treaties, all six standard sections being represented. The implications of this for the unity and authenticity of Deuteronomy are clear. While the suzerainty pattern has been widely recognized in the Decalogue and in Josh 24, there has been a strange lack of acknowledgment of all the obvious facts in the case of Deuteronomy. It is to be hoped that the traditionalistic higher criticism will not long indulge in obscurantism out of regard for the unfortunate circumstance that its seventh-century date for Deuteronomy is the pivot of the massive volume of modern historical studies of Israelite literature and religion.

20. Cf. H. H. Rowley, "Moses and the Decalogue," *Bulletin of the John Rylands Library* 34 (1951–52): 81ff.

or curses and blessings, and often without even an abridged form of the second and fourth words. Similarly, even where there is no bias against the Bible's representations concerning its own origins, the supposition has gained currency that it was an abbreviated version of the Decalogue that was engraved on the stone tables. Such estimates of the contents of the Mosaic tables are clearly unsatisfactory, since the supposed abbreviated forms lack those very features which distinguish the tables as that which comparative study indicates was called for by the historical occasion, and biblical exegesis indicates the tables to be, not a brief ethical catechism, but copies of the Sinaitic Covenant.

The purpose of Israel's copy of the covenant was that of a documentary witness (Deut 31:26).[21] It was witness [[124]] to and against Israel, reminding of obligations sworn to and rebuking for obligations violated, declaring the hope of covenant beatitude and pronouncing the doom of the covenant curses. The public proclamation of it was designed to teach the fear of the Lord to all Israel, especially to the children (Deut 31:13; cf. Ps 78:5ff.).

The secular treaties and the biblical covenant share a perspective of family solidarity reflected in numerous references to the sons and grandsons of the vassal. In the political treaties, sworn commitment is in the terms: "we, our sons, and our grandsons"; and agreeably both curses and blessings are pronounced unto children's children. "Visiting the iniquity of the fathers upon the children unto the third and fourth generation of them that hate me" (Exod 20:5b) is the biblical counterpart, defining the bounds of corporate responsibility in guilt under this covenant administration by the utmost limits of contemporaneity (described here by means of numerical climax, a popular device of Hebrew and Canaanite literature).

Both copies of the covenant were laid before Yahweh as God of the oath. But what was the purpose of Yahweh's own copy in his capacity as covenant Suzerain? In the case of the international treaties, the suzerain would naturally want to possess, preserve, and protect a sealed legal witness to the treaty. It would remind him of the vassal's *adē* for the purpose of enforcement and punishment; for, according to the religious theory which was the legal fiction lending sacred sanction to the treaty, he would be the actual avenger of the oath, the instrument of the oath deities. It would also

---

21. Various types of covenant witnesses other than the divine witness are mentioned. Cf. the Song of Moses, which he had Israel memorize (Deut 31:19, 22; 32:1ff.); the stones with the law written upon them erected on Ebal (Deut 27:2ff.; Josh 8:30–35); and the stone witness of covenant renewal at Shechem (Josh 24:26, 27).

remind him of his suzerain's role as the vassal's protector and of the various specific promises of assistance often contained in such treaties. He had not, however, like the vassal, taken a covenant oath. And human lords being what they are, he would have had considerably less interest in the benefits [[125]] he might bestow on the vassal than in the amount of annual tribute he was entitled to exact from him.

Such, *mutatis mutandis*, was the purpose of Yahweh's own stone table of covenant witness. However, even from the formal point of view there is here a remarkable shift in emphasis arising from the fact that God's suzerainty covenant was an administration of salvation. The form of the blessing suggests the unique emphasis—"showing mercy," and that not merely to the third and fourth generation of them that love him but, contrary to the balance observed in this respect in the curse and blessing formulae of the international treaties, "to a thousand generations" (Deut 7:9). This much more abounding of grace is evidenced even in connection with the function of the stone tables as witnesses against Israel; for since the divine throne under which the tables were located was the place of atonement, the witness of the tables against Israel never ascended to Yahweh apart from the witness of the blood advocating mercy.

The divine Suzerain's condescension in his redemptive covenant at the time of its Abrahamic administration extended to the humiliation of swearing himself to covenant fidelity as Lord of the covenant and Fulfiller of the promises (Gen 15). Mendenhall[22] mistakenly regards the Abrahamic covenant as completely different in kind from the Sinaitic, partly because of God's oath and partly because of an alleged absence of obligations imposed on Abraham. Actually, the total allegiance to his Lord demanded of Abraham (Gen 12:1; 17:1) was precisely that fealty which the treaty stipulations were designed to secure.

Moreover, it is demonstrable that an oath on the part of the suzerain was not incompatible with the genius of the relationship governed by a suzerainty treaty. There is, for example, a treaty with a related deed from Alalakh,[23] [[126]] both concerned with one Abban, the vizier of Hattusa, and his bestowment of certain cities upon his political "servant," Iarimlim. The treaty states that Abban confirmed the gifts in perpetuity by a self-maledictory oath accompanied by the symbolism of slaughtering a sheep. It also stipulates that

22. "Covenant Forms," 62.

23. Published by D. J. Wiseman in *JCS* 12 (1958): 124–29, and in *The Alalakh Tablets*, 25, 26, plate I, respectively.

the territorial gift is forfeit if Iarimlim is disloyal to Abban. The text deeding Alalakh (part of Abban's gift) pronounces curses upon any who would alter Abban's purpose by hostilities against Iarimlim.

All of this corresponds perfectly to God's dealings with Abraham. The Lord covenanted territory to his servant Abraham as an everlasting possession (Gen 12:1, 2; 13:14–17; 15:18) and did so by a self-maledictory oath symbolized by the slaying of animals (Gen 15:9ff.). Moreover, it is clear that by rebellion against Yahweh's word, Abraham would forfeit the promise (Gen 22:16, 17a; cf. Deut 28, esp. vv. 63ff.). And finally, the Egyptians and Canaanites who would oppose this territorial grant were cursed (Gen 12:3; 15:14, 16, 19–21).

God's oath is, therefore, in keeping with the suzerain-vassal relationship. The generic nature of God's covenants with his people remains first and last a declaration of divine lordship, a lordship which may be manifested in the execution of promises or threats. These covenants are sovereign administrations not of blessing exclusively but of curse and blessing according to the vassal's deserts. Since, however, the specifically soteric covenants are informed by the principle of God's sovereign grace, which infallibly effects his redemptive purposes in Christ, they are accompanied by divine guarantees assuring a realization of the blessing sanctions of the covenant.

Now, it would obviously be unsound methodology to give this special feature which belongs to the specifically redemptive covenant administrations a constitutive place when defining the covenant generically. Nevertheless, [[127]] there is not the least incompatibility between divine guarantees of blessing such as God's oath to Abraham, guarantees which, without violating human responsibility, assure the elect vassals that in Christ they will receive that covenant righteousness which is the stipulated way to covenant beatitude, and the nature of suzerainty covenants as they are here defined in terms of divine lordship, enforced in a revelation of law consisting of stipulations and sanctions, both promissory and penal.

Considered in relation to the divine oath and promise, Yahweh's duplicate table of the covenant served a purpose analogous to that of the rainbow in his covenant with Noah (Gen 9:13–16). Beholding this table, he remembered his oath to his servants and faithfully brought to pass the promised blessing. And in that day when the four and twenty heavenly elders worship him saying, "Thy wrath is come, and the time of the dead, that they should be judged, and that thou shouldest give reward unto thy servants the prophets, and to the saints, and them that fear thy name, small and great," then, appropriately, the temple of God in heaven being opened, there is seen in his temple the ark of his covenant, the depository of God's table of remembrance (Rev 11:17–19).

There remains the question of the relevance of our interpretation of the duplicate tables of the covenant for the understanding of their law content. The increased emphasis on the covenantal context of the law underscores the essential continuity in the function of law in the Old and New Testaments. The Decalogue is not offered fallen man as a genuine soteric option but is presented to him as a guide to citizenship within the covenant by the Savior-Lord, who of his mercy delivers out of the house of bondage into communion in the life of the covenant—a communion that eventuates in perfect conformity of life to the law of the covenant. To stress the covenantal "I-thou" nature of this law is to reaffirm the personal-religious character of biblical ethics, as well as to recognize that covenantal religion and its ethics are [[128]] susceptible to communication in the form of structured truth. Yahweh describes the beneficiaries of his mercy as "them that love me and keep my commandments" (Exod 20:6; cf. John 14:15).

Recognition of the completeness of each of the tables provides a corrective to the traditional view's obscuration of the covenantal-religious nature of the laws in "the second table." A hegemony of religion over ethics has, indeed, always been predicated on the basis of the priority in order and verbal quantity of the laws of "the first table," analyzed as duty or love to God, over the laws of "the second table," analyzed as duty or love to man. Nevertheless, this very division of the ten words into "two tables," with the category "love to God" used as a means of separating one "table" from the other, is liable to the misunderstanding that the fulfilling of the demands of "the second table" is to some degree, if not wholly, independent of the principle of love for God.

Our Lord's familiar teaching about a "first and great commandment" and a "second like unto it" (Matt 22:37–40; Mark 12:29–31) has figured prominently in the speculation about the contents of "the two tables."[24] It is, however, gratuitous to suppose that Jesus was epitomizing in turn a "first table" and a "second table" as traditionally conceived.[25] Furthermore, it must

24. In the Westminster Confession of Faith, for example, it is the only proof text cited for distinguishing between the "tables" in terms of duty toward God and duty to man (ch. XIX, sec. II).

25. There is no explicit reference to the two stone tables in the context, which is broadly concerned with the generality of scriptural legislation. Jesus relates his two commandments to the totality of Old Testament revelation (Matt 22:40).

be seriously questioned whether Jesus' commandment to love God's image-bearer, ourselves and our neighbors alike, can properly be restricted after the dominant fashion to the fifth through the tenth laws. The nearest parallel in the Decalogue to the specific language of Jesus is found in the fourth law as it is formulated in Deuteronomy [[129]] (5:14): the Sabbath is to be kept "that thy manservant and thy maidservant may rest as well as thou." And does man not best serve the eternal interests of himself and of his neighbor when he promotes obedience to the first three commandments? Is that not the ethical justification of the Great Commission?

Beyond all doubt, Jesus' "great commandment" must be the heart motive of man in the whole compass of his life. Restricting the principle of love of God to the sphere of worship would prejudice the comprehensiveness of God's absolute lordship, which is the foundation of the covenant order.

That loving God with heart, soul, mind, and strength is as relevant to the tenth commandment as it is to the first is evident from the fact that to violate the tenth commandment is to worship Mammon; and we cannot love and serve both God and Mammon. Or consider the tenth word from the viewpoint of the principle of stewardship, the corollary of the principle of God's covenant lordship. Property in the Israelite theocracy was held only in fief under the Lord who declared: "For the land is mine; for ye are strangers and sojourners with me" (Lev 25:23b). Therefore, to covet the inheritance of one's neighbor was to covet what was God's[26] and so to betray want of love for him. The application of this is universal, because not just Canaan but "the earth is the LORD's and the fullness thereof, the world and they that dwell therein" (Ps 24:1).

The comprehensiveness of Jesus' "first and great commandment" is evident from the preamble and historical prologue of the covenant document. Being introductory to the whole body of stipulations which follow, they are manifestly intended to inculcate the proper motivation [[130]] for obedience not to three or four or five of the stipulations but to them all; and the motivation they inspire is that of love to the divine Redeemer. Why are we to love our neighbors? Because we love the God who loves them; and, according to the principle articulated in the Sabbath commandment (Exod 20:11), the imperative to love God is also a demand to be like him.

---

26. Considered in this light, there is an exact equivalent to the tenth commandment in a Hittite treaty where the suzerain charges the vassal: "Thou shalt not desire any territory of the land of Hatti" (cited by Mendenhall, "Ancient Oriental and Biblical Law," *BA* 17.2 [1954]: 30).

The two commandments of Jesus do not distinguish two separable areas of human life but two complementary aspects of human responsibility. Our Lord's perspective is one with that of the duplicate tables of the covenant, which comprehend the whole duty of man within the unity of his consecration to his covenant Lord.

CHAPTER SIX

Lex Talionis and the Human Fetus

(1977)

The most significant thing about abortion legislation in biblical law is that there is none. It was so unthinkable that an Israelite woman should desire an abortion that there was no need to mention this offense in the criminal code.

There is, however, one law in "the book of the covenant" (cf. Exod 24:7) that deals with a human fetus, and it has naturally received close scrutiny for the light it might shed on the critical question of the nature of the unborn child. This law, found in Exod 21:22–25, turns out to be perhaps the most decisive positive evidence in Scripture that the fetus is to be regarded as a living person. A quite different assessment of the matter is prevalent which alleges that this law assigns to the fetus a status of mere property, not that of a discrete living being. To some extent the prevalence of this view is due to the fact that the other major interpretation, the one that is usually advocated by the "pro-life" position in the current abortion controversy, fails to answer several of the key exegetical questions satisfactorily.

Undeniably, the passage is a Gordian knot formed by an intertwining of several exegetical problems entailing broad issues of legal principle and practice in the Bible. A better solution seems to be available, however, than has been provided in the exegesis presented by either of the opposing sides in the current dispute.[1]

In Exod 21:18–36 there is a series of laws concerned with cases of criminal negligence. The law in verses 22–25 concerns a brawl during which a

1. Several of the major elements contributing to this solution find expression in the study by B. S. Jackson, "The Problem of Exod. 21:22–5 (*Ius Talionis*)," *VT* 23 (1973): 273–304. The point of this law in its canonical form, as I see it, was, according to Jackson, found in a hypothetical earlier form. But it is his contention that the law in its present form no longer bears this meaning and in fact contains self-contradictory elements that betray a history of editorial modifications reflecting an evolution in legal attitude on the issue.

pregnant woman, an innocent bystander, is struck and "her fruit depart(s) from her" (v. 22a KJV). Two varieties of this basic situation are then distinguished, which we will call Case A and Case B. Each of these includes a protasis (v. 22b and v. 23a) depicting one or another consequence of the act described in verse 22a and an apodosis (v. 22c and vv. 23b-25) giving the penalty. The protasis in Case A reads: "yet no mischief (*ʾāsôn*; RSV 'harm') follow" (KJV). In Case B the protasis reads: "if any mischief/harm follow."

According to the interpretation reflected in most modern English translations of this law, miscarriage is involved in the basic situation described in verse 22a as a common denominator of both Case A and Case B. The RSV, for example, translates: "so that there is a miscarriage." The *ʾāsôn* mentioned in verses 22b and 23a can only refer then to the [[194]] woman. Case A thus involves loss of the fetus only, and the penalty (v. 22c) takes the form of monetary indemnification of the woman's husband according to a scale of assessment in which the determining factor is the age of the fetus.[2] In Case B, in addition to the miscarriage the woman suffers *ʾāsôn*, and the penalty clause (vv. 23b-25), utilizing the talion formula, prescribes capital punishment, "life for life," if the woman dies. There is, according to this interpretation, a difference in kind in the penalties for destroying the fetus and for killing the woman, and the fact that a monetary settlement is prescribed for a miscarriage rather than a life being required as in the case of the woman's death means that the fetus was regarded in Israelite jurisprudence as mere property, not as a living person like the woman.

Over against this exegesis stands the interpretation of Exod 21:22–25 widely endorsed in the anti-abortion movement. According to it, miscarriage is not involved in the basic situation described in verse 22a. What comes forth is denoted by the plural of the regular word for child (*yeled*), and it is argued that there is no linguistic warrant for understanding this as a miscarriage.[3] Verse 22a describes the premature birth of a healthy child. The *ʾāsôn* statement in verses 22b and 23a refers in each case to both the mother and the child. Case A involves only some minor harm to the mother, something less than is denoted by *ʾāsôn*, and therefore a pecuniary penalty is sufficient. In Case B, the *lex talionis* applies whether the victim is the mother or the fetus singly or whether both are victims. The fetus is thus treated as a living person, just like the mother.

2. This mode of assessment is attested in a case of miscarriage in the Hittite laws (17, earlier version).

3. Cf., e.g., J. W. Cottrell, "Abortion and the Mosaic Law," *CT* 17 (1973): 604.

While accepting as sound the conclusion concerning the unborn child reached on this second interpretation, I would maintain that that conclusion must be set on a different exegetical base. By way now of developing such an exegesis, attention will first be given here to the penalties in the two apodoses. It will appear that even if it were granted that the first penalty has reference to a miscarriage and the second penalty to harm suffered by the woman, as the dominant interpretation suggests, it would still not follow that the penalty for the destruction of the fetus was different in kind or even in degree from the penalty for harming the woman.

The penalty clause for Case A reads in part: "He shall be strictly penalized; whatever amount the husband of the woman demands of him he must pay" (v. 22b). The verb *ʿnš* denotes punishment.[4] This may take the form of a fine (cf. Deut 22:19), but possibly the verb refers to punishment in general, including physical punishment.[5]

The expression for exacting the fine, literally "lays on him," is [[195]] used again in the adjacent law of the goring ox in Exod 21:28–32. There the owner of the ox is said to be liable to the death penalty (v. 29), but since the offense was one of criminal negligence rather than premeditation the law allows that a ransom for the redemption of his forfeited life be laid on him (v. 30). Exodus 21:22 is similarly concerned with a case of criminal negligence or recklessness, and the use here of the same penalty formula found in verse 30 suggests that the offense in this verse too is a matter of extreme gravity.

The Hebrew expression at the end of verse 22 (*bpllym*) is puzzling. Suggestions that it denotes a process of assessment[6] are linguistically dubious and encounter the difficulty that such a process would contradict the provision by which the setting of the penalty is left completely to the discretion of the woman's husband. Those who understand verse 22c as the penalty for miscarriage often read into *bpllym* the feature found in extrabiblical legislation[7] whereby the penalty is a fine in an amount adjusted to the age of the fetus.[8] But there is no terminological correspondence whatever to support this supposed parallel. Unfortunately, all the biblical contexts where the word in question appears are difficult. I take it in Exod 21:22 to be an adjectival

4. It is used here with the emphatic infinite absolute—hence, "strictly."

5. Cf. Prov 17:26, where the parallel is flogging.

6. Cf. E. A. Speiser, "The Stem *PLL* in Hebrew," *JBL* 82 (1963): 301–6.

7. See note 2 above.

8. Cf., e.g., S. M. Paul, *Studies in the Book of the Covenant in the Light of Cuneiform and Biblical Law*, VTSup 18 (Leiden: Brill, 1970), 72.

form, *pĕlîlî* (cf. Job 31:28), with an enclitic *-m* (as also in Job 31:11). In fact, there is no clear basis for the entry *pālîl* ("judge") in the lexicon of Biblical Hebrew. In Deut 32:31, *pllym* is the plural masculine of this adjective. There the enemies of God's people are described as having incurred guilt that calls for divine vengeance (cf. vv. 34–43). The two instances in Job 31 refer to a crime (*ʿāwôn*) against high heaven (vv. 11, 28) calling for punishment to the depths of perdition (v. 12; cf. Deut 32:22). In every context the reference is thus to an offense of the most serious nature, one that can by no means escape condign punishment. In fact, the meaning could well be liability to death.[9] This meaning of *pĕlîlî* can be seen in Exod 21:22 also. The other terms associated with it there all comport with this emphasis on the extreme gravity of the offense. Instead of contradiction there is clear congruity between *bpllym* and the husband's unrestricted prerogative of assessment.

Further, the preposition *b-* is now readily accounted for instead of being problematic. It is the *bêt* of equivalence (or price). Significantly, this use of *b-* is found in the talion formula in Deut 19:21 (replacing the preposition *taḥat* found in the formula elsewhere): "a life as the equivalent of a life, etc." Of interest also is the usage in a Ugaritic text (1161:3) where this preposition marks the role of three men who become human pledges as bail for two other men. Hence, *bpllym* in [[196]] Exod 21:22 may be regarded as an archaic legal formula expressing the same principle of ransoming a forfeited life that is more fully expressed in Exod 21:30.[10] To parse the final *mēm* in *bpllym* as the emphatic enclitic is preferable to taking it as an abstract plural. The penalty clause states then that the offender must pay whatever is demanded as the equivalent for himself as one who is guilty unto death. How the English translator might best handle this is difficult to say. If the objective is to convey the sense of the original, a translation like "he must pay for his forfeited life" or "he must pay as one deserving of death (or retribution)" might be considered, the first retaining the force of the preposition and the second adhering to the meaning of the adjective.

If our explanation of the penalty clause in Case A is correct, it amounts to very much the same thing as the talion penalty prescribed for the offense in Case B (Exod 21:23–25). In biblical legislation the talion formula, found elsewhere in Lev 24:18–21 and Deut 19:21, does not denote a special type of punishment, i.e., mutilation. It does, of course, express the distinctive judi-

9. Cf. *dāmîm*, "blood guilt," in Exod 22:2, 3 [1, 2].

10. Verse 30 shares with verse 22 the use of the verb *ntn*, "pay," as well as the phrase "lay on him."

cial principle that the punishment must be commensurate with the crime. And it does serve a special function in the legislation, for it is employed in the penalty clause of laws where the protasis does not refer to a single injury but rather to a variety of possible injuries, all of which must be covered by the penalty formulation. The precise nature of the penalty for any specific injury contemplated in the protasis must then be determined according to the analogy of the whole system of penal principles and procedures presented in biblical law. The talion formula itself simply requires that strict, unsparing justice be applied in dealing with whatever injuries are in view.

The phrasing of the talion formula is vividly corporal, and at the level of a capital crime the penalty expressed by "a life for a life" could actually be capital punishment. Since the use of the talion formula is accounted for by the necessity of prescribing succinctly for a variety of offenses, we should not conclude from the use of this formula in place of the usual "he shall surely be put to death" that the penalty intended must be some substitute for capital punishment.[11] On the other hand, the corporal terminology of the talion formula did not necessarily mandate physical punishment of one sort or other. A different kind of penalty might be indicated when all the legally relevant factors were brought to bear on the case. Thus if the offense involved a loss of human life but it was a matter of criminal negligence, not of premeditated murder, the life-for-life formula did not preclude the application of the ransom procedure customary in such cases. While the use of the talion formula does not negate the requirement of capital punishment expressed in Num 35:31, neither does it negate the provision presupposed in that verse for ransom in appropriate cases. [[197]] Thus in Lev 24:18 the life-for-life formula is used in explication of a demand for compensatory payment. Here as always this formula is resorted to because of the variety of offenses comprehended by the penalty clause—specifically, in this case, the variety of the kinds of animal victims for which restitution must be made.

Since the talion formula is not to be understood as necessarily prescribing physical execution when it says "a life for a life," it need not be interpreted literally in the case of the lesser penalties it lists either. In the Lev 24 passage just mentioned, when the talion formula, begun with "a life for a life" in verse 18, is resumed with the list of lesser injuries in verses 19 and 20 (though now with reference to humans rather than animals as in v. 18), the assumption is warranted that the identification of the talion principle with monetary compensation that obtains in verse 18 carries over into the

11. Cf. P. Doron, "A New Look at an Old Lex," *JANESCU* 1 (1969): 26.

continuation of the formula in verses 19 and 20. Hence, the consensus that has prevailed through the centuries that the talion principle in the Bible was never intended to be applied in the form of such literal mutilations appears to be sound.[12] One consideration supporting a non-literal understanding of the talion penalty series is that it will hardly have been the deliberate purpose of an assailant to inflict on his victim precisely one of the disfigurements cited in the talion formula, and intent is taken into account in biblical law when fixing penalties. Another consideration to the same effect is the stereotyped nature of the talion formula. It is particularly obvious in Deut 19:15–21 that there is not a simple literal equivalence between the terms of the talion penalty clause and all the variety of cases in which false witness might figure; clearly we have to do with a fossilized formula whose graphic terms are meant to express only the general principle that the offense must receive a just punishment, neither more nor less. This is evident again in the Exod 21 context, where the kinds of injuries mentioned in the talion formula are not the most likely ones to be encountered in the situation described, and some of them are altogether unlikely.

If the foregoing analysis is substantially correct, there are no essential differences between the penalties prescribed in Case A and Case B of the law in Exod 21:22–25. In both cases the penalty contemplates an offense involving death (as at least one possibility), and in both cases, where a death is involved the penalty may be understood as demanding a ransom for the offender's forfeited life. Therefore no matter whether one interprets the first or second penalty to have reference to a miscarriage, there is no difference in the treatment accorded the fetus and the woman. Either way the fetus is regarded as a living person, so that to be criminally responsible for the destruction of the fetus is to forfeit one's life.

Other features of this law must now be examined. If as mentioned above the penalty in Case A envisages a death (or even a grave injury), the statement in verse 22b about "no *ʾāsôn*" (and its positive counterpart in v. 23a) cannot refer to both the woman and the fetus. One or [[198]] the other is killed, and therefore only one or the other can have escaped *ʾāsôn*. As a matter of fact it will appear that the data are best accounted for if the mother is the victim in Case A and the fetus in Case B.

If a death is involved in Case A it must be mentioned in the description of the basic situation in verse 22a, for it is not mentioned in the special pro-

12. For some of the approaches leading to this interpretation see Jackson, "Problem," 280–83.

tasis of Case A in verse 22b. The force of the verb (*ngp*) used in verse 22a for the blow against the woman has often been slighted. Those who refer the "no *ʾāsôn*" statement in verse 22b to both the woman and the fetus must render *ngp* as "push" or "shove." But this is quite inadequate, for this verb (and its nominal derivatives) is used for fatal divine judgments (see, e.g., 1 Sam 25:38; 26:10) and for slaughter in battle (see, e.g., Judg 20:35; 1 Sam 4:3). In Exod 21:35, *ngp* is used for the fatal attack of the goring ox. Accordingly in Exod 21:22 we are to understand that the victim, whether the mother or her child, is killed. As for the plural form of the verb, this might be a generic plural to cover either of the brawlers (or perhaps both of them) or it might be the indefinite plural active used as a passive, signifying "a pregnant woman is struck." Verse 22a would seem most naturally understood as saying that the woman herself, the immediate object of the blow denoted by *ngp*, suffered the fatal effect in her own person. Also that would most readily account for the reference to the one who imposes the ransom as the "husband of the woman." Though the meaning could conceivably be that the fatal effects of the blow are experienced by the woman in the loss of her child and that it is as family head and father of the child that the husband is brought into the judicial process, this explanation seems less likely than the other.

Since the death assumed in the penalty clause can be accounted for by the verb *ngp*, with the woman herself as the victim, it is not necessary to interpret the expulsion of the fruit of her womb (v. 22a) as a miscarriage. Indeed, as noted above, some would insist there is no warrant for understanding *wyṣʾw yldyh* in terms of a miscarriage. But it is not demonstrable either that this language in itself *must* be understood with reference to a miscarriage or that it *cannot* be so understood. In fact, even those who allege it cannot be taken that way do so themselves when they come to Case B (which, of course, also builds on the foundation of v. 22a). For they relate to both mother and child the *ʾāsôn* (v. 23a) which, according to the penalty imposed, may be fatal. To avoid this dilemma by the arbitrary assumption that this law would not treat the most probable kind of *ʾāsôn* that would befall a fetus under these circumstances, namely death, but only the lesser injuries that sometimes attend such a premature birth, certainly will not do. As noted above, the word translated "fruit" in KJV is the plural of the word for child. The suggestion by those who reject the miscarriage view that the plural takes account of the possibility of a multiple birth does not commend itself. If as is here maintained the first variety of this case (v. 22b) deals with a premature but live birth and the second (vv. 23–25) with a miscarriage, the plural form [[199]] is best understood as a generic plural used with a view to covering both contingencies. The use of the term *yeled*, "child," is particularly suitable for the live birth, and a secondary consideration for the use of the plural is that it is peculiarly appropriate to an aborted fetus, especially at an earlier, more amorphous embryonic stage.

It has been established above that when the protasis of Case A (v. 22b) says there is no *ʾāsôn* it cannot refer to both mother and fetus. The meaning of the term *ʾāsôn*, as well as the location of the statement immediately after *wyṣʾw yldyh*, favors a reference to the fetus. A calamitous loss involving serious injury or even death is denoted by *ʾāsôn*.[13] In the only other biblical context where *ʾāsôn* is found it describes the grievous calamity that Jacob fears might befall Benjamin on the journey to Egypt (Gen 42:4, 38; 44:29). The choice of this unusual word in Exod 21:22 (problematic if the reference were to injury or death of the woman, for which the more common terminology would then be expected) is readily explained if *ʾāsôn* refers to the less everyday circumstance of the calamitous loss of offspring by violently induced miscarriage.

What indications there are point rather definitely and consistently, even if not with absolute conclusiveness, to the view that the mother is the victim in Case A (cf. 1 Sam 4:19–21) and the child in Case B. The sequence of victims in Exod 21:22ff. then corresponds to that in the legislation in Exod 21:28ff., which we have found to be similar in other important respects as well. In the law of the goring ox, the order of the victims is: the man or woman (v. 29), a son or daughter (v. 31), a male or female servant (v. 32). In the law of the striking of the pregnant woman, the victims are in order (on our interpretation): the woman (v. 22), the child (v. 23), and (if we continue into vv. 26–27, which are linked to the preceding law by the transitional talion formula) a male or female servant. Moreover, the treatment of the fetus (on our interpretation of v. 23) corresponds to that of the son or daughter in verse 31 in that the penalty in their case too is identical with the penalty already prescribed for an adult. It may be noted that in one of the Middle Assyrian laws of miscarriage[14] the penalty for striking a woman, whether with non-fatal or fatal result for her, is mentioned first and then the penalty for the loss of the fetus.

Assuming that the statements about *ʾāsôn* refer to the fetus, the use of the talion formula in Case B suggests that the meaning of *ʾāsôn* covers the variety of injuries that might be suffered by a child born prematurely,

13. See ibid., 274–76.

14. Tablet A, law 50.

especially under such adverse conditions, as well as stillbirth. It is possible that only miscarriage is envisaged and that the talion formula was used because it could do double duty by leading transitionally to the following law, which deals with injuries of various sorts inflicted on slaves (vv. 26, 27). It seems more likely, [[200]] however, that the talion formula was used because of its appropriateness to the situation in Case B (v. 23) and that this then prompted the appending of the legislation in verses 26 and 27 as additional instances of criminal negligence (cf. also vv. 20 and 21) for which the talion formula was serviceable.

Since, as we have seen, the penalty for Case B amounts to the same thing as the penalty in Case A, each case involving a fatal injury (either exclusively or as one possibility along with others) and each penalty taking the form of monetary payment, the question arises why the penalty is expressed in such different fashion in the two cases. In the case of the killing of a child by the goring ox, the repetition of the penalty prescribed for killing a man or woman takes the general form: "He shall be dealt with in this same way" (v. 31). The distinctive formulation of the penalties in Case A and Case B of the Exod 21:22–25 law would appear to reflect some significant difference between the two cases. Since the talion formula used in Case B is designed for situations with a variety of possible injuries, we are probably to conclude that Case A, by contrast, deals with the death of the woman exclusively.

To sum up: Case A envisages the death of a mother in giving birth prematurely to a live, uninjured child, and the law prescribes that the assailant must give for his forfeited life whatever the husband demands. In Case B the law requires that if the child suffers calamitous injury or death the penalty payment must be a just equivalent.

On this interpretation of Exod 21:22–25, it is of particular importance for the biblical view of the nature of the fetus that the life-for-life formula is applied to the destruction of a fetus, with no qualification as to how young the fetus might be. The fetus, at any stage of development, is in the eyes of this law a living being, for life (*nepeš*) is attributed to it. To be sure, the life-for-life formula is also used in the case of the death of animals (Lev 24:18), so that this formula by itself does not establish that the referent is a human being. But if it is the fetus of a human mother that is identified by the life-for-life formula as a living being, there can be no question that this living being is a living *human* being. Significantly, the part of the talion formula specifying injuries to eye and tooth and the like is not applied to animals. Only in the case of human beings do these features take on the value that merits legal redress. And surely the living fetus in view when the talion formula mentions the loss of life (v. 23c) must be identified with the human child referred to in the talion formula as suffering the loss of eye or tooth (vv. 24, 25). Consistently in the relevant data of Scripture a continuum of identity is evident between the fetus and the person subsequently born. And Exod 21:22–25 makes clear that this prenatal human being is to be regarded as a separate and distinct human life.

As we observed at the outset, induced abortion was so abhorrent to the Israelite mind that it was not necessary to have a specific prohibition dealing with it in the Mosaic law. The Middle Assyrian laws [[201]] attest to an abhorrence that was felt for this crime even in the midst of the heathendom around Israel, lacking though it did the illumination of special revelation. For in those laws a woman guilty of abortion was condemned to be impaled on stakes.[15] Even if she managed to lose her own life in producing the abortion, she was still to be impaled and hung up in shame as an expression of the community's repudiation of such an abomination. It is hard to imagine a more damning commentary on what is taking place in enlightened America today than that provided by this legal witness out of the conscience of benighted ancient paganism!

15. Tablet A, law 53.

PART THREE

Faith, the Gospel, and Justification

CHAPTER SEVEN

Abram's Amen

(1968)

"And he believed (in) the LORD; and he reckoned it to him as righteousness" (Gen 15:6). Viewing this classic theological text as thus traditionally translated, von Rad concludes that it is the statement of a "mental occurrence on the part of Abraham first and Yahweh second,"[1] a statement with almost "the quality of a general theological tenet."[2] He maintains that this verse is the product of the revisionist's reflection on old narrative materials and that he has inserted it into them as a programmatic index to their theological significance. However, a satisfying explanation does not readily suggest itself as to why such a theological observation would have been introduced at this particular point, where the context has spoken only of Abram's plaint (15:2–3; cf. v. 8), rather than in connection with some other episode where Abram's confidence in the Lord is plainly manifested (as, for example, at Gen 12:3–4 or 14:21–24).

This difficulty remains so long as we hold to the inner, "mental" nature of the verse 6 event. We do not avoid it even when we regard the verse not as an appended editorial opinion but as an actual moment in the particular historical episode described in Gen 15. For while Abram would know his own psychological reaction to God's word of promise and could have introduced an observation concerning his belief into the tradition, this seems improbable. Moreover, even Abram would not have known about an unexpressed, purely "mental" divine reckoning of righteousness to him. And to assume that such an unexpressed response of God to the faith [[2]] of Abram on this occasion was later communicated to either a traditionist or to the

1. *Genesis*, trans. John H. Marks (Philadelphia: Westminster, 1961), 184. Von Rad comments: "The narrator leaves the stargazing man, so to speak, and turns to the reader, to whom he communicates theological opinions of great theological compactness, without describing the actual occurrence upon which these opinions are founded, either in the case of Abraham or in the case of Yahweh" (179).

2. Ibid., 180.

author of Genesis by a special revelation appears too artificial a reconstruction of the course of the inspired recording of the history.

There is reason, therefore, to take another look at Gen 15:6, alert to the desirability of discovering some outward occurrences that will account for what is said about both Abram and Yahweh. The historiographical problem encountered in Gen 15:6 arises, of course, whenever an act of believing is recorded, and a survey of such passages employing *hʾmyn*, particularly when relationship to God is in view, will show that the historian had before his mind some outward faith-manifestation, which is at least implicit in his account. This external expression of belief assumes forms like the voicing of praise and trust in a hymn (Exod 14:31; cf. 15:1ff.), the demonstration of repentance (Jonah 3:5), or, in negative instances, the display of rebellious behavior (Num 14:11; Deut 1:32; 2 Kgs 17:14; Ps 78:22). In the case of Gen 15:6, the indication of an outward act of faith, and thus the key to a more satisfactory exegesis of the verse, will be found, we believe, in the term *hʾmyn* itself.

Delbert Hillers has recently drawn attention to a type of verb in biblical Hebrew that he calls "delocutive," a term previously employed in analysis of Indo-European languages. It is intended to denote the phenomenon of a spoken formula or stock phrase that has been verbalized. Hillers cites, for example, *hiṣdîq*/*ṣiddēq*, "declare righteous," comparing the judicial verdict, *ṣaddîq ʾattâ*, and *ṭihar*, "declare pure," comparing the priestly pronouncement, *ṭāhôr hûʾ*.[3]

Our suggestion is that *hʾmyn* is another of these delocutive verbs and that its delocutive origin is discernible in Gen 15:6 (and elsewhere).[4] This verse will then state not (explicitly) that Abram's inner attitude was one of faith but that [[3]] Abram voiced his "Amen" (*ʾāmēn*) in audible response to the word of God.

The fact that that statement appears in the context of a formal procedure in which such an "Amen" was a customary form of response adds plausibility to the interpretation presented here. Genesis 15 is the account of a solemn covenant ritual and an "Amen" response by the covenant vassal in such ceremonies is attested in the records of both biblical and extrabiblical

3. Delbert R. Hillers, "Delocutive Verbs in Biblical Hebrew," *JBL* 86 (1967): 320–24. Hillers' thesis offers a counterproposal for the customary category of declarative *piel/hiphil*.

4. The delocutive meaning coexists with other meanings of these verbs in the same conjugations. Thus, just as *ṭihar* means both "purify" and "pronounce, 'It is pure,'" so *hʾmyn* means both "believe (in)" and "declare, 'Amen.'"

covenants.[5] Also indicative of the external-procedural rather than internal-psychological level of Gen 15:6 is the terminology of its second clause. The verb *ḥšb*, "reckon," is employed for the rendering of decisions in cultic-judicial process (cf. Lev 7:18; 17:4; Num 18:27). And the substance of the divine reckoning, "righteousness," points to the judicial locution, "You are in the right."[6] Thus, in the case of Yahweh's act, too, intimations of an outward occurrence are present in Gen 15:6 itself.[7]

In order to place the delocutive interpretation of *hʾmyn* in Gen 15:6 in a more adequate context, at least brief consideration must be given to the meaning this verbal form possesses as employed some fifty times elsewhere in the Old Testament.[8] There have been attempts to explain the *hiphil* [[4]] formation of *ʾmn* as causative, but a declarative-estimative or an intransitive (or internal-intransitive) function, or a blend of the last two, is usually favored. Weiser, arguing for a declarative element in the meaning of *hʾmyn*, explains its sense thus: "Gott für נֶאֱמָן [*neʾĕmān*] erklären, oder umschreiben: zu Gott Amen sagen."[9] He apparently does not intend, however, to account for *hʾmyn* as actually a delocutive, but as simply a denominative. The main criticism that is brought against this or any form of declarative or causative interpretation by advocates of the intransitive view is that *hʾmyn* is never followed by the direct object of the one on whom the declarative or causative

5. Cf. Esarhaddon's Nimrud Treaty, lines 494–512 and Deut 27:15ff. See *TGK*, 29. It was this covenantal Amen that first suggested to the writer the possibility of understanding *hʾmyn* in Gen 15:6 as a confessional act. This interpretation was incorporated in a brief commentary on Genesis prepared for a volume not yet published. The reading of Hillers' article prompted the present expanded note, and I would express my gratitude to him, too, for his further clarification of his position in private correspondence. The preparation of the present essay, it will be observed, has survived an unnerving experience that befell its author subsequently—the notice of J. Barr's comment: "Certainly no one is likely to believe that *heʾemin* in fact developed from the practice of saying 'Amen' " (*The Semantics of Biblical Language* [London: Oxford University Press, 1961], 179).

6. See above on delocutive *hiṣdîq*/*ṣiddēq*.

7. The pronominal suffix-object of *ḥšb* is more readily accounted for if there is a particular utterance of "Amen" to serve as antecedent.

8. For a recent useful survey of this much discussed question see H. Wildberger, " 'Glauben', Erwägungen zu האמין," in *Hebräische Wortforschung*, VTSup 16 (Leiden: Brill, 1967), 372–86. The lively current interest in this matter is evidenced by a second article on it in this same Baumgartner *Festschrift*. See R. Smend, "Zur Geschichte von האמין," ibid., 284–90.

9. "πιστεύω κτλ," *TWNT* 6:187.

action terminates (except in the Masoretic Text of Judg 11:20—or, at least, so it has been generally thought).[10]

Right here the delocutive view commends itself by its ability to account on the one hand for certain data that have encouraged declarative interpretations and on the other to explain the absence of the direct object. Repeated contextual association of *hʾmyn* (as well as *nʾmn*) with the covenantal relationship, especially in its formal moments of confessional decision, suggests the likelihood that *hʾmyn* refers to some sort of declarative act.[11] At the same time, the absence of a direct object is compatible with a delocutive *hʾmyn*, for its only possible direct object (the Amen locution) is, so to speak, built into the verb itself, while the person to whom such an Amen is addressed would naturally be indirectly related to the verb by a preposition, which is the actual usage after *hʾmyn*.

Our position is not, of course, that *hʾmyn* has delocutive force every time it is employed in the Old Testament. But while recognizing that in many cases *hʾmyn* has internal-transitive meaning, we do maintain that there are passages [[5]] where that meaning is not applicable or where a translation of *hʾmyn* as "to declare 'Amen'" is, to say the least, preferable, and that these instances are indicative of a delocutive derivation of *hʾmyn*. As for the overall development of the usage of *hʾmyn*, it can be readily understood how, starting with the specific, concrete meaning "declare 'Amen,'" the internalized meaning of "believe" or "believe in" could arise. The same would also be so if there were cases of a declarative-estimative usage of *hʾmyn*. The reverse would not be true in either case. Possibly, however, the diversity of the Old Testament usage of *hʾmyn* represents a more complex development, with a confluence into one common verbal form of more than one tributary source.

Without attempting here to offer a brief for every possible instance of delocutive *hʾmyn* (i.e., of *hʾmyn* with delocutive force), we will simply call attention to the kinds of passages where there appear to be definite advantages in the delocutive interpretation. By way of explaining the use of *hʾmyn b* in Gen 15:6, consideration will be given below to Isa 43:9–10 and note taken of the possible delocutive use of *hʾmyn* there. An especially interesting passage is Judg 11:20, the only one where *hʾmyn* is followed by *ʾt*. This has often been regarded as an anomalous construction and the text has been

10. Cf., e.g., Wildberger, "Glauben," 374ff.; Barr, *Semantics of Biblical Language*, 178.

11. Cf. Weiser, "πιστεύω," 187ff. In the non-religious usage too a connection is found between *hʾmyn* and verbs of saying.

emended from *wlʾ-hʾmyn* to *ymʾn*, "refused," with appeal to possible partial LXX support and to what would be a close parallel in Num 20:21. But it is preferable to accept the preserved text, taking *hʾmyn* as delocutive and the *ʾt* not as the accusative particle but as the preposition "with." Thus, when the Israelite delegation arrived requesting passage through his land, "Sihon did not declare 'Amen' with Israel." This would then be another idiom for expressing the idea of making covenant; other expressions meaning to ratify a covenant also indicate the bilateralism by means of the preposition *ʾt*, or *ʿm*.[12]

[[6]] The seven passages where *hʾmyn* is employed absolutely offer some attractive possibilities of delocutive usage, particularly if it is recognized that *ʾmt* as well as *ʾmn* may be the locution involved.[13] Four of them describe occasions when Israel was confronted with signs or marvelous divine acts in response to which a formal attestation to their divine origin was in order (Exod 4:31; Isa 7:9; 28:16; Hab 1:5). In three of them *hʾmyn* is closely connected with verbs of saying (Job 29:24; cf. v. 22; 39:24; cf. v. 25; Ps 116:10). Covenant confirmation (cf. Gen 15:6 and Judg 11:20) is perhaps the point in two passages. Thus, in Isa 28:16 the decision of those to whom the *hʾmyn* act refers is set in contrast to the making of a covenant with death (vv. 15, 18). And in Job 39:24 what is said about the horse may well parallel the thought expressed concering leviathan in Job 41:4 [40:28], where God asks: "Will he make a covenant with you to take him for your servant forever?" If so, the idea in Job 39:24–25 would be that no display of military terror induces the aroused battle steed to hold back from the fray. He does not utter a yielding vassal's "Amen" at the blare of the trumpet (v. 24b); no, when the trumpet blasts he shrills back a defiant "Aha" (v. 25a). The contrast brought out sharply by the poetic parallelism of verses 24b and 25a comes to focus in the opposing locutions, Amen and Aha.

Another type of context where the usage of *hʾmyn* is easily understood if it is delocutive but which other approaches explain only awkwardly is that involving commands. Response to commands is in terms of assent and obedience, not directly in terms of trust or credence, which are appropriate rather to reports and promises. Agreeably, in the passages under discussion

---

12. Cf., e.g., Gen 26:28; Deut 20:12; 2 Sam 3:12–13. Note also the expression *kōrĕtîm ʾămānâ* in Neh 9:38 [10:1]. Weiser was moving in the right direction on Judg 11:20 with the translation: "to make an agreement with (i.e., to permit)" ("πιστεύω," 186 n. 106). But it is not clear how his general interpretation of *hʾmyn* would warrant the particular meaning which he recognized was called for in this passage.

13. See further below.

(see Deut 9:23; 2 Kgs 17:14; Pss 106:24; 119:66) *hmʾyn* is actually found in series with verbs not of trust but of obedience. Moreover, the practice of accepting a charge by saying "Amen" is evidenced elsewhere.[14]

It would appear, therefore, that a delocutive use of *hʾmyn* in Gen 15:6 would not be an isolated phenomenon but part [[7]] of a fairly widely attested usage that points to a delocutive origin of the *hiphʿil* of *ʾmn*, from which, indeed, all the functions of this verbal form possibly evolved.

The character and orientation of Abram's "Amen" (Gen 15:6) require further scrutiny. What is the significance of *byhwh*, and to what does the "Amen" subscribe?

Elsewhere in the Old Testament *ʾāmēn* functions as a liturgical assent after the praise and blessing of God (1 Chr 16:36; Pss 41:13 [14]; 72:19; 89:52 [53]; 106:48; Neh 8:6; cf. 1 Cor 14:16). It also serves as a formula of consignment under imprecatory oath, particularly in covenant-making (Num 5:22; Deut 27:15–26; Neh 5:13; Jer 11:5).[15] Benaiah's "Amen" before king David was a virtual oath of allegiance, accepting the appointment of Solomon for dynastic succession (1 Kgs 1:36). Faith-subscription to a word of prophetic promise could also be expressed by an "Amen," as may be seen in Jeremiah's mocking "Amen" to Hananiah's false prophecy of restoration (Jer 28:6).[16]

Another locution to which delocutive *hʾmyn* can be related is *ʾĕmet*,[17] "truth." Isaiah 43:9–10 documents the use of *ʾmt* in legal testimony,[18] and perhaps contains another instance of the delocutive use of *hʾmyn*. In this context Yahweh challenges the heathen to present legal testimony in support of the claims of their gods by declaring, *ʾmt*, "It is true" (v. 9). Then turning to his own people, Yahweh identifies them as "my witnesses" (v. 10a). To this is added a statement of the purpose of their appointment, translated in standard English versions, "that you may know and believe me (*wĕtaʾămînû lî*) and understand that I am He" (v. 10b). In the following verses Yahweh's exclusive claims to be God and Savior are proclaimed and the role of his people as witnesses to the validity of those claims is reaffirmed. The context, therefore, suggests that *wĕtaʾămînû lî* (v. 10b) means not just to believe in

14. See the discussion of the function of the Amen formula below, noting especially 1 Kgs 1:36.

15. Note again here the expression in Neh 10:1 for "We make a firm covenant" (cf. note 12 above).

16. A New Testament example of this in sincere mode is the Apocalypse's "Amen" to the promise of Christ's coming (Rev 1:7; 22:20).

17. A contraction for *ʾmnt* from *ʾmn*.

18. Cf. also Deut 13:14 [15]; 17:4; 22:20.

the heart [[8]] but to act as witnesses for Yahweh in judicial process, endorsing his own self-identification by declaring, *ʾĕmet*, "It is true."[19]

Abram's confessional response denoted by *hʾmyn* in Gen 15:6 was not, at least not directly, an *ʾĕmet* of attestation to Yahweh's self-glorification but an *ʾāmēn* of faith-subscription to God's covenant promises. In those suzerainty covenants that were ratified by the vassal's oath of allegiance, the vassal by his "Amen" placed himself under the curse-sanctions of the covenant; he conditionally cursed himself. The Gen 15 covenant, however, was ratified by the Lord's oath-ritual (vv. 17–18), guaranteeing the blessing-sanctions of this covenant. The "Amen" of Abram was oriented, therefore, not to the curse- but the blessing-sanctions; he blessed himself by faith.

Although Abram's response is recorded in immediate connection with the promise of an heir and innumerable descendants (v. 5), it is possible that in this chapter, as often in Genesis and in other biblical narratives, the arrangement of the materials is not simply chronological. If so, the beginning of the covenantal transaction may actually be recorded at verse 7, which contains the Lord's words of self-identification and a historical résumé, for these were the two opening features in the literary pattern of treaties of the second millennium BC. In that case, verses 1b–4 would probably belong to the trance experience of 12ff. (cf. vv. 1b and 12b) and verses 5 and 6 would belong to the somewhat later waking experience (cf. v. 5 with vv. 12 and 17). Abram's faith-claim (v. 6) would then be oriented to the broad complex of God's promises constituting the total beatitude of the kingdom inheritance (cf. vv. 18ff.).

On the delocutive understanding of *hʾmyn*, the following *byhwh* will not have the same force as when *hʾmyn* is translated "believed (in)." What is meant by *byhwh* on this approach may be seen in an Isaianic passage descriptive of the coming time when all the covenant promises have been fulfilled: "He who blesses himself in the land shall bless himself by the God of truth (*bēʾlōhê ʾāmēn*), and he who takes an oath [[9]] in the land shall swear by the God of truth" (Isa 65:16 RSV). To make a solemn affirmation of benediction or malediction by a deity is to acknowledge that he controls one's life and destiny; it is a religious confession. In the stipulations of Yahweh's covenantal rule over Israel the insistence that they swear by his name is coupled as a virtual synonym with the primary demand that they fear

19. Note the description of Yahweh as "a true and faithful witness" (*ʿēd ʾĕmet wĕneʾĕmān*) in the people's oath of obedience before Jeremiah (Jer 42:5) and Christ's self-identification as "The Amen, the faithful and true witness" (Rev 3:14). Relevant in the latter connection is Jesus' familiar formula of validation for his own witness, "verily, verily" (*amēn, amēn*). See too Dan 10:1; Prov 14:25.

and serve him (Deut 6:13; 10:20; cf. Ps 63:11 [12]; Isa 48:1; Jer 4:2; 5:7; 12:16). The Isaianic prospect is that at the consummation of God's reign, when those who have committed their futures to the god of fortune have been confounded but Yahweh's people have experienced his promised deliverance (Isa 65:11ff.), the Lord God will alone be acknowledged in blessings and oath-curses. Like father Abram all God's servants will pronounce their "Amens" in Yahweh's name (i.e., *byhwh*).[20] Yahweh will be the God of the confessional "Amen" (i.e., *ʾĕlōhê ʾāmēn*).

In summary, the meaning of *whʾmyn byhwh* (Gen 15:6a) is that Abram declared "Amen" in the name of Yahweh.[21] His declaration was primarily a confession of faith in the promises of God; it was also a witness to the lordship of Yahweh, the God of the promises. Now the covenant servant who offers such a confessional witness in sincerity, not deceitfully, shall receive blessing from Yahweh, even righteousness from the God of his salvation.[22] This judicial consequence comes to expression in the sequel to Abram's "Amen." For Gen 15:6b records the Lord's verdict of justification pronounced in Abram's hearing during the course of the covenantal ceremony.[23]

To read Gen 15:6 as a general tenet distilled from the theological reflections of the prophetic period[24] is a misreading [[10]] of a simple narrative description of an external occurrence. The ceremonial procedure described is of authentic ancient vintage and the account would not, therefore, supply cause to the documentary theorists to assign the hypothetical source containing it to a relatively late date. By the same token, with the delocutive interpretation of *hʾmyn* in Gen 15:6 we are now in a position to trace the divine disclosure of the truth of justification by faith in a way that accords more than the previous interpretations allowed with the progressive nature of biblical revelation. We need no longer assume the anomaly of a formularized analysis of the inner spiritual-judicial workings of salvation

20. Cf. Gen 12:3; 18:18; 22:18; 26:4; 28:14.

21. Perhaps he used the formula *ḥay-yhwh*, "As Yahweh lives"; cf., e.g., Jer 4:2; 12:16.

22. See Ps 24:4–5; cf. Rom 10:9–10.

23. The reflection of Gen 15:6 in Hab 2:4 suggests the possibility that along with *ṣaddîq ʾattâ* the divine pronouncement to Abram added the word of reward, *ḥāyōh tiḥyeh* (cf. Ezek 18:9), in appropriate complementation to the *ḥay-yhwh* formula possibly used by Abram (cf. note 14).

24. See Smend, "Geschichte von האמין," for a recent statement of this approach, which in its broader application involves the assigning of late dates to all passages where *hʾmyn* is understood in the sense of religious trust.

presented at the earliest stage of that revelation. We may rather see in Gen 15 the descriptive account of a historical episode, the theological implications of which were only later, according to the normal order of Scripture, articulated by inspired prophets and apostles.

Although New Testament quotations of Gen 15:6, following LXX, do not reproduce the overt character of the act denoted by *h'myn*, it is nevertheless possible that the writers involved understood the verse as referring to a confessional act.[25] Certainly the teaching of both Paul and James is congenial to the confessional nature of justifying faith, to which they in effect call attention by appealing to Gen 15:6 in their discussions of the subject. Indeed, the confessional aspect of faith constitutes something of a link between their respective emphases, as Paul counteracts the abuse of Moses and James corrects what amounts to a distortion of Paul.

To James, the confessional appropriation of God's promises would be one way in which true faith comes to that validating, godly expression which distinguishes it from, for example, the shuddering belief of demons. And it would never have occurred to Paul that the sharpness of his distinction between faith and works would be blurred by introducing into the delineation of justifying faith the element of its overt profession. His contrast of faith to works has nothing to do with the distinction between inward and outward, between heart and lips (or hands). His thought rather moves in the judicial [[11]] sphere as he distinguishes between the appropriation of promissory gifts proffered by divine grace and the expectation of wages paid as legal due for services rendered. More than that, Paul explicitly correlates believing in the heart and confessing with the lips as twin aspects of saving-justifying faith. The word of faith which he preached was at once on the lips and in the heart.[26] Perhaps Paul's understanding of Gen 15:6 has been preserved for us in spite of his following the text of the traditional versions in his direct quotations of the verse. For what he says in 2 Cor 1:20 sounds like the faith-witness of Abram's "Amen" transposed into a New Testament key: "For all the promises of God find their Yes in him. That is why we utter the Amen through him, to the glory of God" (RSV).

---

25. See Rom 4:3, 17; Gal 3:6; Jas 2:23.

26. See Rom 10:5ff., especially verses 8–10. Paul thus stood in the tradition of the ancient treaties where we find the emphasis that the taking of the oath must be a matter of both the lips and the heart. See R. Frankena, "The Vassal-Treaties of Esarhaddon and the Dating of Deuteronomy," *OtSt* 14 (1965): 140–41. Cf. Ps 78:36ff.

CHAPTER EIGHT

The Old Testament Origins of the Gospel Genre

(1975)

Was the gospel genre a creation of the New Testament evangelists or can it be traced back beyond the first century AD? In dealing with this form-critical problem we soon find that we are involved with more than the literary form of the gospels. Our form-critical investigation confronts us with fundamental questions about their essential nature, purpose, and message. And to be involved with such questions about the gospels is to be engaged in an analysis of the basic character and structure of biblical religion.

A certain amount of ambiguity attends the use of the term "genre" in form-critical studies.[1] Varying combinations of things like structural pattern, setting, content, mood, and intention are regarded by different form critics as constitutive of genre. The problem of definition may be somewhat simplified at least if we restrict the term to whole documents. The constitutive components of genre as the term will be used here with reference to the gospels are overall form and societal-religious function.

[[173]] To date no scholarly consensus, at least no positive consensus, has emerged from the extensive efforts to identify the canonical gospels with some genre attested in earlier literary tradition. After a perceptive survey of studies along this line, R. H. Gundry endorses the conclusion that from a first-century standpoint the gospels must be pronounced a literary novelty. In his judgment, therefore, it is not legitimate to speak of a gospel genre except in the sense that the four New Testament gospels themselves originated such a genre.[2]

1. Cf. R. Knierim, "Old Testament Form Criticism Reconsidered," *Int* 27 (1973): 435–68.

2. Robert H. Gundry, "Recent Investigations into the Literary Genre 'Gospel,'" in *New Dimensions in New Testament Study*, ed. R. N. Longenecker and M. C. Tenney

At the heart of the problem is the fact that the gospels consist of two very different kinds of material: teaching discourse and historical narrative. They contain accounts of both the words and works of Jesus. Considerable difficulty is already encountered in the attempt to classify each of these two types of material individually in terms of earlier literary forms, quite apart from the problem of accounting for them in combination. The discourses of Jesus include sapiential, legal, polemical, apocalyptic, and other kinds of pronouncements. No single form-critical classification that has been suggested, such as sayings of the wise or manual of community order, manages to comprehend all of this variety. Neither has the search for a specific form of narrative with which to identify the gospel records of the works of Jesus met with success. In particular, the attempt to relate these gospel narratives to aretalogical biography has proven a disappointment on both literary and theological grounds. But the real problem still comes when we try to account for the total form of the gospels, including what they report of both the deeds and sayings of Jesus. In the opinion of the form critics generally, literary antecedents [[174]] are apparently not to be found for the gospel form taken as a whole.

Having reached a negative conclusion as to the existence of literary antecedents of the complete form of the gospels, the form critics have turned to the historical circumstances out of which these documents arose for the explanation of their diverse contents and the evidently new literary form they represent. Some have seen the different kinds of material contained in the gospels as reflecting the variety of activity and concern that made up the life and mission of the early Christian communities to which the gospels were directed. Unfortunately, the tendency of form-critical studies along these lines has been to attribute to the church a creative role with regard to the substance of the gospel tradition.

The more conservative form critics have also appreciated the importance of the ecclesiastical *Sitz im Leben* of the gospels. They have recognized that understanding of the church audience to which a gospel was addressed can help to account for its particular Christological interests and its distinctive selection and arrangement of the available data. The emphasis of the conservatives, however, has fallen on the gospels not as church documents but as lives of Jesus, and they have tended to explain the gospels' peculiar configuration of narratives and discourses, the macrostructure common to all of them, as due ultimately to the actual nature of Jesus' historical career.

(Grand Rapids: Zondervan, 1974), 97–114. Cf. Ralph P. Martin, *New Testament Foundations*, vol. 1, *The Four Gospels* (Grand Rapids: Eerdmans, 1975), 16ff.

Jesus and his mission confronted the world with a unique complex of historical phenomena and it was this uniqueness of Jesus and his redemptive accomplishment that led to the unique Christian kerygma and thus to a new literary genre as that kerygma found documentary expression in the gospels of Matthew, Mark, Luke, and John.

The Book of Exodus and the Gospel Genre

We may readily agree that it would have been fitting for the revelation of the Messiah's mission to be given in [[175]] the form of a brand new literary genre. But is it after all really the case that the gospel genre was a creation of the first century AD?

The Qumran documents have provided fresh evidence of the familiar fact that the Judaism that formed the immediate background of the New Testament appropriated all kinds of literary forms from the Old Testament—apocalypse, history, testament, psalm, and a variety of didactic and legal genres. The suggestion that the New Testament evangelists adopted a genre prominent in their Old Testament Scriptures would, therefore, be altogether compatible with general literary practice in the historical context in which the gospels originated.

In the search for the origins of the gospel genre, the form critics have indeed traced the trajectories of various kinds of gospel materials to Old Testament sources. Nevertheless, they have overlooked the obvious, if I see it aright, in failing to find the origins of the gospel genre as such in the Old Testament, specifically, in the second volume of the Pentateuch.[3] For the book of Exodus appears to have the same thematic focus and to exhibit comprehensively the same literary structure as the gospels. What I hope to show then is, in a word, that the book of Exodus is an Old Testament gospel—the Gospel of Moses.[4]

Coming to the question of the gospel genre from a background of more specialized concern with the form-critical questions of the Old Testament,

3. The section of the Pentateuch we call the book of Exodus is marked off as a unit in itself by the distinctive contents and form of the two sections that immediately bound it (Genesis and Leviticus). Even according to modern higher critical views of the origin of Exodus, it had, of course, emerged and been regarded as a discrete literary entity long before the production of the New Testament gospels.

4. The present essay carries a step further a suggestion I made in *WTJ* 32 (1970): 198; cf. *SBA*, 71ff.

particularly of the Pentateuch, what has impressed me is the similarity of the key problem in the two cases. In both the Pentateuch [[176]] (or more narrowly, Exodus) and the gospels the problem is one of explaining the combination of two major kinds of literary material. Moreover, the two kinds of material are very much the same in the two cases—historical narrative and legislation in the Pentateuch, historical narrative and authoritative sayings in the gospels. The very problem that most perplexes the New Testament form critic at this point thus turns out to be a clue directing him to the goal of his quest.

In the course of the literary criticism of the Pentateuch the documentary theorists, as is well known, have seized upon the difference between narrative and legislative materials as a criterion for the identification of the hypothetical Pentateuchal sources. The partitioning of the book of Exodus between the putative priestly source and the supposed narrative sources has followed for the most part the lines of distinction between legal ordinance and historical narrative. But form-critical study has now disclosed the actual generic unity and identity of the documentary combination of history and law.[5] This combination was a regular feature of the second millennium BC treaty genre. After a preamble introducing the suzerain-author of the treaty, a historical prologue reviewed the past relationships of the covenant partners and this was followed by a law section defining the vassal's duties. The Mosaic covenants, the Decalogue and Deuteronomy, appropriated this international treaty form and thus the history-law complex is found in them too. The combination of narrative and legislation in the book of Exodus does not, therefore, betray a multiplicity of sources behind that document. The conclusion warranted by the form-critical facts is rather that the treaty form adopted by Moses in the Decalogue and Deuteronomy exercised a pervasive influence as he shaped the larger Pentateuchal composition in which he set those treaty texts. It is because Exodus, though not a treaty as such, is an adaptive [[177]] development of the treaty, a creative by-form of the treaty form, that it contains history and law in the peculiar combination that it does.

As observed above, the distinctive combination of narrative and authoritative words is a feature of Exodus and the New Testament gospels alike. As soon as our attention is drawn, whether by this observation or along some other route, to the literary similarity of the gospels to Exodus with its covenantal orientation, the principal elements of that parallelism

5. Cf. *SBA*, 53.

quickly make themselves apparent and we find that the pieces of the gospel genre picture begin to fall into place. What then are these structural features that Exodus and the gospels have in common and justify our speaking of them as a single genre?

In the structure of the gospels the most prominent feature is the long section devoted to the passion narratives. Starting with the transfiguration event (in the Synoptics) and continuing through the resurrection-ascension records, it extends about half the total length of each of the gospels.[6] All that precedes in the gospel story clearly has its face set steadfastly towards this climax in Jerusalem. The passion narratives thus dominate the gospel form thematically and quantitatively.

This feature has its counterpart in the book of Exodus in the dominant position occupied there by the account of the inauguration of the Sinaitic Covenant. Beginning at Exod 19, this climactic section continues on through the entire last half of the book to its conclusion. Here is the record of the awesome scene of theophany and covenant ratification, the divine revelation of the provisions of the covenant, the erection of the tabernacle-residence of the heavenly Suzerain, and the enthronement of his [[178]] glory there in the midst of the covenant community. All the events narrated in the first part of the book lead upwards to this covenantal engagement of Israel at the mountain of God as their high goal. The very topography of the Israelites' journey brings into high relief the ascending literary movement of the book as they proceed from the river valley of Egypt through the depths of the sea, thence along the rising terrain to the heights of Sinai, the lofty setting of the covenant consummation of Exod 19–40.

The correspondence between the dominant second halves of Exodus and the gospels is a matter of content as well as form. For the underlying theme of the passion narratives in the gospels is precisely that of their Exodus counterpart—the inauguration of the covenant. As we shall want to observe further below, the basically covenantal orientation of the sufferings, death, and resurrection of Christ as presented in these narratives is evidenced by explicitly covenantal terminology and, less directly but nonetheless most effectively, by the gospels' extensive appropriation of the exodus-Sinai experiences of Israel as a typological model in the delineation

6. This applies to the Gospel of John as well as to the Synoptics, although John omits the transfiguration episode. On the latter as the opening of the passion narratives, cf. N. B. Stonehouse, *The Witness of Matthew and Mark to Christ* (Philadelphia: Presbyterian Guardian, 1944), 157.

of the messianic history. Incidentally, geographical peaks mark the literary heights in the gospels too. The climactic passion narratives are bracketed by the mounts of transfiguration and ascension, the former of these mountain-top episodes being most realistically related to the parallel Sinai-event of the book of Exodus by the very presence of Moses.

There is a second obvious and major structural correspondence between the gospels and Exodus. It is one that involves the entire first halves of these compositions leading up to the climactic episodes of covenant ratification. In these opening sections both Exodus and the gospels recount the life or at least the public career of the covenant mediator. These accounts of the missions of Moses and Jesus are, of course, not confined to the first halves of the documents but continue on through the [[179]] covenant ratification events related in the second halves. Indeed, it is supremely in the ratification episodes that the mediatorial office is fulfilled. Actually then this aspect of the structural parallelism comprehends Exodus and the gospels in their entireties.

The all-inclusive role of Moses as he is presented in the book of Exodus is plainly that of mediator of the covenant. In the gospels, however, it is not so immediately apparent that the role of covenant mediator is the central and unifying category in the multi-faceted ministry of Jesus. But once it is recognized that the inauguration of the covenant is the governing motif of the passion narratives on which the gospels place such overwhelming emphasis and that covenant ratification is, therefore, to be seen as the culminating achievement towards which Jesus' earlier career moves, the centrality of the mediatorial office in the perspective of the gospels' total portrayal of Jesus and his work can be readily perceived.[7]

It is Jesus' office of covenant mediator that provides the natural and proper explanation of the combination of gospel discourse and gospel narrative that has proved so obstinate an obstacle in the gospel genre quest. For the covenant mediator is prophet as well as ruler and priest; he conveys the words of the Lord's covenant to his people, as well as rescuing them from their enemies and officiating at the ratification rites. The authoritative sayings of Jesus that are interspersed through the narratives of his saving acts are then clearly to be identified as the new covenant equivalents of

7. Even if one did not agree that covenant mediatorship is the controlling motif in the gospels' picture of Jesus' mission, he would still have to recognize that Exodus and the gospels are alike in that their overall outlines are unified by the story of a central protagonist, a great deliverer of God's people.

the covenantal directives of Moses to Israel in Exodus and elsewhere in the Pentateuch.

The structural correspondences that have been noted between the gospels and Exodus are not peripheral but [[180]] fundamental. They take into account the most conspicuous formal features of these documents, features that encompass their entire contents. Moreover, these formal features include distinctive material specifications. The parallelism between these compositions extends beyond the general features that have been mentioned; this is especially true of the material correspondence as to covenantal situation. But the foregoing general comparison of structure and content is an adequate enough basis for stating the conclusion that the New Testament gospels and the book of Exodus are to be viewed as a single genre.

Obviously, every individual specimen of a given genre differs in various ways from all the others; each is to some extent an adaptive variation of the generic form. The flexibility of the gospel genre is displayed by the differences among the four New Testament gospels. As redaction criticism has emphasized, each evangelist had a distinctive Christological perspective which resulted in a distinctive total treatment of those narrative and discourse materials he had at his disposal. Two of the gospels contain accounts of the genealogy and birth of the covenant mediator, while the other two begin in other ways. Luke even made his gospel part one of a two-part work and gave the whole a dedicatory setting according to common formal conventions of his day. Such variations simply reflect the particular circumstances of the origin of each gospel and the special ecclesiastical situation to which each was addressed, as the kerygmatic approach has stressed. They do not forestall the identification of these four gospels as one genre.[8]

Although the differences between the Old Testament book of Exodus and the New Testament gospels with respect to provenience and literary distinctives are certainly much more pronounced than the differences that [[181]] distinguish the New Testament gospels from one another, they are nevertheless not of such significance as to disallow the classification of Exodus with the others as a single genre. Definitions of literary genres cannot avoid a certain amount of arbitrariness at the edges of the idea. As I see it, the somewhat more flexible concept of genre one operates with if he identifies Exodus and the New Testament gospels as one genre is hermeneutically more illuminating than the more rigid concept he adopts if he identifies them as different genres.

---

8. Cf. Gundry, "Recent Investigations," 114.

To suggest a provisional working definition: A document of the gospel genre is one that has as its literary center of gravity an account of the inauguration of a divine covenant, set within a record of the covenant mediator's career and of the law of the community promulgated by the mediator.

There is a functional component that should be added to our concept of the gospel genre. It is implicit in the formal-material elements already mentioned. We shall return to that but wish to take up at this point another feature in the gospels of special relevance for our thesis.

Moses-Exodus Typology in the Gospels

By the citation of Old Testament promise and prediction in their narration of Jesus' life, the New Testament evangelists show that they understand our Lord's mission to be the fulfillment of the Old Testament hope. They also make the connection with the Old Testament revelation by constructing their account of God's epochally new intervention through his Son in such a way as to bring out its typological relationship to the history of the old covenant. They present the saving acts of Christ as a new exodus led by a new Moses.[9]

Many special studies have dealt with various facets of [[182]] this typological use of the Mosaic history in the gospels. Our survey of the matter here will be merely an outline sketch singling out a suggestive selection from among the possible instances of this rather pervasive feature of the gospels.

Our treatment of this vast area can afford to be somewhat tentative in detail since our primary thesis concerning the generic oneness of the gospels and the book of Exodus rests squarely on the major structural parallels between them to which attention has already been called; it is not dependent on the evidence of exodus typology in the gospels. In fact, genre identification is not a matter of historical typology but of literary typicality. For example, the book of Revelation contains a good deal of typological symbolism drawn from the history of the exodus, but it does not exhibit the broad formal-material literary parallelism to the book of Exodus that we have found in the case of the gospels and, therefore, there is no question of identifying Revelation and Exodus as one genre. At the same time, although the gospels' use of the exodus model bears only indirectly on our

9. Messianic prophecy in the Old Testament had already done this. The Qumran sect too regarded its experience as a new exodus.

thesis, it does offer support for our conclusion by confirming the fact that Jesus and his work are contemplated in the gospels from a perspective that is primarily and pervasively covenantal.

The numerous studies of the new Moses and new exodus imagery in the gospels that have been produced over the years have had scarcely any noticeable effect on the concurrent investigation of the gospel genre problem. This is so even though an occasional statement may be found in the typological studies to the effect that the book of Exodus influenced the form as well as the content of the gospel story, or even that it influenced the broad structure of a particular New Testament gospel.[10] [[183]] Perhaps the reason that those engaged in the gospel genre studies have not followed up on this clue is that the typological studies have not faced squarely the form-critical issues of genre definition or have even confused historical typology with literary typicality.

* * * * *

We will deal first with certain general themes found in the gospels' exposition of the messianic salvation.

The word *exodos* (usually translated "departure") appears in the transfiguration episode at the very beginning of the Lucan passion narratives (Luke 9:31). This "exodus" discussed by Moses and Elijah as they spoke with Jesus was soon to transpire at Jerusalem. Suggestions vary as to the precise stage in the Mosaic exodus and the parallel exodus of Jesus that is referred to by the term *exodos*: (a) The Israelites' departure from Egypt; and Jesus' departure from Jerusalem (cf. Rev 11:8), the city doomed to desolation, on his way to Calvary (Matt 27:32; Mark 15:20; Luke 23:26; John 19:17), there to suffer outside the gate, in the wilderness (cf. Heb 13:12). (b) The passage of the departing Israelites through the waters of the sea; and Jesus' undergoing of the baptismal ordeal of his passion (Matt 20:22; Mark 10:38; Luke 12:50; cf. 1 Cor 10:2). (c) The triumphant emergence of the Israelites from the sea, leaving behind the draconic enemy, pharaonic Egypt, buried in the sea; and Jesus' resurrection from the grave in victory over death and the devil (cf. Heb 13:20; Isa 63:11ff.), with his subsequent leading of the disciples forth

10. Cf. Otto A. Piper, "Unchanging Promises: Exodus in the New Testament," *Int* 11 (1957): 16ff.; and Jacob J. Enz, "The Book of Exodus as a Literary Type for the Gospel of John," *JBL* 76 (1957): 208ff.

from Jerusalem (Luke 24:50) to the mount of ascension. Perhaps the *exodos* of Luke 9:31 refers broadly to the whole death-resurrection complex. In that case, this striking term (the name of the book of Exodus in the Septuagint) stands in the transfiguration account as a virtual heading for the entire passion narratives section introduced by that episode.

The messianic exodus, like its Mosaic type, occurred in a [[184]] Passover context. The Last Supper constituted a bond between the Passover and the cross, for it had the Passover feast for its matrix, while it sacramentally celebrated the sacrifice of Christ.[11] The association of the death of Jesus with the Passover is brought out most emphatically in the Gospel of John according to the view (which I find unacceptable) that John describes the crucifixion as taking place on the very day of the Passover sacrifice and that he does this with the intention not of providing chronology but of identifying Jesus' death typologically as the true Passover sacrifice. But the cross of Jesus, like the Mosaic crossing of the sea, was in any case closely conjoined in time with the celebration of the Passover. A possible allusion to the Passover as an image of Jesus' sacrificial death is found in John the Forerunner's description of Jesus as "the lamb of God" (John 1:29, 36), but the referent is not altogether certain.

The terminology of redemption emerges in the narrative of Moses' mission in the book of Exodus (Exod 6:6; 15:13).[12] It is the nature of the exodus as a deliverance from slavery that is in the foreground when it is characterized as a redemption. God heard the cry of the Israelites by reason of their foreign taskmasters; he remembered his covenant with the patriarchs (Exod 2:24; 3:6–10); and he redeemed his people—he acquired them for himself again. Luke draws upon this exodus-redemption imagery in his gospel. He uses the language of redemption in his accounts of Jesus' nativity and youth (Luke 1:68; 2:38). Thus, right from the beginning of his gospel, Luke puts the career of the Lord in an exodus setting. He indicates that Zacharias, father of John the Forerunner, echoing the words of God at the call of [[185]] Moses (Exod 3:6–8; cf. 2:24), prophetically interpreted the salvation to be accomplished by Jesus as a second exodus deliverance from the land of oppression in fulfillment of God's covenant with the patriarchs

---

11. It is noteworthy from the viewpoint of literary analysis that the fact that a memorial feast was instituted on the eve of each exodus resulted in a narrative-disrupting insertion of legislation at a momentous juncture in the conflict (cf. Exod 12:1ff.).

12. Cf. Deut 7:8; 9:26; 13:5; 21:8. Genesis 48:16 is the only pre-exodus instance.

(Luke 1:68–74; cf. Exod 3:8; 5:23; 12:27; 18:4, 8ff.). Elsewhere in Luke's gospel the hope of the remnant in Israel, which was fastening itself upon Jesus for its realization, is summed up in the word "redemption" (Luke 2:38; 24:21). Also, a saying of Jesus is recorded in which he calls the final eschatological deliverance a redemption (Luke 21:28). It is in the Gospel of Luke too that the Nazareth synagogue episode is related, in which Jesus portrays his mission as the fulfillment of the Jubilee symbol (as channelled through the messianic prophecy of Isa 61:1ff.), the symbol of the ultimate redemption from slavery (Luke 4:18ff.).

It was noted above that since the Lord's Supper was instituted during the Passover meal and as an adaptation of it for the church, the death of Jesus memorialized by the Supper is related to the Passover and, through the Passover, to the exodus as its context of meaning. The words of institution of the Supper also interpret the sacrifice of the cross explicitly as a covenantal transaction (Matt 26:28; Mark 14:24; Luke 22:20), and covenant is another exodus-related motif.[13] Covenant and exodus are inseparable in the Mosaic history. Indeed, according to the narrative in the book of Exodus the establishment of the covenant at Sinai was the purpose and goal of the exodus process: Moses was to bring Israel out of Egypt so that they might proceed to the mount of God, there to enter as covenant vassals into the kingdom service of their [[186]] covenant Lord (Exod 3:12; 4:23; and repeatedly; cf. Exod 19:1).

More particularly, at the institution of the Lord's Supper Jesus called the blood of his imminent sacrificial death the "blood of the new covenant," so interpreting it in terms of the covenant-ratifying blood in the ritual described in Exod 24:3–8 (cf. Heb 9:20).[14] Since the symbol adopted by Jesus as the sign of his covenant blood was the sacramental cup of the transformed Passover meal, Jesus' death answers both to the sacrifice offered in preparation for the Passover and to the ratification sacrifices of the Sinaitic

13. This explicitly covenantal exposition of Jesus' death is in itself obviously the most direct evidence for the presence of the covenantal perspective in the passion narratives. But it is being cited at this point for the contribution it makes to the case we are developing in the present section of this essay for the extensive use of exodus typology in the gospels as an indirect argument for the primacy of the covenantal perspective of the gospels.

14. The statement that Jesus' covenant blood was shed for many for the remission of sins involves further ties with the Sinaitic Covenant via intermediate points in the trajectory: the Jeremianic prophecy of the new (law) covenant (Jer 31:31) and the Isaianic prophecy of the new (Mosaic) covenant Servant (Isa 53:12).

Covenant. Thus, the significance of the blood ceremonies that introduced and consummated the exodus-event fuse in the meaning of the cross.

The covenant sacrifice at Sinai was followed by the covenant communion meal of Israel's elders in the presence of God on the mountain (Exod 24:9–11). This aspect of the covenant-making at the Mosaic exodus is clearly present in the communion of the disciples with Jesus at the Last Supper, and again when the chosen witnesses ate and drank with their risen Lord (Acts 10:41) during the forty days before the ascension (Acts 1:3; cf. Exod 24:18).

The occurrence of the resurrection on the morning of the third day is another possible covenantal motif (cf. Exod 19:11, 16; Hos 6:2; Gen 22:4).[15]

The evangelists' predilection for the exodus model has also been claimed as the explanation for the special [[187]] attention called to the wilderness setting in the accounts of certain highly significant episodes in Jesus' life. The suggestion gains plausibility from the fact that the events themselves are strongly evocative of various features of Israel's wilderness experience following the exodus from Egypt; particularly so are the baptism of Jesus in connection with the activities of John the Forerunner, the forty days' temptation of Jesus, and the feeding of the five thousand. If this underscoring of the wilderness setting is indeed designed to set forth Jesus' mission as a new exodus, what needs to be more clearly recognized is that the wilderness of the exodus was above all the place of the covenant-making. It was the place where Yahweh brought Israel into the bond of marriage (Jer 2:2; Ezek 16:8; 20:35–37). The highlighting of the wilderness setting of the opening events of Jesus' career thus advises us from the very outset that we are to view his mission as a leading forth of the new Israel-bride to the ratification of the covenant with the Lord, her husband.

We turn now to observe how the authors of the New Testament gospels brought out the Moses-Jesus parallel in their portrayal of Jesus as mediator of the new covenant. The various Moses-like features may be subsumed under the categories of ruler and deliverer, the functions by which Stephen summarized the role of Moses when he too was drawing a parallel between Moses and Christ (Acts 7:35).

As a preface to this functional comparison we will list certain parallels in the literary structure of the records of the personal origins and the calls of these two covenant mediators. This literary parallelism, though not in

---

15. Cf. W. Brueggemann, "Amos 4:4–13 and Israel's Covenant Worship," *VT* 15 (1965): 1–15; J. Wijngaards, "Death and Resurrection in Covenantal Context (Hos. 6:2)," *VT* 17 (1967): 226–39.

itself typological, is another indication of the evangelists' design of depicting Jesus as a new Moses. It also enforces quite directly our main thesis concerning the literary relationship of the gospels to the book of Exodus.

Birth narratives are prominent in the introductions to the accounts of the old and new mediators (Exod 2:1ff.; Matt 1:18ff.; Luke 1:5ff.). They include a statement of [[188]] the lineage of the child (Exod 2:1; cf. 1:1ff.; 6:14ff., esp. v. 20; Matt 1:1ff.; Luke 3:23ff.), and the genealogy of Moses continues the genealogical tradition of the book of Genesis, which is also incorporated into the genealogy of Jesus. These narratives are set within the international political scene of the day and in particular are related to royal decrees that are directed against the life of Israelite infants and thus threaten the destined deliverer of God's people (Exod 1:15ff.; Matt 2:16ff.). Interestingly, extensive birth narrative appears again in the Old Testament in the history of Samuel, who, among Old Testament figures after Moses, performed most comprehensively the work of a covenant mediator. And at that point in this literary trajectory from Exodus to the gospels is found the song of praise for Hannah's expected child (1 Sam 2:1ff.), of which Mary's Magnificat is reminiscent (Luke 1:46ff.). The birth narratives of both Moses and Jesus also record the naming of the child, and the occasion in each case is evocative of the circumstances of the exodus-deliverance he was later to accomplish (Exod 2:5–10; Luke 2:21).[16]

The earlier life of both Moses and Jesus remains largely hidden from view. But in each case an episode is disclosed that was indicative of the future deliverer's sense of vocation and the failure of others to understand the divine purpose (Exod 2:11ff.; cf. Acts 7:25; Heb 11:24ff.; Luke 2:41ff.). The hidden years of preparation issue in both cases in acts of commissioning, attended by special manifestations of God (Exod 3:1ff.; Matt 3:16–17; Mark 1:10–11; Luke 3:21–22; John 1:32–33). Closely associated with the calls are episodes of personal participation by [[189]] the two leaders in signs of covenantal judgment (Exod 4:24ff.; Matt 3:13ff.; Mark 1:9ff.; Luke 3:21–22). The subsequent narratives relate series of miracles performed by or through Moses and Jesus. In each case these are characterized as "signs" and they serve in part to attest the divine authorization of the mediator's mission (Exod 4:8ff.;

16. In Matthew's account of the flight into Egypt and the return, which he entwines with the birth narratives, he makes an explicit typological connection of the history of Jesus with the exodus by relating the episode to Hosea's observation that God had called his son, the nation Israel, out of Egypt at the time of its national childhood (Matt 2:15; Hos 11:1). Compare also Matt 2:20 and Exod 4:19.

7:3; 8:23; 10:1–2; John 20:30). There are, moreover, striking correspondences in the nature of certain of the signs; compare, for example, the first in each series—Exod 7:19 and John 2:1ff.

The gospels reveal Jesus engaged in a ministry of deliverance that recalls at several significant points the activity of Moses in delivering Israel. Like Moses, Jesus rescued from hostile, threatening forces. His deliverance of the victims of demon possession from the diabolical powers answered to God's deliverance of Israel from bondage by the hand of Moses; for pharaonic Egypt with its gods is viewed in the Old Testament as the realm of the dragon (Ps 74:12ff.; Isa 51:9–10; cf. Ezek 29:3ff.; 32:2ff.). Jesus' saving of the disciples from stormy seas recalls the exodus salvation at the sea (Matt 8:24ff.; 14:24ff.), along with other historic displays of the Creator's sovereign control over the chaotic waters. Because the death of Jesus was prefigured in his baptism, in which the water ordeal symbolism of the Red Sea passage was renewed (cf. 1 Cor 10:1ff.),[17] we may say with biblical propriety that Jesus, like Moses, leads his people through the sea of death.

The figure of shepherd-guide is applied to Jesus and to Moses (Mark 6:34; cf. Ezek 34:5ff.; and Ps 77:20; cf. Num 27:17). Like Moses, Jesus led his followers, supplying their physical needs, going on before them to the promised rest (John 14:2–3; cf. Matt 26:32; 28:7). When Jesus spread a table in the wilderness for the thousands, the provision of the manna and other sustenance in the wilderness during the ministry of Moses found a messianic [[190]] counterpart (John 6:5ff.; cf. Matt 14:15ff.; Mark 6:35ff.; Luke 9:12ff.; and Matt 15:32ff.; Mark 8:1ff.).

Central to Jesus' role as deliverer was the ministry of sacrifice and intercession that came to its chief expression in the final stages of his earthly career, the priestly ministry by which he secured acceptance for his people with God. This too answered to a prototype in the service rendered by the mediator of the old covenant. For though the special priestly office was assigned to Aaron and his line, Moses officiated at the covenant sacrifice (Exod 24:4–8) and engaged in remarkable intercession with God in behalf of jeopardized Israel in the crisis at Sinai (Exod 32:11ff., 30ff.; 34:8–9; Ps 106:23; John 17).

Under the heading of Jesus as ruler, his office as mediatorial representative of God before men comes into consideration. In this capacity he inaugurated the covenant and founded the kingdom, organizing the community of faith and promulgating the law of its life and order. Here is the core of

17. See *BOC*, 56ff.

the matter for the purposes of the present study and here the new Moses typology of the gospels is crystal clear.

Even when stating the contrast between Moses and Jesus Christ in terms of law over against grace and truth, John draws attention to their common mediatorial role. It was "through" Moses and "through" Christ that the old and new covenants came (John 1:17).

Jesus' identity as the prophet like unto Moses, affirmed by Peter (Acts 3:22–23), is reflected in the gospels (John 5:43; 12:48–49; Matt 17:5), and the prophetic role of Moses was precisely his role as mediator of the covenant. The prophetic-legislative passage in the Deuteronomic treaty that instituted the office of the prophet defines it as a continuation of the function of Moses at the Sinai covenant-making (Deut 18:15–19). The prophets of the old covenant down to John the Forerunner were thus primarily covenant messengers, like unto Moses as channels of covenant revelation and as agents of covenant administration. But Jesus Christ was the prophet like [[191]] unto Moses in the full sense that he was the mediator-prophet in the inauguration of the covenant and the establishment of the kingdom. John stresses the uniqueness of the prophetic vision of the Son: only he has seen the Father (John 6:46). But even here John may be alluding comparatively to the special intimacy of the vision of God enjoyed by Moses beyond others in the old economy (Exod 33:18ff.; Deut 34:10; John 1:17–18). Certainly the transfiguration narrative in the Synoptics (Matt 17:1ff.; Mark 9:2ff.; Luke 9:28ff.) contains an impressive set of analogues to the experience of Moses, the prophet-mediator at Sinai. The covenantal perspective is manifested by the presence of Moses and also of Elijah, whose ministry of covenant renewal recapitulated so strikingly various episodes in the life of Moses. The transfiguration transpired on the mountain enveloped by the theophanic Glory-cloud. Was it perhaps in part because Peter was so much under the impression of the similarity of it all to the Sinai event, which had issued in the establishing of God's tabernacle among his people, that, still not sufficiently minding the things of God (Matt 16:23; Mark 8:33), he came up with the suggestion that the transfiguration occasion might immediately have a similar outcome—as though Pentecost might come before Jesus had accomplished his exodus? The voice from heaven commanding, "Hear him," echoed Deut 18:18, so designating Jesus as the Moses-like prophet invested with oracular authority. And the glory shining from the face of the transfigured Jesus was manifestly the transcendent counterpart to the reflection of the glory of the Shekinah that was seen in the face of Moses after he had been in the mount of the covenant (Exod 24:15ff.; 34:29ff.; cf. 2 Cor 3:7ff.).

Also relevant to the gospels' Moses-mediator typology is the identification of Jesus in the gospels as the Isaianic Servant of the Lord, for it was the figure of Moses, the servant of Yahweh in the founding of the Sinaitic Covenant, that Isaiah drew upon in forming the figure of the [[192]] Servant whom God would give as a covenant of the people (Isa 42:6; 49:8).

As ruler of Israel at the inauguration of the covenant, Moses was the human founder of the Old Testament kingdom: he organized the covenant community in its twelve divisions on the basis of the twelve tribal fathers and he communicated to the people the words of God's covenant, the constitution of the kingdom. This model clearly comes into play when the gospels present Jesus as the founder of the kingdom of the new covenant. Jesus gathered and commissioned the twelve to be the apostolic foundation of his church. In his teaching he defined the nature and historical function of his kingdom and set forth the basic principles of its structure and life. The scene of the sermon on the mount, which epitomizes Jesus' authoritative teaching role, recalls unmistakably the figure of Moses at Mount Sinai.

There may be some heuristic value in observing how important strands in the teaching of Jesus fit into the categories of the treaty pattern appropriated in the covenantal writings of Moses.[18] Corresponding to the opening preamble of such treaties, in which the suzerain, speaking in the first person, identifies himself, are Jesus' words of self-identification and especially his "I am" declarations. In all that Jesus said by way of explanation of the Father's redemptive purpose in sending his Son the covenant claims of God upon his people come to expression after the fashion of the reviews of the covenant relationship in the historical prologues of the treaties. And in Jesus' overviews of Israel's history of covenant-breaking, particularly in certain parables such as those of the wicked husbandmen and the marriage of the king's son, we see an adaptation of the historical prologue in the style of the prophetic lawsuit. Treaty stipulations concerning various individual and corporate areas of covenant life find parallels in the instruction given by Jesus. [[193]] Jesus' commandments deal with personal-neighbor relationships, with the authority structure and discipline of the new covenant institution (Matt 16:18–19; 18:15ff.), and with its ministry of word and sacrament (Matt 26:26ff.; Mark 14:22ff.; Luke 22:19–20; Matt 28:18ff.). In a manner analogous to the ceremonial legislation of Moses prescribing the symbols of the cultus, the parables of Jesus present the mysteries of the kingdom in

18. Cf. *SBA*, Part II, Chapter 1 ("The Two Tables of the Covenant") [= pp. 79–92 in the present volume] and Chapter 2 ("Dynastic Covenant").

a figure.[19] Treaty stipulations were followed by treaty sanctions (cf. Exod 23:20ff.; Lev 26; Deut 28–30). It is this tradition of blessings and curses that is resumed by Jesus in his beatitudes and his threats of doom against offenders (Matt 5:3ff.; 7:24–27; 23:13ff.). The eschatological discourses of Jesus also stand in continuity with the treaty-sanction tradition as received through the prophetic channel of Old Testament apocalyptic.[20]

In the gospels' accounts of the final stages of Jesus' earthly ministry there are parallels to the life and work of Moses recorded in the Pentateuch beyond the book of Exodus. The Johannine account of the farewell discourse of Jesus (John 13–17) recalls Moses' Deuteronomic farewell to Israel. In each case it is the hour of covenant ratification. Prominent in the two farewells are similar elements like election of the covenant servants, the Lord-servant relationship, the giving of commandments, the covenant witnesses, and the appointment of a successor for the departing mediator. Both Moses and Jesus make a final disposition through testamentary blessing (Deut 33) or promise (John 14) and intercession (John 17), bestowing on the community an inheritance of peace, joy, and glory in the unity of the name of the Lord. Subsequently, each covenant mediator takes leave of the earthly scene from the site of a mountain top.

[[194]] It was the task of both the old and new covenant mediators, after defeating the forces of Satan and sealing the covenant of God with his people, to erect the sanctuary house of God. The last chapters of Exodus deal with the construction of the tabernacle under the leadership of Moses and the filling of the finished structure by God's Spirit, visibly present in the form of the cloud of glory (Exod 40).[21] While the resurrection accounts in the gospels record the raising up of the temple of the new covenant in the sense that Jesus himself is that temple, it is beyond the gospels in the book of Acts that the further antitypical parallel to the conclusion of the book of Exodus is found. In the Pentecost-event Christ erects the temple of his church and the Holy Spirit fills the house of God (Acts 2:1ff.).

Parenthetically, it may be noted here that both Exodus and the gospels, though distinct literary entities in themselves, belong (or, in the case of the gospels, may belong) to larger literary units into which their

---

19. Cf. Matt 13:10ff.; Mark 4:10ff.; Luke 8:9–10. Ezekiel 40–48 is an intermediate development between the cultic legislation and the parable.

20. Cf. *SBA*, 58ff.

21. Cf. Meredith M. Kline, "The Holy Spirit as Covenant Witness" (ThM diss., Westminster Theological Seminary, 1972), 28ff.

covenant-mediator themes extend. The relation of Exodus to the Mosaic Pentateuch as a whole is formally much the same as that of the Gospel of Luke to the entire Lucan work of Luke-Acts.

Finally, there are new exodus elements in the gospels in which Jesus is presented not as a new Moses but as one who utterly transcends Moses. Jesus, like Moses, provides for his followers and leads them in the way; but Jesus is himself the provision—the true bread from heaven (John 6:35) and water of life (John 4:10ff.; 7:37ff.), and Jesus is the way (John 14:6). Like Moses, Jesus offers the covenant sacrifice, but Jesus is himself that sacrifice. Moses lifted up the serpent on the pole as a symbol of divine judgment; the death of Jesus was that divine judgment in antitypical finality (John 3:14–15; 12:32). Jesus, like Moses, builds the house of God, but Jesus also is himself the [[195]] temple (John 2:19ff.). Jesus and Moses are both covenant servants of the Lord, but Jesus is at the same time the Lord of all covenant servants. He is the Creator Lord who directs the turbulent waters for the salvation of his covenant people, the Angel of the Lord who leads them in the exodus and through the wilderness, the Lord of the covenant who proclaims with original divine authority the law of the covenant and who, in the day of the Lord, administers the covenant's sanctions, the everlasting curse and blessing (Matt 25:31ff.).

* * * * *

It needs to be stressed again that, on the one hand, the presence of the exodus typology in the gospels is not in itself direct evidence for regarding the gospels and Exodus as one literary genre and, on the other, that the thesis of this chapter would not be invalidated if some or even all the instances alleged in the preceding section as examples of that typology should be deemed illusory. However, the data actually do show clearly that the gospels make extensive use of this typological model. Although not direct evidence for our thesis, these data do help to demonstrate that the underlying and unifying factor in the portrayal of Jesus' mission in the gospels is his role as mediator of the new covenant and that the controlling and cohesive motif of the passion narratives is the ratification of the new covenant. The prominence given to the exodus typology by the authors of the New Testament gospels discloses an awareness on their part that they stand as scriptural authors in the line of the transparently covenantal tradition of the book of Exodus.

Canonical Function of the Gospel Genre

The generic identification of the New Testament gospels with the book of Exodus has implications for our understanding of the particular canonical function performed [[196]] by the gospels within the New Testament and thus within the life of the church. For it is a natural assumption that the Lord who authored the covenantal Scriptures will have employed the gospel genre with similar purpose in the canons of the old and new covenants.[22]

The book of Exodus, itself a by-form of the treaty genre, served a purpose in the Israelite community very much like that of the Mosaic treaty documents themselves. In accordance with procedures followed with Near Eastern treaties, the two tables of the covenant and the Deuteronomic document were deposited before the Lord God in his sanctuary to be objective, legal witnesses to the solemn transaction by which the covenant engagement had been entered upon (Deut 31:26).[23] Periodically read to the covenant people, the treaty text kept Israel in remembrance of Yahweh's lordly rights and of the sovereign claims his redemptive grace made upon the allegiance of his redeemed people. The oral republishing of the treaty also kept before the people their specific obligations as Yahweh's servants and the accompanying sanctions of the covenant.

In fact, if we are to understand "the book of the law" which Moses placed by the ark (Deut 31:9, 26; cf. Josh 24:26; 1 Sam 10:25) as the entire Pentateuchal corpus, the book of Exodus would itself be included in the literary deposit to which the function of covenant witness is explicitly attributed. But even if Exodus was not part of the special enshrined covenant documentation, we would be pointed to the same conclusion concerning its purpose in the Old Testament canon by its contents—its dominant account of the ratification of the Sinaitic Covenant and of the establishment of God's rule in the covenant community, set within the broader framework of the narrative of the mission of the covenant mediator. [[197]] And in either case, as part of Israel's Scriptures, copies of which came to be multiplied in the course of time, the book of Exodus (and the Pentateuch as a whole) will have performed this witness function in a form more generally available to the people than a document kept in a sanctuary of extremely restricted access.

If then in adopting the gospel genre once again in the administration of the new covenant, the Lord of the covenant designed that the gospels of

22. Cf. *SBA*, 45ff., 94ff.

23. Cf. ibid., 123ff., 141.

Matthew, Mark, Luke, and John should perform the same function for the church that the Gospel of Moses performed for Israel, their purpose is to provide documentary attestation to the new covenant. Doubling the number of official documentary witnesses provided for the Sinaitic Covenant (i.e., the two stone tablets), the Lord gave the community of the new covenant four such witnesses, and indeed four different rather than duplicate witnesses as in the case of the Sinaitic tablets.[24]

To provide the legal documentary witness to the historically accomplished fact of the ratification of the new covenant by God's action in the mediatorial mission of Jesus Christ—that is the distinctive function of the four gospels in the canon of the New Testament. This witness function of the gospels is to be distinguished from what is usually in view when the gospels are identified as witness documents, as they often are. The point being made here is not that the gospels are the witness concerning Jesus Christ given to the world by the human authors of the gospels or by the church. The kind of witness we have in mind is not a human witness but a witness of God, the Lord of the covenant. It is not a witness to the world but to the church, the community of God's covenant people. It is not a kerygmatic but a legal witness,[25] not kerygmatic-evangelistic [[198]] proclamation of Jesus Christ but legal attestation to God's covenant.

The gospels are, to be sure, of human as well as divine authorship and are, therefore, a human witness too.[26] Moreover, the gospels obviously do testify to Jesus Christ and proclaim the significance of his saving mission. Certainly, too, their contents are to be used in the church's evangelization of the world. But when we consider the structure and the total contents of the gospels, particularly their dominant concern with covenant ratification, and especially when we view the matter in the light of the equivalency of the gospels to the book of Exodus, we are brought to the conclusion that the specific canonical function of the gospels is to be defined from the perspective of God's use of them as legal documents in the administration of his covenant.

---

24. Cf. also Deut 19:15; Matt 18:16.

25. Indeed, kerygmatic witness, though distinguishable from legal witness, always has a legal character; it is a witness borne in the name of the Judge of all the earth.

26. The conscious and express purpose of this human witness to authenticate the historical accomplishment of God's covenant program (cf. Luke 1:1ff.) is clearly in complete congruity with what we have determined to be the purpose of the gospels as divine witnesses.

Understood as covenant ratification witnesses, the gospels have a breadth of purpose that accounts fully for all their contents. It is unnecessary to make a choice, as is usually done, between classifying the gospels as primarily lives of Jesus or as church manuals of one sort or another. The problem thus posed is false and a solution in either direction is bound to be one-sided and inadequate. The covenant reality and the treaty structure, of which the gospels of the old and new covenants are a by-form, provide the comprehensive framework of theological concept and literary pattern within which both types of material, history of Jesus data and community instruction, find their full and proper explanation. The gospels' particular range of subject matter is altogether natural and authentic within the tradition of covenant witness documents.

To define the nature and purpose of the gospels in [[199]] covenantal rather than Christological terms is not to depreciate the significance of Jesus but simply to recognize the specific focus of the Christology of the gospels within their broader covenantal perspective. Certainly there is no tension of interests between the lord of a covenant and his covenant. The covenant documents are precisely the instruments by which a suzerain reveals and enforces his authoritative will. They are exponential of lordship.

That is especially true of the treaty preamble. In the biblical adaptation of the treaty form, the preamble is the revelation of the name of God as Lord of the covenant. This revelation of God's name not only points to the source and foundation of the covenant reality but is itself the ultimate objective of the covenant relationship. And in the gospels, identified as covenantal documents, the Christology performs this supremely significant preamble-like function. It proclaims the name of Jesus, the Lord of the covenant, revealing him as God present with his people, the primary reality of God's covenant relationship to man, and as Savior of his people, the central reality of the redemptive covenant relationship. The covenantal orientation given to Christology in the gospels does not, therefore, detract from its importance but rather enhances it. The kerygmatic impact of the Christology is actually strengthened, for the revelation of the name of Jesus comes in its treaty preamble capacity as a sovereign summons to covenantal commitment, the commitment of believing discipleship under Jesus as sign-attested mediator of the covenant (John 20:31; cf. Exod 4:1ff.; 14:31), indeed as covenant Lord and God.

At the same time, the gospels' preamble-like revelation of the Lord of the covenant is such as to show the wisdom and even necessity of defining the gospel genre in terms broader than Christology. For they reveal the covenant Lord by the name of Father and by the name of Spirit as well as by the name of Son. Their theology proper is not narrowly Christological and it is an advantage [[200]] of the broader identification of the gospels as documents of covenant certification that it can accommodate this more broadly theological character of the texts.

A breadth of perspective along with a centrality of emphasis on Jesus Christ, similar to what we have posited for the gospel documents, is present in the meaning of the word "gospel" (*euangelion*) as it is used in the New Testament gospels. Though this usage is relevant to our present purposes, it does not have as direct a bearing as one might think on the definition of the gospels as documents, since in the evangelists' usage the word does not refer to the documents as such but rather to their central message, the good tidings proclaimed by Jesus and by his followers.

This gospel message is indeed characterized as a message about Jesus Christ (Mark 1:1), but more comprehensively it is designated "the gospel of the kingdom" (Matt 4:23; 9:35; 24:14; Mark 1:14–15). In the Old Testament antecedents of the terminology of heralding the good tidings, those tidings refer prophetically to the reign of the Lord God in the messianic age, to the coming of the Lord to his people in glory to rule with power and justice, rendering to each his recompense (cf. Isa 40:9; 52:7ff.; 60:6; 61:1).

The coming of the kingdom of God announced by the gospel tidings is very much the same event as the inauguration of God's covenant. For a divine covenant "is a sovereign administration of the kingdom of God. Covenant administration is kingdom administration."[27] The establishment of the covenant order is the coming of God to dwell enthroned in a reign of salvation among his people. Therefore, to say the New Testament gospels testify to the ratification of the new covenant is tantamount to saying that they declare the arrival of the age of God's kingdom. It is to say that the gospel documents certify the gospel tidings. Since the gospel tidings, like [[201]] the gospel documents that contain and certify them, are concerned with the broadly theological theme of the kingdom and covenant of God, the adoption of the label "gospels" for the documents themselves, which evidently occurred in the second century AD, was quite appropriate, particularly since the term covenant (or testament) came to designate the New Testament canon as a whole.

The witness of the gospels certifying that God had fulfilled his ancient covenant oath (cf. Gen 15; Deut 32:40ff.) by establishing the new covenant

27. *BOC*, 36.

through his Son is a divine witness. In the gospels, God himself bears witness. More specifically, the divine gospel-witness documents are the witness of God the Spirit to the covenant as now ratified and the kingdom as now realized.

The Scriptures attribute to the Spirit of God the role of divine witness at the making of the Sinaitic Covenant. To appreciate the significance of the relevant biblical data it is first necessary to observe that it is the Spirit in particular who is identified with the theophanic pillar of the Glory-cloud (cf., e.g., Isa 63:11ff.; Hag 2:5; Neh 9:19–20).[28] One passage, Hag 2:5, is of special interest in this regard because it specifically identifies the Spirit with the theophanic pillar functioning as covenant witness. The prophet encourages the people in the rebuilding of the house of God by giving them God's assurance of his presence with them (v. 4b) and of the ultimate completion of his house, which will take place in connection with a new exodus-despoiling of Egypt and a new Sinaitic shaking of the earth (vv. 6ff.). As a support for their confidence in the certain consummation of the covenant, the Lord calls their attention to the divine validation of the covenant relation at Sinai. He reminds them in particular of his treaty word and also of his own visible presence there as a divine witness to the covenant in the form of the glory-pillar: "This is what I covenanted [literally, [[202]] the word I cut] with you, when you came out of Egypt, when my Spirit stood in your midst" (v. 5). Unfortunately, the allusion is lost in the usual versions, which turn the last clause of verse 5 into a statement that the Spirit abode among the Israelites in Moses' day, or, worse still, that the Spirit was abiding among Haggai's contemporaries. The allusion to the Sinaitic pillar of glory, however, is clear. The verb in verse 5b (*ʿāmad*) is the verb used to describe the glory-pillar as standing in Israel's midst (Exod 14:19; 33:9–10). In fact, the noun "pillar" (*ʿammûd*) is derived from this verbal root. The symbolic significance of the pillar form of the theophany may be gathered from the fact that pillars of various kinds served as witness objects for a variety of legal transactions.[29] The pillar form of the Spirit's manifestation thus reveals that he was present at Sinai in the capacity of witness to the covenant.

The Spirit also functioned as covenant witness at Sinai by way of the documentary witnesses of the Sinaitic Covenant, for it was the Spirit of God who, as the Spirit of prophecy, inspired the composition of the covenant

28. For the evidence in full, see Kline, "Covenant Witness"; for the Spirit's covenant-witness function, see 56ff.

29. Ibid., 60–61.

documents. Moreover, the divine agency in the actual inscribing of the two stone tables of covenant witness is said to have been "the finger of God" (Exod 31:18; cf. 8:19), and Scripture elsewhere equates "the finger of God" and the Spirit.[30] This situation illuminates and is in turn illuminated by 2 Cor 3:3, which evidently attributes to the Spirit the writing of the tables of stone.

As the Holy Spirit performs his witness function once again in the divine administration of the new covenant, the phenomena of his coming at Pentecost and his miraculous working in the apostolic church are similar in mode and purpose to his manifestation and wonders in the case of the Sinaitic Covenant.[31] But what is of most immediate [[203]] interest for our analysis of the gospels is the correspondence between the Spirit's activity as divine Inspirer and primary Author of the gospels and his writing of the two stone tablets and inspiring of the canonical witness documents of the old covenant.

Authored by the Spirit, the gospels are the witness of God the Spirit to the historical inauguration of the new covenant through Jesus Christ and to the basic terms of the covenant—its organizational regulations and programmatic commission for the church, its fundamental religious and ethical norms, and its eschatological sanctions. "He that hath an ear, let him hear what the Spirit saith unto the churches."

30. Ibid., 52ff. Compare Luke 11:20 with Matt 12:28.
31. Ibid., 8ff.

CHAPTER NINE

Double Trouble

(1989)

If we speak of the double of something, we might have in mind either twice its amount or its twin. A similar ambiguity in certain biblical words usually rendered "double" has caused interpreters trouble, in part because they have not recognized the presence of the ambiguity or at least have not always reckoned sufficiently with the translation option of "equivalent" or "matching image" rather than "twofold." The most important issue that turns up in an examination of this matter is a theological question concerning God's justice. Through a mishandling of the troublesome "double" words the equity of the divine justice has been beclouded. We will make that theological issue the focus of this study, subordinating the lexical investigation to it. Of the lexical items, primary attention will be given to Hebrew *kāpal* (verb)/*kepel* (noun), but we will also deal with the other "double" terms that figure in passages involving the alleged double divine punishment—namely, Hebrew *mišneh* and Greek *diploō* (verb)/*diplous* (adjective).

Kepel in Isaiah 40

In Isa 40 assurance is given that God's people may expect the coming of the Glory of Yahweh to them (vv. 3ff.), his reward with him and his recompense before him (v. 10), because payment for their sins has been completed (v. 2). By virtue of the full satisfaction of the debt of their iniquity, which had incurred alienation from the Lord and separation from his Presence, the way was now open to restoration. Verse 2 underscores the fact that the punishment for Jerusalem's covenant-breaking has been meted out in full by expressing it in three synonymous statements. The third of these contains the noun *kepel* (dual form) and is usually (mis)translated: "She has received from the hand of Yahweh double for all her sins."

To solve the problem of this apparent imbalance in the scales of divine justice, with two talents of punishment loaded on one side for each talent of sin on the other, resort has been had to various expedients. Some, assuming that the Babylonian exile is the episode in view, suggest that Israel in exile suffered for the sins of the gentiles as well as paying for their own. But this solves one problem by replacing it with another, for a [[172]] role of vicarious atonement impossible for sinful beings to perform is thus attributed to Israel.

Another proposal is that double payment signifies simply full measure. This is theologically innocent enough, and it does catch the general drift of the clause. But its particular assumption about the significance of doubling as simply completeness wants demonstration. Our intention is to show that the problem of the unbalanced scales of divine justice is obviated by the recognition that *kepel* is to be translated "equivalent" rather than "double."

The meaning of the last of the three statements in Isa 40:2 may be approached by examination of the first two, with which the third must be consistent.

According to the first statement, something (denoted by the noun *ṣābāʾ*) has been fulfilled or completed. Usually translated "warfare" or "hard (military) service," *ṣābāʾ* is best understood here as a specified period of labor. The idea is more that of hired or contracted service than rigorous service. Such a meaning for *ṣābāʾ* is found in a series of passages in Job that refer to the day laborer who is obligated to complete a contracted period of service (Job 7:1; 10:17; 14:14; cf. Num 4:23; Dan 10:1). Thus in Job 7:1 the parallel to *ṣābāʾ* is "the days of the hireling," the stipulated time he must work, yearning the while for its completion and his appointed pay (cf. v 2). Similarly in Job 14:14 (cf. 10:17) the picture is that of the laborer waiting for his wages[1] through "all the days of my work term (*ṣābāʾ*)." Here then is the background of the imagery in the first statement in Isa 40:2: a laborer's set period of work with its stipulated wages, its due equivalent according to the current scale. Agreeably the verb (*mālēʾ*) of which *ṣābāʾ* is the subject in this statement is commonly used with terms of time, like days and years, to signify their being completed. The clause may therefore be translated: "Her assigned term of service is completed."

From the second statement in 40:2 we learn that the appointed time that is declared fulfilled is actually a period of punishment for iniquity. Corresponding to the verb *mālēʾ* used in the first clause for completing the work term is the verb *rāṣâ*, which means to make up for, to make good what is

1. On this meaning of *ḥălîpâ* cf. *ḥelep* in Num 18:21, 31.

owed, to acquit a debt. It is used in the Job 14 context mentioned above for the hireling working off his due time of service (v. 6).[2] Of particular importance is the usage in Lev 26. There, in verse 34, *rāṣâ* refers to the land that lay fallow during the time of the Israelites' absence in exile and so made up for the sabbatical years denied to it through the centuries it should have been afforded that rest. Then in verse 41 *rāṣâ* describes the captive Israelites in the land of their enemies making up for their iniquity (both words, verb and object, the same as in Isa 40:2). These [[173]] two ideas are brought together in verse 43: the land making up for its Sabbaths, and the people making up for their debt to divine justice. The effect of that is to give the penal debt that Israel must make good a temporal character; it becomes the judicial sentence of a set period of time to be spent in exile. In the historical event this took the specific form of the seventy years of captivity predicted by Jeremiah (25:11–12; 29:10).[3] Jeremiah's prophecy of the seventy years and the Lev 26 identification of the exile as a time when the land would make up for its Sabbaths are combined in the record of the fulfillment in 2 Chr 36:21. It is this covenant curse of the determined period of exile predictively threatened in Lev 26 that is the underlying, unifying image of Isa 40:2 as a whole. And Lev 26:41 is clearly the primary source of the language in the second of the statements in that verse, which may be translated: "The debt of her iniquity has been paid."

We are now in a position to take up the third statement in Isa 40:2 with its troublesome "double" word, *kepel*. Surely this final pronouncement is to be understood in harmony with the sustained emphasis of the preceding clauses on the fact that sin has received its exactly balancing recompense of punishment. It must make an affirmation consistent with the allusive analogue of the hireling who punctually fulfills the stipulated period of labor as the contractual equivalent of his wages. Hence we translate: "She has received from Yahweh's hand matching punishment as the payment for[4] all her sins."

Not only would the emphatic teaching of an equivalency of punishment and sin found in the preceding statements of 40:2 be contradicted if *kepel* were translated "double" in the last clause, but a survey of the use of *kepel* elsewhere indicates that "duplicate" rather than "double" is consistently its

2. Cf. Job 20:10a, where *rāṣâ* signifies to make good, specifically to indemnify the poor who have been plundered.

3. Note in these passages the use of *mālēʾ* for completing the seventy years and the characterization of the exile as a period of service to the Babylonian master.

4. *Bêt* of cost.

preferable if not its necessary rendering. We will examine that evidence supportive of our interpretation of 40:2 after a concluding expository comment on this prophetic proclamation of comfort to Jerusalem.

The covenant curse of the allotted seventy years of exile as recompense for Israel's apostasy is, as we have said, the underlying image in Isa 40:2, but in accordance with regular prophetic idiom this typological imagery drawn from the old covenant is parabolic of new covenant reality. Through it, Isaiah is prophetically assuring the new covenant beneficiaries of all ages that their debt of sin has been paid and the divine justice perfectly satisfied. This is accomplished by the suffering of that Servant of the Lord whom Isaiah proceeds to set forth in the following chapters. On this One the Lord lays the iniquity of the many, and he endures the curse due to them, making atonement for them (52:13–53:12). Israel's exile sufferings were not typological of the cross as an atoning sacrifice offered by the [[174]] righteous One as a substitute in the place of sinners. Those sufferings were the due punishment for Israel's own sin, like the punishment endured by the lost in hell. However, in that Israel's completion of the allotted time of punishment, the seventy years of captivity, did constitute a full payment, a recompense commensurate with their sins, it could provide a figurative groundwork for the gospel pronouncement of 40:2. Comfort my people: In Christ they have received the hell punishment, the eternal seventy years of banishment from the divine Presence, the just wages, the full equivalent payment that matches and cancels their debt of sin. When it is thus recognized that Isa 40:2 describes God's justice operative in Christ's atonement, it is all the more evident how scrupulously exact the description must be and how inappropriate would be the insertion here of the notion of an inequitable double payment.

Kāpal/kepel in the Old Testament

The conclusion reached concerning *kepel* in Isa 40:2 is confirmed by an examination of the several appearances of *kāpal/kepel* elsewhere in the Old Testament. What we find is that the meaning definitely required in most passages is, for the noun *kepel*, "duplicate, twin, matching equivalent" and, for the verb *kāpal*, "produce a duplicate or duplex," or, with respect to an action, "repeat," while the idea of a double amount is not clearly demanded in any passage.

The verb *kāpal* is used in the book of Exodus with reference to cloth material that is folded over so as to produce a pocket of matching front and back pieces facing each other or twin flaps side by side. Exodus 28:16; 39:9

are concerned with the breastpiece of the high priest's vestments. *Kāpal* here describes the linen as folded double to make the square pouch in which the Urim and Thummim were kept (28:30). The material was not doubled in amount but doubled over, folded in half. The result was a double in the sense of a duplicate or matching face, not twice the quantity.

Similarly, in the case of the directions for the goats' hair covering over the tabernacle in 26:9 the verb *kāpal* indicates what is to be done to the end curtain of the eleven curtains that were joined together, the one at the front of the tent. Obviously there is no thought of doubling its size; all eleven curtains were to be the same size (v. 8). Rather, the curtain in question was somehow folded over, apparently by drawing together its outside edges toward the center of the front elevation of the tent and so producing two matching sides, a kind of diptych.

A striking paronomasia appears in connection with the occurrence of the verb *kāpal* in Ezek 21:14 [19].[5] The paronomasia reinforces the symbolism of the commanded act of clapping palm against palm (*kap ʾel-kap*) [[175]] as an image of the action (*wĕtikkāppēl*) to be performed with respect to the sword of judgment.[6] In the symbolic act one hand meets its mate in a duplicating sort of process, producing a matching pair.[7] Likewise, there is to be a duplicating of the sword; a sword matching the original is to be forthcoming. Such then is the meaning of *kāpal* here, with the resultant translation "the sword will be replicated (or multiplied)." This action denoted by *kāpal* is qualified by *šĕlîšîtāh*, "to a third." Evidently the idea is that the replicating of the sword is to be repeated up to the point[8] of a third sword.[9]

Two instances of the noun *kepel* are found in Job. Though not without its difficulties, Job 41:13 [5] contains a reasonably clear description of a

---

5. The choice of *kap*, not *yad* (cf., e.g., Ezek 25:6), and the expansion of the expression *hikkâ kap*, "clap hands" (cf., e.g., 2 Kgs 11:12), by *ʾel-kap* are dictated by the design of echoing *wĕtikkāppēl*. This argues against repointing *wtkpl* as *qal* instead of *niphal*, which would diminish this sound equivalence.

6. Does the paronomasia even suggest a popular etymologizing of *kepel* as based on *kap*, after the pattern of nouns formed with affixed *lamed*?

7. In Prov 6:1, where the clapping of one's hand to the hand of another accompanies a commitment to become surety for the other, the symbolism might be that as hand matches hand, so a pledge of resources is given by one to match the debts of the other.

8. Thus the force of the appended *-āh* in *šĕlîšîtāh*.

9. If *kāpal* meant doubling the amount, the *šĕlîšîtāh* would mean "to a third time" and the result would be the improbable idea of six swords.

fearful duplex pair in the armament of leviathan. Light is thrown on this verse by the next one, which repeats the same imagery, these two verses together being arranged in an AB//A′B′ pattern. Verse 14 [6] reads: "Who would open the doors of his face? His encircling (*sĕbîbôt*) teeth (are) terror."[10] In this parallel structure, *kepel* (v. 13) corresponds to *sĕbîbôt* (v. 14), and verse 13 [5] is to be read: "Who would open his armored face? Within that pair (*kepel*)[11] of jaws who would enter?" The B-stich in each verse thus refers to the jaws studded with terrifying teeth, and in both cases the point made is not the quantity of the teeth as such (a double amount) but the particular array of this weaponry, the arrangement of the teeth in facing rows, threatening from both sides, from above and below, whatever dared this gantlet. It is this duplex pattern of matching upper and lower jaws that is denoted by *kepel*.[12]

The other appearance of *kepel* is in Job 11:6. The verse is quite obscure but, once more, to interpret *kepel* in terms of double quantity would not seem to fit. Here again structural parallelism may supply an interpretive clue. For verses 5–6a apparently form another AB//A′B′ pattern. Curiously the idea of an opening of the mouth is present here as in 41:13–14. In view this time are not the jaws of leviathan but the lips of God. "But would that God would speak, that he would open his lips like[13] you!" (v. 5). [[176]] Corresponding to "lips" in the parallel B-stich of verse 6a is *kiplayim* (dual). Since *kepel* consistently refers to a matching pair, and especially in view of its use in 41:13 for the duplex form of the mouth, it may be understood here as a poetic synonym for lips. This pairing is corroborated by the use of the dual form *kiplayim*, which answers to the dual *śĕpātāyw*,[14] "lips." Verse 6a is then to be translated: "Would that he would declare to you the hidden things of wisdom, that he would open[15] his lips (*kiplayim*) in understanding!"

10. Possibly the verb "enter" from the corresponding B-stich in verse 13 does double duty here. Translate then: "Who would enter the circle of terror, his teeth?"

11. Cf. the listing *kapallu* in *UT* 422, said to designate an object of apparel that comes in pairs.

12. Even on the interpretation of verse 13 [5] as referring to a two-layered coat of mail rather than two rows of teeth, *kepel* would still signify the matching layers rather than double quantity.

13. By so translating the preposition *ʿim* (cf., e.g., Ps 143:7) we bring out the comparison with the boasting words of Job's lips (v. 2), to which the opening of God's lips is to provide a rebuttal.

14. The suffix pronoun here does double duty with *kiplayim*.

15. The *yiptaḥ* of the parallel B-stich in verse 5 does double duty here.

Another possible explanation of this *kiplayim* would be to see in it a reference to the cosmos-encompassing, paired parameters of God's wisdom—the heights of heaven on one side and the depths of Sheol on the other, which is the theme of the immediately following verses (vv. 7–9). These two solutions could even be combined. For it might be that the lips of God, as a metonymy for the words of his wisdom, are pictured as extending from the upper to the lower ends of creation.[16] In any case, it is the understanding of *kepel* as denoting a positionally matching pair that makes possible a satisfactory explanation of this difficult passage.

Mišneh in Jeremiah 16:18; 17:18

The teaching of a twofold retribution would be found in Jer 16:18; 17:18 if the critical word, *mišneh*, were translated "double," a meaning it has at times (e.g., Exod 16:5, 22; Job 42:10). There is, however, the option of translating *mišneh* "equivalent" rather than "double," as is shown by the use of the term elsewhere. Thus in the Hebrew bondservant legislation of Deut 15 the master is induced to fulfill the requirement to free such a servant in the seventh year by the reminder that during the six years he has received services equal in value (*mišneh*) to six years' wages of a hired servant (v. 18). Though *mišneh* is often translated "double" here, it is difficult to defend the implication that the bondservant would do twice as much work as a regular paid laborer.

Again, in the regulations governing the prospective king of Israel in Deut 17, *mišneh* denotes the "copy" of the Deuteronomic treaty, the covenant law that was to be prepared for the king from the original kept in the sanctuary (v. 18). This, like the two tables of the covenant at Sinai, reflects the practice in ancient treaty diplomacy of providing the vassal with a duplicate of the document while the suzerain retained his copy.[17]

[[177]] This clearly attested option of rendering *mišneh* as "equivalent" deserves the preference in both the passages in Jeremiah that would teach twofold punishment according to customary translations of *mišneh*. The threat

16. Similarly in the Ugaritic myths the lips of Mot, the god of death, are said to extend from heaven to earth, accommodating the host of victims demanded by his voracious appetite.

17. Similar to *mišneh* is the Akkadian term *mištannu* found in one of the Alalakh texts (AT.3), a treaty dealing with the extradition of runaway slaves. *Mištannu* denotes what the owner gives for the returned slave, the stipulated bounty, an appropriate payment in a *quid pro quo* arrangement.

presented to the apostates in Jer 16:18 is then simply that God "will repay them (with punishment) equivalent (*mišneh*) to their iniquity and sin." And the concluding plea in 17:18 is that the petitioner's foes should suffer destruction like that which they intended for him: "Destroy them with a matching (*mišneh*) destruction." So translated, this plea is in keeping with the request in the first part of the verse that the persecutors be dealt with according to the talion principle, the shame and terror they purposed for the petitioner befalling them.

Diploō/diplous in the New Testament

Revelation 18 contains a jubilant vision of God's judgment on the apostate harlot-city of Babylon. In the midst of it a voice from heaven, calling for vengeance on Babylon, clearly specifies that the judgment is to be executed according to the talion principle of punishment equal to the offense. "Give back to her as she has given (v. 6a). . . . Give her as much torture and grief as the glory and luxury she gave herself" (v. 7a).[18] In between the two quoted statements emphasizing proportionate recompense are two others (v. 6b, 6c) in which the relation of Babylon's punishment to its iniquity is denoted by *diploō/diplous*, customarily rendered "double (twofold)" here. Thus NIV: "Pay her back double for what she has done. Mix her a double portion from her own cup." But to translate "double" creates an unacceptable contradiction of the immediately preceding and following call for punishment commensurate with sin. In fact, the imagery of the cup in verse 6c itself seems to underscore the talion principle of equivalence. For it is in the very cup of the harlot's sin, the golden cup full of the wine of her fornication (cf. Rev 14:8; 17:4; 18:3), that her penal potion is to be administered. The idea of pouring her a double amount of punishment would be incongruous with this emphasis on the identity of the vessel of sin and of judgment. Indeed, since Babylon's cup is described as filled to the brim with her abominations (17:4), getting double that amount of punishment into the very same container would be quite a feat. We propose then that "equivalent" be substituted for "double" in the translation of verse 6b and 6c. How *diploō/diplous* acquired in New Testament usage the nuances of *kāpal/kepel* and *mišneh* is readily accounted for by the fact that they are employed to render these Hebrew words in the LXX. Properly translated, Rev 18:6 declares, consistently

18. NIV translation.

with its context, that Babylon's iniquities were to be balanced by their equal weight of punishment in God's scales of justice.

Our rendering of *diploō/diplous* in Rev 18:6 finds support in the two other New Testament appearances of these terms (actually *diplous* in both cases). [[178]] Matthew 23:15 presents one of a series of woes pronounced by Jesus against the scribes and Pharisees. Charging that they made of their proselyte a son of hell, Jesus institutes a comparison between proselytizer and proselyte in terms of that identification. The comparison is expressed by the comparative *diploteros*. If *diplous* means "double" here, the comparative form of the adjective must be ignored, for double is double—there is no such thing as more double. Hence the usual sleight-of-hand renderings "twofold more a son of hell than yourselves" or "twice as much a son of hell as you are." If, however, *diplous* means "matching image," the comparative form becomes more manageable. The idea then is that the proselyte takes on more fully than the Pharisees the likeness of a son of hell.

In 1 Tim 5:17 *diplous* describes the honor of which certain elders are to be considered worthy. The elders in view are those who rule well. If the term *malista* has its meaning of "specifically," the phrase it introduces specifies that these elders are those who labor in teaching the Word. If *malista* means "especially" here, a distinction is drawn between two groups of elders, and the due reception of the contemplated honor by those engaged in teaching is said to be a matter of special importance.

If *diplous* is translated "double," efforts to interpret the verse become problematic and speculative.[19] On the other hand if we translate *diplous* as "equivalent," the problems disappear. For it makes eminently good and simple sense to say that elders who perform their office well are deserving of matching (*diplous*) honor commensurate with their service. In Paul's corroborative observations in verse 18 the pay earned by a laborer illustrates the honor due the elders in verse 17, and this would point to a normal, commensurate (not extraordinary, double) measure of honor, honor matching the elders' labors.

---

19. If *diplous* means twice as much, a comparison is set up with a group that gets a single measure of honor. Since all who rule well are worthy of double honor, there would have to be a group (not mentioned in the verse) who failed to rule well, who would receive the regular amount of honor—a strange thought. To avoid it, "double" might be construed as two kinds of honor (like respect and remuneration) with no comparison made to a group of unsuccessful elders who received only one kind of honor. But the warrant is lacking for that meaning of *diplous*, and the notion of these two kinds of honor would be abrupt, isolated and speculative.

It appears then that the New Testament usage favors the translation of *diploō/diplous* in Rev 18:6 as "render the equivalent" (rather than "double"), and that removes the alleged teaching of a twofold divine retribution from this text too.

Conclusion

On closer scrutiny all the biblical data customarily cited as evidence of the teaching of a double divine punishment for sin dissolves with the discovery that the key Hebrew and Greek terms either never mean "double" or do not have that meaning in the relevant passages.

[[179]] Notice needs to be taken of the fact that in commentary on these texts one finds reference made, in supportive elaboration of the alleged notion of double punishment, to legislation in Exod 22:1, 4, 7, 9 [21:37; 22:3, 6, 8] that stipulates double (or more) payments in cases of theft. Though not directly inflicted by God, these penalties are divinely promulgated. Overlooked in such argument is the fact that two factors are involved in the double payment demanded of the thief: restitution as well as punishment. Return of the original amount is simply restoration. Only the second half of the double payment constitutes punishment, and thus, in keeping with the talion principle, the thief suffers a loss equivalent to that which he inflicted.[20]

Clearly articulated in biblical law, the talion principle of eye for eye and life for life is foundational to the temporal, human administration of justice as prescribed by God in Scripture for both the common-grace state[21] and the Israelite theocracy[22] as well as in the direct execution of judgment by the Lord himself.

---

20. When fourfold or fivefold payment is required (Exod 22:1), aggravation of the crime beyond simple theft is involved, and the additional penalty may be presumed to be commensurate in the divine assessment with the additional degree of guilt.

21. Gen 4:15; 9:6. Cf. Meredith G. Kline, "Oracular Origin of the State," in *Biblical and Near Eastern Studies*, ed. G. A. Tuttle (Grand Rapids: Eerdmans, 1978), 132–41 [= pp. 49–61 in the present volume].

22. Exod 21:23–25; Lev 24:18–21; Deut 19:21. Cf. Meredith G. Kline, "*Lex Talionis* and the Human Fetus," *JETS* 20 (1977): 193–201 [= pp. 93–102 in the present volume].

PART FOUR

Redemption

CHAPTER TEN

The Feast of Cover-over

(1994)

Avian Imagery and Deity

The first metaphor we meet with in the Bible likens the Creator-Spirit to a bird hovering over the deep-and-darkness (Gen 1:2). This same avian image is also a key feature in the Exod 12 account of the paschal event, but it has remained hidden behind the mistranslation of the crucial verb *pāsaḥ*. Not "pass over" but "hover over" is the meaning of this word, as the present essay hopes to demonstrate.

But before investigating *pāsaḥ*, as well as the noun *pesaḥ*, a bit more background on the use of avian imagery for deity. "You have seen what I did to the Egyptians, and how I bore you on eagles' wings and brought you to myself" (Exod 19:4). So the Lord described his guidance of Israel by the Glory-cloud at the exodus. Moses used this figure of the eagle and its young when reviewing these same historical realities in Deut 32:10–11. Significantly, in this Song of Moses God's shepherding of Israel through the wilderness by the theophanic cloud is depicted in the distinctive language of Gen 1:2: as a birdlike hovering (*rāḥap*) over the unstructured world (*tōhû*).[1]

Bird imagery suggested itself naturally for this Glory theophany. First, it was a cloud formation, and clouds and birds belong to the same sphere of the sky, across which they fly. Isaiah parallels the two: "Who are these that fly as a cloud and as doves to their windows?" (Isa 60:8). Also, protective overshadowing is provided alike by the outspread wings of birds (cf. Deut 32:11; Pss 17:8; 91:4) and by clouds (cf. Ps 105:39; Exod 40:35 LXX).

Second, an angelic retinue is integral to the Glory-cloud theophany, and angels also share in the celestial realm of clouds and birds, through which they too are said to fly (Isa 6:6; Dan 9:21; Rev 14:6). Hence in symbolic

1. This is one of numerous indications that the Glory-cloud is a manifestation of the Spirit in particular. For a full discussion of the Glory-Spirit theophany see *IOS*.

representation angelic beings are winged. Most relevant here are the figures of the cherubim guardians of the Glory-Presence in the Holy of Holies (Exod 25:20; 37:9; 1 Kgs 6:24, 27; 8:6–7) and the hosts of winged heavenly creatures seen attending the divine Glory in visionary revelations (Isa 6:2; Ezek 1:6ff.; 3:13; 10:4ff.; 11:22). It is on cherub wings that the Lord soars [[498]] (Ps 18:10 [11]; cf. 2 Sam 22:11). Understandably, then, it is especially the Glory-cloud theophany that attracts avian imagery in the Bible.

Outside the Bible, depiction of deity in avian fashion was common in ancient Near Eastern iconography and literature. Familiar is the use of bird emblems for gods in Egyptian religion. Indeed the hieroglyphic sign of the falcon of Horus on a standard was used as a determinative of gods. An important parallel to the Glory-theophany phenomena in the Bible is the widely attested motif of the winged sun-disk used to represent the divine majesty.[2] Of special significance for the interpretation of the paschal event in Exod 12 is the appearance of this winged symbol of divine glory on door lintels.[3] The entryway formed by such lintels together with their sideposts parallels the biblical gate-of-heaven formation constituted by the Glory-cloud canopy with its two columns (of smoke and fire) and by the cherubim-flanked Glory in the Holy of Holies.[4]

It is within this world of avian and portal symbolism that the meaning of the Lord's paschal act of salvation is to be sought.

The Lord as Avian Shield

Lexical Facts

Two Hebrew verbs, denoting totally different actions, tend to be confusingly blended in the current popular understanding of the Exod 12 event, the meaning of both being expressed as "pass over." The first step in apprehending the true nature of the event is to distinguish these two actions from each other and clarify their relation to one another.

One verb is *ʿābar*. "Pass over" is an acceptable translation for it. It is the word used when the Lord says he is going to go throughout (pass over or through) the land on a mission of judgment (Exod 12:12). Although God

2. Cf. G. E. Mendenhall, *The Tenth Generation: The Origins of the Biblical Tradition* (Baltimore: Johns Hopkins University Press, 1973), 32–56.

3. Cf. ibid., 49, figure 14.

4. Cf. *IOS*, 40.

is in an ultimate sense the subject of this judicial passing over the land, the immediate execution of judgment—the entering into the Egyptian houses and slaying of the firstborn—is attributed to a "destroyer." It is this figure, distinguishable from God (Exod 12:23b; cf. v. 13b), who passes over (*ʿābar*) Egypt. This destroyer would be an angelic agent of God, or even the messianic Angel of the Lord himself.[5] If the destroyer is the Angel of the Lord, the statements that God is the executor of the destructive blows (Exod 12:12, 13c, 23a, 29) find their explanation in the nature of this angel as one who, though distinguishable from God, is identified as God.

The Exod 12 narrative speaks of another action of God that stands in contrast to the destructive passing over the land. This other action is denoted by the second verb traditionally rendered "pass over"—namely, *pāsaḥ* (vv. 13b, 23b, 27b). What is clear is that the action denoted by *pāsaḥ* results in the sparing of the blood-marked Israelite homes from the curse of the
[[499]] tenth plague. The question is: What is the specific nature of this action? Is "pass over" an accurate translation of *pāsaḥ*?

According to the customary approach that renders *pāsaḥ* "pass over," God is viewed as himself the destroyer, and *pāsaḥ* pictures him as not descending in judgment on the houses of the Israelites but as passing over them, as moving harmlessly over and past them. Support for this rendering has been found in the existence of a Hebrew verb *pāsaḥ* that means "limp" (see 2 Sam 4:4),[6] with its related adjective meaning "lame" (see, e.g., 2 Sam 9:13; 19:26; Deut 15:21). On the assumption that *pāsaḥ* in Exod 12 represents this same verbal root, it is suggested that the picture there is of God hobbling or hopping over the spared houses.

That would be a lame metaphor indeed, and there is evidence of (not just another meaning of this verb but probably) another root *pāsaḥ* that yields a far more apt image for the Exod 12 context. To this I shall turn presently, after noting some further problems that beset the traditional interpretation.

One such difficulty is the equating of the destroyer, who passes through (*ʿābar*) the land, with the one who "passes over" (*pāsaḥ*) the Israelite houses. For though, as previously observed, the Lord God is referred to as the subject of the destructive passing through Egypt (either in terms of his being the ultimate author of this judgment or in terms of the divine identity of the destroying angel), nevertheless Exod 12:23 clearly distinguishes Yahweh as the one who performs the *pāsaḥ*-act from the destroyer. Explaining the

---

5. Cf. 2 Sam 24:16–17; 2 Kgs 19:35; Isa 37:36; 1 Chr 21:12ff.; 2 Chr 32:21; Ps 35:5–6.

6. 1 Kgs 18:21, 26 is usually regarded as another instance, but on this see below.

pāsaḥ-act this verse says: "(Yahweh) will not allow the destroyer to enter your houses to strike you." Whatever the precise meaning of *pāsaḥ*, the destroyer is plainly not the subject of the *pāsaḥ*-act.

Another problem for the traditional view is that the *pāsaḥ*-act relates specifically to the door of the house (Exod 12:23b; cf. vv. 13, 27), the door on whose lintel and posts the blood had been daubed. The precise purpose and effect of the Lord's *pāsaḥ*-act is to deny the destroyer access to that blood-marked entryway. *Pāsaḥ* does not denote the taking of a detour but the establishing of a deterrent, not God's bypassing of the house or hopping over the lintel but, on the contrary, his stationing himself squarely and immovably at the door. What the imagery demands is a shielding action—not a separating or distancing of God from the house but an abiding divine Presence, a divine encamping like a guardian at the gate.

A second root *pāsaḥ*, with a meaning that meets the contextual demands of Exod 12, is attested in Isa 31:5. *Pāsaḥ* plainly signifies there a protective action of some kind. Agreeably, "protect" was one of the ancient Jewish interpretations of *pāsaḥ* in Exod 12.[7]

[[500]] The indications in Isa 31:5 are that *pāsaḥ* denotes, more specifically, a sheltering action. In the perfectly balanced structure of the second half of the verse, *pāsaḥ* is one of a pair of infinitive absolutes and its parallel is *gānan*, "cover, shield." Still more precisely, this covering is likened to an action of birds. For the verb *gānan* that is paired with *pāsaḥ* in the second half of the verse resumes the *gānan* in the first half, where it is illustrated by the fluttering or hovering (*ʿûp*) of mother birds over their nests. *Pāsaḥ* is even more directly connected to this avian image if the verse overall is analyzed as a chiasm, with each of the two central lines containing the verb *gānan* and with *ʿûp* and *pāsaḥ* as counterparts in the matching outside lines:

> As birds hovering (*ʿûp*),
>   so Yahweh of hosts will cover (*gānan*) Jerusalem;
>   covering (*gānan*), he will deliver it,
> hovering (*pāsaḥ*), he will save it.

---

7. In the LXX two of the three instances of *pāsaḥ* in Exod 12 are translated "shelter" (*skepazō*, a verb used for a tree shading the earth), and evidence to the same effect is found in the targums and Old Latin. Occasionally, modern commentators have also challenged the now long-entrenched rendering of "pass over." Cf. T. E. Glasson, "The 'Passover', a Misnomer: The Meaning of the Verb *Pasach*," *JTS* 10 (1959): 79–84. Glasson addresses the question of when and how the "pass over" rendering (found in the Vulgate) took hold.

Isaiah 31:5 may well yield something more than evidence of a root *pāsaḥ* meaning "cover/hover over," for it seems to contain an allusion to the original paschal event. The context presents the irony of Israel's looking for help against the Assyrians not to the Lord but to Egypt, the house of bondage from which the Lord had of old redeemed them (vv. 1–3). In verse 4 there is the same aerial perspective as in the judicial passage over Egypt in the tenth plague: God descends from heaven and alights on Zion, encamping over the city for warfare against the attacker. The divine hovering mentioned in verse 5 would thus provide an explanation of God's *pāsaḥ*-action in the paschal episode of Exod 12, interpreting it as a bird-like shielding of his threatened people.

Further evidence of the root *pāsaḥ* meaning "hover over" may be found in one of the passages usually cited under *pāsaḥ*, "limp." Elijah's challenge to the people in 1 Kgs 18:21 has been translated: "How long go ye limping between the two sides?" (ASV) and "How long will you waver between two opinions?" (NIV). The preposition *ʿal*, "on, over," is problematic for translations of this verse requiring "between." Recognizing the difficulty, RSV translates, "How long will you go limping with two opinions?" Though "with" is attested for *ʿal*, the resultant picture is awkward at best. The noun rendered "opinions" is one of a cluster of derivatives from an assumed *sʿp*, "cleave, divide." For the most part the derivatives refer to branches of trees. In Ezek 31:6 the boughs are the nesting place of the birds of heaven. Once we give the verb *pāsaḥ* in 1 Kgs 18:21 its meaning of "hover, flutter," the better-attested meanings of the noun ("branches") and the preposition ("over" or "at")[8] fit perfectly and a convincingly appropriate metaphor is obtained: "How long will you go on hovering like a bird fluttering over two branches? Land on one bough or the other!"[9]

[[501]] A compatible explanation may be suggested for the *pāsaḥ* in 1 Kgs 18:26. It is usually taken as *pāsaḥ*, "limp," and understood as describing the Baal prophets as engaged in a conjectured limping dance alongside the altar. It is possible, however, that the mob of false prophets is pictured as fluttering in a frenzy all over the Baal altar—like the gods in the pagan Babylonian flood tradition who were attracted by the sweet aroma of the offering the flood hero was preparing in thanksgiving for his deliverance and who are said to have swarmed "like flies" over the sacrifice.[10]

---

8. On the use of the preposition *ʿal* with a door (Exod 12:23) cf. Job 31:9; Ezek 46:2.

9. This image of the fluttering bird that does not alight is also in Prov 26:2.

10. Cf. *Gilgamesh Epic* 11.161; *Atraḫasis* 3.5.35.

Contextual Factors

In the light of our findings concerning the verb *pāsaḥ*, the picture in Exod 12 is not one of God's passing over his people but of his coming to them and abiding with them through the dark night of judgment on Egypt. Like a hovering bird spreading its protective wings over its young, the Lord covered the Israelite houses, keeping watch over them. He was their gatekeeper, their guardian against the entrance of the angel of death.

This interpretation of the *pāsaḥ*-action is reinforced by certain contextual considerations. One has to do with the relationship between the act of deliverance from the destroyer and the prior act of expiation. The narrative spotlights the specific place where the sacrificial blood was to be smeared: doorframe, sideposts, lintel (Exod 12:7, 22–23). On the traditional view, no particular connection obtains between the *pāsaḥ*-action and the application of the expiatory blood to this specific location. But the selection of the doorframe as the locus of expiation finds its ready explanation when it is recognized that the *pāsaḥ*-act involved a divine protective presence at that very spot and consisted in a guardianship over that door (12:23). It speaks strongly in favor of the present interpretation that it provides for this mutually illuminating relationship between the saving *pāsaḥ*-action and the specific orientation of the sacrificial act that constituted its forensic basis.

There is another contextual factor that corroborates the shielding nature of the paschal action and its avian portrayal as well. It has to do with the Glory-cloud and specifically with the particular juncture in redemptive history where this form of Spirit-theophany emerged. The Glory-Spirit was present as a feature of the original theocratic order in Eden but withdrew from the fallen world. Then in the days of Moses this form of theophany reappeared, marking the coming of God's theocratic kingdom on earth after its long abeyance during the patriarchal ages.[11] It is at the exodus episode that the biblical narrative introduces the pillars of cloud and fire, the supernatural means by which God led Israel by the way of the wilderness by the Red Sea (Exod 13:21–22; cf. vv. 17–20). Coming immediately before this departure of Israel and serving as a prelude and preparation for it, the paschal event of Exod 12 will most naturally have involved this same divine Presence.

11. See further *KP*, 369–72.

[[502]] Now if the Glory-Spirit, so congenial to avian metaphor,[12] is the divine Presence in the paschal event, this will be what prompted[13] the narrator's use of *pāsaḥ*, "hover over." Also, in view of the fact that overshadowing is a characteristic function of the Glory-cloud,[14] the interpretation of the paschal action as such a protective covering is strengthened by the identification of the Glory-Spirit as the subject of that action.

Moreover, if the Glory-Spirit is the divine actor as early in the exodus history as Exod 12, further credence is lent to our understanding of the *pāsaḥ*-action as a divine guardianship against the destroyer by the strikingly similar role played by the Glory-Spirit in the sequel recorded in Exod 14. It is another night scene, and again the Israelites are under threat of destruction, this time by the pharaoh's pursuing forces. But the pillar of cloud takes up a position behind them, coming between the camp of Egypt and the camp of Israel so that the one does not come near the other all night (vv. 19–20).[15] In this episode, as in the paschal event, the Lord takes his place with his people, stationing himself in such a way as to block the approach of the destroying power. If the Glory-Spirit we see guarding Israel in Exod 14 is the divine actor in Exod 12, it is quite natural that we should find him performing the same function there, as is the case on our interpretation of the paschal event.

Or, turning the matter around, to the extent that it can be shown independently of the evidence for the presence of the Glory-Spirit that the paschal event was a divine guarding of Israel, the resultant twin character of the Exod 12 and 14 events argues compellingly that the Glory-Spirit is indeed the divine actor in Exod 12 as he is explicitly in Exod 14.

There is an important difference between these two formally matching events, which, however, brings out a deeper connection between them. Exodus 12 records a deliverance from the wrath of God; Exod 14, from the

12. See the first section of this article ("Avian Imagery and Deity"), and note the dove manifestation of the Spirit at Jesus' baptism (Matt 3:16; Mark 1:10; Luke 3:22; John 1:32).

13. If, as will be maintained below, the choice of *pāsaḥ* was a consequence of the desire to pun on the noun *pesaḥ*, it might be better to say the presence of the Glory-Spirit contributed to rather than prompted the use of *pāsaḥ*.

14. Again see the first section above, noting also Isa 4:5–6 and the episodes of Jesus' conception (Luke 1:35) and transfiguration (Matt 17:5; Mark 9:7; Luke 9:34).

15. On this occasion the Angel of the Lord does not pose the threat against which the Glory-Presence guards but rather acts in concert with the cloud theophany (Exod 14:19). Together, the Angel and Glory-Spirit perform the dual functions of delivering God's people and destroying the Egyptians (Exod 14:21ff., esp. v. 24).

enmity of the pharaoh, the dragon figure representative of Satan's cause. From the efficacy of the divine shielding against the death angel, agent of the divine wrath, the Israelites were to draw assurance that this same divine guardianship would keep them safe in the hour of the pharaoh's terrible assault.

Jesus, as the paschal lamb who interposes himself between the wrath of God and those who are his own, who while on earth was their Paraclete guardian from the evil one (John 17:12, 15), promised during his last paschal commemoration with them that he would send them another Paraclete [[503]] defender to be present with them forever (John 14:16), even the Spirit, the one who was the Paraclete presence and covering guardian of God's people in the original paschal event. And if God be thus for us, who can be against us? (Rom 8:31).

The Lord as Arboreal Shelter

Pāsaḥ *and* pesaḥ: *Paronomasia*

Along with the verb *pāsaḥ*, the noun *pesaḥ* first appears in the Exod 12 narrative. It is customarily assumed that this noun, used only with reference to the paschal event and its commemorative feast, stems from the verbal root *pāsaḥ*. Thus, on the further assumption that *pāsaḥ* means "pass over," *pesaḥ* is usually rendered "passover." On the view of the verb adopted here, the noun would mean "a covering" or (more abstractly) "protection."

If the noun and verb are cognate, it is certainly better to regard the noun as derived from the verb rather than to regard the verb as a denominative from a noun not known apart from the paschal context. Exodus 12:27 supports this conclusion, for whether the *ʾăšer* in this verse is taken as "who" or "because," it is Yahweh's *pāsaḥ*-act that is immediately cited in explication of the *pesaḥ*-sacrifice. Likewise it is the *pāsaḥ*-act in Exod 12:13 that explains the term *pesaḥ* in verse 11c.

But though Exod 12:13, 27 explain *pesaḥ* in terms of *pāsaḥ*, that does not necessarily mean that the two words are cognate. There is also the possibility that this is a play on words. An obscure word may be introduced into an account and be explained by a pun, using a known word with similar sound and appropriate meaning. A familiar example is Gen 11:9. It tells us that the Shinar tower site bore the name Babel because the Lord there "confounded" (*bālal*) the language of the builders. But according to cuneiform renderings (themselves possibly popular etymology) *bābel* means "gate of god." So in Exod 12 it is possible that a non-Hebrew noun, *pesaḥ*, was chosen to designate the event (and its memorial feast) and that its significance was conveyed by use of the similar-sounding Hebrew verb *pāsaḥ*.

Favoring the paronomasia rather than cognate view is the unlikelihood that a noun would be created from so uncommon a verb as *pāsaḥ* to serve as the name of a notable festival. It is more likely that the unusual verb would have suggested itself in the search for a word that would qualify as a pun on the previously adopted noun *pesaḥ*. Admittedly, it might not be thought much more probable that a foreign term would be chosen as the designation for this Israelite festival in the first place. But on balance that seems to be the more plausible option, at least if a foreign word can be found that fits just right.[16]

Egyptian Etymology

The historical situation of Exod 12 points to Egypt as the most promising source for such an investigation. Various [[504]] possibilities from the Egyptian lexicon have in fact been proposed. They have in common the understanding that the first syllable in *pesaḥ* represents the Egyptian definite article *pꜣ* (attested in the Eighteenth Dynasty and regularly from Late Egyptian on). Noteworthy among such studies is that of B. Couroyer.[17] He discusses several Egyptian words that would satisfy the transcriptional parameters, deciding in favor of *śḫ*, "blow," seen as a reference to the tenth plague, the context of Israel's deliverance. One obvious objection preventing popular acceptance of this proposal is that we expect that the festival commemorating the great paschal salvation would be named after the act of deliverance itself rather than the circumstance that occasioned it.

Omitted in Couroyer's survey is an option for which a more convincing case can be made. It is a word that satisfies the semantic qualifications for a pun relationship to the verb *pāsaḥ*, as required by Exod 12:11, 13, 27. Hence to demonstrate that Hebrew *pesaḥ* represents this Egyptian noun will do two things: it will yield the meaning of *pesaḥ*, and it will at the same time confirm the "cover/hover over" meaning of the verb *pāsaḥ*, used to explain *pesaḥ*.

16. If the meaning of the noun *pesaḥ* can be discovered independently of *pāsaḥ*, this will elucidate the meaning of the verb, even though in Exod 12 their functional relationship is the reverse.

17. B. Couroyer, "L'origine égyptienne du mot 'Pâque,'" *RB* 72 (1955): 481–96.

The Egyptian word is *sḥ*, "arbor, booth," and with the definite article, *pꜣ sḥ*, "the booth." Its determinative sign (which may also serve as an ideogram without the phonetic symbols) delineates the front face or entry of a simple overarching structure with a central supporting pole. Such a covert is the perfect nominal equivalent of the kind of protective covering action denoted by the verb *pāsaḥ*. Arboreal booth connotes the overshadowing function attributed to the Glory-cloud, which was the particular divine Presence in the paschal event. It suggests too the avian image of the overspreading wings of the cherubim guardians of the Glory-Presence.[18] Here then in the *sḥ*-booth of the paschal story would be the model for Scripture's familiar and favorite concept of the Lord God as our refuge, our dwelling place in all generations. So central was this to covenant religion that, as it would now appear, Israel's cycle of feasts was bracketed, spring and autumn, by feasts of booths.[19]

The determinative sign of *sḥ* provides a point of contact with another key feature of the paschal episode in that it portrays not just a booth but the entry face of the structure. For this corresponds to the focal paschal motif of the smearing of the expiatory blood on the entryway. Inclusion of the tent-pole in the determinative sign takes on interest in view of the observation by R. de Vaux that in a springtime sacrifice offered by seminomads (with which commentators have compared various details of the paschal ritual in Exod 12) the blood was put on the tent-poles and later on doorposts.[20]

[[505]] A further link between *pesaḥ* and Egyptian *sḥ* is that both are used in combination with a term for deity. On the Egyptian side is the lexical item *sḥ-nṯr*, "booth of deity, shrine." This is written with the sign (used as either ideogram or determinative) depicting the front elevation of a shrine plus the emblem of divinity. On the biblical side, *pesaḥ* is described repeatedly in Exod 12 as belonging to Yahweh (vv. 11, 27, 48) and is explained in terms of Yahweh's *pāsaḥ*-action (vv. 11–13, 27). The precise force of *lyhwh* depends on whether *pesaḥ* refers to the original event, the feat of covering, or to the subsequent commemorative feast. *Pesaḥ* as an accomplishment

18. Especially the "arbor" meaning of *sḥ* would carry avian associations.

19. Curiously, their designations, *sḥ* and *skwt*, would exhibit assonance.

20. R. de Vaux, *Ancient Israel: Its Life and Institutions* (New York: McGraw-Hill, 1961), 489. T. H. Gaster notes the widespread custom of the erection of sacred trees, sometimes with apotropaic fleeces attached, in spring rituals celebrating the resurrection of the year. One example is the Egyptian festival in which the *djed*-column was raised, representing the resurrection of Osiris (*Thespis: Ritual, Myth, and Drama in the Ancient Near East*, rev. ed. [Garden City, NY: Doubleday, 1961], 313).

is attributed to Yahweh as author, whether the covering is viewed as that which he performs by his personal Presence (vv. 13, 27) or that which he provides by sovereign appointment (i.e., the sacrificial lamb whose blood covers the door, v. 21). Indeed, insofar as Yahweh performs the covering feat by sheltering over the houses himself the *pesaḥ* belongs to him in the sense that he virtually is the *pesaḥ*. When *pesaḥ* refers to the ordinance that is to be kept in perpetuity (vv. 43, 48) *lyhwh* indicates that the feast with its offerings belongs to Yahweh as a remembrance of him to be observed in his honor (see, e.g., Lev 23:5; 2 Chr 30:1, 5; cf. Exod 13:6; Lev 23:6, 34; Deut 16:10). There are aspects of this complex of ideas that we shall want to reflect on further below, but the point at present is simply that the recurring combination of *pesaḥ* with *lyhwh* appears to be a reflection of *sḥ-nṯr* and so supports the proposed Egyptian etymology of *pesaḥ*.

Additional correspondences appear between *sḥ-nṯr* and important elements in the paschal narrative. Above we remarked on the biblical account's emphatic focus on the doorframe as the place of expiatory covering and as the station of the divine Coverer. While the determinative of *sḥ* does depict the front face of the booth, the entry area, the determinative of *sḥ-nṯr* reflects the architectural focus on the Exodus account more specifically, for prominent in the shrine façade (its hieroglyphic sign) is the actual doorframe. In fact the façade is essentially an expanded doorframe.

The correspondence of these Egyptian and Israelite "booths of deity" extends beyond their shared focus on the doorway to the fact that this entrance is in each case the site of cultic ritual. In Exod 12 it is precisely the cultic act of daubing the blood of the *pesaḥ* sacrifice on the doorposts and lintel that sets the entrance door in the center focus of the event. Similarly there are Egyptian offering texts that speak of the offerings being presented at the face or front (*ḫnty*) of the *sḥ-nṯr*. Indeed it was on the doors and lintels of *sḥ-nṯr* structures that these formulaic offering texts were written.[21]

Still another feature of the paschal situation parallels the doorframe motif of the *sḥ-nṯr*. As observed above, the cherubim-flanked Glory formation [[506]] of the paschal Presence was conceptualized as a doorframe, more specifically as the gate of heaven.

The parallelism with the *sḥ-nṯr* goes beyond a correspondence in various details and involves a formal equivalence in overall structural identity. For inasmuch as the divine Presence was itself the *pesaḥ*-covering, this

21. A. Gardiner, *Egyptian Grammar* (London: Oxford University Press, 1964), 170–71.

pesaḥ was a divine *pesaḥ*, a booth of God, a *sḥ-nṯr*. And so too each Israelite house, sanctified by the enveloping divine covering, was a *sḥ-nṯr*, a divine sanctuary-booth.

Along such lines the case can be made to explain the biblical *pesaḥ* as Egyptian *pꜣ sḥ*. But why this *ad hoc* appropriation of an Egyptian term? Would no Hebrew word do? Perhaps *sḥ* was more suitable than Hebrew *sukkâ*, "booth," because the Egyptian term, especially in the form *sḥ-nṯr*, could refer to the more substantial structures involved in the original paschal event—that is, the Israelite houses transformed into shrines. Another advantage of *sḥ-nṯr* over *sukkâ* is that it connoted, particularly through its hieroglyphic determinative, the doorframe in the front elevation, which was so prominent in the Exod 12 episode.[22] A Hebrew term that would denote that front façade is *pānîm*, "face." It is used in the description of Ezekiel's temple (Ezek 41:14; cf. v. 21), which mentions as part of "the face of the house" the doorposts (41:21) and as part of the entrance of the house "the lintel" (47:1).[23] But façade was a secondary meaning of *pānîm*. Moreover *pānîm* would not convey the requisite basic idea of covering. In the last analysis, however, the strength of the case for the Egyptian etymology is not the lack of a fully satisfactory Hebrew term but the compelling character of the remarkable reverberations and resonances between the Egyptian *sḥ-nṯr* and the whole complex of phenomena in the paschal event.

Sepulchral Sanctuary

There is another point of correspondence that supplements the evidence for our proposed etymology of *pesaḥ*. But it is adduced here primarily by way of indicating how awareness of the Egyptian source may sharpen our perception of the paschal event.

The Egyptian offering formulae in which the *sḥ-nṯr* was mentioned as the site of the ritual were funerary texts. The doors and lintels on which they were written were in mortuary structures. The gods who are referred to in the texts as the givers of the boon or (later) as recipients thereof are chthonic deities.[24] The *sḥ-nṯr* was thus a tomb shrine.

22. If *sḥ* figured in the name of an Egyptian spring festival familiar to the Israelites during their long sojourn there, that would help to account for the adoption of the foreign term for their paschal feast.

23. For this translation of *miptān* see *IOS*, 40 n. 32.

24. Cf. Gardiner, *Egyptian Grammar*, 171.

Correspondingly, houses of death fill the scene in the drama of the *pesaḥ lyhwh* in Exod 12. Every house in Egypt was turned into a house of death that night (12:30, 33). Most literally, the house of the pharaoh, residence of a divine king according to Egyptian ideology, became a funerary *sḥ-nṯr*. And is that not what the Israelite houses became also, marked as they were with [[507]] the blood of the lamb? The verb used to denote the destroyer (*šāḥaṭ*) is the one used for the killing of the lamb (12:21). Its death was the equivalent of the judgment death inflicted on the Egyptian firstborn. By the striking[25] of the lamb's blood on the Israelite houses they were stamped with the sign of death. They were rendered houses of death, houses that had experienced the divine judgment. Each such house was, like the Egyptian *sḥ-nṯr*, a tomb shrine—but with an extraordinary redemptive twist.

This death-signifying blood—that is, the lamb slain—was at the same time the *pesaḥ*, the covering that protected from the death stroke. The antecedent of *pesaḥ* in Exod 12:11a is the lamb, the subject of verses 3–10. And again, the reference in the command to "kill the *pesaḥ*" (v. 21) is clearly to the lamb. To ask how the slain lamb can represent at once the death judgment of God inflicted and a protective shielding from that blow is to inquire into the judicial heart of the gospel of justification by grace. The answer lies in the nature of the death judgment suffered by the lamb. It was a vicarious, expiatory act of sacrifice, a suffering of divine wrath in the stead of others, so providing them with a place of refuge from that wrath passing over the world.

The wonder of grace deepens when we recall that by reason of his personal Presence hovering (*pāsaḥ*) over the Israelite houses, the Lord himself was their shielding shelter (*pesaḥ*). The lamb is the *pesaḥ* and the Lord is the *pesaḥ*. Both are true because the Lord becomes the lamb. And John bore witness to Jesus, the Word become flesh, the one who was before him, his Lord, and said, "Behold the lamb of God that takes away the sin of the world" (John 1:29). The Lord shielded his people from his own wrath by himself intercepting the death angel's thrust as he stood guard at the door of their dwellings.

By virtue of their Lord-lamb covering, the Israelite house tombs were sanctuary sepulchres, places of refuge in which those redeemed by the blood of the lamb were sealed until the night of judgment had passed. Though a sign of death, the blood on the doorframe was an emblem of salvation, for it

---

25. The application of the blood to the doorframe is described by the verb *nāga*^{c}, from which is derived the noun *nega*^{c} used in Exod 11:1; 12:13 for the plague of slaying the firstborn. The noun is explicated in 12:13 by *šāḥaṭ*. On *nāga*^{c} cf. Gen 12:17; 32:25 [26]; Isa 6:7; 53:4, 8.

was the blood of a triumphant sacrifice. The offerings that were the subject of the Egyptian notices on the mortuary lintels were imagined to be a contribution to the ongoing life of the deceased. In a formally similar fashion the paschal blood on the lintels of the *sḥ-nṯr* dwellings of the Israelites also spoke of life beyond death, but this word of promise was the word of the living God, their God, he who is not the God of the dead but of the living. The lamb's blood on these sanctuary tombs presaged their becoming empty tombs in the morning. Their blood-covered doors would be opened and their redeemed occupants would emerge as the children of the resurrection day.

An unmistakable allusion to these paschal sanctuary tombs is found in Isaiah's celebration of God's resurrection victory over death. He prophesies of that day when the Lord will come to punish the inhabitants of the earth [[508]] for their iniquity and to slay the leviathan, the monster in the sea—not Egypt's pharaoh this time, but the dragon with the power of death (Isa 26:21–27:1). In that day death itself, the last enemy, will be vanquished. The insatiable swallower will be swallowed (25:8). The covering shroud that covers all the nations (25:7) will be removed and no more cover the dead (26:21b). In light of that resurrection prospect the grave is transformed. For God's martyr-people it becomes a refuge into which they are welcomed: "Come, my people, enter into thy chambers and shut the doors about thee; hide thyself for a little moment until the indignation pass over (*ʿābar*)" (26:20).[26] Like the blood-smeared house tombs of the Israelites, the realm of death is for the saints of the Lord a safe sanctuary, a passage to heaven. For those who sleep in Jesus, the souls under the altar (Rev 6:9), the living Lord is their covering in death, their *pesaḥ*-covert.

Hover Over and Cover-over

We have determined that the noun *pesaḥ* means "the booth," and this corroborates our other conclusion that the verb *pāsaḥ* in Exod 12 means "hover/cover over." A question of English translation, however, arises with respect to the *pesaḥ*-feast. If we translate "the Feast of the Booth," we fail to distinguish it clearly from the autumnal Feast of Booths. In the Hebrew

26. Isaiah 26:20 also reflects God's sealing of the Noahic remnant in the ark, as in a sanctuary tomb that would be a refuge for them until the judgment passed over the earth and the covering of the ark was removed. For a discussion of the Isaiah context see Meredith G. Kline, "Death, Leviathan, and the Martyrs: Isaiah 24:1–27:1," in *A Tribute to Gleason Archer*, ed. W. C. Kaiser Jr. and R. F. Youngblood (Chicago: Moody, 1986), 229–49 [= pp. 217–37 in the present volume].

text the use of two different terms for booth, *pesaḥ* and *sukkâ*, obviates the problem. We might similarly use some synonym of booth, like hut, for the spring feast. But a truly successful translation will want to bring out, if possible, the paronomasia of *pesaḥ* and *pāsaḥ*. It would also be an advantage if a suggested new name for this feast would connect with, even while correcting, the traditional "Passover." "Feast of Cover-over," however odd its ring, would at least satisfy these desiderata. It shares the terminal "over" with "Passover." And it captures the *pesaḥ-pāsaḥ* pun, thus: the feast was called Cover-over because there the Lord hovered over his people.

Paschal Paradigm

Further confirmation of our conclusions concerning both *pāsaḥ* and *pesaḥ* is afforded by certain canonical echoes of the paschal event. These are later passages in which the paschal incident is used as a metaphorical model for subsequent redemptive realities and that include the motif of divine sheltering. To the extent that such a passage is distinctly allusive to the Exod 12 record, its inclusion of the concept of God's overshadowing presence may be fairly regarded as an interpretive reflection of *pāsaḥ/pesaḥ* in the original paschal episode. A pair of such echoes, one from the Old Testament and one from the New Testament, may serve as a suggestive sampling.[27]

[[509]] The use of avian imagery in Ps 91 for God's watch care over his people (vv. 1, 4) is one of this psalm's similarities to the Song of Moses in Deut 32, where, as noted above, that metaphor refers to the overshadowing Glory-cloud at the exodus.[28] The mention of angels as agents of the divine guardianship in verses 11–12 reinforces the avian metaphor. This theme of God as a secure dwelling, refuge and shield opens and governs the psalm (vv. 1–2, 4, 9). The perils from which Yahweh protects his own (vv. 3–10) recall the plagues on Egypt, especially the last night of judgment: ten thousand fall at the side of God's people, but the plague does not come near their dwelling, as the Lord sovereignly directs the activity of angels during the night of terror. Since Ps 91 thus depicts the redemptive covenant relation as an extended paschal experience, its dominant motif—God's birdlike

27. For other examples of such later illuminating allusions see the discussion of Isa 26:20ff. and 31:5 above.

28. Book 4 of the Psalter, especially Pss 90–100, has been identified as a "Moses book" reflective of the exodus and wilderness experiences. Cf. M. E. Tate, *Psalms 51–100*, WBC 20 (Dallas: Word, 1990), xxvi.

overshadowing presence—will be an expository reflection on the paschal role of the Lord denoted by *pāsaḥ/pesaḥ*.

As is generally recognized, the disasters threatened in the various judgment series in the book of Revelation are adaptations of the ten plagues on Egypt. The diptych vision of Rev 7 presents, first, the protection of God's elect in the midst of earthly calamities (vv. 1–8), and then the continuation of this condition of security into the eternal state (vv. 9–17). As in the paschal-exodus history, the plagues are inflicted through angelic agency (vv. 1–3). The church is delineated under the form of the covenant community in Egypt, the twelve tribes of Israel (vv. 4–8; cf. Exod 1:1–5). Moreover the muster of the tribes in Rev 7 echoes the military imagery of Exod 12, which speaks of the twelve tribes setting out on their journey as armies (vv. 17, 41, 51).[29] Identification of the church in glory as those who have experienced an exodus[30] out of great tribulation (v. 14a) recalls Israel's severe oppression in the Egyptian house of bondage.[31] By the application of the paschal blood as a seal to the lintels and doorposts, the Israelites were marked off as exempt from judgment. Likewise the putting of the seal of God on the foreheads[32] of the 144,000 preserves them from the four angels with power to harm land and sea (Rev 7:2–3; cf. 9:4). As a result of the paschal presence of God, forensically grounded in the expiation accomplished by the lamb, the Israelite *pesaḥ*-house was transformed from tomb shrine to sanctuary from wrath, with promise of resurrection victory over the grave. Similarly the redeemed of the Lamb in Rev 7 are assured that the Lord will wipe away all tears from their eyes (v. 17), a prospect always associated with the elimination of death (cf. 21:4; Isa 25:8; 65:19). Otherwise stated, the Lamb-shepherd will guide them to the [[510]] waters of life in the heavenly paradise (v. 17a; cf. 21:6; 22:1–2, 17) as he, the Angel of the Presence, led the exodus generation on to the earthly paradise of Canaan.

In short, Rev 7 represents a remarkably comprehensive and detailed echo of the paschal episode.[33] And inevitably at the heart of it is the declara-

29. The listing of Judah first in Rev 7:5 might be due, at least in part, to the lead position of the tribe of Judah in the march of conquest (Num 10:14).

30. The verb in Rev 7:14a, *erchomai ek*, reflects the use of *exerchomai* in the climactic summation of the paschal triumph (Exod 12:41 LXX).

31. Cf. Exod 4:31 (LXX), which, like Rev 7:14a, uses *thlipsis*.

32. For the symbolic equivalence of forehead and lintel in the matching models of the tabernacle/temple architecture and the high priest's vestments see *IOS*, 44–45.

33. It is understandable that features from the twin autumnal Feast of Booths should be interwoven (Rev 7:9).

tion that God spreads his tent over the white-robed multitude (v. 15; cf. Rev 21:3; Isa 4:5). Covered by the cosmic canopy of Glory, they are the fulfillment of the typological pattern of the Israelites under the overshading theophanic cloud (Rev 7:16; cf. Isa 4:6). The covering presence of God in Rev 7:15 is the eschatological antitype of the central reality of the paschal event, the Lord's *pāsaḥ*-act of spreading his wings as a sheltering cover (*pesaḥ*) over those sealed by the blood of the lamb.

At Golgotha, where the true paschal Lamb was slain, the sovereign ordering of God arranged a reproduction of the typological paschal scene of the doorway smeared with the blood of the lamb. This new doorway involved a great redemptive irony. To Jesus belonged the Glory of the Father. His proper place was the throne above the ark, above the lintel of that gate of heaven, with the holy cherubim on either side framing the entrance with golden splendor. At Golgotha the cherubim were replaced by two criminals crucified with him, on either side one, the vertical posts of their crosses the sideposts of this new paschal doorframe. And in the center, on the horizontal beam of Jesus' cross, the lintel of this doorway, was posted his indictment. No epiphany of glory for him here—rather, the epitome of scorn.

Yet even the indictment on the lintel proclaimed in spite of itself the proper majesty of the Lord-lamb: "King of the Jews." Though the Golgotha entryframe, stained by his blood, was a place of death, a sepulchral entryway, the tomb of the paschal victim was opened. And he came forth as the paschal firstfruits from the dead, the Easter victor, the Lord of life. The paschal door of Calvary proves to be the very gate of heaven. All who are called and come are welcomed there into the true and heavenly *sḥ-nṯr* to abide forever under the shadow of the Almighty.

CHAPTER ELEVEN

Trial by Ordeal

(1985)

Investigation of the juridical dimension of the book of Job has intensified of late, stimulated perhaps by current interest in legal aspects of Old Testament literature in general. Several dissertations are among the studies of this subject produced during the last decade.[1] Moving beyond the earlier recognition of forensic phraseology as a metaphor occasionally used by the various speakers in Job, some of the more recent studies find that judicial patterns are detectable in the form of the book. Such form-critical analysis may even reach the conclusion that not merely an individual section here and there but the central literary structure of the book exhibits a lawsuit form. Even where that is so, however, there seems to be little inclination to bring into the picture the juridical data found in the prologue of Job.

If we extend the analysis back into the prologue, we discover there a more ultimate level of legal conflict behind the judicial confrontation of God and Job that unfolds from the third chapter onwards. The present study will be concerned with the specific character of the judicial strife that emerges in the prologue—the controversy between God and Satan—and with its relationship to the subsequent lawsuit between God and Job. To have a grasp of this matter is to have the key to a satisfactory understanding of the fundamental meaning and message of the book of Job.

In this "drama," as we shall see, the scene itself is all-important. How the legal conflict finally turns out is already implicit in the setting in which it takes place. The court of heaven, where the conflict first erupts, continues to be the setting for the action throughout. Though it is not always the foreground of

1. Cf. G. Many, "Der Rechtsstreit mit Gott (*Rîb*) im Hiobbuch" (PhD diss., Katholisch-Theologische Fakultät der Ludwig-Maximilian Universität, Munich, 1970); S. H. Scholnick, "Lawsuit Drama in the Book of Job" (PhD diss., Brandeis University, 1975); M. B. Dick, "Job 31: A Form-critical Study" (PhD diss., Johns Hopkins University, 1977).

the story and is not even continuously unveiled to our view, the scene of Yahweh's enthronement as Judge of all the earth remains the constant background of all that transpires. The judicial scene of the heavenly council, eternally sovereign [[82]] and unshakably permanent, is the fixed panoramic backdrop behind the temporal stage properties in the changing foreground.

There at the throne of heaven the Adversary was obliged to present himself to hear the King set the bounds of his existence and freedom (Job 1:7). It was the Lord who initiated the battle by a self-glorifying, challenging claim: "Hast thou considered my servant Job . . . a perfect and an upright man, one that feareth God . . . ?" (Job 1:8). In effect, God was telling Satan that the ancient curse pronounced against him in Eden (Gen 3:14, 15) was in process of inexorable fulfillment: out of mankind in its covenant of death with the devil God was reconciling to himself a new mankind, called to engage in holy war against the Serpent and promised in that warfare an ultimate absolute triumph. In the land of Uz lived a man who was, the Lord maintained, clear evidence that the promise of his primordial decree was sure and its word of doom on the devil certain. Let Satan behold this trophy of divine redemptive grace, this true and faithful servant of the Lord, and admit that the enmity of the woman's seed against him had been effected, that their covenant with death had been annulled and their covenant with God renewed.

Challenged to confess the Lord's redemptive power and to acknowledge as the corollary of that his own inevitable destruction, Satan refused. Turning accuser instead, he called in question the genuineness of Job's religious commitment, thereby denying God's power to set free the captives of hell (Job 1:9). Worse, Satan in effect charged the Judge himself with deceit and fraud (Job 1:10). Blasphemy flung at the very throne of God invited fearful retribution, but Satan is aware of the times and seasons. Contradictory spirit that he is, he must have recognized in the secret abyss of his being the infallibility of the decree declared in Eden, even while he publicly branded it an empty lie. He would, therefore, realize that his destined doom must be delayed until that particular seed of the woman who should engage him in the climactic battle had visited the earth in the fullness of time. He was accordingly prepared to meet any sign of premature judgment with the prayer he teaches his demonic disciples to pray: "Art thou come hither to torment us before the time?" (cf. Matt 8:29).

Meanwhile, Satan pressed this advantage (this boon of delayed doom) to his disadvantage by precipitating a struggle with the Almighty that could only speed forward the redemptive movement he denied towards the dreaded time of his own final torments. He proposed that God's claims concerning Job be put to the test (Job 1:11). And the Lord granted permission to Satan to begin the trial by ordeal. For such it was. The legal dispute that had arisen between them in the divine assembly was to be settled by resort to combat designed to demonstrate whose power actually prevailed in the life of Job.

In the ancient world the judicial impasse resulting from lack of evidence or [[83]] conflicting testimony might be resolved by an appeal to the gods. One could make such appeal by oath, exposing oneself to the oath-deity's curse on false witnesses. Dread of the curse would deter the guilty from taking the oath and his silence would betray and condemn him.[2] Insofar as an oath contemplates direct revelation of the divine verdict in an external act of judgment, it falls into the category of trial by ordeal.

A more spectacular form of this judicial procedure went beyond mere verbal description of the oath-curse or even the symbolic dramatization of the curse that frequently accompanied the oath. It prescribed a physical ordeal, pitting the oath-taker against some element which the deity would employ to punish the perjurer. A familiar example was the river ordeal, of special interest because it was part of the symbolic tradition behind the new covenant sign of baptism.[3]

Even more spectacular than an individual's undergoing of an ordeal by means of an impersonal power, like water or fire, was the technique of ordeal by combat, which required the legal opponents to face one another in a duel of some kind. A biblical illustration of this sort of thing is the judicial contest between Aaron and Korah's two hundred and fifty related in Num 16 and 17. All the disputants, censers with burning incense in hand, presented themselves before the Lord at the entrance of the tent of meeting to see whom he would choose for his holy service. And Yahweh, God of ordeal judgment, revealed his verdict against Aaron's challengers in earthquake

2. For the biblical practice see Exod 22:11 [10]; 1 Kgs 8:31, 32; cf. Exod 20:7; Eccl 9:2; Heb 6:16. This cultic-judicial procedure is reflected in psalms that contain protestations of innocence and appeals for the heavenly Judge to rise up in judgment for the suppliant (e.g., Pss 7:3ff. [4ff.]; 17:1ff.; 26:1ff.).

3. Cf. *BOC*, 55–60. In Israelite legal praxis the procedure is clearly illustrated by the jealousy ordeal of Num 5:11–31. The similarity between the judicial techniques of Israel and other ancient nations is informative, but there was, of course, an essential difference too: while the effectiveness of the technique elsewhere lay in psychological conditioning by subjective factors, in Israel the living Lord, the God of creation and history, was pleased to render his judgment through the ordeal medium in accordance with the terms he had appointed.

and fire, subsequently confirming his choice of Aaron in the supplementary contest of the budding rod. From outside the Bible another example of resort to combat to settle a dispute over a position of leadership is found in a mythological Egyptian text which is concerned with contention over the inheritance of the divine kingship of Osiris. The claimants are Horus, the son of Osiris, and the evil Seth, brother of Osiris. The struggle takes place in the presence of the divine tribunal, the Ennead. Before judgment is at very long last given in favor of Horus, the two rivals engage each other in a boat race, which quickly degenerates into a [[84]] novel sort of naval battle, and in a variety of other combat-ordeals.[4]

In the controversy between God and Satan over the question of Job's religious allegiance, the ordeal was in a sense an individual one for Satan. He had to encounter the ordeal power of God the Judge in the specific form of God's redemptive might at work in the life of Job. Satan must try to undo what God claimed to have done in Job—or make it appear that it had never been done in the first place. Viewed from this perspective, the strange fact emerges that as Satan stalked the saint of God, trying his soul, the tempter was himself under trial. Or, stated in terms of the general experience of the people of God, the history of the church is the arena of the devil's trial by ordeal.

But since Satan had in reality directed charges against the Lord as well as Job, the Lord was one of the litigants in this case. Because of this dual role of the Lord as Judge and litigant, for Satan to struggle to prevail over the ordeal power of the divine Judge, the God of the ordeal, was at the same time to enter into personal combat against the one who was his legal adversary. In this lawsuit, then, Satan was engaged in a judicial ordeal by duel with the Lord God.

On the Lord's part, no inconsistency with his own divine nature was involved in his entering into a trial by ordeal-combat with Satan. For there was no temporary suspending of his absolute claims to be the God of truth while attempting to establish that identity on some other grounds. There was no entertaining of the possibility that his word might return to him void, not even while he was engaged in judicial ordeal with Satan to settle where the truth lay with regard to that very matter. For it was the very essence of this judicial process as an ordeal undertaken before the heavenly

4. For a translation of some of this tale and a digest of the rest see *ANET*, 14–17. Other varieties of trial by combat-ordeal of special relevance for the book of Job will be mentioned later in this essay.

throne that it made appeal to the God of that throne for a sovereign revelation of judgment. The combat proceeded on the assumption of the absolute veracity, justice, and power—the divinity—of the enthroned Judge. The very possibility of contending over the question of whether God's word was truth depended on the acknowledgment that he was the true God, the God of truth. When the Lord swore the ordeal oath he swore by himself because he can swear by no greater (cf. Heb 6:13). He can validate the truth of his judgment by no other name.

Deviously implicit in Satan's allegations that Job was a hypocrite and the Lord's claim concerning him a fraud was, of course, the ultimate denial that the Lord was God, the Judge of all the earth. But Satan's accusatorial innuendoes did not change the actual judicial realities. They did not alter the fact that this was an ordeal undertaken before the Lord, seated as God on his judgment [[85]] throne. And God did not step down from his throne in order to grapple with his adversary. When the Lord God engages in judicial apologetics, he does not bear false witness against himself. He does not put his Godhood in abeyance, not even for a little while in order to fight to win it back again—perhaps and somehow. The Judge does not play the devil's advocate by denying himself, hoping it will not occur to the devil—and the theologians—that there is a contradiction between this "God" who "is," the self-denying, emptied deity of the apologetics ordeal, and the eternal God who was and is to come, the unchanging Creator-Judge, Alpha and Omega. There is no abdication in heaven. In the ordeal by combat with Satan, God remained on the throne as the God of the ordeal, consistently maintaining from the outset on through the final subjugation of the dragon his true self-identification as God, infinite, eternal, and unchangeable, the same today as yesterday and tomorrow.

By the same token, Satan did deny himself. He contradicted the contention he presented in court in the very act of entering into a trial by ordeal before the throne of God. The outcome was inherent in the fact that this was a trial by ordeal conducted before the eternal throne of the Lord God of heaven. That is what was meant by our earlier comment that in this drama of the book of Job the scene is all-important.

As we trace the course of this great ordeal between God and Satan we come upon another ordeal, an ordeal within the first ordeal. The two are distinguishable and yet the second belongs to the first and the outcome of the second is determinative of the outcome of the first. Understanding the relation of these two ordeals to one another is a matter of seeing just where the figure of Job fits into the picture of the supraterrestrial combat.

Ancient armies sometimes elected to let the issue of the day be settled by combat between their individual champions.[5] What made this seemingly cavalier or even reckless manner of deciding serious causes seem altogether reasonable and appropriate was the notion that the gods were involved in the warfare. Since this divine aspect of the battle must be the decisive factor, it was of secondary importance whether the battle at the human level was between entire armies or individual champions. "The LORD saves not with sword and spear: for the battle is the LORD's, and he will give you into our hands." So David, youthful champion of Israel, faithfully confessed before Goliath in the hearing of the assembled armies.[6] It was a battle in the holy war of Yahweh, God of Israel, and because the judgment of Yahweh was sovereign, the champion of Israel must prevail as he went to the combat in the name of Yahweh of hosts. In [[86]] the judicial ordeal of battle the Lord would render a verdict in favor of his people by blessing their champion—his champion—and by returning upon the giant from the ranks of the uncircumcised his own defiant oath-curse (1 Sam 17:44–47).

Like David (except that David was aware of his role), Job came to the field of battle as God's champion. In the ordeal of judgment into which the Lord had entered with Satan he had entrusted the honor of his holy name and the vindication of the validity of his redemptive work to this mortal. Job, the champion of God—no greater nobility than that![7]

With whom then did Job contend in this ordeal? With Satan? Yes, of course with Satan. God had opened the gates of hell and the great dragon that deceives the nations and accuses the holy brethren had been let loose upon the man from the land of Uz (Job 1:11). Of Job too it was true—his wrestling was not against flesh and blood, not against the Chaldeans and Sabaeans, not against the three friends, but against the rulers of darkness, the spiritual hosts of evil, against the wiles of the devil (cf. Eph 6:11, 12).

But if we stop with that we are still in need of making the discovery Jacob at last made at Peniel. In his night ordeal there Jacob learned that ultimately a man's wrestling is with God. Not by an unscrupulous bargain with Esau, not by crafty deception of Isaac, not at all by outwitting or over-

5. See Yigael Yadin, *The Art of Warfare in Biblical Lands* (New York: McGraw-Hill, 1963), 2:265–67.

6. Pertinent again at this point is the concluding observation in note 3 above.

7. How undiscerning is the exegesis that sees here only what it describes with supercilious profanity as "the idea of a God who allows human suffering for the purpose of winning a heavenly wager"—so S. Terrien in his commentary on Job in *IB* 3:888.

powering man but by wrestling with God and prevailing with tears and supplications must Jacob win the name Israel and become patriarch in the succession of Abraham and Isaac in God's covenant of redemption (cf. Gen 32:24–30; Hos 12:3, 4). Likewise, Job's wrestling was in the last analysis not with man, nor with the lightning and the wind, nor with his festering flesh; it was not ultimately even with the devil that Yahweh's champion must prevail but with the Lord God himself.

That is where our second ordeal comes in—the ordeal within the ordeal. For this wrestling of Job with God had the character of a judicial ordeal in that it led to a revelation of God's judgment with respect to Job, particularly over against the friends who, however unwittingly, had in effect been playing the part of the devil's champions.

How curiously complex this interlocking, three-cornered combat becomes! In one way or another each of the three principals contends with both the others. God confronts Satan in ordeal and Job as God's champion fights against Satan too. But that ordeal of God and Job against Satan is to be decided by God's ordeal with Job: to subdue Satan by the hand of Job, God must subdue Job. Yet, [[87]] so entangled have victory and defeat become that if Job as God's champion is to overcome Satan he must prevail with God. However, Job can prevail with God only as he is brought to his knees in suppliant submission before God. Hence it is also true that Job can subdue Satan only by being himself subdued by God. Not Job but God is the real conqueror of the dragon.

As if things were not already sufficiently intricate, before it was all over God was to commission yet another champion to represent him in combat, but not this time against Satan (at least, not directly so). This second champion was to face none other than God's first champion, Job. That collision of champions was part of the trial in which Job's ordeal, the ordeal within the ordeal, came to its climax.

Though the trial turned out to be of a kind that Job had hardly anticipated, it was at his own clamant insistence that his ordeal struggle with the Lord eventually took on more particularly the character of a court trial. Throughout the debate with the three friends Job voiced ever more desperately his plea for such a trial. Let come what may, he must have the privilege of a judicial audience with God.[8] Guilty Adam had hidden from

---

8. Cf., e.g., Job 13:13ff. The plea is so insistent it has been called a summons. See J. J. M. Roberts, "Job's Summons to Yahweh: The Exploitation of a Legal Metaphor," *ResQ* 16 (1973): 159–65.

the parousia of his Judge (cf. Job 31:33; Gen 3:8), but innocent Job let it be known that he had no intention of behaving like Adam, if ever God would grant his request for a fair trial.

This clamor for a hearing issued in a final passionate protestation of innocence, an oath of clearance remarkable for both its form and content (Job 31). It is an unusually long oath but even more striking is its use of the complete oath form, including the apodosis specifying the curses, rather than the more conventional truncated oath formula.[9] Still more noteworthy is the penetrating perception of the inward and spiritual depths of God's holy requirements that is displayed in the catalogue of sins of which Job declares himself innocent.[10]

Such an oath protesting innocence would sometimes accompany a defendant's appeal for a public trial before a third party when efforts towards achieving a private settlement had failed. The plaintiff would thereby be obliged to produce evidence to substantiate his accusations and to justify whatever coercive measures he might have meanwhile applied.[11] [[88]] Clearly, Job desired that God would specify the charges against him. He wanted to have the indictment in writing, and it was his boast that he would then be able to prove his innocence, charge by charge, and so turn the document of indictment into a crown of honor (Job 31:35–37).

And at last God did deign to come and speak to Job, the forerunner Elihu having first prepared the way for the advent.[12] God came as Judge. He had not stepped down from the throne to do judicial combat with Satan, and neither did he deny himself in the process of engaging in litigation with his servant Job. He came as the God of ordeal judgment in response to Job's ordeal-oath. He did not give any accounting for the mysterious treatment that had been accorded to his servant and there was therefore no opportunity for Job to defend himself against any imagined charges. There was instead simply the divine challenge: "Gird up now thy loins like a man" (Job 38:3a; cf. 40:7a).

According to the language of that challenge the encounter was evidently to be a belt-wrestling bout such as was employed at times in the ancient

---

9. S. H. Blank, "An Effective Literary Device in Job XXXI," *JJS* 2 (1951): 105–7, calls attention to the rarity of the complete oath-formula, citing Pss 7 and 137.

10. For a discussion of questions arising from the fact that Job's asseveration of innocence kept pace with so spiritual a probing of sin, see my commentary on Job in C. F. Pfeiffer, ed., *The Wycliffe Bible Commentary* (Chicago: Moody, 1962), 482 (hereafter, Kline commentary).

11. Cf. M. B. Dick, "The Legal Metaphor in Job 31," *CBQ* 41 (1979): 37–50.

12. For this interpretation of the Elihu section see Kline commentary, 483–86.

Near East as a form of legal procedure.[13] Job must fasten the wrestling belt about his waist and set himself to grapple with God. He must become locked in the grip of the ordeal power and fight to prevail in judgment. However, unlike Jacob's struggle with the Angel, the combat in Job's case was not, of course, to be an actual physical wrestling. That imagery in the challenge was merely a literary figure by which the Lord pictured this judicial ordeal more graphically. As Job presently discovered, it was not by his prowess in physical combat that he was to be tried but by his ability to hold his own in a test of knowledge (cf. Job 38:3b; 40:7b).[14]

The wisdom contest was a popular ancient diversion. Josephus reports a royal exchange of riddles, with wagers on the side, between kings Solomon and Hiram.[15] In the realm of literature a favorite type of fable consisted of a verbal clash of wits between personified creatures of various sorts. For example, the dispute between the ox and the horse or the contest between the tamarisk and the palm. In comparing these with the wisdom ordeal of God and Job it is of [[89]] particular interest that according to the standard form of such fables the debate concluded with a judgment scene in which the god settled the question.[16]

Since wisdom was Job's forte, he might have been momentarily elated to learn that his ordeal would be of a kind that proved his mettle in that area. The opening words of the voice from the whirlwind were, however, disquieting: "Who is this that darkeneth counsel by words without knowledge?" (Job 38:2). So Job was apprised that though he might point with pride to his performance as a counselor in his community (cf. Job 29:7ff.), in the probing of the question of his own sufferings his contribution had been less than consistently illuminating. Then, after depicting the imminent encounter as a

13. For a discussion of a legal text from Nuzi in which the judges call for a belt-wrestling ordeal to settle a dispute brought before them see C. H. Gordon, "Belt-wrestling in the Bible World," *HUCA* 23 (1950–51): 131–36. Cf. Gen 30:8; Job 31:22, 23.

14. At the same time, the questions addressed to Job are like the opening challenge with its belt-wrestling figure in that they imaginatively confront Job with situations in which the extent of his power as over against that of his Creator is brought under consideration. This is particularly prominent in the second round of the "wrestling." In this questioning, the possession of power to exercise physical control over the realm of nature is equally with the possession of knowledge about the world regarded as an expression of wisdom. Wisdom *is* power.

15. *Antiquities of the Jews* 8.5.3. Cf. also 1 Kgs 10:1ff.

16. See W. G. Lambert, *Babylonian Wisdom Literature* (Oxford: Clarendon, 1960), 150ff.

belt-wrestling ordeal, as we have seen (Job 38:3a), the Lord set Job on guard for the thrust and parry of the wisdom contest: "For I will demand of thee, and answer thou me" (Job 38:3b).

Form-critical investigation of the questions that God proceeded to put to Job suggests that he was imitating the technique of a scholarly master instructing a student.[17] It has been observed that the interrogative formulae used by the Lord are similar to those found in an Egyptian document of the late second millennium BC, in which an official, one Hori, gives instruction in the geography of Syria by a catechetical method, evidently in a school for the training of government officials. There are, moreover, Egyptian treatises of an encyclopedic nature listing natural phenomena and objects, professions, etc., the kind of material a teacher would produce or consult when preparing to instruct his class.[18] Interesting parallels in the selection and sequence of topics have been noted between one such text and the contents of Job 38:4ff.[19] It would appear then that while Job had concluded his debate with his friends by adopting the posture of the teacher towards them (cf. Job 27:11), the Lord now assumed that role and assigned Job the place of a disciple. Since this ordeal presupposed that all wisdom belongs to God, and since its purpose was not to destroy Job but to establish and edify him, the master-disciple format was altogether appropriate.

God's questions ranged over the earth (Job 38:4–21) and heaven (Job 38:22–38) and the animal kingdom (Job 38:39–39:30), spanning the reaches of time from the singing of the morning stars at the laying of the foundations of the earth [[90]] to the shouting of captains in the latest tumults of human history. For his part, Job was quite unable to interrupt the stream of questions with any information that might support a decision in his favor in this wisdom contest. When eventually the questions ceased, he could only lay his hand upon his mouth (Job 40:1–5). God had prevailed in the first stage of the ordeal.

---

17. See G. von Rad, "Hiob XXXVIII und die altägyptische Weisheit," in *Wisdom in Israel and in the Ancient Near East*, ed. M. Noth and D. W. Thomas, VTSup 3 (Leiden: Brill, 1955), 293–301; English translation in G. von Rad, *The Problem of the Hexateuch and Other Essays* (New York: McGraw-Hill, 1966), 281–91.

18. The genre of the noun list classifying phenomena in related groupings probably originated among the Sumerians. This process of classification is thought to have led to the comparisons of opposite pairs, and this in turn to the disputation fables.

19. The heading of this text reads: "Beginning of the teaching about all that Ptah has created." See note 17 above.

Then a second time the summons was issued: "Gird up thy loins now like a man: I will demand of thee, and declare thou unto me" (Job 40:7).[20] As the ordeal resumed Job was invited to exalt himself to the dignity of king of creation and to demonstrate his ability to deal with the world's problems, in particular, to subdue all the proud forces of evil (Job 40:10–14).[21]

It was of course unthinkable that Job should assay thus to fill the role of deity, and that suggestion was not developed further. But in order that Job might learn still better the lesson of his human limitations, God made another proposal, apparently a more feasible one, for it reduced the test from heavenly to earthly dimensions. He indicated that he was prepared to accept a handicap, as it were. Instead of continuing to engage Job in combat himself, God now commissioned one of his creatures, indeed, a creature of a lower order than man, to serve as his champion in the ordeal.

"Behold now behemoth, which I made as I made you" (Job 40:15). Here was a fellow creature of Job's—let him measure the competence of his wisdom-power over against it. Was not this an answer to his prayers? He had pleaded for a trial in which he would not be smitten with the paralysis of dread at the terrors of God's theophany (cf. Job 9:34, 35; 13:21). Here was his chance. All he need do is cope with a dumb brute. Surely Job should fare more successfully against a subhuman opponent, even though it was a king of the beasts, than he had hitherto against God, the King of kings.

That is how it happened that God's champion Job found himself with another champion of God arrayed against him in battle.[22] For deity to be represented by a bestial champion in a quarrel was not unheard of in ancient

---

20. It is in keeping with the conduct of the sport of belt-wrestling that the Joban imagery suggests that the contest involved more than one "fall."

21. See again note 14 above.

22. I have assumed here the interpretation of behemoth and leviathan (cf. Job 41:1 [40:25]) as two terms for just one creature, probably the crocodile (see Kline commentary, 488). Of interest for that identification is an Egyptian text that describes an oracular situation in which the penalty for infidelity in an oath was to be cast to the crocodile (see the account of the text by John A. Wilson in "The Oath in Ancient Egypt," *JNES* 7 [1948]: 137–38). But the point that God used a champion in his ordeal with Job does not depend on the specifics of my interpretation of behemoth-leviathan. On the other hand, the fact that the role of behemoth-leviathan in the judicial ordeal was that of God's representative champion against Job is a serious difficulty for the interpretation of it/them as a mythological symbol for Satan. It is also a problem for the view that sees in it/them a consoling didactic image of the struggle Job had undergone in his sufferings. Cf. John G. Gammie, "Behemoth and Leviathan: On the Didactic and Theological Significance of Job

literary tradition. [[91]] There is, for example, the well-known episode in the epic of Gilgamesh where the enraged goddess Ishtar constrains her father, Anu, to create the Bull of Heaven and commissions it to descend to Erech, there to do battle for her against Gilgamesh, who had spurned her romantic approaches. As it turns out, her champion proved no match for the dragon-slayer Gilgamesh and his companion Enkidu. Though the Bull of Heaven achieved an auspicious beginning by annihilating armies with the mere blast of its nostrils, when it met up with the heroes they dispatched it with a well-directed sword thrust between the neck and horns.[23] There is more to the story, because offended goddesses do not give up too easily, but as for Ishtar's champion, the Bull of Heaven, it succeeded only in bringing disgrace upon its divine sponsor, while the human heroes gained honor at its expense.

It was quite otherwise with behemoth-leviathan, the champion of God. "Will he swear a covenant oath to you; will you take him as your permanent servant? . . . On earth is not his equal, created fearless. He looks upon whatever is haughty; he is king over all proud creatures" (Job 41:4, 33, 34 [40:28; 41:25, 26]). Thus challenged by God, Job succumbed, acknowledging as too wonderful for him the wisdom of the Creator embodied in the champion that confronted him (Job 42:1–6).

Right here redemption springs its surprise. Overwhelmed in the divine ordeal, Job nevertheless receives a verdict of justification (Job 42:7–9) and the blessing of twofold restoration (Job 42:10–17). Job the vanquished is Job the triumphant. Like Jacob-Israel, Job triumphed by the tears and supplications of his vanquished, contrite heart. By the confession, "I abhor myself and repent" (Job 42:6), he prevailed with God.

The meaning of this repentance and the explanation of the mystery of this justification are to be found within that interpretation of the history of man and God revealed in the book of Job's canonical context, with its pattern of creation, fall in the first Adam, and promise of redemption through the coming heavenly mediator. Such was the personal faith-framework of Job's repentance. At the close of his final oath, mankind's fall in Adam and

---

40:15–41:26," in *Israelite Wisdom*, ed. J. G. Gammie, W. A. Brueggemann, W. L. Humphreys, and J. M. Ward (Missoula, MT: Scholars Press, 1978), 217–31.

23. An additional feature in the parallelism of this epic tradition with the Joban behemoth-leviathan context is that (as often in the portrayal of heroic combat with monsters) the conflict of Gilgamesh and Enkidu with the Bull of Heaven found iconographic depiction as a belt-wrestling bout.

the cursing of the earth were present in his thoughts (Job 31:33, 40). His believing apprehension of the promised eschatological deliverance from sin and from the curse of death through a divine Redeemer and by means of sacrifice for sin came to expression in his priestly ministry at the altar (Job 1:5; 42:8–10) and in the [[92]] prophetic insights to which he gave witness (e.g., Job 16:18ff.; 19:25ff.). That is the biblical world of ideas to which the faith of Job and of the book of Job belong, and it is within that universe of theology that the outcome of Job's ordeal-combat with God must be understood. The justification of vanquished confessing Job was in accordance with the redemptive wonder of the grace of the God who is just and justifies the ungodly who believe in Jesus (Rom 3:26; 4:5).

In the trial by ordeal, God's claim that Job was his servant had been fully vindicated, the religious commitment of Job being judged by the terms of the ordeal precisely as defined by Satan himself at the outset.[24] According to those terms, genuine devotion to God was devotion that did not admit of any suspicion of its being prompted by interest in temporal benefits. It is, therefore, of the utmost significance that at the time of Job's repentant submission to the Lord he was still in a condition of unrelieved misery and without the hint of an intimation of any improvement in his temporal circumstances. Expecting only the continuation of his sufferings down to the grave, he nevertheless gave himself anew in unreserved commitment to his God and so demonstrated conclusively that Satan's allegations of hypocrisy in Job and fraud in God were false and that God's claim was true. Beyond contradiction, Job did in fact serve the Lord "for nought."

Throughout the course of the argument with the friends it becomes increasingly evident that what was of supreme import to Job was that the Lord God was his God. What was shattering to him was not his loss of temporal blessings but his fear (groundless though it was) that he had lost his God. The whirlwind theophany had not answered the question of the *why* of his particular sufferings or extended any hope of temporal relief, but it had served as a means of grace to confirm Job's assurance that, fallen son of Adam though he was, God was his God in the divine purpose and promise of redemption. And by his unconditional repentance Job showed that he was prepared to serve God for God's sake alone, purely and truly, in singleness of heart.

---

24. On this point see Matitiahu Tsevat, "The Meaning of the Book of Job," *HUCA* 37 (1966): 74.

By his victory in his wrestling ordeal with Job, the Lord proved victor in his ordeal-conflict against Satan.[25] In this fateful ordeal, the Lord, the God of judgment ordeal, the Judge of all the earth, had spoken. He had revealed decisively through his champion Job's victory over the draconic Adversary that his gospel-decree of Gen 3:14, 15 was sovereign and true: God the Creator [[93]] would at last destroy the devil and by redemptive re-creation raise up a new mankind consecrated forever to the service of his glory.

The history of Job was not, of course, the end of the history of redemption, but the way the ordeal of this champion of God ends is the way the whole history of redemption ends. The issue of Job's ordeal was a triumphant reiteration of God's original claim concerning him. Here again, at the end of the ordeal, God calls Job, "my servant" (Job 42:7, 8)—and we hear no more from the silenced Accuser. That was a sign for all the promised seed of the woman who, with Job, resist the devil, steadfast in faith, that God, their God, will perfect, establish, and strengthen them, and shortly bruise Satan under their feet (cf. Rom 16:20; 1 Pet 5:9, 10). Likewise, the unannounced temporal restoration by which the Lord vindicated his faithful champion was a sign that in the end God will be clearly revealed as compassionate and of tender mercy (Jas 5:11).

A comprehensive study of the book of Job from the legal perspective would have to deal with additional matters scarcely alluded to here, some of them rather large issues like the nature of the disputation with the three friends and the significance of the mediator figure in Job's speeches. In the foregoing analysis our purpose has been simply to bring forward into view and hopefully into the ongoing discussion the usually ignored forensic realities of the Joban prologue. It is only as we are prepared to give a proper place to the basic legal controversy disclosed in that prologue, the trial by ordeal of God and his champion Job against the satanic Adversary, that we can expect to achieve a juridical reading of this Old Testament wisdom book that is true to it in its canonical literary wholeness and its canonical theological integrity as part of the redemptive revelation in the Scriptures.

25. It was a final irony for the defeated dragon, the old serpentine leviathan, that God vanquished him by using as his representative agent in overcoming Job a member of the animal kingdom (cf. Gen 3:1), and indeed another leviathan.

CHAPTER TWELVE

The Rider of the Red Horse

(1990, rev. 2001)

The symbolic scene depicted in Zech 1:8 contains the essence of the prophet's night visions and, indeed, of his entire prophecy. His overall theme, developed in visions, oracles, symbolic actions, sermons, and "burdens," is the restoration and consummation of God's kingdom. Analysis of the structure of the book shows it to be unified by a repeating sequence of three main topics. First and primary is the return and presence of God's Glory in the midst of his people as their strength and salvation. The other two are the promised consequences of the first: the second in the triadic pattern is the elimination of evil, the evil of oppression from without and perversion within; and the third is the redemptive establishment of the Zion community as an expression and embodiment of God's universal sovereignty.

Involved as principals in this historical drama are the Glory-Presence of the Lord, the satanic world, and the redeemed covenant community. These three appear in Zech 1:8 in the symbolic guise of the rider of the red horse, the deep, and the myrtles, respectively. Each of these becomes the focus in one of the three following interpretive sections of the first night vision: the deep, in the report of the horsemen (1:9–11); the myrtles, in the Angel's intercession (1:12); and the Glory-Presence, in the Lord's response (1:13–17).

Present as the Heavenly Warrior

Messianic Angel of the Presence

When the apostle John received his apocalyptic vision on Patmos, the opening revelation confronted him with the figure of the Son of Man in the transfigured brilliance of heaven's glory (Rev 1:13–16). Similarly, Zechariah in his opening vision beheld the commanding presence of a man riding a red horse, a man who was the Angel of the Lord, the pre-incarnate revelation of the coming Christ. That this man and the messianic Angel are in fact one and the same individual is brought out clearly by the pointed identification of the "the Angel of Yahweh" in verse 11 as "the one stationed among the myrtles," the phrase already used twice to describe the man-figure (vv. 8 and 10). Moreover, like this man, the Angel is the one with immediate authority over the other horsemen.

[[2]] A second angel appears in this and subsequent visions, repeatedly described by Zechariah as "the angel who was talking with me" (1:9, 13, 14, etc.). Such an interpreting angel was also sent to other recipients of apocalyptic visions (cf., e.g., Dan 8:16ff.; Rev 22:8ff.). But the Angel of the Lord is unique among the angels. He is the Lord of angels. In the course of Zechariah's visions we find the same evidence of this Angel's divine attributes and prerogatives that appears elsewhere in the Scriptures and has led to the general recognition of this figure as a form of theophany; more specifically, as a manifestation of the second person of the Trinity. One such indication of the divine identity of the Angel of Yahweh in the present context is the reference to him in verse 13 as simply "Yahweh."

In this man-Angel the coming Messiah-Lord was revealing at the very outset of these visions his immediate presence with his people. He was there with them in their historical struggle, exercising his sovereign power in their behalf (cf. Isa 63:9 and 43:2). That personal presence of the Lord of Glory in the midst of the covenant community on earth was the all-important reality. To make known the meaning of the presence and mission of this messianic Angel is what Zechariah's visions are all about. They are an unveiling of the secret of the covenant, an apocalypse of the mystery of the divine Presence.

Mounted Warrior

The appearance of the divine Angel to Zechariah in this opening vision recalls his appearance to Joshua near Jericho at the beginning of the conquest of Canaan. Even in their literary form the accounts of the two appearances (Josh 5:13 and Zech 1:8) correspond closely, with similarities both in sentence structure and vocabulary. Like Zechariah, Joshua looks, and behold a man, standing over against him. The martial purpose of his presence, indicated by the drawn sword in his hand, was confirmed by his self-identification as commander of the army of Yahweh. His deity was revealed in his declaration that the place was sanctified by his presence (vv. 14, 15; cf. Exod 3:5). Similarly, the divine man-Angel who confronted Zechariah was readily identifiable as an agent of God engaged in a military undertaking, mounted as he was on a red horse among the other supernatural world-traversing horsemen. He was the commander of these heavenly troops. It was to him they reported after their reconnoitering of the nations prior to a campaign of judgment (Zech 1:11; cf. the spying out of Canaan in Josh 2:1ff. and 7:2ff.). Zechariah's subsequent visions would develop the theme, but already in the first vision it was evident from the mode of the initial appearance of the man-Angel that his mission was one of bringing God's judgment on the hostile world powers and so making a place for the kingdom of the saints of the Most [[3]] High—precisely as was the case when he appeared to Joshua at the launching of the holy war to take possession of Canaan.

We should at least mention in this connection two other episodes involving the Angel of Yahweh with drawn sword in hand for possible further illumination of his appearance in Zechariah's first vision. Numbers 22:22ff. tells how shortly before the appearance to Joshua, before Israel had crossed the Jordan, the Angel took his stand opposing Balaam on his way to curse Israel. And 1 Chr 21:16 (cf. 2 Sam 24:16ff.) relates that David looked and saw the Angel of Yahweh, standing between heaven and earth, his drawn sword stretched out over Jerusalem, which he was in the process of destroying with the plague. Background for these angel-and-sword episodes is found in the cherubim associated with the flaming sword in their assignment of guarding from profanation the original holy land of Eden (Gen 3:24; cf. Job 37:11, 12).

It is not only in Zechariah's opening vision that the Scriptures represent the Messiah as a mounted figure. Closest of the other instances to the imagery of Zech 1:8ff. is the representation of Christ as rider on a white horse in Rev 19:11ff. (cf. Rev 6:2). There too Christ, the richly diademed King of kings, commands other horsemen, the armies of heaven, as he proceeds to judgment-battle against the beast, false prophet, and kings of the earth. Blended there with the mounted warrior symbolism of Zech 1 is the man-and-sword imagery of Josh 5, for out of the rider's mouth issues a sharp sword with which to strike down the nations (v. 15). Different historical hours are in view in the two passages, Rev 19 envisaging the final eschatological conflict and Zech 1 an earlier stage, but the warrior-judge role of the messianic horseman is the same in both.

Of a piece with the representation of the mounted Messiah is the portrayal of Yahweh, the divine warrior, driving his victorious horses and chariots (Hab 3:8). "The One mounted (or riding) on the clouds" is an epithet of Yahweh (Ps 68:4 [5]; cf. Isa 19:1), as it was of the Canaanite storm god Baal. Yahweh is also depicted as riding or mounted on the cherub (Ps 18:10 [11]) and on the heavens (Deut 33:26; Ps 68:33 [34]).

Later in the book of Zechariah the messianic king once again appears as a mounted figure.[1] This time, however, he rides a donkey rather than a horse (Zech 9:9). Resumed there is the patriarch Jacob's testamentary blessing on Judah (Gen 49:8–12), in which Shiloh, the coming one, tethers his donkey to the vine. A special designation for the donkey, shared by these two passages alone in the Old Testament, has been found to refer to [[4]] a particular kind of animal that was used in the death-ritual by which ancient covenants were ratified.[2] Accordingly, in the fulfillment of the prophecy of Zech 9 at the triumphal entry of Jesus into Jerusalem (Matt 21:4, 5), the donkey on which the Lord rode presaged the cross and the shedding of the blood of the new covenant. This donkey colt identified the lion of Judah as the lamb of God. Summed up in the two images of the mounted Messiah in Zech 1 and 9, the rider of the red horse and the rider of the donkey colt, is the dual status of Jesus as covenant Lord and covenant Servant; his double advent for sacrificial atonement and judicial conquest; his two-stage career of humiliation and exalted glory.

Heaven's Legions

With the mounted man-Angel were other horse(men). Represented by this equine symbolism here, and again in the seventh vision (Zech 6:1–8), are contingents of celestial beings. These heavenly hosts, who are seen surrounding the throne of God in visions of the divine court, take part in the deliberative assembly there, but they are also pictured as accompanying the King of Glory when he goes forth to battle on a day of the Lord. (Similarly, the members of the divine council in Canaanite mythology have a dual role, constituting an army when occasion requires.)

Such attendant heavenly forces are mentioned in those passages where we have found Yahweh depicted as a mounted warrior. For example, at the beginning of the blessings of Moses in Deut 33, the Lord is said to have come with an army of myriads of holy ones as he advanced from Sinai to Canaan in his warfare in behalf of Israel (v. 2). Celebrating the same occasion,

---

1. The literary-thematic pattern of the night visions is repeated in the "burdens" (Zech 9–14), the overall structure thus being a diptych. The two passages portraying Messiah as a mounted figure (1:8 and 9:9) occupy corresponding positions in this parallelism.

2. See ARM II, 37:5–14. An English translation of the text is available in *ANET*, 482c.

Ps 68 numbers in the thousands of thousands the chariotry forces among whom the One of Sinai proceeded (v. 17 [18]). Zechariah himself, echoing this opening vision at the close of his book, foretells the final advent of the Lord God in judgment with all the holy ones (14:5). Again, with specific reference to the parousia of Christ, biblical prophecy portrays the final judgment event as a coming of the Son of Man in the glory of the Father with all the holy angels (e.g., Matt 16:27; 25:31; Mark 8:38; Luke 9:26; cf. Jude 14, 15). As in Zech 1 and 6, equine imagery is used at times for these angelic forces elsewhere in the Bible. It may be merely implicit in references to chariotry or it may be explicit, as in the familiar episodes in the careers of Elijah and Elisha recorded in 2 Kgs 2 and 6.

What Zechariah saw was a symbolic representation or actualizing of the divine epithet "Yahweh of hosts," which is used repeatedly in the context of these night visions. The rider of the red horse was a personal [[5]] manifestation of Yahweh in angelic mode and the horsemen belonged to the hosts of Yahweh's angel legions (cf. Matt 25:31; Rev 12:7). The prevalent military connotation of the "Yahweh of hosts" title is not lost in this symbolic restatement, even though the mission of the horsemen is not one of battle. They are in fact engaged in world reconnaissance and it is likely the speed with which they executed their mission that is particularly emphasized by the imagery of horses. In Zechariah's day, the far-flung Persian government was noted for its rapid communications via a system of horsemen stationed along the roads of the empire. Nevertheless, the role of the horsemen of Zech 1 is not just that of general government administration, for their rapid gathering of information concerning the nations was part of a judicial process to assess the ripeness of the world for judgment and to determine the hour for the Lord of hosts to go forth to war.

Three (or perhaps only two) groups of horses are mentioned, distinguished from each other by different colors. The size of each group is not indicated. One group is chestnut-red, like the mount of the Angel of Yahweh. Another group is white. The other color-term, the second in the sequence of three, is usually thought to denote a lighter red and is rendered "bay" or "sorrel." These are all natural colors for horses and there are no convincing grounds for regarding these colors in themselves as symbols for specific, different destinations or missions; indeed, they all shared the same task of world surveillance. It may well be, however, that the palette selection of red(s) and white was designed to create the impression of flames and light. A desire to produce such a bright, fiery image would then explain why black horses, which are found in the seventh vision, are absent from this first one. Also, the second color-term, *śĕruqqîm*, evidently derives from a verbal root that is used for the shining of the sun. Now this term is possibly to be construed as in apposition to the first color. (Similarly, the term *ʾămuṣṣîm*, "strong ones," is annexed to the four color-terms used for the chariot horses in Zech 6:2, 3.) But whether it designates a distinct color group of horses separate from the other two or whether it is appositional to the first color and defines the red hue more precisely, it would highlight the fiery, brightly luminous appearance of these horses. This imagery would thus be an equivalent in prophetic vision for the fiery horses with the chariots of fire which were seen in similar yet distinctive visionary mode at Elijah's ascent into heaven (2 Kgs 2:11) and again later by Elisha and his servant when the forces of the king of Aram menaced Dothan (2 Kgs 6:17). This would not be the only place in biblical revelation where a bright hued color scheme was employed to produce the impression of flames of fire. Flame colored linen was used for the inside covering of the tabernacle (cf. [[6]] Exod 26:1, 31, 36). There too it was a matter of giving visual expression to the Name of God, Yahweh of hosts, in an earthly replica of the Glory-court of heaven, where the heavenly hosts were represented by cherubim figures, portrayed in the fiery curtains as well as in gleaming golden sculptured form above the ark. In the imagery of his first vision, Zechariah saw the same reality that was found in the tabernacle, that reproduction of the Glory-Spirit realm where Yahweh reigns on chariot throne as a flaming fire, amid ten thousand times ten thousand of holy ones (cf. Ezek 1:4, 13; Dan 7:9, 10).

Conveyed to Zechariah in this vision of the man-Angel with the other supernatural horse(men) was, therefore, the assurance of the earthly presence of the heavenly reality in its full panoply of power. The divine Presence, which Israel had in the past experienced as the visible Glory-epiphany, though not outwardly observable in Zechariah's day, was nevertheless really present—the Lord of Angels and his holy retinue. Zechariah beheld this Presence in the Spirit.

Present by the Deep

Background Imagery of the Divine Warrior and the Deep

If we follow the Masoretic tradition for the vocalization of the noun *mṣlh* in Zech 1:8, there is no reason to translate it "ravine" or otherwise to depart from the regular meaning of *mĕṣûlâ*, or *mĕṣôlâ* (cf. *ṣûlâ*, Isa 44:27), namely, the depths of the sea, the watery deep. This is the meaning it has, for example, later in the book of Zechariah itself (see 10:11, where the plural *mĕṣûlôt* is used) and Ps 68:22 [23], the context of which is similar to Zech 1 in that it portrays the Lord as a riding figure (v. 5 [6]) accompanied by a myriad of forces (v. 17 [18]). For the rendering of the preposition (*bêt*) as "by" in connection with a body of water, see, e.g., 1 Sam 29:1 ("by the spring") and Ezek 10:15, 20 ("by the river"), the latter being of special interest because there too we find the motif of a Glory-theophany by the waters. The LXX rendering of *mṣlh*, "(the mountains) of the shadows," would reflect a reading *mĕṣillâ*, from a root meaning "be dark." If this reading were being considered, one might note the Akkadian term *maṣallu*, used for the canopied area of a royal garden, a baldachin, and translate "the myrtles which serve as [*bêt essentiae*] a canopy-shade." But the clearly attested *mĕṣûlâ* of the Masoretic tradition is to be preferred over other possibilities not attested elsewhere in biblical Hebrew. Zechariah saw the Lord of the angels of heaven standing between (or among) the myrtles by the deep. God's message of comfort and hope for his faithful was distilled in that cryptic, symbolic scene.

[[7]] To unfold that message we examine first the association of the Glory-theophany of the divine horseman with the watery deep. The significance of this imagery may be determined by tracing it to its sources in earlier biblical revelation. Immediately obvious is the connection with the exodus event. There we find all the elements of Zechariah's scene, the equine figures as well as the Glory-theophany of God's cloud-chariot and, of course, the sea. The very term *mĕṣôlâ* is used in the Exod 15 hymnic celebration of the victory of Yahweh, the divine warrior, who triumphed over the horse and rider and all the military might of Egypt. Yahweh hurled pharoah's horses and chariots into the sea, the depths covered them, they descended into the deeps (*mĕṣôlôt*) like a stone (v. 5). *Mĕṣûlâ* (or equivalents) is also found in later reminiscences of the Lord's salvation triumph at the Egyptian sea (Neh 9:11; cf. Ps 68:22 [23]). It is also used for the watery depths when exodus imagery is applied to a later exodus-like redemptive event, as in the reference to "all the depths of the Nile (or river)" in Zech 10:11.

Closely linked to Israel's passage through the Egyptian sea was their crossing of the Jordan. These twin episodes under the leadership of Moses and his successor Joshua (Josh 4:23) are blended in passages like Exod 15:13–17; Ps 114:3–5; and Hab 3:8. We have cited the appearance of the man to Joshua (Josh 5:13–15) as part of the tradition of Angel of the Lord theophanies that illuminates the significance of the Angel-rider figure in Zech 1. Now we note another point of connection between that episode and

Zechariah's vision in the fact that the depths of the Jordan just traversed by Israel (Josh 3 and 4) formed the backdrop for the theophany of the commander of the Lord's hosts to Joshua (Josh 4:19; 5:10).

Zechariah's imagery finds its explanation then in the exodus event and the exodus-like passage of the Jordan, each involving a theophany by the watery depths. The meaning of these events can in turn be more fully uncovered and thereby a more complete explanation of Zechariah's symbolism secured if we take the phenomenon of the Glory-theophany by the deep back beyond the exodus to the earliest instance of it, and then follow the development of this revelational motif forward in history to the exodus and on to Zechariah's era.

The Deep in Creation

Glory-theophany over the deep is first encountered in the creation record. After the declaration of the absolute beginning of the invisible heaven and the visible world in Gen 1:1, the narrative focuses in verse 2 on the earth at an unstructured stage of unbounded deep and darkness and reveals there, hovering eagle-like above, [[8]] the reality of the Glory of heaven's King, the Lord of heavenly hosts. This Glory-Presence is here called the Spirit of God, an identification attested elsewhere as well (cf., e.g., Gen 3:8; Neh 9:19, 20; Isa 63:11–14; Hag 2:5). By virtue of the presence of this Glory-Spirit the darkness and deep would become bounded and formed into ordered realms (the theme of the first three days of the creation account), and those realms would abound with creatures who were to rule over them (the theme of the second three days, which are arranged in matching sequence to the first triad of days, so that rulers occur parallel to their realms).

Acted upon by the Spirit of life (cf. Ps 104:30; Ezek 37:1–14), the lifeless primeval deep would become a double source of life, the fructifying rain reservoirs above (Ps 104:13ff.) and the enlivening waters of springs and rivers below (Gen 2:6; Ps 104:10ff.). They would become the seas teeming with creatures (Ps 104:25, 26). In Eden the dark, dead deep would be transformed into the river that watered the garden of God and the tree of life, the primal typological reality behind the biblical image of the river of life that flows from the throne of God (Ezek 47:1ff.; Rev 22:1, 2).

Hence the presence of the King of Glory above the waters was a pre-indication that the dark deep would be subdued and filled, that the kingdom of God would emerge with royal earthlings made in the image of God and reigning in his name, commissioned, in imitation of their Creator, to the continuance of the kingdom program of subduing and filling the earth (Gen 1:26–28). Moreover, because the Glory constituted a Spirit-temple and functioned as a heavenly paradigm as well as a divine power in creation, the presence of Glory gave promise that an ectypal likeness of the archetypal sanctuary would be reproduced in the visible world. Inchoate deep and darkness would be transformed into a cosmic temple for the enthronement-revelation of the divine Glory-light. More than that, a living temple of God-like spirits would be brought forth and fashioned into a holy habitation of the Lord of hosts. In short then, the Glory-Spirit over the waters was a revelation of the absolute sovereignty of the Creator-King, a guarantee that whatever the conditions that seemed unruly and contrary, they would be overcome and God's kingdom would be established and consummated in the form of a living and everlasting temple, the Omega-likeness of the Alpha Glory-Spirit.

The Deep in the Deluge

At the Noahic flood we once again find the theophanic Spirit present over the deep in a creation or, more specifically, a re-creation event. The narrative of the episode in Gen 6–8 is so constructed that it reflects in various ways the form of the creation record [[9]] in Gen 1:1–2:3, so inviting the reader to see the flood as another creation episode—as Peter did and so expounded it in 2 Pet 3:5–7.[3] Strikingly reproduced in the physical phenomena of the flood was the process of the original creation. There was a return to the deep-and-darkness of Gen 1:2 in the flood's reversal of the separation and bounding of the waters above and below, described in day two of Gen 1 (cf. Gen 7:11–12). Then followed a recapitulation of the creation sequence of the abatement and bounding of the waters; the reappearance of the dry land and vegetation; and the ultimate re-emergence of animals and mankind in the re-created world, the heavens and earth that now are, as Peter calls it (2 Pet 3:7). It is of particular interest that the biblical account of this re-creation event narrates it in a way that recalls the Spirit (*rûaḥ*) of Gen 1:2. Genesis 8:1 marks the turning point between the watery chaos produced by the flood and the reconstruction of the cosmos by observing that *rûaḥ* (wind) was sent from God over the flooded earth. The theophanic presence of the Creator-Spirit of Gen 1:2 suggested by the word play on *rûaḥ* in Gen 8:1 is also disclosed by the episode of God's sealing the remnant in the ark (Gen 7:16). This presence of the Spirit over the waters in the re-creation event of

3. For a full discussion of this, see *KP*, 220–25.

the flood signified his lordship over the waters (cf. Ps 29:10) and announced that he was ready to bring forth the new world-order out of chaos.

Further, re-creation since the fall is necessarily by means of redemptive judgment; a work of destruction must clear the way for redemptive reconstruction. Re-creation involves de-creation (cf., e.g., Isa 65:17; Dan 7:11–14; Rev 20:11–21:1; 21:4, 5). Hence, in the re-creation event of the flood, the deluge waters from which God brought forth the new world were first employed by him for the de-creation of the old world.

The flood depths, though a return to the dark deep of Gen 1:2, had additional symbolic nuances. The primeval deep was dead in the sense of without life forms, but the deluge deep was not just devoid of life, it was the destroyer of life. It was the realm of the dead. For those in the ark, the flood experience was a death passage, a death and burial. Hence God's mighty act with respect to the flood waters may be construed not simply in terms of re-creation but of resurrection. In subsequent biblical revelation the deep is a familiar synonym for death and Sheol. (A reflex of this in Canaanite mythology is the confusingly similar roles of the gods Death and Sea as adversaries of the hero-god Baal.) Psalms 18:4 [5] and 69:1, 2, 14, 15 [2, 3, 15, 16] contain pleas for deliverance from death-Sheol envisaged as the breakers, torrents, and miry depths of the sea (cf. also Pss 42:7 [8]; 88:6 [7]). In the New Testament application of Ps 69 to Jesus, the overwhelming waters become a figure for Messiah's death-sufferings. Psalm 18 is [[10]] especially relevant to the Zech 1:8 imagery because in response to the prayer of the psalmist for salvation from the breakers of death, Yahweh appears in Glory-theophany as a mounted warrior and snatches the suppliant from the deep waters (vv. 8–19 [9–20]). Again in the psalm of Jonah (Jonah 2:2ff. [3ff.]) the prophet's descent into the heart of the seas is described as an experience of Sheol, so that the Lord's deliverance of him was a bringing him up from the underworld. Accordingly, the New Testament applies this (as it did Ps 69) to the death-burial-resurrection of Christ (Matt 12:40). In the resurrection scene in Rev 20:13, the sea is paralleled by death and Hades—each giving up the dead that were in it. And in the vision of the new heaven and earth in Rev 21:1ff. this parallelism recurs: the sea is no more (v. 1) and death shall be no more (v. 4). Present in Rev 20 and 21 is the theophany of the glory of the God of the great white throne (Rev 20:11) and heavenly sanctuary (Rev 21:1–5, 11). Manifesting himself as the Re-Creator of the new heaven and earth, he shows himself, over against the sea of death, to be the God of resurrection power, who can break open the bars of the deep and swallow up the watery depths of death in victory.

The waters of the flood also functioned as God's instrument for the destruction of rebellious mankind and thereby for the deliverance of the covenant remnant from the oppression of the wicked. The mighty waters were the servant of the almighty Lord in his execution of redemptive judgment. In terms of judicial procedure, they were the ordeal waters by which a verdict of justification was rendered for the godly remnant and condemnation was declared and punishment executed against the ungodly. Accordingly, the theophanic Spirit over these waters was a revelation that the King of Glory was in sovereign control over the threatening situation, even making the destructive deep itself serve to accomplish his will as he took action in remembrance of his covenant promise (Gen 8:1a). The heavenly Presence over the flood waters proclaimed that the Creator was also the sovereign Judge of all the earth and the faithful Redeemer of his people.

Elsewhere in biblical revelation envisaging the final judgment ordeal by fire (2 Pet 3:6, 7), the baptismal ordeal-waters of the deluge (cf. 1 Pet 3:20, 21) become an ordeal stream of fire (Dan 7:9–11). Like the river of life, the river of fire flows from God's throne, for the Glory-Spirit is the executor of the dual sanctions of the covenant, of both the blessing and the curse potential of the baptismal judgment ordeal (cf. Matt 3:11). In the eschaton, the stream of fire, the ordeal instrument, becomes the lake of fire, the realm of perdition, the second death (Rev 20:14; 21:8). Thus the story [[11]] of the appearance of the Glory-Spirit over the primeval waters leads in the course of biblical symbolism to a double eschatological reality, to both a river of life and fiery lake of death.

The Deep in the Exodus

This brings us back to Israel's exodus from Egypt, which, we may now observe, was a creation event, a redemptive re-creation, like the flood. We can now appreciate the significance of the fact that it was at this historical juncture that the Glory-Spirit reappeared (cf. Exod 14:21, 22), to be in this new age a continuing visible divine presence in the midst of the covenant people. By thus manifesting himself in this Glory-Spirit theophany at the sea, the Lord identified himself as the God of the original creation—and of the diluvian re-creation—and gave notice that his present intention was to accomplish a kingdom-inaugurating re-creation.

Such is the reading of the situation in Deut 32:10, 11. In this song Moses interprets the exodus as a redemptive recapitulation of Gen 1, and he does so precisely in terms of the presence of the Shekinah-Glory in the exodus history. For he employs the key features of Gen 1:2 to describe Israel in the wilderness by the sea, under the ruling, guiding Glory-cloud. The intention to portray the exodus history as a replay of Gen 1:2 is made clear by the use in Deut 32:10, 11 of two rare words (the noun *tōhû* and the verb *rḥp*), found in the Pentateuch only in these two passages. In the Song of Moses, the wilderness becomes the new *tōhû*, the waste land, equivalent to the primeval deep-and-darkness, and it is the Shekinah-cloud that is referred to as hovering (the verb *rḥp*) over Israel in the wilderness-*tōhû*. (This corroborates our understanding of Spirit in Gen 1:2 as one of the instances where it denotes the heavenly Glory.)

As in the flood narrative, so in the exodus account we read of the *rûaḥ* (wind, breath, spirit) as God's agent in dealing with the deep (Exod 14:21; 15:8), again evoking the *rûaḥ* (Spirit) of the original creation (Gen 1:2). Once more there is a dividing of the waters so that the dry land appears, and once again there is the fashioning of a kingdom people who are established in a paradise land under a covenant of works. With respect to this divine work of redeeming Israel from Egypt and forming them into his holy kingdom, the Lord is subsequently identified in Scripture as Israel's Creator (Isa 43:15) or Maker (Isa 45:11; cf. Gen 2:7).

Like the deluge waters, the sea of the exodus was not only to undergo a creational kind of division and bounding, but was to be wielded by the Lord as an agent of judicial ordeal, as a weapon in an overwhelming [[12]]
judgment on the Egyptians. The parousia of God in the Glory-cloud over that sea heralded, therefore, a work of destruction as well as of re-creation. It proclaimed the advent of a day of the Lord.

An additional turn is given to the meaning of the Egyptian sea in some biblical allusions to the exodus in that rather than viewing the waters as a means of judgment, as the waters of a baptismal ordeal, they use the sea as a figure for the objects of judgment. The sea, in the guise of a monster of the deep, is made to represent the forces of Satan, pharaoh and his army, the enemy power that is vanquished by Yahweh. Appearing in his storm chariot of Glory to perform miracles of redemptive judgment for the salvation of his people, the divine warrior slays the dragon, Sea. "It was you [O God] who split open the sea by your power; you broke the heads of the monster in the waters. It was you who crushed the heads of Leviathan" (Ps 74:13, 14a NIV). "Was it not you who cut Rahab to pieces, who pierced that monster through? Was it not you who dried up the sea, the waters of the great deep, who made a road in the depths of the sea so that the redeemed might cross over?" (Isa 51:9b, 10 NIV).

In explanation of this development in the symbolism of the sea, there is the fact that at the exodus the sea stood as an obstacle in the way, threatening the existence of the fleeing Israelites. But it is also evident that the biblical authors are adapting the ancient mythological drama of a hero-god who vanquishes an evil deity depicted as draconic sea, and in the process creating the world or at least establishing world order and his own preeminence in the council of gods. Pagan myth thus comingled and perverted the truths of God's creation of the world and his subsequent overcoming of evil. When the biblical authors draw upon this imagery, they empty it of its mythological substance, employing it simply as a literary figure to portray the realities of God's warfare against Satan and his earthly allies in the course of redemptive history. Most familiar is the use of this imagery in the book of Revelation to portray the conflict of Christ and Satan. Applying this dragon-sea figure to Egypt and its king exposes the satanic dimension of their hostility to the covenant people, while the imagery of Yahweh slaying the leviathan suggests the re-creation aspect of the exodus event.

In tracing the complex development of the biblical symbolism of the deep, it has been found that the sea represents both death and the draconic adversary, Satan. This combination is understandable for there is a close connection between the devil and death. Scripture applies the same name, Belial, to both (cf. Ps 18:4 [5] and 2 Cor 6:15) and refers to both as enemies
[[13]] of the Lord's people and as devourers of their victims. Satan is indeed said to be the one who has the power of death (Heb 2:14).[4]

Summing up thus far, revelation of Yahweh in Glory-theophany by or over the sea proclaims him Creator and Re-Creator, judge of the world, victor over Satan, and redeemer of his people. Such a parousia-epiphany heralds a day of the Lord, the manifestation of God's supreme sovereignty over everything in heaven and earth, and the coming of his kingdom, crowned by his royal house and holy temple.

Exile Visions of Theophany by the Deep

These conclusions will find further substantiation as our attention is called to the fact that Zechariah's vision of theophany by the deep belongs to a cluster of such prophetic visions, all from the sixth century BC. Zechariah's

4. See further my "Death, Leviathan, and the Martyrs: Isaiah 24:1–27:1," in *A Tribute to Gleason Archer*, ed. W. C. Kaiser and R. F. Youngblood (Chicago: Moody, 1986), 235–36 [= pp. 225–27 in the present volume].

vision, received soon after the restoration began, was preceded by similar visions seen by Ezekiel and Daniel in the midst of exile. It was in his opening vision by the Kebar River, where Israelite exiles had been settled in the land of the Babylonians, that Ezekiel beheld the fiery whirlwind coming of the chariot-enthroned Glory (Ezek 1:1ff.). By waters in the land of exile, Daniel too had visions of the divine Presence—by the Ulai near Susa (Dan 8:2, 16ff.) and on the bank of the Tigris (Dan 10:4ff.; 12:5ff.).

This was a time when the world power dominated the covenant people, having attacked and overcome them and brought to an end the theocratic dynasty and kingdom. Israel's political status had in effect reverted to the situation when the Egyptians oppressed the Hebrews, before the establishment of the theocratic kingdom and the emergence of the messianic dynasty of David. It was natural that in this period of exile the symbolism of the sea as a figure for the contemporary kingdoms dominating the covenant community should come to the fore again in the imagery of prophetic vision. These kingdoms were viewed as monsters of the stormy deep, like leviathan Egypt of old. Such was the form they assumed in Daniel's night vision (Dan 7:2ff.). In the apocalyptic perspective of this vision (read in the light of its interpretive restatement in Rev 13:1ff.) the world kingdom enterprise takes on the character of a counterfeit creation. Satan, standing by the waters, like the Glory-Spirit over the deep in Gen 1, summons from the chaotic sea of the nations monstrous world kingdoms fashioned in his draconic likeness. The waters thus symbolize the satanic source of evil powers, hostile to the God of heaven and his people.

In this historical and literary context, the Kebar and Ulai and Tigris, the sites of the visions of Glory-theophany seen by Ezekiel and Daniel, are [[14]]
to be recognized as representing the kingdoms through which they flowed, those ungodly world powers that held sway over God's covenant land and people. And as for the appearance of the theophanic Glory above these waters of exile, it sealed the promise of a new exodus deliverance and triumph like that achieved by the Shekinah-Presence at the waters of the Egyptian sea. The presence of Israel's God in majestic splendor above these foreign waters gave reassurance that he was King of kings, ruler of all nations, and that the proud world kingdoms would therefore be brought down under his judgment, while his redemptive kingdom, though now lowly, would surely gain the upper hand and be exalted at last.

Zechariah's vision of theophany by the deep is to be understood as of a piece with those seen by Ezekiel and Daniel shortly before. To a limited extent restoration from exile had taken place in Zechariah's day, but the political conditions were not fundamentally changed. Persia, the second beast power from the deep in Dan 7, still ruled over the heritage of covenant promise. In addition to the shared imagery of theophany by the waters and the basic similarity of the historical situation, there are other correspondences between Zechariah's vision and those of Ezekiel and especially of Daniel, particularly the visions recorded in Dan 10:4ff. and resumed in 12:5ff.

Some of those correspondences between the Zechariah and Daniel passages are matters of details in literary form, others concern the essential message. A date formula of similar construction introduces both visions (Zech 1:7; Dan 10:1, 4; cf. 8:1). Note also the more than minimal identification of the seers, and the reference to them by the rare pronoun *hallāz* (Zech 2:4 [8]; Dan 8:16). (Common to both is a revelatory process in which an interpreting angel assists the human recipient in the understanding of the vision [Zech 1:9, 13, 14; Dan 10:10ff.; cf. 8:16]. Compare too the similar affects of the visionary experience on the recipients [Zech 4:1; Dan 10:9, 10].) Of larger import, each theophany vision begins with the statement that the seer looked, and behold a man (Zech 1:8; Dan 10:5; cf. Ezek 1:26, 27). And that man in both cases is a manifestation of the divine Presence. In Daniel the man is identifiable with the figure called Michael your prince (Dan 10:21) and Prince of the host, or Prince of princes (Dan 8:11, 25), the same Prince of the host whose appearance to Joshua (Josh 5:14) served as a model for the appearance to Zechariah of the man, the mounted leader of the celestial contingent. Moreover, in both visions this messianic Angel-Prince figure is involved in military engagement with the world kingdoms, in particular with Persia (Zech 1:7, 11; Dan 10:13, 20). Further, the correspondence extends to the [[15]] central burden of these visions, namely, their concern with the delay of God's decisive redemptive intervention. That eschatological concern, already intimated by the symbolic imagery of Zechariah's vision (particularly, the myrtles by the sea), is clearly voiced in the report of the horsemen and the intercession of the Angel (Zech 1:11ff.), pointedly so in the plea, "How long?" (v. 12). Precisely this same concern over the duration of the world's oppression of the covenant community is sounded in Daniel's parallel vision, there again expressed in the plaintive "How long?" (Dan 12:6).

It would be in the Lord's response to the Angel-rider's intercession at the end of Zechariah's first night vision that the ultimate triumph over the oppressive world power was reassuringly proclaimed. But the very presence of the messianic warrior by the sea, revealed in the opening symbolism of Zech 1:8, was already a sure token of the coming deliverance and victory.

Present in the Midst of the Myrtles

In our previous comments on the symbolism of Zech 1:8, we have treated the deep in connection with the figure of the rider of the red horse. In the text, it is the myrtles that are explicitly identified as being by the deep. The Angel-rider is by the deep because he comes and takes up a position in the midst of the myrtles. And that is the main point of this symbolic disclosure. While his people are in the world wilderness facing the satanic deep, while they are in the throes of their historic earthly struggle, Immanuel, mighty God, is present with them.

Myrtles as Paradise Trees in the Wilderness

Though a shrub, myrtles are sometimes listed in the Bible with trees. (Facilitating this is the fact the Hebrew *ʿēṣ* signifies wood as well as tree.) Myrtles grow to some nine feet and thus as seen here probably stood at the height of the mounted horseman. With their delicate, star-like, white flowers and fragrant, bright green leaves the hardy evergreen myrtle naturally appears in idyllic pictures of the fertility and luxuriance of the earth in the messianic age (cf. Isa 41:18, 19a; 55:13). Also suggesting that the myrtles by the deep are a paradisaical image is the fact that paradise by the deep is a feature of those historical episodes of creation, exodus, and Jordan crossing which we have noted as the background for understanding the symbolism of theophany by the deep.

At creation, the Glory-Spirit brought forth paradise out of the primordial deep and darkness to be mankind's dwelling place. The dead deep itself was transformed into the river of Eden that watered the garden with its trees, including the very tree of life, beneath the mountain of the Glory-theophany. From the beginning, luxuriant trees, in association with [[16]] theophany by waters, are a conspicuous feature of paradise, and trees of life, flourishing on either side of a river of life, appear in apocalyptic visions of Eden's paradise at last redemptively restored and perfected (Ezek 47:12; Rev 22:1, 2).

Paradise by the deep is also found to be an element of the exodus re-creation event. After recording the song of Yahweh's triumph over the deep (Exod 15:1–21), the narrative hastens to tell of Israel under the directing hand of the Glory-theophany coming to Elim and encamping there by the twelve springs of water among the seventy palm trees (Exod 15:27). As part of the larger Mosaic context in which the exodus wilderness experience is represented as a creation event, and in particular the wilderness is identified with the *tōhû*-deep (cf. Deut 32:10, 11), the description of the Elim oasis in Exod 15:27 at once evokes the paradisaical waters and trees of the garden of Eden. Also suggestive of Elim's equivalency to Eden is the linkage with the mountain of theophany of the covenant Lord (cf. Exod 16:1).

Glory-theophany over Jordan's flooding deep in the days of Joshua was again the prelude to paradise, the paradise of the promised land flowing with milk and honey (cf. Josh 5:6), with the oasis of Jericho and its perennial spring, the city of palm trees (Deut 34:3), as an identification sign at the border. In the passage of Jordan's deep, Israel moved from the sphere of wilderness into a paradise realm (cf. Josh 5:12).

It thus appears that the myrtles by the deep in Zech 1:8 reinforce the other creation and exodus motifs already observed in the imagery of this vision. They do so by adding the element of the paradise land which the Creator-Redeemer provides as the dwelling for his people and as the site of his theophanic Presence. In his lordship over the deep the Lord God transforms it into a fructifying source for the arboreal blessings of his holy garden, the homeland of his people.

More particularly, the myrtle trees point to Eden's tree of life. Being evergreens, the myrtles were a natural symbol of everlasting life. Moreover, since the eternal paradisaical life they represent is a life which in redemptive re-creation the Lord brings forth from the sea of death, the myrtles represent life from the grave, resurrection.

As to the precise picture in Zech 1:8, it is difficult to determine whether the Angel-rider stands between two myrtles or in the midst of a larger group. Eden contained two special trees and paired trees of life flank [[17]] the river of life in prophetic pictures of paradise restored. Also, visions corresponding to the first vision of Zechariah in the literary arrangement of the night visions contain symbolic pairs. In the seventh vision, the agents of Glory emerge from between two mountains (which evidently led the LXX translators to read "between the mountains" [instead of myrtles] in Zech 1:8). And in Zech 4:2, 3, we read of the lampstand (*mĕnôrâ*) with an olive tree on either side. Further, a deity standing between two trees is a common Near Eastern image. It may well be then that the Zech 1:8 imagery is that of the Glory-theophany flanked by two paradise trees of life. The messianic Glory-Angel would thereby be identified as the Resurrection and the Life, as the divine Savior of Ps 18, who raises up his suppliant people from death's deep waters.

If the myrtles between which the messianic Angel stands allude specifically to the original two special trees of Eden in their two distinct identities, then Zechariah's imagery would be informed not only by the tree of life symbolism but by the significance of the tree of judicial discerning between good and evil (cf. Gen 2:9). That tree represented the dominical authority with which man was invested as image of the sovereign Glory-Spirit. A claim was made by the Son of man to what both the trees of Eden symbolized when he said that it was given to him by the Father to have life in himself and authority to execute judgment (John 5:26, 27). This twofold messianic endowment with life and judicial authority was also represented by the two symbolic items associated with the two tables of the covenant in the ark of the covenant—the manna, heavenly bread of everlasting life (cf. John 6:32ff.), and the budded rod of Aaron, the sign of his authority in God's courts (cf. Zech 3:7; Heb 9:4; Num 17:10). Significantly, these symbols were located within the paradisaical decor of the holy of holies, beneath the Glory, flanked by cherubim, themselves peculiarly identified with life and holy authority.

Of the several instances of paradise by the deep that we have cited as background for the symbolism of Zech 1:8, Israel's encampment at the Elim oasis brings out most vividly the truth that the presence of God's Glory, the source and provider of the life and beatitude of holy paradise, may be enjoyed by his people while they are still in the wilderness, not yet arrived at their promised inheritance. The wilderness setting is mentioned just before and just after the Elim episode (Exod 15:27). From the sea of the exodus salvation to Elim was the journey through the wilderness of Shur (Exod 15:22–26). Then leading from Elim to Sinai was the journey through the wilderness of Sin (Exod 16:1ff.). Likewise in Zech 1:8, the wilderness is the setting of the myrtles of paradise and the Angel-rider's [[18]] appearance there. This becomes evident when it is recognized that in the figure of the myrtles there is an allusion to the Feast of Tabernacles, or Booths, that graphic memorial of Israel's life in the wilderness. We shall trace the intricate web of this myrtles-Tabernacles connection, observing in advance that the wilderness, the common context of the Elim paradise, the Tabernacles experience, and the myrtles by the deep in Zech 1:8, is an appropriate metaphor for the political-eschatological situation confronting not only Zechariah but the church to the end of this present world.

Myrtles and Tabernacles—Consummation Glory

When the Feast of Tabernacles was celebrated in the days of Israel's return from exile, myrtles were designated along with olive and palm trees as meeting the requirement written in the law of Moses for the construction of the shelters in which the people lived during the week of celebration (Neh 8:14ff., esp. v. 15; cf. Lev 23:39ff., esp. v. 40). One criterion in the law for the selection of trees for this purpose was their practical suitability for constructing the huts; with this in view, trees with broad fronds of leafy branches were specified. The second criterion was ornamental appearance indicated by the phrase, "trees of *hādār* (glory or beauty)." Of the several designated trees, the flowered myrtle would best serve this function. The choice of the myrtle for the Zech 1 imagery might then be to direct attention primarily to the glory aspect of the tabernacles, while their protective function remained secondary. Highlighting this connection and further prompting the selection of the myrtles here would be a word play that obtains between *hādār* (glory) and *hădas* (myrtle).

To catch the full force of the myrtles image in Zech 1, we must then inquire into the typological meaning of the Feast of Tabernacles. It was celebrated at the close of the agricultural year when all the fruit of the land had been harvested and was accordingly called the Feast of Ingathering (Exod 23:16; 34:22). Its date in the seventh month and its seven day duration, initiated and concluded (on a crowning eighth day) with days of solemn rest, emphasized its sabbatical-consummatory significance. Tabernacles was thus a typological prophecy of the completion of God's kingdom through the final universal ingathering of the elect of all nations to worship the Lord with joy as the King over all the earth, the Lord of hosts. Agreeably, Zechariah at the close of the book, returning to this theme of his opening vision, declares that in the eternal day the redeemed remnant of all the national families of the earth will from year to year come before God's throne to keep the Feast of Tabernacles (Zech 14:16). Employing the customary prophetic idiom of Old Testament typology, he thus indicated that beyond the final eschatological conflict (Zech 14:1ff.) [[19]] what Tabernacles had adumbrated will be realized. This would also be the fulfillment of the prophecy of Zechariah's contemporary, Haggai, dated on the last day of the most recent Tabernacles feast, shortly before Zechariah's visions (cf. Hag 2:1; Zech 1:7), declaring that the Lord would bring the glory of the nations into his house (Hag 2:6–9). Similarly, the apostle John saw the universal harvest of the worshippers of the Lamb (cf. Rev 14:14–16), an innumerable multitude out of every people and nation, with palms in hand engaged in Tabernacles celebration before God's throne (Rev 7:9), covered there by the tabernacle of God (Rev 7:15). The three annual festivals all featured pilgrimage of God's people to his house, but the connection of Tabernacles with the final completion of harvest made the Tabernacles pilgrimage to Jerusalem the premier sign of the final universal pilgrimage and permanent assembling of the covenant people of all ages at the heavenly Zion.

Myrtles and Tabernacles—Present Glory in the Wilderness

A curious feature of the Feast of Tabernacles is that while its place in the annual and agricultural calendars made it a sign of the consummation of the kingdom, the situation to which it pointed as a historical memorial and which it dramatized by the peculiar manner of its observance identified it with an earlier, emphatically pre-consummation stage in the redemptive process. This intriguing combination of contrasting concepts finds expression in the two names of the festival—Ingathering and Booths. The former, as we have seen, speaks of the final harvesting into the heavenly assembly (cf. Rev 14:14–16). The latter refers to the pre-consummation condition of God's people. The name Booths reflects of course the requirement that during the festival the pilgrims were to dwell in structures of leafy branches in imitation of the Israelites' mode of life while they were on the move in the wilderness between the salvation event at the Egyptian sea and their entrance into Canaan, the prototype of the Sabbath-paradise to come (Lev 23:43). The rough simplicity of the booths underscored the unsettled, impermanent character of the wilderness situation. The huts occupied during the Tabernacles festival were only a temporary arrangement, like the booths that used to be set up in the fields by harvesters. This comparison suggests the possibility that an original connection of the two names, Ingathering and Booths, is to be found in some old harvest festival celebrated in such temporary shelters in the field. If the Mosaic ordinance of the Feast of Tabernacles is an adaptation of such a harvest festival, it has invested the old form with a totally new, redemptive-historical significance.

The transient nature of Israel's experience in the wilderness was further reflected in the kind of dwelling the Lord prescribed for himself at Sinai. As [[20]] a gracious expression of his Immanuel-Presence with his people, the Lord adopted a form of residence similar to their own. The temporary nature of even this more elaborate tabernacle of the Lord is emphasized in the narrative of David's proposal to build a permanent house for the ark of God (2 Sam 7:1ff.). From what the Lord says on that occasion about his continuing use of the tabernacle-form of sanctuary, it is evident that the transitory character of Israel's existence extended beyond the wilderness journeying into the tumultuous days of their penetration of the land and the troubled period of the judges, down to the emergence of the Davidic dynasty and the obtaining of rest from all the enemies round about. A wilderness-like, impermanent state of affairs continued all the while God's dwelling place retained its temporary tent-form, until that very time when the Lord was arranging through covenant with David for the constructing of a temple-house by David's son (2 Sam 7:13).

Of course even under Israel's theocratic kings the kingdom of God did not yet attain its true permanence. After all, Canaan was not the true Sabbath land but only a prototype, and Jerusalem was not the heavenly city but only a foreshadowing of it. Celebrating the Feast of Tabernacles in those days would have been a reminder of this. There in Jerusalem, on the roofs and in the open court of the city of the Great King, the Israelites had to set up and reside in the temporary booths—a declaration that this was not the eternal city itself and this was not the time or place for the saints' everlasting mansions of glory. Did not the (apparent) preservation of the portable wilderness tabernacle within Solomon's temple (cf. 1 Kgs 8:4) serve as a similar reminder, as a sign that even this more durable structure on fixed foundations was only a typological prefiguration of the truly permanent temple to be built by the Greater than Solomon? Though Israel enjoyed a privileged position in the typological order of things they were not thereby prematurely transported out of the basic circumstances of this present world. From the fall until the inauguration of the world to come at the consummation, life for the people of God is always a pilgrim journey through an alien wilderness under the shadow of death. So it was in Zechariah's day. So it is in ours.

Two different moments in the redemptive journey are symbolized in the Feast of Tabernacles, signified by the two names, Booths and Ingathering. It reminded God's people that they were pilgrims and aliens in this world (Booths) and simultaneously promised them that they were the heirs of heaven (Ingathering). But the symbolism of this festival was even more richly complex in its portrayal of the eschatological nature of the existence of God's people in this world. It did not simply declare that the [[21]] promised goal of the consummation of redemption would at last be reached; it said something too about a present realization of that eschatological hope.

The actual character of the process of redemptive eschatology is such that heaven breaks into the history of this world beforehand, particularly in the reality of the presence of the Spirit, re-creatively fashioning God's people in the image of his Glory. It is especially (though not for the first time) in the present age of the church that this semi-eschatological situation obtains, the consummation being already experienced in the inner glory of the supernatural presence and renewing power of the Spirit, even while the consummation in its external dimensions of glory is not yet attained. And this realized eschatology of the inner glory of the Spirit, experienced even in the time of our tabernacling in the wilderness of this present age, we find to have had a place in the rich symbolism of the Feast of Tabernacles. (Of interest here is the way Paul combines the teaching of the gift of the Spirit as a present earnest of glorification with the representation of our temporal, mortal condition by the figure of a tabernacle [2 Cor 5:1–5; cf. 2 Pet 1:13, 14].) To see how it was that the Feast of Tabernacles signified this additional feature of a present participation in the promised future glory, we must explore further the symbolism of the booths. In the process, we will also discover further confirmation of our interpretation of the myrtles in Zech 1 as containing an allusion to these booths.

Myrtles and Tabernacles—Replicas of the Glory-Spirit

Crude in form, hastily set up, and thus apt symbols of the impermanence of the wilderness era, the booths were nevertheless designed to be replicas of the theophanic Glory itself. Materials prescribed for construction of the booths are described in Lev 23:40–42 (cf. Neh 8:15) by terms that call attention to their likeness to the Glory-cloud. Trees of splendor (*hādār*), or majestic trees, were to be used. The term *hādār* is a synonym of *kābôd*, "glory," repeatedly serving as its poetic parallel in descriptions of the majestic radiance and beauty of the theophanic appearance of the heavenly King (cf. Pss 90:16; 96:6; 104:1; 145:5; Isa 2:10, 19, 21; 35:2). God's kingship over all the earth is dominant in these contexts. Of special interest in connection with the symbolism of Zech 1:8 is Ps 104:1, where the *hādār* is identified with the theophanic light of the Lord (v. 2), who is pictured as riding on his cloud chariot (v. 3). Other than Lev 23:40, *hādār* is applied to trees only in Isa 35:2. There it refers to the splendor of Carmel's wooded range and Sharon's dense vegetation, in parallelism with the *kābôd* of Lebanon's majestic cedars. And significantly the verse concludes by paralleling this *kābôd* and *hādār* of majestic trees to the *kābôd* and *hādār* of Yahweh, our [[22]] God. It is in the wilderness that this divine glory and arboreal splendor are said to appear. This forecast of the renewal of paradise in the wilderness is also found in Isa 41:19, which mentions the myrtle along with the cedar and other trees that will characterize the once dry wilderness now turned into springs and pools of water (v. 18) by the Lord's re-creating hand (v. 20, cf. *br*ʾ). Such, we have seen, was the promise of the imagery of the myrtles by the deep in Zech

1:8, another link in the connection between these myrtles and the booths of Lev 23:40–42 (cf. Neh 8:15).

In light of this usage of *hādār*, the requirement that the booths of the Tabernacles festival be made of trees of *hādār* apparently had in view their serving as symbolic images of the Glory-Spirit. To the same effect is the stipulation in Lev 23:40 that the wood for the booths be selected from leafy trees, trees of densely interwoven foliage (*ʿābôt*). Here again, this time more subtly through the device of paronomasia, a connection is made with the Glory-cloud. For *ʿābôt* also appears as the plural of *ʿāb* ("dark cloud mass," also a "wood thicket"), which is the term found in Exod 19:9 for the theophanic cloud of Sinai. It is similarly used elsewhere, and in particular for the clouds as the chariot on which the Lord rides (Job 22:14; Pss 18:11, 12 [12, 13]; 104:3; Isa 19:1). The Ps 18 example is of special importance because of its close relationship to the Zech 1:8 imagery of the mounted divine warrior who comes to deliver his people from the deep (cf. Ps 18:10, 16 [11, 17]).

The connection between the booths of glory-wood and the Glory theophany is also made from the other side. That is, not only are the booths described in Glory-cloud terms, but the Glory theophany is referred to as a booth (*sukkâ* the plural of which, *sukkôt*, is the name of the festival). One instance is the very verse (v. 11 [12]) in Ps 18 just cited in illustration of the usage of *ʿāb* ("thick cloud"). Here God's *sukkâ* ("covert," cf. the parallel *sēter*, "hiding place") is in fact identified as those dark water-clouds of the sky (cf. Job 36:29). Psalm 31:20 [21] extols the Lord whose Presence is the hiding place (*sēter*), the *sukkâ* for those who take refuge in him (v. 20 [21]). In the preview of the day of Zion's consummation in Isa 4:2–6, it is said that when Yahweh engages anew in creation (cf. *bārāʾ*, v. 5) the Shekinah pillar of cloud and fire (v. 5), the Spirit (cf. *rûaḥ*, v. 4) of the original creation, will overshadow the mountain of God and the assembly of the redeemed. Over everything the Glory (*kābôd*) will be a canopy (v. 5) and a covert (*sukkâ*, v. 6).

We can further demonstrate the identification of the shelters of the Tabernacles festival as replicas of the Glory theophany and at the same [[23]]
time clarify the choice of the myrtle in Zech 1:8 as a symbolic cipher for these booths by tracing the matter to its ultimate roots. Hovering over the mountain of God in Eden, the Glory-cloud was a shelter, a shade by day and light by night, a roof and a lamp. God was man's original dwelling place. This is the picture that informs prophetic views of the paradise of the new creation (Isa 4:5, 6; Rev 22:5). A natural replica of this supernatural shelter was at hand in the trees the Lord made and among which he placed man in the garden. Trees, especially those with dense foliage, afforded a covering,

a lodging place protected from the elements, a shade from the heat and a covert in the storm (cf. the cosmic tree of Dan 4:10–12, a dwelling place for all the creatures of the earth). And trees in their kindled state provided the light and warmth of fire, the benefits of the sun captured from the air and embodied in the living tree and then released into the air again in the tree sacrificed in the flames. Like the luminous, overshadowing Glory-cloud, trees were a house, a protecting roof and an illuminating torch-lamp. In other respects too there was likeness. Like the Glory-theophany in its majestic beauty, the trees were a delight to the eyes. Like the Glory-Spirit, the source of life, the trees provided the fruit of life; they were good for food. Indeed God invested one tree with special symbolic meaning as a tree of life, and another tree with the significance of the judgment tree, reflecting the judicial dominion of the Glory-Spirit. These two trees were sacramental means facilitating the full development of man as the image of God, the likeness of the Glory-Spirit.

The character of trees as natural poetic images of the Glory-canopy may explain the significance of the frequent appearance of trees as cultic objects at places of worship. But here we want to note that what the Lord prescribed by way of dwellings en route to the promised land and in the commemoration of this in the Feast of Booths was essentially an adaptation of the native role and simile-value of trees.

The tents in which the Lord and the Israelites tabernacled in the wilderness and the huts provided for the Feast of Booths are structurally quite similar. They are alike impermanent, wooden frame construction with non-rigid coverings. In so far as the tent coverings were made of cotton or linen cloth, as in the case of the inner curtains of the Lord's tabernacle, they were like the booths of the festival in having coverings of plant material. The wood and foliage of the trees were incorporated in ruder form in the huts, while the tree and other plant products used as material in the tents underwent more processing by the artisans. But that difference is simply disregarded as insignificant when booths are appointed for the feast as equivalents of the tent-dwellings occupied by God's people in the [[24]]
wilderness (Lev 23:40). The booths and tents were much the same, and both were in form and material essentially modified tree shelters. That being so, the myrtle trees of the Zech 1:8 vision were all the more a natural symbol to evoke the Feast of Tabernacles and in particular the booths, revealing behind them a more fundamental level of symbolism in the trees of Eden and so illuminating their nature as replicas of the divine Glory, for such were the trees of the garden of God.

Moreover, the fundamental structural equivalency of the booths and the particular tent that the Lord prescribed as his own dwelling in the midst of the tents of Israel brings into still clearer focus the nature of the booths as replicas of the Glory-canopy. For the holy tabernacle was precisely and on a most elaborate scale the ectypal earthly replica of the archetypal heavenly Glory-temple that appeared on the mountain of God. It was the Council Tent (*ʾōhel môʿēd*), so named as symbolic copy of the heavenly council (*môʿēd*) of the Lord of hosts. Because of the presence of this divine council on the mountain (*har*) of God, the latter was called *har môʿēd* (cf. *harmagedōn*), Council Mountain. Har Magedon is the mountain of God's enthronement and the mountain of judgment. The likeness of the booths of the Tabernacles festival to the holy tabernacle, therefore, reinforces the evidence previously presented identifying the booths as symbolic replications of the Glory-Spirit (namely, the shared designations of the booths and the Glory-theophany as alike canopies of royal beauty and their common relation to the trees of Eden). The picture that emerges in the Tabernacles festival is then one of the Glory-Spirit re-creatively overshadowing the redeemed Israelite community in the wilderness, fashioning them in his own glory-likeness. Consequently, the exodus typology depicts the mission of the coming Christ as a work of new creation, especially the creation of the new humanity in the image of God, a transformation perfected at last in their glorification and reception into the heavenly tabernacle.

Myrtles and Tabernacles—Transfiguration and Tabernacles

A foretaste of the ultimate restoration of the Glory-image and at the same time a dramatic exposition of the meaning of the Tabernacles festival along these lines was given in the episode of our Lord's transfiguration. Various features of the transfiguration relate that event to the Feast of Tabernacles, even while others identify it as a messianic counterpart to the encounter of Moses with the Glory theophany on Sinai. The transfiguration was a wilderness event, apart on a high mountain. Redolent of the wilderness too were both the visitors seen with Jesus, Moses, and Elijah. Also, there is the possibility that the introductory time detail, "after six days" (Matt 17:1; Mark 9:2; cf. Luke [[25]] 9:28, "about eight days"), refers to the time leading from the Day of Atonement to the Feast of Tabernacles. The exodus context of Tabernacles is echoed in the topic of conversation, the *exodos* ("decease" or "departure") about to be accomplished by Jesus (Luke 9:31). Above all, the mention of the booths, which Peter suggested be constructed for Jesus, Moses, and Elijah, recalls the wilderness shelters of the Israelites and the imitative reconstructions thereof prescribed in the Feast of Tabernacles. (On the rendering of *skēnē* as "booths," cf. the LXX use of it for *sukkâ* in Lev 23:42–43 and the LXX use of *skēnopēgia* to designate the Feast of Tabernacles in, e.g., Zech 14:16.) Especially important for the understanding of the festival booths as images of the Glory-cloud is the way the booths and the overshadowing cloud are brought together in the transfiguration narrative. Peter's suggestion about the booths was made as Moses and Elijah were departing (Luke 9:33a). So far as it made sense at all (cf. Mark 9:6; Luke 9:33c), the idea apparently was that these two might be persuaded to stay on, continuing this "good" arrangement. As specifically stated in Matt 17:5 and Luke 9:34, it was while Peter was proposing the man-made shelters that the theophanic cloud, the divine covering, overshadowed the scene. In this combination of earthly booths and heavenly cloud the transfiguration answers to the Israelite booths and the Glory-cloud in the wilderness and to the imitative commemoration of that wilderness situation in the Feast of Tabernacles.

That the transfiguration was indeed antitypal to the Tabernacles symbolism becomes plain once we have recognized that the festival booths were designed to be images of the Glory-canopy, for the transfiguration itself consists in precisely such a replication of the divine Glory. The physical glorification of Jesus was a fashioning in the likeness of the bright theophanic cloud (cf. Matt 17:5) that overarched the holy mountain. This majesty of Jesus was a revelation of him as the Son, the image-likeness of the Father, as the voice from the majestic Glory declared (cf. 2 Pet 1:16, 17). In the case of the first Adam, likeness to the Glory-Spirit was never completed, the component of physical glory not having been attained. But the glory-image is perfected in the second Adam, as the firstfruits of a new humanity, and that ultimate consummating of the reproduction of the divine image in man was anticipated in the transfiguration.

Additionally, the theme of renewal in the image of Glory is associated with both of those who appeared with Jesus in glory at the transfiguration. As a result of his approach to the overshadowing Glory on Sinai, the countenance of Moses was transfigured. And Elijah, who had his own close encounter with the Glory on the mountain of God, also experienced a [[26]] remarkable foretaste of physical glorification in his deathless exodus, borne aloft by the fiery chariots and horses of Glory. These two who participated in the transfiguration with Jesus were the only two in the history of Israel qualified by both these credentials of theophanic encounter and physical transformation for appearance at this antitypal event of Glory replication.

So Peter spoke better than he knew in introducing the Tabernacles motif of the booths into the transfiguration episode. Of course, the Son from heaven was here and it was therefore not a time for earthly symbols but for the heavenly reality. Nevertheless the transfiguration was indeed a new covenant counterpart to Tabernacles. Hence in the antitypal transfiguration event the image-relationship of the Tabernacles booths to the Glory as replicas to a divine paradigm received the bright illumination of historical fulfillment.

Glory-Presence in the Midst of the Myrtles by the Deep

We have found that the Feast of Tabernacles as a harvest festival was a promise of the final ingathering, the hope of ultimate glorification, and that its requirement to live in rustic booths simultaneously reminded worshippers of the wilderness-like, not-yet-arrived nature of their life in the present world. These very same booths were designed, however, to be replicas of the theophanic Glory and so were affirmations of the Creator's redemptive renewal of his people in his image, a re-creation that begins here and now during the wilderness journey, even if the perfecting of the Glory-likeness awaits arrival at the heavenly destination. The booths thus portray the complex eschatological character of the present existence of the saints as both already and not yet. By symbolizing the believers' present participation in the heavenly glory in the Spirit, the booths indicate that their life on earth, awaiting the future consummation of glory, is already in measure one of realized eschatology.

What is true of the Tabernacles booths will also be true of the imagery of the myrtles in Zech 1:8. The myrtles by the deep recall the Elim oasis in the wilderness and like it give promise of the glorious paradise inheritance at the end of the journey. As a promissory sign of the restoration of paradise at the consummation, they correspond to the prophetic ingathering aspect of the Feast of Tabernacles. But they also correspond to the booths as symbolic replicas of the Glory-covering. When we were tracing a common rootage for the symbolism of the booths and the myrtles in the trees of the garden of Eden, we reflected on the character of these trees as natural images (and, in the case of the two special trees, as sacramental images) of the Glory-canopy over paradise. So perceived, the [[27]] myrtles by the deep emerge as signs of God's redemptive re-creating of his image in the new humanity. Like the booths of Tabernacles, the myrtles teach an already/not yet eschatology of the anticipation of heaven in the course of the earthly pilgrimage of the redeemed, a realized eschatology of the Spirit's renewing of the glory within before the parousia of the Glory without. They tell of a glory experienced by God's children even while laboring on through the wilderness over against the deep.

By portraying the replication of the divine image in the symbolism of the booths, the Feast of Tabernacles was a reminder of the presence of the Glory-Spirit himself, the archetypal Shekinah-shelter which hovered above the community in the wilderness. Tabernacles was thus a celebration of God's presence in the midst of his people. In the case of the equivalent symbolism of the myrtles in Zech 1:8, that reality of the divine presence took visible form in the appearance of the Lord of Glory in the figure of the Angel of the Presence, the rider of the red horse, seen by Zechariah as accompanied by the other agents of the divine council and stationed in the midst of the myrtles. This presence of the Lord himself among his myrtle-people is the glory of the covenant, the secret of all life and beatitude, a guarantee that the Glory within will be followed by the Glory without. For the people of God, the bearers of the Father's image, this Presence is an earnest of the transfiguration change awaiting them in the Sabbath land beyond the wilderness at the parousia-revelation of God's Glory.

Glory-Angel in the Midst of the Myrtles and in the Burning Bush

Zechariah's opening vision answers in its imagery and message to the inaugural revelation of the old covenant order by which Moses was called to lead Israel out of Egypt, through the wilderness, to its promised inheritance (Exod 3). Zechariah saw the Angel of the Lord, commander of the fiery heavenly beings, in the midst of the myrtle shrubs by the deep. Moses saw the theophanic fire, identified with the Angel of the Lord, in the midst of the desert shrub in the wilderness over against the Egyptian sea. These two episodes are linked through their mutual relationship to the appearance of the Angel to Joshua near Jericho, recounted in Josh 5. We have observed above the interrelation of the Zech 1 and Josh 5 appearances. The connection between the encounters of Moses and Joshua with the divine Angel is strengthened by the common feature of the divine command to each man to remove his footwear because the site of the Angel's presence was holy (Exod 3:5; Josh 5:15). A closer look at the theophany of Exod 3 should open another window on the message of the vision of Zech 1:8.

[[28]] Clear direction for understanding the significance of the theophany of the burning-but-unconsumed bush emerges from a comparison of that event (narrated in Exod 3) and the Sinai theophany witnessed by Israel (as reviewed in Deut 4 and 5). Both events involve a fiery theophany and both transpire at Horeb, the mountain of God (Exod 3:1; Deut 4:10; 5:23). Possibly there is a word play on Sinai in the term *sĕnê*, "bush," in Exod 3. In any case, both the bush and Sinai are described by the same phrase, "burning with fire" (Exod 3:2; Deut 4:11; 5:23), and both passages speak of people "approaching" (Exod 3:5; Deut 5:23) to "this great sight/fire" (Exod 3:3; Deut 5:25; 18:16). Certainly, then, the fire in the burning bush is not symbolic of the fiery trials of oppressed Israel, but is the manifestation of the presence of the Lord, who is a consuming fire (Exod 19:18; 24:17; Deut 4:24; cf. Deut 33:16). This is stated explicitly in Exod 3:2 if we translate: "The Angel of Yahweh appeared to him as [*bêt essentiae*] a flame of fire." And this leads to the meaning of the bush and the wonder of its not being consumed. At Sinai a covenant was established between Yahweh and Israel as a nation, a covenant that brought the consuming fiery Presence of the Lord of Glory into the midst of the covenant community. In the Exod 3 anticipation of Sinai, the bush in which the flaming theophany appears must then represent God's people. What depicts the afflicted condition of the Israelites is not the fire in the bush, but the nature of the bush itself: a lowly desert shrub. If, as often conjectured, it is a thorny type of bush, that fact and its wilderness location might be suggestive of the sin-cursed world outside Eden, in which God's people, along with all the rest of mankind, have their existence until the end of the days (cf. Gen 3:17–19, 23, 24).

But the key question of interpretation concerns the great wonder that the bush is aflame, yet not consumed by the flames. It is the meaning of this, in particular, that is clearly explained by the comparison of Exod 3 and the Deut 4 and 5 account of Sinai. It turns out that the main problem was not how the Israelites could manage to endure in the face of the world tyrant. Rather, the fundamental issue was the ultimate religious question of how sinners can survive in the parousia-Glory presence of God and his consuming holiness. Israel's election to privileged covenant relationship, by bringing the Glory of the Lord into their very midst, seemed to threaten them with fiery destruction. Yet they were not consumed. That was the wonder, a mystery of redeeming love and grace. They expressed it in fearful amazement: "Behold, Yahweh our God has showed us his Glory and his Greatness and we have heard his voice from the midst of the fire. We have seen today that God can speak with man and he can still live!" (Deut 5:24). The Glory-flame descends upon the bush but [[29]] does not consume it. The bush still lives. This miracle of grace was not to be presumed upon as a covenant guarantee regardless of Israel's covenant keeping or covenant breaking. Alert to the continuing threat of the holy Presence, the Israelites hastened to request some distancing of themselves from it through the provision of a mediator. They plead: "Why should we die? This great fire will consume us" (Deut 5:25).

After Israel's rebellion in the matter of the golden calf, the Lord expressed a reluctance to expose Israel to this danger inherent in the presence of his Glory-theophany in their midst. He proposed instead to send with them his Angel unattended by the Glory (Exod 33:2, 3). For if God were to go with them in the Shekinah Glory, he might destroy them (v. 5). At the intercession of Moses, the Lord relented and promised: "My Presence will go with you" (Exod 33:14). However, precisely what Israel feared and God warned would happen did happen. One such divine judgment came in response to Israel's further rebellion against the covenant on their departure from Sinai, an episode that was memorialized by naming the site Taberah ("consuming," a designation that embodies the verbal root *bʿr*, used for the burning bush in Exod 3:2, 3). The blessing of the covenant, the wonder of grace, is that the bush burns (*bʿr*), but is not consumed or devoured (*ʾkl*). Describing the curse of the covenant against repudiators of grace at Taberah, the biblical narrative employs the terminology of Exod 3:2 in an ironic reversal. Numbers 11:1 relates that fire from the Lord burned (*bʿr*) among the Israelites and devoured (*ʾkl*) some of them.

The old covenant canon closes not long after Zechariah's night visions with this theme of the crisis of the divine fire in the thorn bush. Malachi predicts the advent of the Angel of the covenant as a refiner's fire, a day that burns (*bʿr*) like a furnace, and raises again the ancient, cardinal question facing the sinner: Who can survive at his fiery parousia (Mal 3:1, 2; 4:1 [3:19])? As for the arrogant who do not fear the Lord, the prophet warns the fire will totally consume them (4:1 [3:19]). But he knows that the fiery Glory-Spirit is the executor of the blessings as well as the curses of the covenant. He has not forgotten the sign at the inauguration of the old covenant, the miracle of the Glory-flame in the bush that still lived. Accordingly he likens the parousia-Glory not only to the burning furnace but to the sun of righteousness which rises with healing in its wings for those who fear God's name (4:2 [3:20]). The imagery of the winged sun-disc belongs to an ancient iconographic tradition that represented the majesty of the divine presence as a luminous glory between winged or other objects. It is a prominent motif in the symbolism of Zechariah's night visions, with a form of it, as noted above, possibly in the opening vision of [[30]] the Glory Angel between the myrtles.

Present in the midst of the myrtles, the Angel-Commander of the fiery horses of heaven promises life and peace, vindication over against the satanic forces of the deep, and exaltation from wilderness existence into the glory of the consummated city of God. Like the burning bush, these myrtles are aflame with the presence of divine glory, but they are not consumed. This wonder seen by Zechariah is a sign confirming God's faithfulness to his covenant with Abraham and his seed, the covenant of promise not disannulled by the law (Gal 3:17). It speaks of the Immanuel-mystery, which is most fully revealed in the new covenant, whose mediator is the Glory-Angel become God-man, the incarnate rider on the red horse.

John, the seer of the New Testament Apocalypse, also saw a version of the sign of the burning bush (Rev 1:12–20), a version adapted from another Zecharian form of it (cf. Zech 4)—the transfigured-glorified Jesus, the light of the world, standing among the seven lamps, burning but not consumed, symbol of the church renewed in the luminous image of Christ, blessed by the presence of Glory within even during its present existence in the wilderness, bound for the Glory of the New Jerusalem. The Angel of fire in the bush, the Angel-rider in the midst of the myrtles, the glorified Christ in the midst of the lampstands—each represents the already/not yet stage in the process of the formation of the eternal temple-city, the stage of the covenant people's life in the present world wilderness.

PART FIVE

Resurrection and Consummation

CHAPTER THIRTEEN

Death, Leviathan, and the Martyrs: Isaiah 24:1–27:1

(1986)

A series of Isaianic oracles concerning the nations (chs. 13–23) culminates in a section popularly known as the Isaiah apocalypse[1] (chs. 24–27). From 27:2 on, the focus of this section is on Israel, its fall and fullness.[2] (More than is generally recognized, Paul tapped this vein for his discussion of Israel in Rom 9–11.) In Isa 24:1–27:1 there is a broader, universal perspective.[3] The present essay will concentrate on this first part of the "apocalypse," treating it as a distinct composition and attempting to show how the subject of death, or better, the Lord's conquest of death, permeates and structures its contents. Some contribution may thereby be made to the higher critical debate, at least as to the unity of the material. But my primary interest is in opening up exegetically Isaiah's pastoral theology of death and resurrection and judgment. And in the process, I also want to explore the extraordinary influence exercised by 24:1–27:1 on subsequent biblical revelation, particularly on certain major eschatological passages in the New Testament.

Victory Over Death

Three passages celebrating Yahweh's victory over death occupy the key positions in the structure of Isa 24:1–27:1.[4] They frame the composition [[230]] with

1. The form-critical assessment expressed by this label is disputed, other genres (including cantata) being proposed.

2. At the close, however, the focus seems to widen (cf. 27:13).

3. Isaiah 24:1–27:1 and 27:2–13 are alike in their eschatological extension to the final divine advent.

4. The customary chapter partitioning (except for the separation of 27:1 from ch. 26) appropriately marks the main divisions.

introduction (24:1–3) and conclusion (26:19–27:1) and form its central apex (25:6–8). Each, by means of its own distinctive image, graphically depicts a dramatic reversal that overtakes the realm of death.

The Devourer Devoured

I shall start with Isa 25:6–8, the centerpiece of the composition,[5] and its picture of the eschatological banquet. To appreciate the point of this imagery it is necessary to recall the reputation of the grave as the great devourer. Sheol opens wide its spacious maw and swallows down victims insatiably.[6] But at the banquet for all peoples "in that day" (cf. v. 9) a remarkable reversal will take place. The Lord will become the devourer[7] and death, the famed and fearful swallower, will itself be swallowed up (v. 8).[8]

Perhaps the banquet scenario in 25:6–8 was prompted by the desire to exploit the identity of death as the swallower.[9] However, the divinely hosted banquet is a standard feature in visions of the life to come in biblical and extrabiblical literature. Moreover, the victory banquet is a regular element in the epic pattern of the conflict of the hero-deity and the monstrous power of disorder and death, which is in evidence elsewhere in the passage. In any case it was the communion meal of the elders of Israel on the mountain of God after the Exodus-triumph over the dragon (Exod 24:9–11)[10] that provided the specific typological model for Isa 25:6–8. For "on this mountain," the location assigned to the banquet in 25:6–7, refers back to the 24:23 scene of the Glory epiphany before the elders on Mount Zion, and that in turn clearly recalls the banquet scene at Sinai (cf. Exod 24:10–11).

---

5. Within chapter 25 itself this passage stands in the center between two confession sections (vv. 1–5; 9–12).

6. Isaiah 5:14 speaks of Sheol making wide its throat (or enlarging its appetite) and opening its mouth without limit to engulf the multitudes descending therein. In the Ugaritic texts Mot, the god of death, is similarly described (*UT* 67, i 6–7). Cf. also Exod 15:12; Num 16:30, 32, 34; 26:10; Deut 11:6; Ps 106:17; Prov 1:12; Hab 2:5.

7. It is particularly as the consuming theophanic fire that God is the devourer (cf., e.g., Exod 24:17; Deut 4:24; 9:3; Ps 21:9 [10]; Isa 29:6; 30:27, 30).

8. Announcements of God's judgments on his enemies frequently involve such radical reversals. The evil that they have purposed or perpetrated boomerangs against them.

9. Variations on this image recur as a kind of leitmotiv of the haunting presence of death throughout this composition.

10. Use of the dragon-conflict pattern for the Exodus history in poetic portions of the Bible is well known.

The image of death as the swallower, alluded to in Isa 25:6–8, leads naturally to the further image of death as a cover. Thus in the Num 16 narrative the earth opens its mouth and swallows the rebels (v. 32) and then closes over them and covers them (v. 33; cf. Ps 106:17). The covering, concealing aspect of the grave is prominent in the concluding treatment of the victory over death in Isa 26:21, but it is probable that here in 25:7 there is also reference to the grave, the swallower, as a cover over all peoples. In parallel with God's swallowing of death (v. 8) we read of his swallowing "the face of the wrapping that enfolds[11] all peoples, the woven thing woven over all the nations" (v. 7). This woven covering is most likely a shroud.[12] But this is apparently a figure for the grave, the universal shroud that covers all humanity in their common lot of death.[13] It could then be that the explanation of the "face"[14] of the shroud is to be found in the common expression "the face of the earth," inasmuch as it is this face, [[231]] or surface, of the earth that constitutes the covering shroud over Sheol's occupants.[15] The two instances of Yahweh's swallowing (bl^{c}) would then together encompass as their twin objects death (v. 8) and Hades (v. 7).

Quoting Isaiah's forecast of the swallowing of death (25:8), Paul identifies this banquet of everlasting victory with the believers' ultimate putting on of the glory of incorruption and immortality (1 Cor 15:54).[16] And the apostle John portrays this death of death in his account of the resurrection (the "second resurrection" in the first/second death/resurrection scheme of Rev 20–21)[17] as a casting of death and Hades (or the "first death" in that same scheme) into "the second death," the lake of fire (Rev 20:14; cf. 21:4).

11. Cf. the use of *lwṭ* in 1 Sam 21:9 [10]; 1 Kgs 19:13.

12. Some take it as a mourning veil, others as the net by which death ensnares its victims, a widely attested image.

13. Cf. Hab 2:5; Josh 23:14.

14. The "face" of the shroud in Isa 25:7 might also allude to the face-portraits on mummy cases and on coffins with anthropoid lids.

15. To be judged to eat dust forever was for the serpent to be cursed with death. But Yahweh's swallowing of the earth-cover of death and the grave is a banquet of resurrection life forever, a devouring-death of death. Anticipating this eschatological banquet is the sacramental supper of the Lord, in which a feasting on Christ's death celebrates his victory of life.

16. Cf. also 2 Tim 1:10.

17. Cf. Meredith G. Kline, "The First Resurrection," *WTJ* 37 (1975): 366–75 [= pp. 239–47 in the present volume].

The Vessel Emptied

Anticipating the master theme of Isa 24–26, the opening verses (24:1–3) foretell the Lord's mighty overthrow of death. The theme is expressed in terms that suggest that here at the beginning death is already being thought of as the greedy, gluttonous devourer, filled with generations on generations of mankind. In 25:8 the great reversal is a matter of the swallowing of the swallower. Here it takes the form of the upending and emptying out of what had been a filled container.[18]

"See, Yahweh pours out the netherworld and empties it out; He turns it upside down and scatters out its occupants" (v. 1). The verb *bqq*, "empty out," onomatopoetically imitates the gurgling sound of water plopping out of a bottle. It is here reinforced by the similar sounding *blq*: *bôqēq . . . ûbôlĕqâ*.[19] The use of *ʾereṣ* for the netherworld is now well recognized.[20] In the present general context note, for example, "the realm (*ʾereṣ*) of the shades" (26:19).[21] The "face," *pānêhâ*, combined here with the verb *ʿwh*, "bend low,"[22] to express "turn upside down" apparently refers to the ground as surface of the grave,[23] which is compared to the top of a vessel bent over or upturned to pour out its contents.

According to the customary view of 24:1–3, it introduces the theme of the desolating of the earth, which is then traced further in the rest of chapter 24. But as interpreted above, this opening passage depicts the ultimate repair of the situation lamented in the immediately following verses and

18. Jeremiah 51:34 combines the imagery of Isa 24:1–3; 25:6–8 in one picture of destruction in terms of devouring, monster-like swallowing, filling the maw, and emptying a vessel.

19. Nominal derivatives of these two verbs appear as synonyms in Nah 2:10 [11], a passage descriptive of the judgment of Nineveh, which has just been likened to a pool draining away (v. 8 [9]). Also the emptying process in both passages is equated with a plundering (*bzz*) of the plunderer (Isa 24:3; Nah 2:9 [10]). Cf. Jer 48:11–12.

20. The word *ʾereṣ* does not thereby denote two entirely distinct entities. It is rather that the earth as the receptacle and covering of the dead becomes functionally the grave or netherworld as one aspect of its total historical identity.

21. A parallel phrase in 26:19 is "the dwellers (*šōkĕnê*) of the dust," an equivalent of "its [the netherworld's] inhabitants (*yōšĕbêhā*)" in 24:1.

22. Cf. Ps 38:6 [7].

23. On the possible resumption of this concept of the face of the earth in 25:7 see above. The Sumerian myth *Inanna's Descent to the Netherworld* (117, 123) refers to an entrance gate Ganzir, called the "face" of the netherworld. The familiar imagery of the gates of death is found in Isa 38:10. Cf. Ps 9:13–14 [14–15]; Matt 16:18; Rev 1:18.

hence serves as an introduction not to chapter 24 alone but to the entirety of Isa 24–26. The interpretation of this passage as an opening statement of the main overall theme of the resurrection victory is corroborated by its closing formula: "For Yahweh has spoken this word" (v. 3). [[232]] Such an assurance of the certainty of fulfillment is better accounted for if what has just been foretold is not merely the desolation of the earth but the astounding prospect of the termination of the sway of death. Moreover, the one other place within Isa 24–26 where essentially this same formula of divine utterance appears is at the close of the climactic assertion of the resurrection in 25:6–8.

The resurrection-judgment, according to 24:1–3, is universal. This is suggested by the paired listing of the representatives of opposite ends of the socioeconomic spectrum of mankind (v. 2).[24] Subsequently the theme of the termination of death becomes more specifically occupied with the resurrection of the people of God. Thus in 25:6–8 and 26:19 and following, this theme finds expression within the genre of hymnic praise, the saints celebrating the resurrection as God's saving triumph that delivers them from the satanic hosts. Not merely excluded from that salvation, the wicked are viewed along with death as the enemy from whom God rescues his own. But before the focus is narrowed down to the meaning of the resurrection for the redeemed, 24:1–3 presents the broader picture of a general resurrection, an emptying out of all the contents of the death-vessel without distinction.[25] All that death has swallowed down will be cast out at the resurrection. So death's historical role comes to an end: the first death undergoes the second death.

24. Similarly in Rev 20:12 "the great and the small" indicates the totality of the dead who are delivered up by death and Hades and the sea to stand before the judgment throne (cf. also 19:18). The appearance of the sea with death and Hades in 20:13 is one of numerous instances of the conceptualization of death as the waters of the deep. This identification of the netherworld with the waters of the sea perhaps contributed to Isaiah's imaging of death as a bottle or skin whose liquid contents are to be poured out. Conceivably Rev 20:12–13 reflects such an understanding of Isa 24:1–3. Cf. B. F. Batto, "The Reed Sea: Requiescat in Pace," *JBL* 102 (1983): 27–35; "Red Sea or Reed Sea?" *BAR* 10.4 (1984): 57–63.

25. Nevertheless the resurrection experience means different things for the godly and the wicked, as appears in the perspective of 25:6–8; 26:19ff. In the language of Rev 20, what is the second resurrection for those written in the book of life is the second death for those who are not.

The Veil Removed

The covering aspect of Sheol, the natural concomitant of its identity as the devourer, is once again present in the final picture of the resurrection-victory over death in 26:19 and following. Previously the face of the earth (or netherworld) was viewed as the cover of a vessel (24:1) or as an enveloping shroud-cover (25:7), but here it is a veil-like covering that conceals the dead (26:21b). The blood of the slain sinks into the earth. The dead disappear into Sheol, concealed behind earth's covering of soil and stone. Death is the "hidden" place (Job 40:13). Resurrection is then an uncovering, an unveiling, a revealing of the concealed. "The earth shall disclose her blood and no more cover her slain" (Isa 26:21b).

It is clear from the context that the slain in view are the martyrs, as typical of all the faithful. For the passage opens with the declaration that the dead who belong to the Lord shall arise in joy (v. 19), and it continues with a special encouragement to God's people in contemplation of their experience of death (v. 20).[26] Moreover, immediately connected with this revealing [[233]] of the blood of the slain is the assurance of the divine advent to punish their wicked oppressors (v. 21a).

In this connection I want to point out the Isaianic roots of a misunderstood Pauline concept in Rom 8. To do so it will first be necessary to discuss the relationship of the context of Isa 26:19 to the context of 24:4. With its announcement of the uncovering of the earth and the resurrection-manifestation of the saints, the former passage answers redemptively to what the latter says about the earth in mourning over the curse of death and especially over the polluting stain of innocent blood. One indication that this mourning does have to do with death is the contrastive correspondence between the situation mourned in the context of 24:4 and the celebration of the conquest of death in chapter 25, especially verses 6–8. A comparison shows sorrow replaced by joy, sighs by songs of praise, the languishing of earth's fruit by a lavish feast of fat things full of marrow and flavorful wine, well refined. In Isa 24 the curse that is grieved over is one that "devours the earth," decimating its population (v. 6). This is the motif of death as the never-sated devourer, which 25:6–8 takes up in its answering prophecy of the devouring of the devourer.

In the context of 24:4, what makes the earth groan is that it is obliged to become the grave, to cover over the human dead. But the relationship of that passage to 25:6–8, which has a redemptive focus on God's people,

26. On this see further below.

argues for a special (even if not exclusive) concern with the death of the righteous in the former. Pointing in the same direction is the explanation given in 24:5 for the entrance of death and the resultant mourning of the earth: "The earth is profaned (*ḥānĕpâ*) under its inhabitants." In view of the use of *ḥnp* elsewhere for polluting the ground by spilling innocent blood on it,[27] it appears that the sin against God's covenant by reason of which the earth suffers defilement and mourns is hostility vented on the covenant faithful, resulting in their martyrdom.

When the profaned, mourning earth of the 24:4 section is understood in this way, it becomes apparent that 26:19 and the verses that follow, like 25:6–8, answers directly to the earlier passage, proclaiming the resurrection-conquest of death as the resolution of earth's grievance.[28] Earth's accursed role as concealing the grave of the not-yet-vindicated people of God comes to an end when the martyrs are revealed and arise and the cry of their blood is heard and honored in heaven.

Until that deliverance from death's curse, the earth bemoans its role as netherworld. Isaiah 24:4 pictures the realm of nature as joining together [[234]] with man in sighs over death. This brings to mind at once the similar thought in Rom 8. Paul says that creation groans together with those who have the firstfruits of the Spirit (vv. 19–23). Even the more precise image of the groaning of birth-travail (Rom 8:22) reflects the Isa 24–26 context. For in 26:16–18 God's people, struggling in the warfare against the enemy until God grants them the resurrection deliverance (v. 19), are likened to a woman crying out in birth pangs.[29] Moreover, just as the groaning of travail in 26:17–18 is followed by the resurrection-revealing of God's people (vv. 19–21), so in Rom 8 creation's groaning in birth pangs (v. 22) is in expectation of the resurrection of the children of God mentioned in the next verse (v. 23). Indeed, quite an extensive correspondence can be traced between these Pauline and Isaianic passages. Other features of 26:19–27:1 to be dealt with below are reflected in the latter part of Rom 8, such as the justification of believers in the face of satanic accusation and the persuasion of God's presence and love in the experience of death. It is also remarkable that just as

---

27. See Num 35:33; Ps 106:38.

28. The use of *nĕbēlâ*, "corpse," in 26:19 echoes *nābĕlâ*, "it [the earth] withers (or dies)," in 24:4. The verb *nābēl* contributes to the alliterative quality of 24:4, but its choice there was probably also prompted by the preceding imagery of the emptied pitcher (cf. *nēbel*, "skin bottle") and the following motif of the silenced music (cf. *nēbel*, a musical instrument).

29. A similar combination of ideas and imagery is found in Hos 13:13–14.

Isaiah moves from these themes into the question of Israel, its fall and fullness, in chapter 27, so does Paul in Rom 9–11 and (as we have observed) in such a way that his line of thought and imagery show dependence on Isa 27.

From this mutually illuminative relationship of Isa 24–26 and Rom 8 one perceives that the "bondage of corruption" over which, says Paul, the creation groans (Rom 8:21) is the earth's being subjected to the fate of covering the blood of the innocent and concealing the corpses of the saints.[30] The term for corruption, *phthora*, is the one that describes physical death in the resurrection context of 1 Cor 15,[31] another passage with clear connections with Isa 24–26.[32] And in Rom 8, as we have seen, what the earth looks forward to in hope as its deliverance from this corruption is precisely the resurrection of the righteous. As the repeated references to their resurrection in verses 19, 21, and 30 indicate, that event is not merely the occasion of the earth's deliverance but is itself the liberation from the corruption over which the earth groans.[33] By reason of the swallowing up of death in resurrection-victory, "the reproach of God's people"—the vanity of corruption from which until now the earth groans to be released—"is removed from all the earth" (Isa 25:8).

---

30. Whatever wider reality might be suggested by "the whole creation" (Rom 8:22), the critical element in the idea is the earth's character as grave of the saints. If one is not persuaded that the earth's groaning in Rom 8:21 is specifically due to its entombment of the martyr-righteous, preferring still to see this verse as a reflection on Gen 3:17 (i.e., as a general curse affecting all mankind), then it must at least be recognized that that curse consists particularly in the reversal of the earth's original subservient relationship to mankind whereby man now is overpowered by the earth and ultimately reduced to the condition of "dust unto dust" (Gen 3:19).

31. See verses 42, 50.

32. Note particularly the quotation of Isa 25:8 in 1 Cor 15:54. Verse 55 continues with a quotation from Hos 13:14, which falls within a section of Hosea's prophecy where extensive interdependence with Isa 26–27 has been noted. See note 29 above and J. Day, "A Case of Inner Scriptural Interpretation: The Dependence of Isaiah 26:13–27:11 on Hosea 13:4–14:10 (Eng. 9) and Its Relevance to Some Theories of the Redaction of the 'Isaiah Apocalypse,'" *JTS* 31 (1980): 309–19.

33. In Rom 8:19 the "revealing (*apokalypsis*) of the sons of God" for which creation waits is customarily identified as the manifestation of the saints with Christ in glory; cf., e.g., Col 3:4. But discovery of the relation of Rom 8 to Isa 24–26 and of its concern with the earth's deliverance from profanation through the corruption of death suggests that the *apokalypsis* is the emergence of the righteous from their concealment in the earth (as in Isa 26:21), the uncovering that is the prelude to the manifestation in glory. Cf. J. Plevnik, "The Taking Up of the Faithful and the Resurrection of the Dead in 1 Thessalonians 4:13–18," *CBQ* 46 (1984): 274–83.

This discussion should not be closed without attention being drawn to another connection between Isaiah and Paul. Specifically, it again concerns Isa 24–26 and Romans. There is a general persuasion abroad that Gen 3 is without influence on theological developments in the rest of the Old Testament.[34] And when Gen 3 is thus regarded as an isolated, [[235]] unfruitful phenomenon, Paul's federal-covenantal reconstruction in Rom 5 is left without a supportive canonical linkage. But Isaiah at least (not to assess other suggested connections) can be adduced as a bridge between Moses and Paul in this matter. What the prophet says in the context of 24:4 must be recognized as a significant source for the covenantal theology of death in Rom 5:12 and the verses that follow. Isaiah deals there with death as a curse. Like Paul, Isaiah teaches that death entered the world through the entrance of sin—indeed, through the sin of breaking "the ancient covenant" in Eden—and that death so passed unto all men, devouring the earth's population, generation after generation (24:5–6; cf. v. 20).

Vindication of the Martyrs

Associated with death in Isa 24–26 as allied enemies of the saints are Satan and, more conspicuously, his human accomplices. And the final proclamation of the resurrection in 26:21 depicts it not only as a redemption of believers from the prison of death (v. 21d) but as a vindication of the martyrs against these satanic persecutors: "The earth shall disclose her blood" (v. 21c). The cry of the martyrs' blood will be heard. At the resurrection they will have their day in court.[35] For the Lord will come forth "to punish the inhabitants of the earth for their iniquity" (v. 21ab). Vindication of the Lord's people will not stop short of taking vengeance on their primeval adversary, the serpent-devil (27:1). What is said in 26:21–27:1 about the coming vindication of the saints is a concluding summation; the theme of the enemies and their subjugation is under development throughout chapters 24–26. This material will be examined, dealing in turn with Satan and his demonic hosts and then with the evil world-power.

---

34. For a recent representative statement see L. R. Bailey, Sr., *Biblical Perspectives on Death* (Philadelphia: Fortress, 1979), 53. He insists that, apart from the possible exception of Gen 2–3, mortality is not associated in the Old Testament with guilt and punishment.

35. Cf. Gen 4:10–11; Job 16:18; Rev 6:9–11; 8:3ff.; 11:18; 19:2.

Judgment on Leviathan

Included in the final portrayal of the resurrection triumph over death is the judgment of leviathan (Isa 27:1).[36] This serpentine symbol in the Bible often signalizes the demonic dimension of a situation. Sometimes the dragon is a figure for Satan himself, as in Rev 12:9; 20:2, and here in Isa 27:1.[37] Inasmuch as the devil is the one who has the power of death (Heb 2:14),[38] it is understandable that he and death should be found together here in common undertaking and common judgment. The same combination is found in Rev 20:10–14.

There is indeed a curious overlap in the attributes and activities of death [[236]] and the devil in biblical representations of them. They even share the same name, or epithet: Belial.[39] Like death, the devil is depicted as the swallower, if not through the Belial designation then at least in Rev 12:4, where the dragon is seen ready to devour the messianic child, and in 1 Pet 5:8, where the Adversary is compared to a lion on the prowl,[40] seeking to devour believers. Similarly, Satan's human agents are portrayed as Sheol-like swallowers of the godly. The description of these enemies in Ps 73:9 with gaping mouth reaching from heaven to earth reflects strikingly the

36. Isaiah 27:1 continues the judgment theme of 26:21 (note *pqd*, "punish," in both verses). Together the two verses deal with the final judgment of the evil occupants of both earth and heaven. Cf. 24:21–22. "In that day" in 27:1 forms an *inclusio* with 26:1. (It is a question whether the same phrase at the beginning of 27:2 introduces the following vineyard song, as is likely, or possibly belongs with 27:1.)

37. Isaiah 27:1 closely resembles a passage in a mythological text from Ugarit (*UT* 67, i 1–3). Such mythological use of the dragon figure is a corruption of the tradition of the serpent-agent of Satan in the fall episode. In biblical texts like Isa 27:1 the dragon imagery is a demythologized, poetic adaptation.

38. This characterization of the devil is explained by his critical role in the entrance of sin into the world, through which death also found entrance. Moreover a continuing agency of Satan in the infliction of death is suggested in Job 2:6 (and, on one interpretation, in 1 Cor 5:5).

39. Note the parallelism of death and Belial in Ps 18:4 [5] and 2 Sam 22:5. Belial (or Beliar) is used for Satan in 2 Cor 6:15. This is of special interest for this Isaiah context. If *blyyʿl* is derived from *blʿ*, "swallow," cf. Isa 25:7–8. If it is explained as *bly* plus *ʿlh*, "none comes up," cf. 26:14. In Job 7:9 *lōʾ yaʿăleh* describes the one who descends into Sheol. Isaiah 26:14 uses *qwm*, not *ʿlh*, but in Ps 41:8 [9] *qwm* with negative stands parallel to *blyʿl*.

40. Behind this usage is probably the judicial surveillance conducted by Satan with a view to his accusing function, as in Job 1:7 and 2:2.

description of Mot in the Ugaritic mythology.[41] And like the devil they are more specifically compared to lions eager to devour the righteous.[42] Death, on its side, shares with the Satan-Adversary in his identity as the enemy. Paul in his discussion of the resurrection in 1 Cor 15 characterizes death as "the last enemy" (v. 26), and possibly there is some (or even considerable) precedent in the Psalms for designating death as the foe.[43] Quite natural then is the conjunction of death and the devil in Isa 24:1–27:1. In particular, the aptness of Isaiah's concluding word on the judgment of leviathan (27:1), appended to his final account of the resurrection-victory over death, can be appreciated.

The disclosure concerning leviathan in 27:1 is adumbrated in 24:21–22. It is indicated there that the saints' warfare is on two levels. For behind the hostility displayed by earthly oppressors is a hidden, demonic enemy on high: "In that day Yahweh will punish the host of the height on high and the kings on the ground below" (v. 21). On high an army of evil beings is associated with the devil in his cause (cf. Rev 12:7–9). God's judicial intervention[44] against them will come "after many days" (v. 22b), at the final cosmic catastrophe (v. 20) and the revelation of the parousia-Glory (v. 23).[45]

---

41. Cf. *UT* 67, ii 1–3.

42. See, e.g., Pss 10:9; 17:12; 35:17, 25; cf. 5:9 [19]; 124:3–6.

43. Cf., e.g., Pss 31:8 [9]; 61:3 [4]. For a survey of the evidence in the Psalms adduced by M. Dahood for death as the foe see N. J. Tromp, *Primitive Conceptions of Death and the Nether World in the Old Testament* (Rome: Pontifical Biblical Institute, 1969), 110–19.

44. The verb *pqd*, "punish," used in the first colon of verse 21 is repeated at the close of verse 22 as an *inclusio*. Hence the same judgment is in view in each case. "After many days" (v. 22b) is equivalent to "in that day" (v. 21a).

45. "Before his elders will be the Glory" (v. 23). After the introduction (24:1–3) two sections on earth's desolation (vv. 4–13; 16b-22) alternate with two brief sections describing the final epiphany and the response thereto (vv. 14–16a; 23). Verses 14–16a form an intricate chiasm produced by lexical and morphological pairings. In the terminal parts of the chiasm the eschatological theophany is denoted as the Majesty (*gʾwn*) and the Beauty (*ṣby*), in the middle parts as the Name (Yahweh). The Glory (*kbwd*) of verse 23 is the corresponding reference to the parousia in the second epiphany section. Further on in 24:15 the *ʿl-kn* is perhaps to be taken as a divine title, "the Most High, the Upright." Following a suggestion of L. Viganò, W. H. Irwin argues for this in "The Punctuation of Isaiah 24:14–16*a* and 25:4*c*-5," *CBQ* 46 (1984): 215–19. A chiastic structuring is, however, still preferable to Irwin's overall stichometric analysis.

This judgment of the demonic host on high is the same as the judgment of leviathan announced in 27:1.[46]

Something of the nature of the judgment on leviathan referred to in 27:1 may be discerned from the equivalent disclosure in Rev 20:10a. There the devil's doom takes the form of the lake of fire, the second death. That realm is one of forever-continuing torment (v. 10b), and accordingly, the fate of Satan and others relegated to it is not absolute erasure from existence. The second death is existence on the other side of an impassable gulf from the cosmos proper. To be cast into the lake of fire is to cease to figure or function in heaven and earth as the consummated kingdom of God. Satan slain, or banished to the second death, no longer participates in the creation proper. He no longer functions as the power of death or otherwise [[237]] affects the glorified saints.[47] Such existence, cut off from rapport with God's realm of life, is a death-existence.

Implicit in the nature of the resurrection of God's people as a judgment-victory over the devil (27:1), the one who has the power of death, is the justification aspect of the vindication of the godly. For inseparable from Satan's identity as possessor of the power of death is his role as "the accuser of our brethren . . . who accuses them before God day and night."[48] It is through his tempting to sin and then prosecuting for sin (the ultimate duplicity) that he has come to wield the power of death. Therefore God's resurrection-conquest of Satan as possessor of the power of death is at the same time a triumph over him as the accuser of the brethren. And in the judicial ordeal

46. A question arises as to the relation of the imprisonment in 24:22a and the binding of Satan in Rev 20:2–3. If that imprisonment is equated with the judicial intervention announced in verse 21 and again in verse 22b, then it will not correspond to the thousand-year confinement of the devil in Rev 20:2–3 but to his subsequent eternal doom (20:10). If, however, the imprisonment of verse 22a is understood as pluperfect with respect to the judgment of verse 21 (and thus too as preliminary to the same judgment as mentioned again in v. 22b), it would then be equivalent to Rev 20:2–3, and the "many days" could correspond to the "thousand years." In this case the subject of the imprisonment might better be viewed as only the demonic host, not the earthly kings. The word *bôr*, "pit," often used as a synonym of Sheol, also denotes a place of confinement and torment for demons. See Luke 8:31 (cf. Matt 8:29); Rev 9:1, 2, 11; 11:7; 17:8; 20:1, 3.

47. The Son of God came so that through death he might "render inoperative" him that had the power of death (Heb 2:14) and death itself (1 Cor 15:26; 2 Tim 1:10).

48. It is just after a reference to Satan in terms distinctly reminiscent of 27:1 that this identification of him as the Accuser is given in Rev 12:10. The echo of 27:1 is all the clearer if the disputed adjective *bārîaḥ* means "primeval" and thus corresponds to the "ancient" serpent of Rev 12:9.

before God's throne, to defeat the accuser in his quest for a verdict of condemnation is to seal the verdict of justification in behalf of the accused.[49]

The conclusion that the resurrection-victory of God's people involves their justification is also arrived at if the resurrection as a victory over death is considered. For death entered the world through sin, in condemnation for the breaking of the primeval covenant. Hence deliverance from death through resurrection in Christ is a reversal of condemnation. It publicly registers the verdict of justification secured by the merits of Christ. This verdict answers to the prayer of the blood of the martyrs that is disclosed at the resurrection (26:21), inasmuch as that blood has been pleading not only to be avenged through the judgment of the enemy but to be recognized as righteous blood, righteous through the advocacy of the blood of the Lamb (cf. Heb 12:24; Rev 12:11a). Agreeably, in the vision of the intermediate state in Rev 6:9–11, the martyrs awaiting the final avenging of their blood on the earth-dwellers already receive a foretaste of that judgment by being acknowledged as justified through the bestowal of white robes, emblematic of their righteousness (cf. Rev 19:8).

It follows that what 26:14, 19 say about not participating or participating in this resurrection may be construed as legal pronouncements of condemnation and justification respectively. These two verdicts are formulated as a clearly matching contrastive pair. The wicked dead, true to their name "sons of Belial/perdition," will not rise again (v. 14).[50] But God's dead, something of a contradiction in terms according to the argument of Jesus for bodily resurrection,[51] shall come to life (v. 19).[52] The promise of resurrection,[53] "your dead shall live" (v. 19a), is a verdict of justification. It is comparable to "the just shall live," the justifying verdict pronounced on
[[238]] the righteous believer in Hab 2:4. There too we find a contrasting verdict against the wicked.[54] The *lōʾ-yāšĕrâ* in verse 4a (however the grammar as a

49. Cf. Zech 3.

50. Context must be ignored to take this as a denial of a universal resurrection. See the discussion of 24:1–3 above and note 78 below.

51. See Matt 22:32; Mark 12:27; Luke 20:38; cf. John 5:21.

52. For this meaning of *ḥyh* see 1 Kgs 17:22; 2 Kgs 13:21; Job 14:14; Ezek 37:3, 5, 6, 9, 10, 14.

53. For a recent survey of the evidence for interpreting 26:19 and context in terms of physical resurrection see F. C. Hasel, "Resurrection in the Theology of the Old Testament Apocalyptic," *ZAW* 92 (1980): 271–76.

54. Hebrews 10:37–38 connects Isa 26 and Hab 2 by (apparently) introducing its citation of Hab 2:4 with the "yet a very little while" of Isa 26:20 (LXX). Cf. the

whole is construed) must refer to God's verdict of condemnation[55] on the proud sinner, a verdict to which "shall live" in verse 4b corresponds. And Paul, citing this passage in Gal 3:11, confirms not only that "shall live" is a verdict but that it is indeed a verdict of justification. For he parallels this life obtained by the righteous through faith in Jesus Christ with the verdict of justification, which, he asserts, was not obtainable through the principle of works operative in the law.[56]

Subjugation of the World-City

The ancient dragon directs his assault on the faithful through the earthly agency of the dragon-like beast (cf. Rev 12:17–13:7). Inevitably, at the judgment, the beast shares the dragon's doom in the lake of fire (cf. 20:10). The place prepared for the devil and his angels is the fitting fate of the seed of the serpent, for throughout history they have exhibited their father's spirit of self-assertion in blasphemous defiance of God and murderous hatred of his people.[57] An antichrist propensity infects the apostate city of man from the days of Cain onwards, erupting virulently in the reign of the sons of the gods at the climax of prediluvian history (Gen 6:1–4) and in the final manifestation of the beast in the man of sin.

This two-tiered structure of the satanic enterprise has already been encountered within Isa 24–26. In 24:21 the kings of the ground below and the demonic hosts above are listed together as the joint objects of divine vengeance.[58] Elsewhere Isaiah suggests the bond of identity between these

---

echo of Isa 26:11 in Heb 10:27. Also note in Hab 2:5 the reference to the insatiable appetite of death, devourer of all peoples, the central concern and pervasive image of Isa 24–26. Further, the patient waiting in faith for the eschatological divine intervention encouraged in Hab 2:3 is a major emphasis in the Isaiah passage (e.g., 25:9; 26:3, 4, 8, 9, 20).

55. Preponderantly the verb *yšr* is used in the registering of assessments. Such is also the tradition of interpretation reflected in the LXX as quoted in Heb 10:37.

56. The function of resurrection to life as the rendering of a verdict of justification should be borne in mind in dealing with Paul's expression "justification of life" (Rom 5:18) and his statement that Jesus "was raised for our justification" (4:25). On the principle of works in the Mosaic economy see Meredith G. Kline, "Of Works and Grace," *Presbyterion* 9 (1983): 85–92.

57. See note 42 above for the attribution to these human enemies of the same lionlike rapacity that distinguishes the devil and death.

58. What is depicted as a single judgment episode here in 24:21–22 is related twice in the book of Revelation because of the thematic arrangement of its visions:

companies by applying to the earthly forces of evil the term *mārôm*, which in 24:21 distinguishes "the host of the height on high" (*hammārôm bammārôm*). Thus 24:4 notes that even the "height (*mĕrôm*) of the people of the earth" are among the death mourners.[59] And 26:5 prophesies judgment against "the ones who dwell in the height (*mārôm*)," further identified as "the lofty city."

Under the present major heading of the vindication of the martyrs it is the enmity of Satan's earthly agents against God's people that calls for particular attention. Isaiah 25:10–12 contains a distinctive treatment of this enmity. Moab, inveterate foe of Israel, serves as representative of the hostile world. Disdainful of the presence of the Glory-hand of God on "this mountain" (v. 10), that is, Zion (cf. 24:23; 25:6), Moab extends[60] its grasping hands "in the midst of it" (v. 11a), to seize all it can from Israel.[61] The [[239]] full extension of its clutching embrace is compared to a swimmer's stretching forth his hands in a sweeping stroke (v. 11b). In this greedy grabbing by Moab a replication of the insatiable appetite of Sheol-death[62] is again met with. Moab's rapacious lust is totally frustrated, however, as God brings down into the dust "his pride with the catch[63] of his hands" (v. 11c).

The enmity of the world-power is also mirrored in the prayers of the saints. Out of the midst of their struggle against the overwhelming might of the oppressor they raise their cry, seconding the call of the martyrs' blood

---

once in Rev 19 from the perspective of the beast and kings of the earth, and a second time in Rev 20 from the perspective of the career of Satan.

59. Pretensions to deity by mortals are repeatedly mocked by reminders of mortality. See Gen 6:3; Isa 14:9ff.; Ezek 28:9; cf. Ps 82:7.

60. This same idea is again expressed by the verb *prs* in a similar context in Lam 1: "The adversary has spread out his hands over all her [Jerusalem's] desirable things" (v. 10a). Interestingly, the adversary who thus profanes the sanctuary is further defined in verse 10c in terms of the law of Deut 23:3 [4] forbidding the Moabites and Ammonites to enter the assembly of the Lord. Also note Moab's involvement in the destruction of Judah (2 Kgs 24:2).

61. For this same imagery elsewhere in Isaiah see 10:10, 14; 11:14.

62. In the motif of Mot's prodigious appetite, his hands figure as scoops (cf. *UT* 67, i 19–20). By them he also grasps his victims (cf. *UT* 2059, 21–22). For similar biblical references to the hands of Sheol see Ps 89:48 [49]; Hos 13:14.

63. Like *pēras* earlier in verse 11, *ʾorbôt* is followed by "his hands" and should be understood in a way that brings out this connection. That is achieved if one regards the noun as related to *ʾrb*, "lie in ambush," and as denoting plunder or prey—here the treasure that had been seized by Moab's outstretched hands. This results in a further point of likeness of this agent of the devil to death, for the latter is pictured as ensnaring its prey (cf., e.g., Ps 18:5 [6]). So too is the devil (2 Tim 2:26).

for divine retribution. Isaiah 26:8–9ab describes the constancy of the saints in such expectant prayer for God's decisive acts of judgment,[64] indignant as they are at the obdurate obtuseness of the unrepentant, unrelenting wicked in the absence of such judgments (vv. 9cd, 10).[65] Verses 7 and 11 articulate their actual petitions.[66]

Again in 26:17–18 the antagonism of the world-power is reflected in the confession by the godly of their helplessness to prevail in the battle against the foe. In childbirth, as it were, they manage to bring forth only wind (vv. 17–18ab). They acknowledge: "Victory we cannot achieve (*naʿăseh*) on the earth; the inhabitants of the earth do not fall" (v. 18cd).[67]

But what God's people cannot achieve for themselves he accomplishes for them: "Every achievement in our behalf (*maʿăsênû*) you have accomplished for us" (26:12). The section on their powerlessness to overcome the enemy (26:16–18) leads at once into the closing prophecy of the resurrection as the Lord's redemptive triumph, vindicating his people over against the world-power (26:19ff.).

---

64. "Yes, for the way of your judgments we call upon you, Yahweh; our soul's longing is for (the revelation of) your memorial Name. In my soul I long for you in the night; yes, in my inmost spirit I yearn for you in the morning." In verses 8, 9b God's "judgments" are his judicial acts of deliverance. The "Name" (v. 8) is the theophanic Presence or Parousia. Note the chiastic structure with the repetitive *taʾăwat-nāpeš* (v. 8b) and *napšî ʾiwwîtîkā* (v. 9a) in the center and the corresponding *ʾap* clauses with their semantically matched verbs in the first and fourth cola (vv. 8a, 9b).

65. "Only when your judgments are on the earth do the inhabitants of the world learn righteousness. If the wicked is shown compassion, he does not learn righteousness; in a land of fair dealings the one who is evil does not see the majesty of Yahweh." In verses 9d, 10a *ṣedeq* refers to God's acts of judgment. In verse 10b the *waw* of *ûbal* is emphatic with postposition of the verb. Thus understood, an excellent parallelism obtains between the two cola of verse 10. In verse 9c, W. H. Irwin reads *kĕʾaššēr* "correct, set right," instead of *kî kaʾăšer*; cf. his "Syntax and Style in Isaiah 26," *CBQ* 41 (1979): 246.

66. "Let there be a way of justice for the righteous, O Upright One, may you make level the path of the righteous" (v. 7). "Yahweh, let your hand be lifted high; let those who do not see see. Let them be dismayed at the fury of your forces; by the fire of your enmity consume them" (v. 11). Verse 7 is an example of the form in which the b-element is a single word (here, as often, a vocative) serving both a-sections. The first colon contains an interrupted construct chain. Possibly *mêšārîm* refers to the concrete *mēšarum*-act. Verse 11 is a further petition for the parousia (cf. the "hand" of God and the angelic armies). Note again the theme of Yahweh as the true devourer who consumes the hostile would-be devourers.

67. On this see further below.

One subtle device tying the resurrection announced in 26:19 to the preceding description of the saints' battle with the world-power (v. 18) is the double use of the verb *npl*, "fall,"[68] to highlight the contrast being drawn. In verse 18d the godly lament their inability to make their enemies "fall" dead in battle. Then in verse 19 God is said to make his dew "fall" on the dead, bringing them to life.

Renderings of verse 19 as though it continued the figure of childbirth (v. 18ab) are unacceptable. The figure has meanwhile shifted in verse 18c to that of military salvation or victory. Moreover, *npl* is not attested elsewhere in biblical Hebrew for childbirth, whereas it is used for battle casualties (cf. Num 14:29; Jer 9:21). Also, consistently in this context "the inhabitants of the world" are the wicked foe (cf. esp. vv. 9, 21).

Again, to interpret *tpyl* in verse 19b as "give birth," with "earth" as subject, is to undo the parallelism between verses 19c and 19d and particularly [[240]] to lose the obvious relationship, both sonant and semantic, between *tappîl* and *ṭal*, "dew." For the use of *npl* for the falling of dew on the ground see 2 Sam 17:12. Therefore verse 19cd should read: "For the dew of dawn[69] is your [God's] dew, and on the land[70] of the shades you make it fall."[71] The "land of the shades" continues the focus of verse 19ab on "the dwellers in the dust," the martyred saints called "your [God's] dead." Restored by God's revivifying dew, they sing in the exultation of their vindication.

Most directly and emphatically the retribution-vindication aspect of the resurrection of the martyrs is expressed in 26:21. God's decisive intervention

68. Enhancing the *npl* wordplay in 26:18 is the use of *nĕbēlâ*, "corpse" (v. 19). As observed above (note 28) this also recalls the verb *nbl* in 24:4, another context that is concerned with death and mourning and also contains a case of paronomasia using *npl* and *nbl*. Note the use of *npl* in 24:20 (itself a parallel to 26:14).

69. On *ʾôrôt* as "lights, dawn" cf. *ʾūrîm*, "East" (24:15). Dawn fits well with waking from sleep (*hāqîṣû*). For the association of dew and dawn cf. Exod 16:13; Judg 6:38; Ps 110:3. On resurrection and dawn cf. Hos 6:2–3. On light and life cf. Job 3:16; 33:28; Pss 49:19 [20]; 56:13 [14]. Whether *ʾôrôt* is understood as dawn, or herbs, or (Elysian) fields (so Mitchell Dahood, *Psalms I*, AB 16 [Garden City, NY: Doubleday, 1966], 222–23), the idea is that of the enlivening effect of dew.

70. Cf. note 21 above.

71. Dahood, *Psalms*, 1:223, takes *tpyl* from the verb *nbl*: "But the land of the shades will be parched." On this basis Irwin ("Syntax," 258) suggests a wordplay with *tappîl* calling to mind *tabbîl*, i.e., the earth gives birth to the shades it had parched. Earlier he took *tappîl* from *pll*, "moisten": "It will moisten the land of the shades" (*Isaiah 28–33: Translation with Philological Notes*, BibOr 30 [Rome: Pontifical Biblical Institute, 1977], 20).

will take the form of a descent from his heavenly temple (v. 21a; cf. Mic 1:3) for the purpose of exacting recompense (v. 21b), and that with immediate reference to the appeal of martyrs' blood revealed (v. 21c) and the witness of God's slain released from the grave (v. 21d).

Once and again in Isa 24–26 the city is used as a figure for the hostile world-power. Judgment is in store for this city (24:10–12; 25:2, 12; 26:5–6) and its kings (24:22; 26:5, 14). In the case of both the city (25:12; 26:5–6) and its proud citizenry (26:5), these prophecies of final retribution are couched in the imagery of the primeval curse on the serpent (Gen 3:14–15), the humbling in the dust and the trampling under foot. Isaiah thus anticipates the apostle John's theme of the dragonlike beast sharing the dragon's doom. He makes the same point more explicitly in his prophecy of the powers in the heavens and the kings on earth imprisoned together in the pit (24:21–22).

Perhaps the delineation of the judgment of the world-city is intended to conjure up the netherworld scene. The realm of the dead was conceptualized as a city with its entrance gates (cf. 24:12),[72] and various characteristic features of the netherworld appear in the picture of the devastated world-city in chapters 24–26. It is a joyless desolation (24:7–12),[73] an eternal[74] ruin (25:2),[75] laid low in the dust (25:12; 26:5–6).[76] On this interpretation the

72. Cf., e.g., Ps 9:13 [14], which contrasts the gates of death with the gates of Zion (v. 14 [15]), and Isa 38:10. On Mot's city cf. *UT* 51, viii 11.

73. Cf. Ps 73:18–19; Ezek 26:20.

74. On the use of "eternity" for the netherworld (including its gates) in the Old Testament and literature of the biblical world see A. Cooper, "Ps. 24:7–10: Mythology and Exegesis," *JBL* 102 (1983): 37–60.

75. If the Masoretic Text is followed, the third colon in 25:2 should be translated: "(You have turned) the city into a palace of strangers." The *mēʿîr* of the first and third cola are thus treated identically. The full pattern, "from . . . to," established in the first colon continues with ellipsis of "from" in the second colon and "to" in the third. For the role of "strangers" as desolators see verse 5 (cf. Isa 1:7). In the Sumerian composition *Lamentation over the Destruction of Ur* the goddess Ningal bewails the fact that a "strange city" and "strange house" have replaced her demolished dwelling. The fall of Jerusalem is bemoaned in almost identical fashion in Lam 5:2. J. A. Emerton emends the *mēʿîr* in Isa 25:2c to *muʿar*, *hophal* participle of *ʿrr*, translating "the palace of foreigners is destroyed" ("A Textual Problem in Isaiah 25:2," *ZAW* 89 [1977]: 72). Cf. Isa 23:13 for *ʿrr* with *ʾarmôn*, "palace," paralleled moreover by *sym* and *lĕmappēlâ*, as in 25:2ab.

76. Cf., e.g., Gen 3:19; Job 10:9; 17:16; 21:26; 34:15; Pss 22:15 [16]; 90:3. In the Akkadian myth *Descent of Ishtar to the Netherworld*, dust and clay are said to be the fare of the netherworld (obv. 8). A fate decreed there is the curse of having the "food of plows" as food (rev. 23–24). Cf. Gen 3:14.

world-city is mocked with the irony of its downfall. It conspired with the prince of death to usurp the status of Zion, heavenly city of life, but it ends up as a necropolis, the netherworld city of the dead.[77]

From this land of no return the persecutors of the saints do not arise (26:14; cf. 24:20).[78] The contrast between their fate and the resurrection affirmed for the martyrs (26:19) underscores the vindicatory nature of the latter.

In sum, then, according to Isa 24–26 an army of enemies is associated with death in warfare against the saints, but divine vengeance will befall them all on the day of resurrection. A similar perspective informs Paul's [[241]] teaching on the resurrection: death is "the last enemy" to be abolished by Christ in a process that involves his putting "all His enemies under His feet" (1 Cor 15:25–26).

Invitation to the Martyrs

Even before death is ultimately abolished, it undergoes for the martyr-people an intermediate transformation. In the light of their coming resurrection-vindication, death assumes for them a different face. It becomes something that can be welcomed. The language of invitation becomes appropriate for it: "Come, my people, enter into your inner rooms and close your doors about you. Hide yourselves for a brief moment, until the wrath has passed by" (Isa 26:20). The term *ḥeder*, "inner room," used for private rooms like the bedchamber, is combined with death in Prov 7:27: "the chambers of death."[79] The house or room, particularly a sleeping chamber, is a natural image, elsewhere attested, for Sheol.[80] Certainly then the invitation of Isa 26:20, embedded as it is in a context of death and resurrection, is to be understood as welcoming God's people into the inner room of death, as into a sanctuary.

---

77. This same ironic reversal becomes a major motif in Ezekiel's prophecy of Gog (Ezek 39:11–16). Gog aspires to the mount of God but must settle for the immortality of the cemetery city of Hamonah.

78. Their resurrection experience is a passage from Sheol to the second death. They do not return to their historical freedom vis-à-vis the godly. They are not present in God's eternal cosmic kingdom of life to threaten again the peace of the righteous. Cf. above the discussion of the judgment on leviathan; cf. also notes 25, 50.

79. Cf. *ḥdry šʾwl* in 1QH X, 34. In Phoenician and Punic *ḥdr* means "grave, netherworld."

80. Cf. Tromp, *Primitive*, 156–59.

Quite clearly Isaiah is alluding to the enclosure of the Noahic family within the ark-house[81] for their passage through the waters of death. In the flood narrative Noah receives an invitation from God to enter[82] the virtual burial chamber (Gen 7:1). There is a fastening of the door behind the occupants (Gen 7:26).[83] The ark as burial room functions as a refuge until the time of wrath on the hostile world-power has passed.[84] Meanwhile the occupants of the ark anticipate their eventual resurrection-exit and the perfecting of their vindication.

According to Isa 26:20 death for the redeemed has been radically altered, from confining covering to covert.[85] This same view of the death of the righteous is expressed in 57:1–2. There it is seen as a gathering away from evil and an entering into peace and rest.[86] Sheol's repute as an "eternal house" is refuted by the interim character and indeed relative brevity attributed to its continuance in 26:20. Implicit in the temporal limit of "a brief moment" is the hope of the resurrection, when all the enemies have been abolished and there is no longer need for the refuge provided by death.[87] Meanwhile death has lost its terror. The great enemy is obliged to serve the saints as a friend. Yahweh's triumph over Mot has begun.

Subsequent biblical revelation concerning death reflects quite specifically the Isaianic disclosures, with the perception of death as a veritable blessing [[242]] and the invitation to experience it as a temporary sanctuary until the resurrection-vindication.

In Dan 12:13 the invitation, "Come my people," of Isa 26:20 is made individually personal. Daniel is invited: "As for you, come!"[88] Under discussion in the context are the persecution of the covenant people and the ultimate resurrection of glory for "the wise." The invitation is immediately preceded by a beatitude pronounced on those who wait in faith for the time

81. Cf. *KP*, 225–27.

82. As in Isa 26:20, the verb is *bwʾ*.

83. As in Isa 26:20, the verbal phrase is *sgr bʿd*.

84. Isaiah 26:20 also recalls the securing of the Israelites behind their blood-smeared doors in Egypt while the Lord's judgment passed through (*ʿbr*, Exod 12:23, as in Isa 26:20).

85. Cf. Job 14:13–15. Job longs for Sheol as a temporary hiding place from wrath until the resurrection.

86. Cf. Pss 36:7–12 [8–13]; 57:1 [2].

87. Hebrews 10:37, apparently citing Isa 26:20, identifies the brief time as that still remaining until the second coming of Christ. Cf. note 54 above.

88. As in Isa 26:20 the imperative is *lēk*.

of deliverance. That Daniel's invitation does indeed contemplate his death becomes evident once the verse is properly punctuated. "Until the end you shall rest.[89] And then at the end of the days you will stand [or arise] in your allotted inheritance."[90] In the first instance, as in the second, "the end" refers to a historical climax of collective eschatology, not to the individual end of Daniel.[91] It is rather the verb "rest" that refers to his death, in agreement with the earlier Isaianic assessment of the death of the godly.[92]

A series of passages in the book of Revelation presents again this distinctly Isaianic perspective on the death of the righteous: 2:10; 6:9–11; 14:13; 20:4–6.[93] In all these passages the godly are viewed as under persecution. The beast power, or even the devil himself, appears in the nearby contexts. But the saints are faithful unto death, and their martyr blood cries out for avenging.[94] Also, the intermediate state of death is perceived as a royal sabbatical resting until the historical strife is over.[95] This interval of waiting will be short.[96] And finally, the continuity of John, the New Testament seer, with Isaiah, the Old Testament prophet, is exhibited in their common portrayal of death as having been fundamentally changed for the redeemed of the Lord. In Rev 20:4–6 this transformation is expressed by identifying the Christian's death as "the first resurrection."[97]

---

89. The key to the verse division is this emphatic *waw* with postposition of the verb.

90. For *gôrāl* in this sense see Judg 1:3; Ps 125:3; cf. Col 1:12.

91. On *qēṣ* see also Dan 12:4, 6, 9, noting especially the correspondence of verses 4 and 13.

92. As in Isa 57:2 the verb is *nwḥ*. Cf. Job 3:17.

93. Rev 14:13; 20:6 are in the form of beatitudes. Cf. Dan 12:12.

94. See Rev 6:10.

95. Esp. Rev 6:11; 14:13.

96. Esp. Rev 6:11; cf. 2:10.

97. See Kline, "The First Resurrection" [= pp. 239–47 in the present volume]. Cf. Rev 12:11. There the martyr victims are proclaimed victors. It is in and through their faithfulness unto death that they are overcomers, secured from the second death, assured of the second resurrection (cf. Rev 2:11).

CHAPTER FOURTEEN

The First Resurrection

(1975)

One of the critical points in the exegesis of Rev 20 is the interpretation of *prōtos* in the phrase, "the first resurrection" (v. 5). Premillennarians understand it in the purely sequential sense of first in a series of items of the same kind. They interpret both "the first resurrection" and the resurrection event described in verses 12 and 13 of this chapter as bodily resurrections. The contextual usage of *prōtos*, however, does not support such an exegesis; it rather points compellingly to an interpretation of "the first resurrection" found in (so-called) amillennial exegesis.[1]

The Meaning of *prōtos*

The vision of the recreation of the world in Rev 21:1ff. will be a good starting place for our survey of the relevant data concerning *prōtos*. This word is employed here as the opposite of "new." The consummation of history brings "a new heaven and a new earth" (v. 1) and a "new Jerusalem" (v. 2). Indeed, God as Consummator will make "all things new" (v. 5). And the word "first" is used for that which is superseded by the "new": "the first heaven and the first earth were passed away" (v. 1). Indeed, when God makes all things new, all "the first things" pass away—tears, death, sorrow, crying, pain (v. 4). In this passage to be "first" means to belong to the order of the present [[367]]

1. Two articles on Rev 20 appearing in the forum of *The Westminster Theological Journal* within the last two years (cf. *WTJ* 35 [1973]: 281–302 and 36 [1974]: 34–43) were in agreement on the negative conclusion at least that "the first resurrection" is not a bodily resurrection. I find that the supplementary evidence for that conclusion to be offered in the present comments is not altogether unanticipated in the commentary literature, but I wish to call attention to it because it seems to be generally overlooked in current discussions and because it has, I believe, a quite decisive bearing on the whole millennial issue.

world which is passing away. *Prōtos* does not merely mark the present world as the first in a series of worlds and certainly not as the first in a series of worlds all of the same kind. On the contrary, it characterizes this world as different in kind from the "new" world. It signifies that the present world stands in contrast to the new world order of the consummation which will abide forever.

An alternate term for "new" in Rev 21 is the word "second." The death that is identified with the lake of fire and is the eternal counterpart to the death that belongs to the order of "first things" (v. 4) is called "the second death" (v. 8). Thus "second" as well as "new" serves as the antithesis of "first." Whatever accounts for the preference for "first" over "old" in describing the present world, the use of "first" naturally led to the use of "second" alongside of "new" for the future world, particularly for the future reality of eternal death for which the term "new" with its positive redemptive overtones would be inappropriate.

In this antithetical pairing of first death (an expression virtually contained in v. 4) and "second death" (v. 8), Rev 21 confronts us with the same idiom that we find in Rev 20 in "the first resurrection" (vv. 5, 6) and the second resurrection (an expression implicit in this chapter). The arbitrariness of the customary premillennial insistence that "the first resurrection" must be a bodily rising from the grave if the second resurrection is such is exposed by the inconsistent recognition by premillennial exegesis that, although the first death is the loss of physical life, "the second death" is death of a different kind, death in a metaphorical rather than literal, physical sense.

Before tying the data of Rev 21 into the interpretation of Rev 20 more closely, it will be useful to take notice of certain other New Testament instances of the use of *prōtos* in antithetical pairs, these too descriptive of comprehensive historical-eschatological structures.

In the book of Hebrews the terms "first" and "new" are used to distinguish the Mosaic and the messianic administrations of God's redemptive covenant (cf. 8:7, 8, 13; 9:1, 15, 18; 10:9). The new covenant is also called "the second": "He taketh away the first, that he may establish the second" (10:9). Here then in this terminology for the two-covenant pattern is the identical [[368]] pairing of terms, including the same alternate for "new," that we find in Rev 20 and 21.

Although the term "second" appears along with "new," it is "new" that predominates as the counterpart to "first." Accordingly, the significance of "first" in this context is not so much priority in a series but opposition to the idea of "new." *Prōtos* thus functions here as an equivalent for "old," our traditional designation for the Mosaic covenant. Indeed, the author of Hebrews expressly observes that when God speaks of a "new covenant, he hath made the first old," adding, "Now that which decayeth and waxeth old is ready to vanish away" (8:13). This contrast between the first and new covenants does not correspond exactly to that between the first and new worlds in Rev 21, but in both cases the reality described by the term "first" is one that passes away. In Hebrews as in Rev 21 *prōtos* is used for the provisional and transient stage in contrast to that which is consummative, final, and enduring.

A similar usage of *prōtos* is found in connection with Paul's treatment of the theme of resurrection in 1 Cor 15. Once again there is a binary pattern with contrasting parts which together span all history. In contraposition in this pattern stand the two Adams. The "first man Adam" (v. 45; cf. vv. 46–47) is not first in the sense of heading an indefinite series of Adams but first in the antithetically qualitative sense of being counterpart to the "last Adam" (v. 45). Here again "second" appears as an alternate term of contrast to "first": "the second man is the Lord" (v. 47). By eliminating the thought of any intermediate Adams between the "first" and "last" Adams, the term "second" here, as in the Hebrews and Rev 21 passages, underscores the binary (as over against indefinitely seriatim) framework within which *prōtos* is functioning and derives its specific meaning.

The first Adam is earthy and psychical; the last Adam is heavenly and spiritual (vv. 45, 47). Because of the federal positions occupied by the two Adams the qualities of each one also inform the life sphere at the head of which he stands (vv. 44–49). "First" is thus correlated with the preliminary, pre-consummative phase of kingdom development over against the eschatologically final stage of the kingdom which bears the image of the last Adam. The connotative force of *prōtos* in this passage is [[369]] further articulated in the distinguishing elements of the world order that emerges out of the fall of the first Adam: dishonor, weakness, corruption, death (vv. 42–43).

Instructive linguistic and theological parallels to the usage of *prōtos* in Rev 21 are thus afforded by the exposition of the covenant theme in Hebrews and by the Pauline treatment of the two Adams. Like Rev 21, Hebrews uses "first" for a historical stage that passes away. Like Rev 21, Paul uses "first" and its opposite in 1 Cor 15 for a twofold structure comprehensive of cosmic history. In none of these passages does *prōtos* function as a mere ordinal in a simple process of counting objects identical in kind. In fact, precisely the reverse is true in all three passages; in each case it is a matter of different kinds, indeed, of polar opposites. Whatever idea of priority still attaches to *prōtos* in these passages, it is thoroughly subordinated in all of them to the function of expressing in combination with an antonym ("new," "second," or "last") a sharp antithesis. As for Rev 21 itself, the framework within which *prōtos* performs its antithetical function is that age-spanning structure of biblical eschatology which divides universal history into the two stages: this world and the world to come. To be called "first" within that pattern is to be assigned a place in this present world with its transient order. That which is "first" does not participate in the quality of consummate finality and permanence which is distinctive of the new kingdom order of the world to come.

The Meaning of "The First Resurrection"

An interpretation of *prōtos* in keeping with the usage and meaning of the word found in Rev 21 is required in Rev 20, specifically in the expression "the first resurrection." The proximity of the Rev 20 and 21 contexts and the general thematic continuity between the two chapters would be enough to suggest and indeed to create a presumption in favor of such an interpretation. But the matter is put beyond reasonable doubt by the striking fashion in which the first-(second) resurrection pattern is interlocked in the "thousand years" context with the (first)-second death pattern of Rev 21.

Thus, in the account of the postmillennial resurrection for [[370]] final judgment in Rev 20:13ff. the issue of that judgment for those not found in the book of life is "the second death," "the lake of fire" (v. 14). And, most to the point, "the second death" formula is directly conjoined with "the first resurrection" formula in the very verses where the latter expression appears: "This is the first resurrection. Blessed and holy is he that hath part in the first resurrection: on such the second death hath no power" (vv. 5b, 6a). "The second death" is thus utilized right within the explanation of what "the first resurrection" is. Clearly the usage of *prōtos* in the first-(second) resurrection pattern must be the same as the usage of *prōtos* in the intertwined (first)-second death pattern, which is itself part of the broader first-new things pattern of Rev 21.

"The first resurrection" is not, therefore, the earliest in a series of resurrections of the same kind, not the first of two (or more) bodily resurrections. The antithetical usage of *prōtos* in this context requires a conclusion diametrically opposite to the customary premillennial assumption. If the second resurrection is a bodily resurrection, the first resurrection must be a non-bodily resurrection.

The specific meaning *prōtos* bears in this context, as well as its grammatical function, contradicts the interpretation of "the first resurrection" as a bodily resurrection. For bodily resurrection is man's introduction into the final order of the world to come. That which is constituted through the experience of bodily resurrection is permanent; it belongs to the sphere of consummated things. But the meaning of *prōtos* in this context is, as we have seen, antithetical to consummation and permanence. That which is "first" belongs to the order of the present passing world. "The first resurrection" must then be something this side of bodily resurrection, some experience that does not bring the subject of it into his consummated condition and final state.

What then is meant by "the first resurrection"? The answer must certainly be sought in terms of the striking paradoxical schema of which the expression is an integral part. In this arrangement two binary patterns are combined into a complex double pattern with antithesis between the parts within each pair (i.e., the first-new contrast) and also between the two pairs themselves, the one having to do with death and the other with resurrection. As we shall see, there is also a criss-crossing pattern [[371]] of connections between the two pairs, "the first resurrection" and "the second death" being the explicit and metaphorical members of the two pairs, while the first death links with the second resurrection, both being implicit and literal.

Within this schematic pattern, where we would expect to find mention of the second resurrection we find instead "the second death." When describing the event of bodily resurrection that at least includes if it is not exclusively concerned with the unjust (v. 13), the author deliberately does not refer to it as a "resurrection." For the true significance of the event is to be found in the destiny in which it issues and in the case of the unjust the grave delivers them up (v. 13) only to deliver them over to the lake of fire (v. 15). Hence, the real meaning of the resurrection of the unjust to physical life is conveyed by the paradoxical metaphor of death, "the second death" (v. 14).

The proper decipherment of "the first resurrection" in the interlocking schema of first-(second) resurrection and (first)-second death is now obvious enough. Just as the resurrection of the unjust is paradoxically identified as "the second death" so the death of the Christian is paradoxically identified as "the first resurrection." John sees the Christian dead (v. 4). The real meaning of their passage from earthly life is to be found in the state to which it leads them. And John sees the Christian dead living and reigning with Christ (vv. 4, 6); unveiled before the seer is the royal-priestly life on the heavenly side of the Christian's earthly death. Hence the use of the paradoxical metaphor of "the first resurrection" (vv. 5–6) for the death of the faithful believer. What for others is the first death is for the Christian a veritable resurrection!

This interpretation of "the first resurrection" is consistent with the contextual force of *prōtos* as descriptive of the pre-consummation stage of things. For bright as is the prospect that is opened up by the identification of dying in Christ as a resurrection to heavenly glories with exemption from the power of the second death assured (v. 6), that state is still not the ultimate glory of the Christian. It stands on this side of consummation. It is only the intermediate, not the final state.

The other major amillennial interpretation of "the first resurrection," which views it as regeneration or baptism into Christ, would also meet the contextual requirement that *prōtos* refer to [[372]] an experience within the present course of history. However, it does not handle satisfactorily the paradoxical schema we have been examining; in particular, it misses the clear correlation of first death and "first resurrection" in this pattern. It also encounters other difficulties. If "the first resurrection" were regeneration, the death of which "the first resurrection" was the triumphant reversal would be fallen man's death in sin, his unregenerate state. But the living and reigning (v. 4) which is "the first resurrection" (v. 5) is surely to be regarded as answering to the death experience described earlier in the same verse, the death of Christian martyrdom: "(I saw) the souls of them that were beheaded for the witness of Jesus . . . and they lived." Though this martyrdom imagery is apparently a concrete, typical individualization of a more general kind of experience and is in that sense figurative, it is clearly a Christian experience that this figure portrays. Martyr death would obviously be a most unsuitable figure to depict death in sin. It would be incongruous even for the Christian experience of dying to sin. Those who participate in "the first resurrection" are not those who are dead in sins but those who are righteous in Christ. Their martyrdom is not the kind of death for which spiritual regeneration would be the remedy, but it is itself a consequence and seal of a spiritual regeneration that has been manifested in faithful Christian witness (cf. Rev 2:10; 12:11). The same problem surfaces in the reference to "the rest of the dead" who do not take part in "the first resurrection" (v. 5). On the interpretation under criticism this would be another group of the unregenerate and verse 5 would then become a rather pointless statement to the effect that the unregenerate are unregenerate during the thousand years. However significant the theological observation that triumphant Christian death belongs to a spiritual process whose source is regeneration, spiritual resurrection from death in sin simply is not what is meant by "the first resurrection" in Rev 20:5–6.

The Beatitude of the Christian Dead

For the Christian, to die is resurrection. This interpretation of "the first resurrection" finds further confirmation in the fact that the blessedness of Christian death is a recurring theme in [[373]] the Apocalypse, as was to be expected in a book of its origin and purpose. The support is the stronger in that the parallelism between Rev 20 and the other occurrences of this theme involves the literary form in which it is expressed. In fact, the parallels in concept and terminology are so close as to make the identification quite unmistakable.

In Rev 20 "the first resurrection" prospect takes the shape of a beatitude: "Blessed and holy is he that hath part in the first resurrection: on such the second death hath no power, but they shall be priests of God and of Christ, and shall reign with him a thousand years" (v. 6). This is one of the seven beatitudes of the Apocalypse (cf. 1:3; 14:13; 16:15; 19:9; 22:7, 14). Christian death is also the subject of the second beatitude in this series: "Blessed are the dead which die in the Lord from henceforth: Yea, saith the Spirit, that they may rest from their labours; and their works do follow them" (14:13). This Sabbath blessing is very much the same as the millennial blessing of Rev 20:6. For the biblical concept of Sabbath rest includes enthronement after the completion of labors by which royal dominion is manifested or secured (cf., e.g., Isa 66:1). The Sabbath rest of the risen Christ is his kingly session at God's right hand. To live and reign with Christ is to participate in his royal Sabbath rest. In Rev 20:6 this blessedness is promised to those who have part in "the first resurrection" and in the Rev 14:13 equivalent it is pronounced on the dead who die in the Lord. A similar promise of rest is given to the martyr-souls in the vision of the opening of the fifth seal (Rev 6:11).

The letter to the church in Smyrna in Rev 2 contains a section that closely parallels Rev 20:4–6 in its treatment of the blessedness of Christian death. Like the Rev 20 passage it speaks of martyrdom and promises that through such death the "crown of life" will be secured, a life exempt from "the second death": "be thou faithful unto death, and I will give thee a crown of life . . . He that overcometh shall not be hurt of the second death" (vv. 10b, 11b). An additional point of resemblance is the contextual reference in both passages to the activity of Satan (2:9, 10 and 20:2–3, 7ff.). There is also the intriguing possibility of a relationship between the numerical symbols of the ten days of tribulation (2:10) and the thousand years of reigning (20:4, 6). The intensifying of ten to a thousand [[374]] together with the lengthening of days to years might then suggest that the present momentary tribulation works a far greater glory to be experienced even in the intermediate state as the immediate issue of martyrdom. The equation of the state of Christian death referred to in this letter with "the first resurrection" state of Rev 20 is of course firmly established by the common contextual mention of "the second death" (not found in any other context), the same assurance of deliverance from this "second death" being given in both cases. But the "crown of life" promise in Rev 2:10 is also a strong confirmation of this equation. The crown, *stephanos*, though it might be the festive garland might also be the royal crown. If the latter image is intended here, the "crown of life" promised to the Christian dead is precisely the nominal equivalent of the verbal "they lived and reigned" in the account of the experience that attends "the first resurrection" in Rev 20:4ff.

The way "the first resurrection" is identified with living and reigning with Christ a thousand years in Rev 20:4–6 has the effect of connecting the qualifying force of *prōtos* quite directly to "the thousand years." The millennium as such is virtually called a "first" age. It falls within the days of this present passing world characterized by "the first things." The parousia with its concomitant consummative events of resurrection and judgment must then follow these "thousand years." The premillennial view of the second advent is excluded.

The postmillennial view will not do either. If the "thousand years" are, as postmillennarians hold, a late concluding phase of the interadvental age, and if (as is then the case) Rev 20 is the only place in the book where this special phase of kingdom development is mentioned, it would not seem possible to discover a satisfactory explanation for the almost exclusive focus of this one and only millennial disclosure on the intermediate state, while nothing is said, beyond what might be implied in the prior binding of Satan, about the distinctive situation of the church and the nations on earth during the thousand years. This same difficulty obtains on the premillennial view. On an amillennial approach, earthly developments in church and world during the time denoted by the "thousand years" are dealt with all through the book. The special attention given to the church in heaven in Rev 20 is then simply [[375]] a supplemental emphasis and quite understandable in this book, as we have noted.

If the postmillennial view were to account at all plausibly for the almost total concentration on the intermediate state in the Rev 20 description of the millennium, the justification would have to involve the assumption that the features here assigned to the intermediate state were at least peculiar to the millennial phase of it. But if the millennium is restricted to a late phase of the present church age, such an assumption is quite unacceptable. For in this book the beheaded faithful who provide the individualizing image for the Christian company who are said to live and reign during the thousand years (20:4) will naturally be understood to include those persecuted first century believers with whom the author identified himself as a companion in tribulation for the testimony of Jesus. And certainly, according to the perspective of the series of Apocalyptic beatitudes to which Rev 20:6 belongs, the Christian dead have participated in the blessedness of the millennial "first resurrection," the blessedness of the intermediate state of royal rest with Christ, from the time of the church's beginnings when the Apocalypse of Jesus Christ was revealed on Patmos. For the voice from heaven said to John: "Write, Blessed are the dead which die in the Lord from henceforth" (14:13).

CHAPTER FIFTEEN

The First Resurrection: A Reaffirmation

(1976)

The characteristic courtesy of Ramsey Michaels in discussion, even when the discussion is a disagreement, is amply evidenced again in his Response to my earlier article.[1] I admire the virtue and appreciate this particular instance of it, but as one notably deficient in irenic grace I could almost wish he had set a less noble example! Despairing of matching it, I tender my apologies beforehand, ere the ardor of offensive defensiveness has quite carried me away.

So far as formal exegesis is concerned, Professor Michaels' Response is not so much a criticism of my article (the distinctive point of which he in fact endorses) as it is a novel proposal of his own setting himself against the commentators of all millennial schools on what has been a point of fundamental, if formal, agreement among them. Though he characterizes his approach as a "rather conventional premillennial" one, at this critical point it is anything but conventional.

He charges the commentators on all sides with complicating the picture in Rev 20:4–6 by reading as a double pair of first and second death and first and second resurrection what he wants to restrict to the single pair of first resurrection and second death. In spite of the bold manner in which this proposal is introduced as being "of course" what John says, it must strike most readers of the book of Revelation as a strained exegesis, unnatural in the extreme.

How he arrived at such a position seems to be clear enough, however. Having acknowledged the validity of my observation that in the Rev 20 and 21 context "first" and "second" do not refer simply to mere sequence but denote a qualitative difference, he then perceives that if that fact is

1. J. Ramsey Michaels, "The First Resurrection: A Response," *WTJ* 39 (1976): 100–109. The "earlier article" referred to is Meredith G. Kline, "The First Resurrection," *WTJ* 37 (1975): 366–75 [= pp. 239–47 in the present volume].

incorporated into the double binary pattern interpretation that has all along been accepted on all sides, it will have to be admitted that there is a difference in kind between the first and second resurrections as [[111]] well as between the first and second deaths. That, he is also aware, spells the end of the premillennial exegesis—and millennial opinions go down swinging!

It is under point two that the Response takes up this decisive issue, asserting that Rev 20:4–6 does not contain the idea of two death experiences and two resurrection experiences but only one of each. The Response says that John does not pair "first" with death or "second" with resurrection, and it then makes the quite unfounded assumption that if first death and second resurrection are not present as explicit terms in the text they are not present in the thought of the text either. But the attempt of the Response to avoid the force of the fact that the concepts of first death and second resurrection are found in this context is evasive and futile. The concept or experience of the first death is, in fact, brought into immediate juxtaposition to the term "second death" every time the latter is used (Rev 2:10, 11; 20:4–6; and 20:13, 14). This is not fortuitous. Whatever proleptic or parenthetical aspect may be involved in the use of "second death" in these passages, its use in combination with the concept or experience of the first death is still eminently appropriate in each instance, and thus rather clearly deliberate. The concept of a second resurrection is also prominent in the context where the term "first resurrection" is used (Rev 20:12ff.). These data flatly contradict the contention of the Response that we are not to think (as we find ourselves naturally inclined to do) of a first death and second resurrection in Rev 20:4–6 in order to fill out the pattern that is initiated there by the explicit terms "first resurrection" and "second death" and is further intimated by the reference to the experience of the first death in this very passage (v. 4) as well as in the surrounding context. These data are far more than an adequate basis for recognizing the double binary pattern; they are completely compelling, and it is this that accounts for what has been the general consensus on the subject.

Beyond this it should be noted that the Response hardly gives an adequate account of all the facts concerning the explicit usage of the term "first" in Rev 20 and 21 when it says that "first" is paired only with "resurrection" and not with "death." Revelation 21:4 says that death and the related phenomena of sorrow, crying, and pain will be no more in the new world and [[112]] explains this absence of death by the statement: "for the first things are passed away." The death in view here is identified as one of the "first things" (i.e., as belonging to the pre-consummation order). The facts are obscured when this evidence is dismissed with the ambiguous and misleading remark that "Kline can point to the use of the word 'death' in 20:13f. and 21:4 as evidence that the *concept*, though not the term, 'first death' is present in the context." The fact is that Rev 21:4 does virtually use the *term* "first death." And accordingly the assumption of the Response discussed above is not merely unfounded and contradicted by contextual data, but it (and the whole argument of point two) is quite pointless.

But before turning to other sections of the Response it should be noted that its own positive exegetical proposal will not bear close scrutiny. As previously mentioned, Michaels agrees that a qualitative contrast is denoted by the first-second pair in Rev 20 and 21. But he ignores the particular nature of that difference as a contrast between old, pre-consummative and new, consummative. On his view of a single pair, namely, first resurrection and second death, "first" and "second" denote the bare notion of difference, supposedly underscoring the polar contrast between death and resurrection. In the attested usage in the context, however, the first-second pair is used primarily and essentially to contrast the old and the new varieties of one entity (like apples), i.e., death *or* resurrection, not, as in Michaels' view, to denote in some abstract way the contrast between totally different entities (like apples and rocks), i.e., death *and* resurrection. Michaels has not faced up to the real nature of the contextual evidence, which offers no justification for interpreting "first" and "second" as he does. Moreover, stripped of the specific antonymic significance (i.e., old and new) which they have in the context and even of every trace of sequential force, as they are in Michaels' view, it is not evident how the terms "first" and "second" would convey the notion of contrast at all. The idiom would be quite opaque and would not, therefore, serve to reinforce the inherent contrast between death and resurrection but only, by perplexing the reader, to blur it. In fact, as Michaels expounds "first" and "second," they do not express difference but similarity. The "first resurrection" is said to be so named because it is the only one to deserve the name. Apparently, then, [[113]] "first" means the real thing. And the "second death" is said to be so designated because it has finality. So, "second" seems to mean final. But "real" and "final" are, if comparable at all, synonymous, not antonymic. It is a question, therefore, whether the exegetical proposal of the Response is intelligible, let alone credible.

Revelation 20:4–6 does, then, contain the idea of two kinds of death experiences and two kinds of resurrection experiences, so that we all have to come up with identifications for these—and there are no options in sight that would salvage the premillennial exegesis. The Response contends under points one and three that the particular experiences with which my article identified the two kinds of death and resurrection are not different kinds but just one kind of each.

Under point one, the Response argues that the second death is not different in kind from physical death, which introduces man into the intermediate state, but only finalizes it. This is a strange contention which obliterates the significance of the bodily resurrection and the consummation. For if the second death simply finalizes physical death, man's disembodied condition would be perpetuated; there would be no resurrection of the wicked. Michaels does not wish to deny the resurrection of the wicked and, in fact, he acknowledges elsewhere that it is the resurrection of the wicked that is paradoxically called "the second death," since it is "only formally a resurrection."

Certainly a death that consists in disembodiment differs in kind from death as re-embodiment to suffer eternal perdition. The book of Revelation introduces a new image, the lake of fire, to portray the new, eternal kind of death. Revelation 20:14 depicts death—death in the sense of the grave and intermediate state—as being terminated by means of this very lake of fire, the new kind of death to which it gives way. This is, of course, one of the places where the context compels us to think of a first death as the intended contrast to what is called "the second death."

Whether we do well to speak of this second death as "metaphorical" is no doubt debatable. If that term suggests the mistaken idea that the second death is not a real future event or that it is spiritual death in distinction from an experience of the total person raised from the grave, that is a serious disadvantage. [[114]] On the other hand, since it is the resurrection (of the wicked) that is called "the second death," the appropriate adjective for this usage does not seem to be "literal." But whatever adjectival term we use to distinguish them, we are dealing here with two very distinct kinds of death.

In the discussion of the two kinds of resurrection under point three, the Response again betrays a lack of appreciation for the decisive significance of the resurrection-consummation event. My article took the position that just as "the second death" is the paradoxical designation for the resurrection of unbelievers, so the death of believers is paradoxically called "the first resurrection." The two support and really demand each other. Michaels accepts the first but balks at the second (an inconsistency that is necessary if one is not to give up premillennialism). He maintains that "first resurrection" is a contradiction in terms, if "first" is understood as pre-consummative.

Professor Michaels' argument here succeeds in showing only how seriously he has been influenced by the Kantian dialectic, to which as a matter of fact he refers with approval. He speaks of a "first resurrection *as resurrection*" and says that we cannot speak of a particular "resurrection" as consummative and at the same time as belonging to the present order (in an intrusive-anticipatory sense). The resurrection (and consummation) concept of the Response is radically Kantian, not biblical; it is an ideal abstraction of the noumenal realm that cannot enter the phenomenal realm and participate in history. Hence, time with its chronological distinctions of earlier and later has no significance for it. It floats immune above history's eschatological movement from this world to the consummation world. The familiar biblical eschatological structure of already not yet ceases to be the biblical structure when it is reinterpreted within the Kantian system. Set in that framework, the already and the not yet can only stand as abstract entities in dialectical tension; they cannot come together as coordinate dimensions of individual historical experiences. It is only in terms of such a profoundly unbiblical approach that it could be denied that there is a difference in kind between the "resurrection" which the Christian experiences when he passes into the intermediate state at death, absent from the body though at home with the Lord, and the resurrection he experiences at the day of the redemption of [[115]] his body and glorification. It is precisely because my colleague and (I hope still) friend has let himself come under this alien Kantian-Barthian influence that we repeatedly find that the biblical reality of the consummation does not come into its own in his thinking.

Regrettably, a personal note must be intruded here. For in this connection the Response links my hermeneutics with the Kantian world view, and I may not let my Christian witness be thus compromised. To dispel any false impression that might exist, let me say there is no later Kline, only an older version of the Van Tilian Reformed, Covenantal, garden variety of Christian he was in the 1948–65 Westminster period. I still reprobate the Kantian dialectic that comes to expression in Barthian hermeneutics, exemplified in a commentary like that of Caird on Revelation, and I can only deplore its insidious influence within evangelical circles.

One's judgment on the exegetical question under discussion will have been determined on the basis of the decisive issues already reviewed, but the remainder of the Response calls for comment. In point four the problem once again is the logical one of unfounded assumptions. The Response isolates Rev 20 from Rev 21, identifying chapter 20 (quite erroneously) as the "climactic vision of the Christian hope," and arbitrarily insists that the topic of the bodily resurrection of believers must be dealt with within these literary confines, suggesting—the last desperate swinging of the premillennial cause now becomes very wild indeed!—that otherwise the scent of incipient gnosticism will contaminate Rev 20.

Involved here, of course, are larger questions about the structure of the book of Revelation and the theme of chapter 20 and how it fits into the total structure. I would just briefly observe that, as I understand it, Rev 20 is one part of an extensive section of the book in which the final disposition of all the major figures who have appeared is dealt with, each in turn. Revelation 20 is Satan's turn, and it is no wonder then that this chapter does not feature the final resurrection of the redeemed. Their turn comes in Rev 21:1–8, the last part of the long section of final judgments. If one is going to speak of a "climactic vision of Christian hope," a more appropriate selection would be Rev 21:9ff., which does present the resurrection-consummation [[116]] event under the imagery of the revelation of the bride of the Lamb in the glory of the eternal city. This theme is also present in Rev 21:1–8. Whether or not one accepts precisely this analysis of the structure, it should be apparent that one cannot just blithely proceed on the basis of the unvalidated assumptions made in point four of the Response.

As for point five, the Response slights the relevance of Rev 2:10–11 and 14:13, especially the "from henceforth" in 14:13. In the comparison of Rev 6:9–11 with Rev 20:4–6, faulty logic is again in evidence. Noting that these two pictures of the church differ in that the number of the Christians is incomplete in the vision of the intermediate state in Rev 6, the Response argues that if the relation between the two is not that of simple identity but rather of continuity, Rev 20 "must refer" to a subsequent stage which "can only be" the bodily resurrection beyond the intermediate state.

But the logical options are obviously not so limited. There is indeed progression in the perspective from incompleteness to completeness as we move from Rev 6 to Rev 20, but both passages portray the intermediate state. Revelation 20:4–6 views the entire period of the church in the intermediate state as a whole, while Rev 6:9–11 sees it at a particular (early) point. And, contrary to the Response, the eschatological position and posture of the Christians is precisely the same in both passages. A judgment has already been rendered in favor of the martyrs in Rev 6, just as for the martyrs in Rev 20. It is attested by the bestowal of white priestly robes, indicative of the verdict of righteousness. And like the saints in Rev 20, who share with Christ in the reign of his sabbatical session on the heavenly throne, so too the overcomers of Rev 6 (cf. Rev 3:5) are granted royal sabbatical repose.

The priestly aspect of the service of the church before the throne is also present in both passages. Moreover, in each case, while favorable judgment has already been rendered for the martyrs, the punitive vengeance of God against their wicked slayers is still future. In Rev 6 the martyrs pray for that ultimate vindication and in Rev 20 that consummation of divine judgment is yet to come after "the thousand years." This full and striking parallelism between Rev 20:4–6 and the vision of Rev 6:9–11, which admittedly refers to the [[117]] intermediate state, is a powerful confirmation that "the first resurrection" of Rev 20 refers to the experience of death through which the Christian enters that blessed and holy state.

As an appendix to the foregoing review of the Response, I shall venture a few comments on certain broader aspects of the millennial question.

The policy adopted in some of our Reformed churches allowing considerable confessional latitude on the subject of the millennium would suggest that this is an isolable exegetical question, not affected by the general body of Reformed doctrine and not necessarily affecting the latter in any confessionally significant way. But that stance might well stand some rethinking. Of special interest is the way the doctrine of common grace fares in different millennial reconstructions, for that doctrine is a cornerstone of the Reformed view of history.

The world order of common grace is covenantally formalized in the postdiluvian revelation to Noah (Gen 8:15–9:17). This covenant of God with all the earth granted to the just and the unjust in common a measure of the blessings of earthly life, including the provision of the judicial structure of the state. And God defined this arrangement as one that would continue valid and operative until the termination of the present cosmos. The consummation will introduce through cosmic re-creation a world order in which no blessings of any kind are apportioned as a common gift in which the unjust participate but all blessings are for the beneficiaries of special redemptive grace alone. Until that re-creation, however, the order of common grace is firmly established by divine stipulation and decree. It is open to penetration at points by the world order to come, but it is not subject to eclipse until the consummation.

The millennium envisaged by classical premillennialism is in conflict with the terms of the covenant of common grace. It features a theocracy on earth before the consummation, a universal kingdom of Christ in which those blessings hitherto received in common by all men and often in greater measure by the unjust than the just are no longer apportioned according to the principle of common grace but according to a policy of special favor to the people of God. The redeemed are in fact already in possession of glorified natures and experience their public vindication over against the world of unjust men. The premillenarian's [[118]] millennium would thus abrogate the common grace order prior to the consummation, in contradiction of God's covenantal guarantees.

The cogency of this criticism might be questioned on the grounds that history has already witnessed an earthly theocracy established by divine appointment. But theocratic Israel under the old covenant was a limited, local kingdom. Other nations coexisted with Israel and the common grace order thus continued uninterrupted, true to the terms of God's covenant. In the case of the millennial theocracy of classical premillennialism, however, there would be a universal suppression of the common grace principle with its judicial order of the state, because this theocracy would itself be a universal world order.

There are, of course, non-classical forms of premillennialism that would, or at least could, avoid this difficulty since they foresee a millennial theocracy that is not universal but a restoration, with messianic overtones, of the limited Israelite institution of Old Testament days. Such varieties of premillennialism, however, contravene Reformed theology even more blatantly in other vital respects. (See my remarks in *WTJ* 36 [1974]: 245–47.)

In so far as postmillennialism joins premillennialism in locating the realization of messianic kingdom prophecies in an earthly millennial kingdom, it too is incompatible with the covenant of common grace. Moreover, because of the particular nature of the millennial theocracy of postmillennialism, the postmillennialist is lured into a misinterpretation of the theocratic covenant mediated through Moses.

On the premillennial view, the millennial kingdom is a church-kingdom ruled over by Christ, who, on this view, has returned before the millennium. On the postmillennial view, Christ does not return with the glorified church until after the millennium and meanwhile the millennial kingdom is a state-kingdom. Now if a theocratic state fulfills the prophetic blessing ideal of the old covenant, it must also fulfill the legal stipulation ideal of that covenant. Covenantal prophecy and law must agree with each other. Hence, the covenant which God gave Israel as the constitution for the Old Testament theocratic kingdom will be interpreted by a consistent postmillennialist as though it were the constitution for an ordinary state kingdom. What was meant to [[119]] apply to the special redemptive institution of the theocracy—the demand to confess God, the guarantee that obedience to the covenant stipulations will be rewarded with earthly prosperity and power, etc.—must all be regarded by the postmillennialist as normative for the state, any state. And he looks to the millennium for the universal realization of this supposed ideal of old covenant law. In this postmillennial compounding of errors the biblical concepts of the common and the holy are confounded. What the covenant of common grace makes secular is sacralized and what the covenant of redemptive theocracy makes sacred is secularized.

It appears then that certain varieties at least of premillennialism and postmillennialism are not compatible with the biblical doctrine of common grace, so important in Reformed theology. The amillennial position, on the other hand, is altogether consistent with it.

To propose that ecclesiastical policy should be changed so as to curtail or even reduce confessional liberty as to millennial position is no doubt to propound an idea whose time has not yet come. Nevertheless, that policy is a symptom of the neglect that the area of eschatology has suffered in the enterprise of systematic theology, which is mandated by the unity of biblical truth. Perhaps, ready or not, we are being drawn indirectly into a more thoroughgoing integration of eschatology into the Reformed system of theology. For within the Reformed community movements have emerged, admirable for their concern and, in many ways, achievement in formulating a Christian world view and analyzing biblical law, but radically flawed by their failure to do justice to precisely those principles we have found to be critical for a systematic treatment of eschatology, the biblical principles of the common and the holy.

CHAPTER SIXTEEN

Har Magedon: The End of the Millennium

(1996)

Some sixty years ago C. C. Torrey published a study of Har Magedon that has not received the attention it deserves.[1] His explanation of the Hebrew terms transliterated into Greek as *har magedōn* (Rev 16:16) is accepted in the present article and additional evidence for it adduced. Further, it will be shown how this interpretation leads to the recognition that Har Magedon is Mount Zaphon/Zion and that the Har Magedon battle is the Gog-Magog crisis of Ezek 38–39. This in turn proves to be of critical significance in the millennium debate. For it adds a final, decisive point to the traditional amillennial argument for the identification of the conflict marking the end of the millennium (Rev 20:7–10) with the climactic battle of the great day of the Lord to which the Apocalypse repeatedly returns, as in the Rev 16:12–16 account of the Har Magedon encounter itself and the Rev 19:11–21 prophecy of the war waged by the messianic judge.[2]

Har Magedon, the Mount of Assembly

Derivation from har môᶜēd

Har is the Hebrew word for mountain. The meaning of *magedōn* is disputed. The most common view, following the variant reading *mageddōn* in Rev 16:16, identifies it as Megiddo, site of notable battles in Israel's history (Judg 5; 2 Chr 35:22–25) and thus an apt designation for the place where "the

---

1. C. C. Torrey, "Armageddon," *HTR* 31 (1938): 237–48.

2. See also Rev 6:12–17; 11:7–13, 18; 13:7; 14:17–20; 17:11–14. Cf. Meredith G. Kline, "A Study in the Structure of the Revelation of John" (unpublished). A full exposition of the recapitulatory structure of Revelation is found in G. K. Beale, *The Book of Revelation: A Commentary on the Greek Text*, NIGTC (Grand Rapids: Eerdmans, 1999).

battle of the great day" occurs. In addition to the frequent objection that there is no mountain of Megiddo, the area being rather a vast plain, Torrey stressed the fact that the vicinity of Jerusalem is where biblical prophecies uniformly locate the eschatological crisis in which the armies of the nations assemble against God and his people.[3] He cited passages like Zech 12 and 14, Joel 3 [4], Isa 29:1–7, and, of particular relevance, Rev 14:14ff. (esp. v. 20) and 20:7ff. (esp. v. 9), which parallel 16:14–16 in the structure of the Apocalypse.[4]

[[208]] Torrey's own solution, developing an earlier conjecture by F. Hommel, was to trace *har magedōn* to the Hebrew *har môʿēd* (cf. Isa 14:13), "Mount of Assembly." He noted the appropriate association of *har môʿēd* with Jerusalem and dealt with the question of transcriptional equivalence. The apparent differences between the Hebrew *har môʿēd* and the *har magedōn* rendering can be readily accounted for. Representation of the consonant *ayin* by Greek *gamma* is well attested. Also, in Hebrew *-ôn* is an afformative to nouns, including place names.[5]

Antipodal to the Abyss

Supportive of the derivation of *har magedōn* from *har môʿēd* is the fact that each of these expressions in its single biblical appearance is paired with Hades as its polar opposite on the cosmic axis. In the Isa 14:13 context the contrast is drawn between the heights to which the king of Babylon aspires as the site of his throne and the depths to which he is actually to descend. He will not ascend to the *har môʿēd*, above the stars of God, to the *yarkĕtê ṣāpôn*, "heights of heaven," as he boasts (vv. 13–14), but will be brought down to the *yarkĕtê bôr*, "depths of the Pit" (v. 15).[6] Correspondingly, in the book of Revelation *har magedōn* (16:16) is contrastively paired with *Abaddōn* (9:11), another Hebrew term, here the name of the angel of the Abyss, and in its Old Testament appearances a synonym of Sheol (Job 26:6; 28:22; 31:12; Ps 88:12; Prov 15:11; 27:20). The Abaddon of Rev 9:11 is then the equivalent of the Sheol and Pit of Isa 14:15. And the *har* (mountain) element in *har magedōn* (Rev 16:16) of course contrasts with the Pit of Abaddon, as does the *har* in *har môʿēd* (Isa 14:13).

3. The prophetic idiom is typo-symbolical, not literal, but that is a separate issue.

4. Cf. Ps 48:1–8 [2–9]; Isa 24:21–23; Mic 4:11–13; Zeph 3:8.

5. Examples especially pertinent in the present context are *ṣāpôn*, *ʾăbaddôn*, and the spelling of Megiddo as *mĕgiddôn* in Zech 12:11.

6. For further discussion of the terms *yarkĕtê* and *ṣāpôn* see below.

That *har magedōn* is to be perceived as paired with *Abaddōn* even though they do not appear in the same immediate context is indicated by certain factors besides their antipodal semantic relationship. One is that in the book of Revelation these two terms, and these alone, are described as *Hebraisti*, "in Hebrew."[7] Another factor is their parallel placement in the literary structure of the Apocalypse: within an overall chiastic arrangement they appear in the corresponding series of the trumpets and the bowls of wrath, in each case at the climax.

In short, then, we find that in Isa 14 and the book of Revelation there are matching antonymic pairings of *har môʿēd* and *har magedōn* with the pit of Hades. Within the framework of this parallelism the *har môʿēd* of Isa 14:13 is the equivalent of the *har magedōn* of Rev 16:16 and as such is to be understood as its proper derivation and explanation. Accordingly, *har magedōn* signifies "Mount of Assembly/Gathering" and is a designation for the supernal realm.

As an appendix to this point we would note that the term *môʿēd*, if seen as the Hebrew behind *magedōn*, provides a further point of linkage for the
[[209]] pairing of *har magedōn* and *Abaddōn*. For in Job 30:23 the Death/Sheol realm denoted by *Abaddōn* is called the *bêt môʿēd*, "house of gathering." Though Job longs to come to God's place of judgment, the heavenly council gathered on the *har môʿēd*, he is sure only of being brought down with all who live to their common appointed gathering, their house of gathering (*bêt môʿēd*) in Sheol. The association with *môʿēd*, "gathering," thus shared by Abaddon and Har Magedon intensifies the irony of those biblical passages where someone finds himself in Abaddon/Sheol who had laid claim to Har Magedon or gathered forces against it.[8]

Hebraisti

There is another overlooked clue to the meaning of *har magedōn* in Rev 16:16 itself. As noted in the discussion of the relationship between *har magedōn* and *Abaddōn*, each term is identified as *Hebraisti* (which can refer to Aramaic as well as Hebrew). Our clue has to do with a stylistic feature characterizing the appearance of such transliterated words in the Greek

---

7. Perhaps a desire to flag the correspondence with *Abaddōn* prompted the addition of -*ōn* to *magedōn*.

8. For a similar situation involving the *ʾōhel môʿēd*, the tent of gathering, compare the experience of Korah in Num 16.

text of the New Testament: these words are regularly accompanied by an explanation of some sort, even by a translation sometimes. The *Abaddōn* counterpart to *har magedōn* in Rev 9:11 is a good example: "They had a king over them, the angel of the Abyss, whose name in Hebrew is Abaddon, and who has in Greek the name Apollyon (Destroyer)."

By way of further illustration it will suffice to mention those instances where the transliterated word is specifically identified as *Hebraisti*. These turn out to be all the more apropos in that this use of *Hebraisti* is an exclusively Johannine trait within the New Testament, with four instances in John's gospel besides the two in Revelation.[9] In three of the cases in the gospel the word in question is the name of a place. In each case the context furnishes at least an identification of the place thus denoted, even if not a translation. In John 5:2 Bethesda (with variants Bethsaida, Bethzatha, Belzetha) is identified as a particular pool in Jerusalem having five porches or colonnades. Similarly, in John 19:13 the Aramaic *Gabbatha* (of uncertain meaning) is identified by the Greek term *Lithostrōton* ("stone pavement or mosaic"), the designation of Pilate's judgment seat to which *Gabbatha* is appended. In the case of the reference to the site of the crucifixion in John 19:17 the Greek name *Kraniou* ("of the skull") affords the translation of the Aramaic name *Golgotha*, which is added to it.[10] In John's resurrection narrative the Aramaic *rabbouni* is at once explained by the Greek *didaskale*, "teacher" (John 20:16).

This consistent pattern creates a strong presumption that an accompanying explanation will be found in Rev 16:16 for *har magedōn*, the place name there with the *Hebraisti* label. Such an explanation can be shown to be present once it is recognized that *har magedōn* is based on *har môʿēd*. The [[210]] semantic connection is between *Magedōn* and the main verb in the statement: "And he gathered (*synēgagen*) them into the place called in Hebrew Har Magedon." The verb *synagō* interpretively echoes the noun *magedōn*—he gathered them to the Mount of Gathering. In effect it translates *magedōn*, establishing its derivation from *môʿēd*, "gathering." *Synagō* is indeed the verb used in the LXX to render *yāʿad* ("appoint"; *niphal* "assemble by appointment"), the root of *môʿēd* (an appointed time or place of assembly).

An instructive parallel is found in Num 10, where an interpretive wordplay affords an explanation of *ʾōhel môʿēd*, "tent of meeting/gathering," which symbolically points to the same heavenly reality that the *har*

---

9. Cf. *nai, amēn* (Rev 1:7).

10. The explanatory role of the Greek is clear in the Aramaic-Greek sequence found in Matt 27:33; Mark 15:22.

môʿēd represents.[11] Directions are given to Moses that at the sounding of a certain trumpet signal "the whole assembly (*ʿēdâ*, from the root *yāʿad*) shall gather (*yāʿad*) unto you at the entrance to the Tent of Meeting (*ʾōhel môʿēd*)" (v. 3). The verb of gathering that brings out the significance of *ʾōhel môʿēd* is rendered in the LXX of Num 10:3 by the same *synagō* that explains *har magedōn* in Rev 16:16.[12] Numbers 10:3 thus corroborates our view of how *synagō* functions in Rev 16:16.

We conclude that the evidence of the *Hebraisti* clue in Rev 16:16 clinches the case for the *har môʿēd* derivation of *har magedōn*.

Har Magedon, Mount Zaphon/Zion

Appositional to *har môʿēd* in Isa 14:13 is the phrase *yarkĕtê ṣāpôn* (Zaphon). Accordingly, what is disclosed about *ṣāpôn*, and particularly *yarkĕtê ṣāpôn*, in this and other contexts will contribute to our picture of the *har môʿēd* and thus of Har Magedon. The data that emerge through the Zaphon connection will also be found to confirm further the derivation of *har magedōn* from *har môʿēd*.

Zaphon, Realm of Deity

In texts from Ugarit on the north Syrian coast, Zaphon is the name of a mountain about thirty miles north of Ugarit that was regarded as the residence of Baal.[13] As a localized representation of the cosmic abode of the gods, Mount Zaphon shared its designation with the celestial realm. In the Old Testament, *ṣāpôn* means "north."[14] But it may also denote Zaphon, the terrestrial mountain;[15] or Zaphon, the mythological realm of the gods;

11. On this see further below.

12. For other examples of *yāʿad* translated by *synagō* in the LXX cf. Neh 6:2, 10; Ps 48:4 [5].

13. "Zaphon" has been traced to *ṣpw/y*, "to look out" (used, e.g., in Ps 66:7 for God's surveillance of the nations from the heights of heaven), or to *ṣpn*, "to hide." Opinions differ on whether its application to Mount Zaphon was direct or secondary, with a (storm)wind as the primary designee.

14. Most now explain this as another instance of naming quarters of the globe after prominent topographical features, in this case after Mount Zaphon to the north of Israel.

15. Ezek 32:20; Ps 89:12 [13] are possible instances of this usage.

or, as a demythologized figure, the heaven of the Lord God; or the holy mountain of God, Zion, as the visible earthly projection of God's heaven.

The phrase *yarkětê ṣāpôn* appears in Ps 48:2 [3]; Isa 14:13; Ezek 38:6, 15; 39:2. Its meaning is clearly seen in Isa 14, where it stands in apposition [[211]] with phrases (including *har môʿēd*) that refer to the heavens to which the king of Babylon aspires and in opposition to the *yarkětê bôr* into which the king will actually be cast. Some commentators, especially those who see a reference not to Zaphon the mountain of Baal but to a mountain of El farther north, would translate "the distant north." It is evident, however, from the contrastive pairing with *yarkětê bôr*, the Pit of Sheol, that *yarkětê ṣāpôn* concerns a vertical, not horizontal, dimension. It refers not to a quarter of the earth but to a level of the cosmos, denoting the supernal realm, the celestial zenith, while its antipodal opposite, *yarkětê bôr*, denotes the infernal region, the netherworld nadir. In these phrases *yarkětê*, which in the singular means "side" and in the dual "recesses, extreme parts," signifies the remotest reaches, the utmost height or depth.[16]

There are other passages where *ṣāpôn* has been understood as referring to the celestial realm. One is Ps 89:12 [13]. Above, it was cited as a possible instance of *ṣāpôn* as Mount Zaphon. Favoring that is the conjoined mention of mounts Tabor, Hermon, and Amanus (taking *ymn* as an alternative for *ʾmn*), the mountain of El. Another view is that *ṣāpôn* here signifies "clouds," an appropriate pairing being produced by emending *yāmîn* to *yammîm*, "seas." Problematic for the rendering "the north and south" is the absence of a concept parallel to this in the context. What does parallel God's creating of *ṣāpôn* and the south (v. 12 [13]) is God's founding of the heaven and earth (v. 11 [12]). This favors understanding *ṣāpôn* as the heavens, with its lower cosmic counterpart designated "south" as a play on the meaning of *ṣāpôn* as "north." Note also this psalm's emphasis on God's heavenly throne site (vv. 5–8, 13–14 [6–9, 14–15]).

Job 26:7 is one of two passages in Job that contain a similar use of *ṣāpôn*.[17] Here again the perspective is cosmic with references to the upper and lower extremes of creation in illustration of the universal scope of God's

---

16. The semantic equivalent of *yarkětê ṣāpôn* is found in the Ugaritic *ṣrrt ṣpn*, apparently meaning "insides/heart of Zaphon." Interestingly, one text in which this expression appears deals with a pretender to the divine throne—namely, with Ashtar the Rebel's futile attempt to ascend to Zaphon and occupy the throne of Baal.

17. The other is Job 37:22; on this see below under the discussion of Ezek 1:4, another such passage.

providential control. Sheol and Abaddon appear in verse 6 representing the lower region, and verse 7 then adds: "He spreads out *ṣāpôn* over emptiness; he suspends the earth on nothing." Clearly, a vertical rather than horizontal dimension is in view. The *ṣāpôn* is the sky above the earth.[18] But beyond that, as the preceding mention of Sheol/Abaddon suggests, the visible heavens point to the invisible heaven of God's abode.

The Zaphon with which *har môʿēd* (and thus *har magedōn*) is equated in Isa 14 is the celestial realm of deity. It should also be noted that through the tying in of the heaven-defying king with the *yarkĕtê ṣāpôn* in [[212]] this passage, the antichrist associations of Har Magedon in the Rev 16:16 episode begin to come into focus here.

Zaphon/Zion

In Ps 48 the *yarkĕtê ṣāpôn* connection yields the identification of Har Magedon with Zion, the earthly counterpart of the heavenly dwelling of Israel's God-King. The opening verses of this psalm introduce its celebration of the supremacy of Yahweh, the Suzerain, and his mountain-city: "Great is Yahweh, and greatly to be praised, in the city of our God (v. 1 [2]a, b, c); the mountain of his sanctuary, paragon of peaks, joy of all the earth (vv. 1 [2]d, 2 [3]a, b); Mount Zion, the heights of Zaphon,[19] city of the Great King (v. 2 [3]c, d, e)."[20] Linking the city and mountain of God, this passage declares Zion/Jerusalem to be the *yarkĕtê ṣāpôn*. This establishes that *har môʿēd* (appositional to *yarkĕtê ṣāpôn* in Isa 14:13) is Mount Zion, and thereby that *har magedōn* is related to the city of Jerusalem (and not to be explained by Megiddo).

This identification of *har môʿēd* is also attested by passages (like Ps 74:4; Lam 2:6) that speak of Zion as the place of God's *môʿēd* and the assembled

---

18. The astronomical reference in verse 7a is to the pole of the ecliptic, devoid of stars (so Meredith M. Kline in unpublished address). Another view is that *ṣāpôn* refers to the clouds suspended in the sky. Cf. J. De Savignac, "Le sens du terme *Ṣāpôn*," *UF* 16 (1984): 273–78.

19. There is no comparative preposition before *yarkĕtê ṣāpôn* and no need to take this as *comparatio decurtata* (cf. GKC 118r).

20. This arrangement (contrary to the numbered verses) into three triplets (A.B.C.) brings out some artful poetic features: the correspondence of the three cola (a.b.c.) of B and C (on the equivalence of Bc and Cc, cf. Isa 24:10–11); the summary *inclusio* provided by Cc with Aa–c. In biblical and mythological texts reference to the exalted throne-city of deity tends to prompt clusters of descriptive phrases in apposition.

congregation (*ʿēdâ*) of his people, and most graphically by the locating of the *ʾōhel môʿēd*, "tent of meeting," and its temple continuation in Zion.[21] In the *ʾōhel môʿēd* God met (*yāʿad*) and spoke with his people (Exod 25:22; 29:42–43; Num 17:4 [19]), his presence being mediated through the Glory theophany enthroned amid the cherubim. The tent was thus an earthly replica of the divine council in heaven, where the Most High sits as King surrounded by his assembled hosts.[22]

The relevance of Ps 48 for Har Magedon extends beyond its identification of *yarkĕtê ṣāpôn*, the *har môʿēd* equivalent, with Zion/Jerusalem. This psalm also relates how the rebellious kings gather (*yāʿad*) there against Yahweh (v. 4 [5]), who shatters their advancing forces and secures the eschatological peace of his city (vv. 5ff. [6ff.]). All the key elements of the Har Magedon event of Rev 16:16 are united here in connection with the *har môʿēd* (Zaphon) site, a signal corroboration of the explanation of *har magedōn* as *har môʿēd*.[23]

Har môʿēd/magedōn is then the place of God's royal presence, whether heavenly archetype or earthly ectype, where he engages in judicial surveillance of the world (Lookout Mountain); where he gathers the gods (cf. Ps 82:1) for deliberation (Council Mountain); where he musters his armies for [[213]] battle (Marshal Mountain); where he assembles the company of his holy ones, spirits of just men made perfect with myriads of angels (Ecclesia Mountain).[24] Echoing Ps 48, Heb 12:18–29 displays these varied facets of Har Magedon, Mount of Gathering, and identifies it as Zion, heavenly Jerusalem, city of the living God, the Great King.

The story of the earthly Har Magedon goes back to the beginnings of human history when this mountain of God rose up as a cosmic axis in Eden. There the battle of Har Magedon was joined as Satan challenged the God of the mountain and overcame the first Adam, the appointed guardian of the garden-sanctuary.[25] In redemptive history Zion was a typological renewal of Har Magedon, the setting at the dawning of the new covenant age for

21. Cf. Ps 15:1. Similarly in Canaanite mythology the tent of the deity and his mountain are conjoined.

22. Cf. Ps 78:69. On the replication of the heavenly archetype in the tabernacle see *IOS*, 39–42.

23. The same situation obtains in Ezek 38–39, to be examined presently.

24. In secular texts both the Greek *ekklēsia* and equivalents of *môʿēd* are used for a civil assembly. An example of the latter is the designation of the Byblos assembly in the Wen-Amun text.

25. See *KP*, 121–22.

another momentous encounter in the continuing warfare, this time resulting in a decisive victory of Jesus, the second Adam, over the evil one. The typological Zion/Jerusalem provides the symbolic scenery for prophecies of the climactic conflict in the war of the ages. Through his antichrist beast and his allied kings gathered to Gathering Mountain, Satan will make his last attempt to usurp Har Magedon. But the Lamb, the Lord of the mountain, and his assembled armies will triumph in this final battle of Har Magedon, the battle of the great day of God Almighty (Rev 16:14–16; 19:11–21; 20:7–10).

Har Magedon and Magog

Following the trail of *har magedōn* back to *har môʿēd* has led us to examine a set of Old Testament passages containing the phrase *yarkětê ṣāpôn*. From the first two (Isa 14; Ps 48) it has appeared that *har môʿēd/magedōn* is identifiable with Mount Zaphon/Zion. Ezekiel 38–39 is a third such passage, and here we discover a fundamental correspondence between the Zaphon/Magedon and Gog-Magog concepts. That means that the Har Magedon crisis of Rev 16:14–16 (and the series of parallel passages in Revelation) is to be identified with the millennium-ending Gog-Magog event of 20:7–10. For the Rev 20 passage is replete with allusions to Ezek 38–39, including, along with the explicit mention of Gog and Magog, the distinctive central theme of Ezek 38–39, the universal gathering of the world forces to destroy God's people and their catastrophic overthrow by the descent of fiery judgment from heaven.[26] Accordingly it is generally acknowledged that Ezekiel's prophecy and the vision of the loosing of Satan after the thousand years in Rev 20 describe the same eschatological event.

A main consideration in establishing the identity of the Rev 16 Har Magedon crisis and the Ezek 38–39 Gog crisis (and thus the Rev 20 Gog crisis) is the antichrist element common to both.[27] The antichrist [[214]] identity of the dragon-like beast in the Har Magedon episode would be acknowledged by most, irrespective of their millennial preferences. For the continuity of this beast of Rev 16 with the fourth beast of Dan 7 (in the final phase of its little-horn expression) is obvious, and in Daniel an alternative representation of this bestial eschatological foe is the self-deifying king of Dan 11:36,

26. For further details see below.

27. "Antichrist" is used here in the popular sense, as a designation for the man of sin figure referred to in 2 Thess 2:3–10.

the figure interpreted by Paul as the antichrist (2 Thess 2:4). It remains now to show that the antichrist element is also conspicuously present in Ezek 38–39 among the other major features of this Gog-Magog prophecy that appear again in the Apocalyptic accounts of Har Magedon.[28] Gog's antichrist characteristics may best be elicited through an examination of his provenance and his destination.

Provenance of Gog

A description of Gog's place of origin is included in the opening account of his hostile advance with his military forces against the community of God's people (Ezek 38:1–13). A condensed recapitulation of this portrayal of Gog appears as an introduction (38:14–16) to the next section, which presents God's judgment on Gog (38:17–23), and once again by way of introduction (39:1–2) to the final section, which contains a double elaboration of the divine judgment (39:3–8; 39:9–29).[29]

Whatever details are omitted from the two abbreviated recapitulations of the opening section, one feature included each time is Gog's provenance, the *yarkĕtê ṣāpôn* (Ezek 38:6, 15; 39:2). It is from the heights of Zaphon that God brings Gog with all his armies to overthrow them on the mountains of Israel. Gog is characterized by the antichrist syndrome: he is a pretender to the throne of heaven. The correspondence of his experience to the king of Babylon typology in Isa 14 is seen in the ironic motif of the polar contrast between his pretensions and his actual fate. Challenging Yahweh's sovereignty on Zion, Gog would take possession of the mountain heights of Israel. But he ends up with his vast military array in the depths of a valley. He lunged for a heavenly throne but plunged into a netherworld grave. Not the lofty polis (city) of the divine Suzerain but a necropolis was his destiny.

The ironic reversal is underscored by puns. Instead of the glory of *ṣiyyôn* (Zion), Gog's hallmark will be *ṣiyyûn* (Ezek 39:15), the marker that flagged

---

28. It may be recalled that such Har Magedon features were observed in the other *yarkĕtê ṣāpôn* passages. Psalm 48 relates the marshaling of enemy forces against Zaphon/Zion, and in Isa 14 the antichrist aspect of the Rev 16:16 episode is articulated in the aspirations of the king of Babylon, a prototypal antichrist who claims for himself supremacy on *har môʿēd*.

29. The two elaborations on the destruction of Gog are arranged in thematic parallel, each treating in turn (1) the destruction of Gog's weaponry (vv. 3, 9–10), (2) death-burial (vv. 4a, 11–16), (3) banquet (vv. 4b–5, 17–20), and (4) devastation of the nations (vv. 6a, 21).

for burial the corpses of his forces. The valley where his armies were buried is called the valley of the *ʿôbĕrîm* (Ezek 39:11), "those passing through or across," a term used for the dead, those who cross over from this world to the next.[30] In that sense will they turn out to be *ʿôbĕrîm* who set out to be *ʿôbĕrîm* in the sense of invaders traversing the land of Israel as [[215]] conquerors.[31] Another name given to the burial valley is *gêʾ hămôn gôg* (Ezek 39:11),[32] "valley of the multitude of Gog." It recalls God's wordplay interpretation of the new name, Abraham, he gave to Abram as a gift of grace: *ʾab hămôn gôyîm* (Gen 17:4–5), "father of a multitude of nations." In quest of such name-fame Gog mustered his multitudes, but his *hămôn*-name proclaimed his shame. Whereas *ʾab hămôn gôyîm* prophesied of Abraham's innumerable descendants out of all nations, elect in Jesus Christ and co-heirs with him of the kingdom of eternal life, the similar sounding *gêʾ hămôn gôg* signified the mountains of skeletons of Gog's hordes, cleared from God's kingdom land and cast into *gêʾ hinnōm*, the Gehenna valley of the dead, where the fire is never quenched.

The antichrist character of both the king of Babylon in Isa 14 and Gog in Ezek 38–39 is brought out by their connection with the *yarkĕtê ṣāpôn*. Gog, however, is not just an Old Testament prefiguration but the antichrist of the final crisis. In Rev 20:7–10 the Gog-Magog assault on Zion marks the end of the millennium. Within Ezek 38–39 indications also abound of the eschatological finality of the Gog crisis. As in Rev 20, it comes after a long age of secure preservation for God's people (Ezek 38:8)—in New Testament terms, after the age in which the church, though sorely persecuted, is preserved by the Lord to complete the great commission task (cf., e.g., Rev 11:7). And as the judgment on Gog in Rev 20 merges with the resurrection of the dead for final judgment (20:11–15), so God's judicial deliverance of his people from Gog in Ezek 38–39 institutes for them the eternal state of unending, never-again-disturbed felicity (39:21–29).

"Your [Gog's] place" (*mĕqômĕkā*) stands in Ezek 38:15 (within the first recapitulation section) as a substitute for the previous "land of Magog" (Ezek 38:2; cf. 39:6). Indeed, the term is probably an etymological play on Magog. *Māqôm* would interpret the *mā-* in Magog (explained either by the Akkadian *māt*, "land of," or as the Hebrew noun prefix signifying

30. Cf. Job 34:20; Ps 144:4. See M. S. Odell, "The City of Hamonah in Ezekiel 39:11–16: The Tumultuous City of Jerusalem," *CBQ* 56 (1994): 479–89.

31. Cf. Ezek 14:17; Zech 9:8.

32. Cf. *hămônâ* (Ezek 39:16).

"place").[33] The second syllable would then be taken as the name Gog, a name borne by an earlier Anatolian king (Gugu or Gyges) and here created out of Magog to serve as a symbolic pseudonym for the future antichrist foe. Even if "your [Gog's] place" is not intended as an etymological explanation of Magog, it certainly functions in this context as an equivalent of Magog. And since "your place" is identified as *yarkĕtê ṣāpôn* in Ezek 38:15,[34] its equivalent, Magog, is likewise identified as *yarkĕtê ṣāpôn*—and thus as *har môʿēd/magedōn*.

In fact *māqôm* could by itself, like *yarkĕtê ṣāpôn*, carry the idea of divine dwelling site. In Deuteronomy *māqôm* is used repeatedly for the place God would choose for his throne and residence—namely, Jerusalem (e.g., Deut 12:5, 14; 14:22–23; 15:20). In 2 Chr 36:15 it is used by itself as the designation of God's temple. It is equated with the mountain of Yahweh (Ps 24:3) [[216]] and refers to God's royal abode in heaven (Isa 26:21; Mic 1:3). In the light of this usage, "your [Gog's] place" in Ezek 38:15 would by itself seem to signify the position of supreme divine authority that Gog claimed. Along with *yarkĕtê ṣāpôn* it would be an expression of Gog's antichrist pretensions. The theme that thus emerges in Ezek 38–39 is that of Gog's coming from his place to challenge God at his place.

The Ezek 38–39 account of Gog's Zaphon provenance harks back to the Noahic chapter in the story of the mountain of God. The list of nations gathered by Gog begins and ends with northern nations near Gog's land of Magog (Ezek 38:2–6). Also, in the basic passage identifying Gog (38:2–3) and in the second recapitulation of it (39:1) Gog is titled Prince-Head of (Anatolian) Meshech and Tubal. Included in the mountainous territory of these northern nations was the Ararat region where Noah's ark came to rest.

Noah's ark was designed as a replica of the three-story universe, the cosmic city-temple of God (cf. Isa 66:1).[35] Established in sabbatical rest on the Ararat mountaintop, the ark was a redemptive restoration of the mountain of God in Eden, itself a replica of the heavenly Zaphon.

Supportive of the allusive relation of Ezek 38–39 to the flood event is the fact that the list of the seven military nations gathered by Gog, along with the three mercantile peoples introduced in 38:13, is patently based on the Gen 10 list of nations that developed in the postdiluvian movement of

33. As in *māqôm* itself.

34. Cf. Ezek 38:2–6, where Magog (v. 2) and *yarkĕtê ṣāpôn* (v. 6) form an *inclusio* for the survey of nations gathered by Gog.

35. See *KP*, 225–27.

the Noahic families out from Ararat. Indeed, the northern nations more closely associated with Gog, and Magog itself, appear at the head of the Gen 10 list (vv. 2–3).

Understood against this Ararat background, Gog's pretensions are again exposed as nothing less than claiming for himself the headship over the traditional mount of deity in his ancestral land in the north. Genesis 11 reports that the Babel-builders attempted a rebellious restitution of the lost Eden/Ararat mountain of God. Gog takes the challenge against the God of Zaphon to the ultimate, antichrist stage.

Destination of Gog

As related in Ezek 38–39, Gog's antichrist challenge takes place according to God's preannounced purpose and his sovereign orchestration of the event. Lured by the Lord to this final confrontation, Gog advances against "the mountains of Israel" (39:2, 17). It is God's chosen Mount Zion in the heart of these mountains that is his central point of attack. As in the case of the mustering of the bestial armies in Rev 16, the destination and intended target for Gog and his hosts is Har Magedon, where the Lord's Anointed is enthroned at his right hand.

The indications for this are clear, even though Zion is not mentioned by name in Ezek 38–39. God does speak of the mountains of Israel as "my mountains" (38:21) and of the land of Israel as "my land" (38:16). Implicit in that is the royal mountain-city where Yahweh dwells and rules over the mountainous domain he claims as his own. Also, such a capital city on the cosmic mountain was regarded as the center of the earth, and in 38:12 [[217]] Gog is described as scheming to assault the people of God dwelling at "the center (lit., navel) of the earth."[36] In that concept Gog's real objective is exposed—Yahweh's Mount of Assembly, rival to Gog's pseudo-Zaphon. In the Rev 20 version of Ezek 38–39, Gog's armies are explicitly said to compass "the beloved city" (v. 9), which is Jerusalem/Zion.

Though the term *ṣāpôn* is not applied to the mountain of God's Presence in Ezek 38–39, it is so used at the beginning of the book to denote the divine source of the prophet's visions. In Ezek 1:4 the storm-wind (*rûaḥ sĕʿārâ*),[37] the fiery cloud (*ʿānān*) that is the theophanic chariot, is said to

36. Cf. Ezek 5:5.

37. The combination of *rûaḥ* with *sĕʿārâ* involves a play on *rûaḥ* as both wind/breath and Spirit, frequent in references to the Glory-Spirit theophany.

come from Zaphon.[38] The same term for storm, *sĕʿārâ*, is used for God's golden whirlwind confrontation of Job (Job 38:1; 40:6), for the theophanic chariot in Elijah's translation into heaven (2 Kgs 2:1, 11), and for the storm chariot of the divine warrior advancing above his people as their defender (Zech 9:14). Ezekiel saw the theophany "coming" not as a storm moving across the earth from the geographical north[39] but as a parousia advent out of heaven. Ezekiel 1:4 is an expansion of the introductory statement (v. 1) that heaven was opened and Ezekiel saw visions of God. The storm-cloud theophany of verse 4 corresponds to the visions of God in verse 1, and the *ṣāpôn* of verse 4 is the heavens of verse 1. Divine appearances are comings, advents. Anticipatively setting the scene for Yahweh's revelation to Job out of the theophanic storm (*sĕʿārâ*, Job 38:1), Elihu announced that God's awesome golden majesty was "coming." Indeed, it was "coming from *ṣāpôn*" (Job 37:22).[40] The *ṣāpôn* of Ezek 1:4 is then the heavenly site of God's Glory, the celestial place of God's enthronement,[41] here opened up to be accessed by Ezekiel, as was characteristic of the call experience of Old Testament prophets. It is therefore in keeping with an attested concept and terminology of Ezekiel if we interpret the Ezek 38–39 scenario as a coming of antichrist Gog from his pseudo-Zaphon to challenge Yahweh on his true Zaphon. Agreeably, Gog's coming is portrayed in 38:9, 16 as a coming like a storm-cloud over the land and thus as a counterfeiting of the storm-cloud parousia of God's Glory by a pseudo-parousia.

The antichrist identity of the Gog figure of Ezek 38–39 is evidenced by the identification of this archenemy with the pseudo-Zaphon in the north and by his gathering of his universal hordes against Mount Zion, the authentic Zaphon/Har Magedon.

[[218]] Some detect in this motif the influence of the myth of the conflict between the gods of order and the chaos powers. In Ugaritic texts, for ex-

38. *Haṣṣāpôn* exhibits the use of the definite article for unique objects, like the sun; cf. GKC 126, 2(c).

39. This is the common interpretation of *haṣṣāpôn*. Confusingly it identifies *sĕʿārâ* as the stormy approach of enemies from the north (a recurring theme in Ezekiel, to be sure) after first recognizing that it is the Glory theophany of Yahweh.

40. See the comments above on the use of *ṣāpôn* in Job 26:7 for the cosmic north, heaven, the polar antithesis of Sheol/Abaddon.

41. In Ezek 3:12 this locus of God's Glory is called "his place," another term for the seat of divine sovereignty. The vision of the Glory-Spirit in Ezek 43 (explicitly linked, v. 3, to the prophet's opening vision) describes it as "the place of my throne" (v. 7).

ample, it is in connection with Baal's sovereign station at Zaphon that he must do battle against such rival divine beings. And with respect to Ezek 38–39 in particular, M. C. Astour suggests a more specific inspiration in the Cuthean Legend of Naram-Sin, which relates the ordeal of that king against northern hordes that are the embodiment of chaos demons.[42] But whatever imagery of the chaos myth has been taken up into the Scriptures, it appears there as demythologized figures of speech. In the Bible the conflict is not cosmological-existential but redemptive-eschatological.

Millennial Applications

According to the premillennial position, the thousand-year era of Rev 20:1–6 with the Gog-Magog episode at its close (vv. 7–10) follows chronologically the judgment of the antichrist beast portrayed in Rev 19:11ff. A common and telling criticism of this view calls attention to various points of identity between the Rev 20:7–10 crisis and the one referred to in 19:11ff. (and the series of parallel Apocalyptic passages, including 16:14–16).

The war (*polemos*) of Rev 20:8 is certainly "the war of the great day of God, the Almighty," the battle of Har Magedon described in 16:14–16. In each case it is the war to which Satan, the dragon, gathers the nations of the whole world. This universal gathering against the Lamb and the city beloved of the Lord is also referred to as Satan's deception of the whole world through the signs wrought by his agents, the beast from the sea and, particularly, the false prophet. Indeed, this theme of the deception-gathering appears in a series of five passages in the Apocalypse, concentrically arranged according to the subject(s) of the action, with 16:13–16 the centerpiece and 20:7–9 the concluding member. Satan as the ultimate deceiver is the subject in the first member of the chiasm (12:9) and in the last (20:7–9), where the deception is specified as the gathering. The false prophet, acting in association with the dragon-like beast, is the subject in the second member (13:14), which speaks of his world-deceiving signs, and in the fourth (19:17–20), where his deceptive signs are identified with the gathering of the kings of the earth against the messianic horseman and his armies. At the center of the chiasm (16:13–16) all three subjects appear together as the source of the demonic signs by which the kings of the whole earth are gathered to Har Magedon for the great war. This identification of Satan with his two agents

42. M. C. Astour, "Ezekiel's Prophecy of Gog and the Cuthean Legend of Naram-Sin," *JBL* 95 (1976): 567–79.

in the disastrous enterprise is also brought out in the fifth member of the chiasm (20:10).[43]

The identity of the war of 20:7–10 with the antichrist-Har Magedon battle is further indicated by other parallels between Satan and the beast. In [[219]] Rev 20 Satan emerges from his imprisonment in the Abyss, instigates his final challenge against the Lord and his city, and goes to his doom (vv. 7–10). The beast comes up out of the Abyss in the climactic stage of the eighth king, makes war against the witnesses of the Lamb in the true Jerusalem, and goes to his destruction (17:8–14; cf. 11:7–8; 19:20).

Our thesis at this point is that Ezek 38–39 proves to be the common source behind Rev 20:7–10 and the series of passages in Revelation referring to the antichrist-parousia event. Cataloguing the details that substantiate this will at the same time underscore and supplement the evidence cited above for the correspondence of Rev 20:7–10 and the other Apocalyptic passages with one another.

The relationship of Rev 20:7–10 to Ezek 38–39, obvious enough from the adoption of the Gog-Magog terminology in Rev 20, is also evidenced by a set of basic similarities: the marshaling of hordes from the four quarters of the earth (Ezek 38:2–7, 15; 39:4; Rev 20:8); the march of the gathered armies to encompass the saints in the city of God, center of the world (Ezek 38:7–9, 12, 16; Rev 20:9); the orchestration of the event by God (Ezek 38:4, 16; 39:2, 19; Rev 20:3, 7); the timing of the event after a lengthy period in which God's people were kept secure from such a universal assault (Ezek 38:8, 11; Rev 20:3); the eschatological finality of the crisis (Ezek 39:22, 26, 29; Rev 20:10ff.); and the fiery destruction of the evil forces (Ezek 38:22; 39:6; Rev 20:9–10).[44]

Just as clearly, the Gog-Magog prophecy of Ezek 38–39 is a primary source drawn on by Rev 16:14–16; 19:17–21 and the other Apocalyptic prophecies of the final conflict. Prominent in these passages is the major feature that marked the dependence of Rev 20:7–10 on the Ezekiel prophecy—namely, the universal gathering of the enemy armies (Rev 16:14–16; 17:12–14; 19:19; and compare 6:15 with Ezek 39:18–20), including too the historical setting of that event at the close of this world-age (Rev 6:12–17; 11:7–13; 16:16–17 [cf. 17:10–14]; 19:15–21), following an era in which it is given to the church to fulfill its mission of gospel witness (11:3–7; cf. 12:6, 14).

43. The NIV foists a pluperfect sense on the verbless clause that refers to the fate of the beast and false prophet.

44. Some of these points were mentioned earlier by way of demonstrating that the Gog of Ezek 38–39 is the final antichrist.

Further (and of central interest in this essay), the Har Magedon of Rev 16:16 is identifiable with Mount Zaphon, the provenance of Gog in Ezek 38–39. Particularly important is the significance of this location for the identity of Gog. His claimed lordship over the Zaphon site of the divine council, a challenge to the true Lord of Har Magedon, reveals the Gog of Ezek 38–39 to be the bestial antichrist agent of Satan in the Apocalyptic prophecies of the war of the great day. Such self-exaltation over all that is called God is the affront of this man of sin that provokes the parousia of the Lord Jesus to overthrow and destroy him (2 Thess 2:3–10). The pseudo-parousia attributed to this antichrist, a spectacle of satanic deception (2 Thess 2:9), is another feature found in Ezekiel's prophecy where, as we have noted, Gog's coming is portrayed as an advent in storm-cloud theophany (Ezek 38:9, 16). [[220]] Also, beast symbolism is used for the antichrist phenomenon in Revelation, and beast imagery is applied to Gog in Ezek 38:4; 39:2. Extensive evidence of the Ezekiel source is afforded by the Apocalyptic accounts of God's judgment on the beast. Instruments of judgment mentioned by both Ezekiel and John include earthquake (Ezek 38:19–20; Rev 6:12; 11:13; 16:18–20), sword (Ezek 38:21; Rev 19:15, 21), and destructive hail and fiery brimstone (Ezek 38:22; 39:6; Rev 16:21; 19:20). Most striking is the distinctive motif of God's summoning the birds and beasts to feed on the carcasses of the defeated armies Gog had gathered, the banquet theme elaborated in Ezek 39:4, 17–20 and incorporated into the account of Christ's victory over the beast and his assembled armies in Rev 19:17–18.

The conclusion is amply warranted that Ezek 38–39 is the common source of Rev 20:7–10 and the passages earlier in Revelation that deal with the eschatological battle. This confirms the standard amillennial contention that the Gog-Magog episode of Rev 20:7–10 is a recapitulation of the accounts of the Har Magedon crisis in these other passages. And the capstone for that argument is what we have discovered about the equation of Har Magedon (*môʿēd*) with Gog's place, Magog, the equation established by the Zaphon connection in Isa 14:13; Ps 48; Ezek 38–39. It now appears that the very term *har magedōn* itself identifies the Rev 16:14–16 event as the Gog-Magog event of 20:7–10.

Revelation 20:7–10 is not, as premillennialists would have it, an isolated, novel episode, not mentioned elsewhere in the book of Revelation. Rather, it belongs to a series of passages, including Rev 19:11–21, which premillennialists rightly regard as referring to the antichrist-Har Magedon crisis and the parousia of Christ. It therefore follows that the thousand years that precede the Gog-Magog crisis of Rev 20:7–10 precede the Har Magedon-parousia event related in the other passages. Har Magedon is not a prelude to the millennium, but a postlude. Har Magedon marks the end of the millennium. And that conclusion spells the end of premillennialism.

The conclusion that Har Magedon is the end of the millennium also contradicts the preterist approach to the Apocalypse. Preterists interpret the series of passages (except for Rev 20:7–10) that we have taken as prophecies of the final conflict as referring instead to past events, like the fall of Jerusalem or the collapse of the Roman empire. This approach with its drastic reductions of the Apocalyptic emphasis on the final global Gog crisis is understandably popular with postmillennialists, whose distinguishing notion is that the present age, the millennium, is—at least in its latter phase—a time not only of surpassing evangelistic success for the church but one of outward prosperity and peace.[45] Indeed, postmillennialism of the theonomic reconstructionism variety, in keeping with the theonomic insistence that Torah legislation enforcing the theocratic order is definitive of the church's [[221]] duty today, anticipates that the millennial success of the church's mission will involve its worldwide political dominance and the forcible elimination of public practice of non-Christian religions. They expect a fulfillment in this church age of the Old Testament prophecies of the restoration of the kingdom in the dimension of external dominion to the ends of the earth.[46]

For such postmillennial expectations, the biblical forecast of a global surge of anti-Christian forces as the immediate precursor of the parousia is obviously a problem. The postmillennialists' strategy is to confine the problem to Rev 20:7–10 by adopting the preterist approach and then to try to minimize the enormity of the crisis described in that passage. But once the preterist option is removed, their exegesis loses all plausibility as they attempt to deal with the whole series of Har Magedon-Gog passages and the recurring, progressively elaborated theme of the worldwide suppression of the gospel witness in which the millennium issues. Actually, Rev 20:7–10 by itself refutes the postmillennial projections, for it is evident there that the nations of the world have not become officially "Christianized" institutions

---

45. The postmillennial label is often given to those whose optimism is limited to the evangelistic sphere. See below for a suggested revision of millennial terminology.

46. Cf. D. Chilton: "All nations are absolutely required to be Christian, in their official capacity . . . Any nation that does not submit to the all-embracing rule of King Jesus will perish; all nations *shall* be Christianized . . . in this world as well as in the next" (*The Days of Vengeance* [Fort Worth: Dominion, 1987], 489), commenting on Rev 19:16.

during the millennium.[47] That is in accord with the consistent eschatological pattern of Scripture. In the visions of Dan 2 and 7, for example, the imperial power clearly retains its beast-character throughout history, ultimately prevailing against the saints. Not until the parousia of the Son of Man and the final, total elimination of the bestial empire do the people of the Most High receive the kingdom of glory and universal dominion.

Recognition of the identity of the Har Magedon and Gog-Magog events thus proves to be decisive for the rejection of any view, premillennialist or postmillennialist, that understands the millennium as an age that witnesses the fulfillment (at least in a provisional form) of the Old Testament prophecies of the coming of God's kingdom in external earthly grandeur. The kingdom of glory does not come until final judgment is executed against antichrist/Gog, and therefore not before the end of the millennium. There is no transitional stage in its appearing between the first and second advents of Christ. The glory kingdom comes only as a consummation reality and as such it abides uninterrupted, unchallenged for ever and ever.

Here is the fundamental difference in the eschatology of the several millennial views, the difference that our names for them should reflect. Two of the views are pre-consummation. They hold that a (transitional) realization of the Old Testament prophecies of the kingdom as an external imperial power occurs during the millennium and thus before the consummation. These two can be distinguished from each other in terms of how they relate the millennium [[222]] to the parousia as pre-parousia (the postmillennialists) and post-parousia (the premillennialists).[48] The amillennial position alone represents the post-consummation view of the coming of the kingdom of glory.[49]

---

47. This problem drives some to the so-called consistent preterist position, which extends the preterist hermeneutics to Rev 20:7ff. and so regards as past history what all others recognize as events that will usher in the world to come.

48. Their shared pre-consummation status signalizes a hermeneutical kinship between theonomic postmillennialists and (dispensational) premillennialists: both fail to understand the typological nature of the Israelite theocracy.

49. Within the post-consummation view there is room for differing expectations as to the extent of the church's missionary success and of Christian influence on culture, as long as the latter is perceived within the limits imposed by the terms and guarantees of God's covenant for the common order (cf. esp. Gen 8:20–9:17). It is a basic theological flaw in all pre-consummation views that their millennial scenarios entail violations of those divine covenantal commitments.

Bibliography

Astour, M. C. "Ezekiel's Prophecy of Gog and the Cuthean Legend of Naram-Sin." *JBL* 95 (1976): 567–79.
Bailey, L. R., Sr. *Biblical Perspectives on Death*. Philadelphia: Fortress, 1979.
Baltzer, K. *Das Bundesformular: Seine Ursprung und seine Verwendung im Alten Testament*. WMANT 4. Neukirchen: Neukirchener Verlag, 1960.
Barr, J. *The Semantics of Biblical Language*. London: Oxford University Press, 1961.
Batto, B. F. "Red Sea or Reed Sea?" *BAR* 10.4 (1984): 57–63.
———. "The Reed Sea: Requiescat in Pace." *JBL* 102 (1983): 27–35.
Beale, G. K. *The Book of Revelation: A Commentary on the Greek Text*. NIGTC. Grand Rapids: Eerdmans, 1999.
Blank, S. H. "An Effective Literary Device in Job XXXI." *JJS* 2 (1951): 105–7.
Blocher, H. *In the Beginning*. Downers Grove, IL: InterVarsity Press, 1984.
Brown, W. P. *Structure, Role, and Ideology in the Hebrew and Greek Texts of Genesis 1:1–2:3*. Atlanta: Scholars Press, 1993.
Brueggemann, W. "Amos 4:4–13 and Israel's Covenant Worship." *VT* 15 (1965): 1–15.
Chilton, D. *The Days of Vengeance*. Fort Worth: Dominion, 1987.
Clark, W. M. "The Flood and the Structure of the Pre-Patriarchal History." *ZAW* 83 (1971): 184–211.
Clifford, R. J. *Creation Accounts in the Ancient Near East and in the Bible*. Washington, DC: Catholic Biblical Association of America, 1994.
Cohen, A., ed. *The Soncino Chumash: The Five Books of Moses, with Haphtaroth*. London: Soncino, 1956.
Collins, C. J. "How Old Is The Earth? Anthropomorphic Days in Genesis 1:1–2:3." *Presbyterion* 20 (1994): 109–30.
Cooper, A. "Ps. 24:7–10: Mythology and Exegesis." *JBL* 102 (1983): 37–60.
Cottrell, J. W. "Abortion and the Mosaic Law." *CT* 17 (1973): 602–5.
Couroyer, B. "L'origine égyptienne du mot 'Pâque.'" *RB* 72 (1955): 481–96.
Dahood, M. "Eblaite *ì-du* and Hebrew *ʾēd*, 'Rain Cloud.'" *CBQ* 43 (1981): 534–38.

———. *Psalms I*. AB 16. Garden City, NY: Doubleday, 1966.

Day, J. "A Case of Inner Scriptural Interpretation: The Dependence of Isaiah 26:13–27:11 on Hosea 13:4–14:10 (Eng. 9) and Its Relevance to Some Theories of the Redaction of the 'Isaiah Apocalypse.'" *JTS* 31 (1980): 309–19.

Delitzsch, Franz. *New Commentary on Genesis*. Vol. 1. Edinburgh: T&T Clark, 1888.

De Savignac, J. "Le sens du term *Ṣāpôn*." *UF* 16 (1984): 273–78.

Dick, M. B. "Job 31: A Form-critical Study." PhD diss., Johns Hopkins University, 1977.

———. "The Legal Metaphor in Job 31." *CBQ* 41 (1979): 37–50.

Dillmann, A. *Genesis*. Vol. 1. Edinburgh: T&T Clark, 1897.

Doron, P. "A New Look at an Old Lex." *JANESCU* 1 (1969): 21–27.

Driver, S. R. *A Treatise on the Use of the Tenses in Hebrew*. 2nd ed. Oxford: Clarendon, 1881.

Elliott, R. H. *The Message of Genesis*. Nashville: Broadman, 1961.

Emerton, J. A. "A Textual Problem in Isaiah 25:2." *ZAW* 89 (1977): 64–73.

Engnell, I. *Studies in Divine Kingship in the Ancient Near East*. Uppsala: Almqvist & Wiksell, 1943.

Enz, Jacob J. "The Book of Exodus as a Literary Type for the Gospel of John." *JBL* 76 (1957): 208–24.

Fraine, J. de. *L'Aspect religieux de la royauté israélite*. Rome: Pontifical Biblical Institute, 1954.

Frankena, R. "The Vassal-Treaties of Esarhaddon and the Dating of Deuteronomy." *OtSt* 14 (1965): 122–54.

Frankfort, H. *Kingship and the Gods*. Chicago: University of Chicago Press, 1948.

Gammie, John G. "Behemoth and Leviathan: On the Didactic and Theological Significance of Job 40:15–41:26." Pages 217–31 in *Israelite Wisdom*. Edited by J. G. Gammie, W. A. Brueggemann, W. L. Humphreys, and J. M. Ward. Missoula, MT: Scholars Press, 1978.

Gardiner, A. *Egyptian Grammar*. London: Oxford University Press, 1964.

Gaster, T. H. *Thespis: Ritual, Myth, and Drama in the Ancient Near East*. New York: Schuman, 1950. Rev. ed., Garden City, NY: Doubleday, 1961.

Gemser, B. "The Importance of the Motive-Clause in Old Testament Law." Pages 50–66 in *Congress Volume: Copenhagen, 1953*. Edited by G. W. Anderson et al. VTSup 1. Leiden: Brill, 1953.

Glasson, T. E. "The 'Passover,' a Misnomer: The Meaning of the Verb *Pasach*." *JTS* 10 (1959): 79–84.

Goldbaum, F. C. "Two Hebrew Quasi-Adverbs: לכן and אכן." *JNES* 23 (1964): 132–35.
Gordon, C. H. "אלהים in Its Reputed Meaning of *Rulers, Judges*." *JBL* 54 (1935): 139–44.
———. "Belt-wrestling in the Bible World." *HUCA* 23 (1950–51): 131–36.
———. "Homer and Bible." *HUCA* 26 (1955): 43–108.
———. *Ugaritic Handbook*. Rome: Pontifical Biblical Institute, 1948.
———. *Ugaritic Manual*. Rome: Pontifical Biblical Institute, 1955.
Green, W. H. "The Sons of God and the Daughters of Men." *PRR* 5 (1894): 654–60.
———. *The Unity of the Book of Genesis*. New York: Scribner's, 1910.
Gundry, Robert H. "Recent Investigations into the Literary Genre 'Gospel.'" Pages 97–114 in *New Dimensions in New Testament Study*. Edited by R. N. Longenecker and M. C. Tenney. Grand Rapids: Zondervan, 1974.
Hasel, F. C. "Resurrection in the Theology of the Old Testament Apocalyptic." *ZAW* 92 (1980): 267–84.
Heidel, A. *The Babylonian Genesis*. Chicago: University of Chicago Press, 1963.
———. *The Gilgamesh Epic and Old Testament Parallels*. Chicago: University of Chicago Press, 1949.
Helfmeyer, F. J. "אוֹת." *TDOT* 1:167–88.
Hillers, Delbert R. "Delocutive Verbs in Biblical Hebrew." *JBL* 86 (1967): 320–24.
Hooke, S. H., ed. *Myth, Ritual, and Kingship*. Oxford: Clarendon, 1958.
Hummel, C. E. *The Galileo Connection*. Downers Grove, IL: InterVarsity Press, 1986.
International Congress for the History of Religions. *La Regalità Sacra—The Sacral Kingship*. SHR 4. Leiden: Brill, 1959.
Irwin, W. H. *Isaiah 28–33: Translation with Philological Notes*. BibOr 30. Rome: Pontifical Biblical Institute, 1977.
———. "The Punctuation of Isaiah 24:14–16*a* and 25:4*c*-5." *CBQ* 46 (1984): 215–22.
———. "Syntax and Style in Isaiah 26." *CBQ* 41 (1979): 240–61.
Jackson, B. S. "The Problem of Exod. 21:22–5 (*Ius Talionis*)." *VT* 23 (1973): 273–304.
Jacob, B. *Das erste Buch der Tora—Genesis*. Berlin: Schocken, 1934.
Jacobsen, Thorkild. *The Sumerian King List*. Chicago: University of Chicago Press, 1939.

Johnson, A. R. *Sacral Kingship in Ancient Israel*. Cardiff: University of Wales Press, 1955.

Joüon, P., and T. Muraoka. *A Grammar of Biblical Hebrew*. Rome: Pontifical Biblical Institute, 1993.

Kline, Meredith G. "Job." Pages 459–90 in *The Wycliffe Bible Commentary*. Edited by C. F. Pfeiffer. Chicago: Moody, 1962.

———. "A Study in the Structure of the Revelation of John." Unpublished manuscript.

———. "Of Works and Grace." *Presbyterion* 9 (1983): 85–92.

Kline, Meredith M. "The Holy Spirit as Covenant Witness." ThM diss., Westminster Theological Seminary, 1972.

Knierim, R. "Old Testament Form Criticism Reconsidered." *Int* 27 (1973): 435–68.

Korošec, V. *Hethitische Staatsverträge*. Leipzig: Hinrichs, 1931.

Kraeling, Emil G. "The Significance and Origin of Gen. 6:1–4." *JNES* 6 (1947): 193–208.

Lambert, W. G. *Babylonian Wisdom Literature*. Oxford: Clarendon, 1960.

Lightman, A. *Ancient Light*. Cambridge: Harvard University Press, 1991.

Maatman, R. *The Bible, Natural Science, and Evolution*. Sioux Center: Dordt College Press, 1970.

———. *The Impact of Evolutionary Theory: A Christian View*. Sioux Center: Dordt College Press, 1993.

Many, G. "Der Rechtsstreit mit Gott (*Rîb*) im Hiobbuch." PhD diss., Katholisch-Theologische Fakultät der Ludwig-Maximilian Universität, Munich, 1970.

Martin, Ralph P. *New Testament Foundations*. Vol. 1, *The Four Gospels*. Grand Rapids: Eerdmans, 1975.

Mendenhall, G. E. "Ancient Oriental and Biblical Law." *BA* 17.2 (1954): 26–44.

———. "Covenant Forms in Israelite Tradition." *BA* 17.3 (1954): 50–76.

———. *The Tenth Generation: The Origins of the Biblical Tradition*. Baltimore: Johns Hopkins University Press, 1973.

Michaels, J. Ramsey. "The First Resurrection: A Response." *WTJ* 39 (1976): 100–109.

Muilenburg, J. "The Form and Structure of the Covenantal Formulations." *VT* 9 (1959): 347–65.

Murray, John. "Calvin's Doctrine of Creation." *WTJ* 17 (1954): 21–44.

———. *Principles of Conduct*. London: Tyndale, 1957.

Odell, M. S. "The City of Hamonah in Ezekiel 39:11–16: The Tumultuous City of Jerusalem." *CBQ* 56 (1994): 479–89.

Paul, S. M. *Studies in the Book of the Covenant in the Light of Cuneiform and Biblical Law*. VTSup 18. Leiden: Brill, 1970.

Piper, Otto A. "Unchanging Promises: Exodus in the New Testament." *Int* 11 (1957): 3–22.

Plevnik, J. "The Taking Up of the Faithful and the Resurrection of the Dead in 1 Thessalonians 4:13–18." *CBQ* 46 (1984): 274–83.

Rabast, K. *Die Genesis*. Berlin: Evangelische Verlagsanstalt, 1950.

Rad, G. von. *Genesis*. Translated by John H. Marks. Philadelphia: Westminster, 1961. Originally published as *Das erste Buch Mose, Genesis* (Göttingen: Vandenhoeck & Ruprecht, 1956).

———. "Hiob XXXVIII und die altägyptische Weisheit." Pages 293–301 in *Wisdom in Israel and in the Ancient Near East*. Edited by M. Noth and D. W. Thomas. VTSup 3. Leiden: Brill, 1955. Translated in *The Problem of the Hexateuch and Other Essays* (New York: McGraw-Hill, 1966).

Ramm, B. *The Christian View of Science and Scripture*. Grand Rapids: Eerdmans, 1954.

Rengstorf, K. H. "σημεῖον." *TDNT* 7:200–269.

Richardson, A. *Genesis I–XI*. London: SCM, 1953.

Ridderbos, N. H. *Is There a Conflict Between Genesis 1 and Natural Science?* Grand Rapids: Eerdmans, 1957.

Roberts, J. J. M. "Job's Summons to Yahweh: The Exploitation of a Legal Metaphor." *ResQ* 16 (1973): 159–65.

Roth, D. L. "Genesis and the Real World." *Kerux* 9 (1994): 30–54.

Rowley, H. H. "Moses and the Decalogue." *Bulletin of the John Rylands Library* 34 (1951–52): 81–118.

Rushdoony, R. *The Institutes of Biblical Law*. Nutley, NJ: Craig Press, 1973.

Scholnick, S. H. "Lawsuit Drama in the Book of Job." PhD diss., Brandeis University, 1975.

Simpson, C. "The Book of Genesis." *IB* 1:437–829.

Smend, R. "Zur Geschichte von האמין." Pages 284–90 in *Hebräische Wortforschung*. VTSup 16. Leiden: Brill, 1967.

Speiser, E. A. "*ʾed* in the Story of Creation." *BASOR* 140 (1955): 9–11.

———. "The Stem *PLL* in Hebrew," *JBL* 82 (1963): 301–6.

Stonehouse, N. B. *The Witness of Matthew and Mark to Christ*. Philadelphia: Presbyterian Guardian, 1944.

Tate, M. E. *Psalms 51–100*. WBC 20. Dallas: Word, 1990.

Terrien, S. "Job." *IB* 3:877–1197.

Torrey, C. C. "Armageddon." *HTR* 31 (1938): 237–48.

Tromp, N. J. *Primitive Conceptions of Death and the Nether World in the Old Testament*. Rome: Pontifical Biblical Institute, 1969.

Tsevat, M. "The Meaning of the Book of Job." *HUCA* 37 (1966): 73–106.

———. "The Neo-Assyrian and Neo-Babylonian Vassal Oaths and the Prophet Ezekiel." *JBL* 78 (1959): 199–204.

Vaux, R. de. *Ancient Israel: Its Life and Institutions*. New York: McGraw-Hill, 1961.

Vos, G. *Biblical Theology*. Grand Rapids: Eerdmans, 1954.

Waltke, B. K., and M. O'Connor. *An Introduction to Biblical Hebrew Syntax*. Winona Lake, IN: Eisenbrauns, 1990.

Warfield, B. B. "Christian Supernaturalism." Pages 25–46 in *Studies in Theology*. New York: Oxford University Press, 1932.

Weinfeld, M. *Deuteronomy and the Deuteronomic School*. Oxford: Clarendon, 1972.

Weiser, A. "πιστεύω κτλ." *TWNT* 6:174–230.

Wenham, G. J. "Legal Forms in the Book of the Covenant." *TynBul* 22 (1971): 95–102.

Wijngaards, J. "Death and Resurrection in Covenantal Context (Hos. 6:2)." *VT* 17 (1967): 226–39.

Wildberger, H. " 'Glauben,' Erwägungen zu האמין." Pages 372–86 in *Hebräische Wortforschung*. VTSup 16. Leiden: Brill, 1967.

Williams, J. G. "Concerning One of the Apodictic Formulas." *VT* 14 (1964): 484–89.

Wilson, John A. "The Oath in Ancient Egypt." *JNES* 7 (1948): 129–56.

Wiseman, D. J. "Abban and Alalaḫ." *JCS* 12 (1958): 124–29.

———. *The Alalakh Tablets*. London: British Institute of Archaeology at Ankara, 1953.

———. *The Vassal-Treaties of Esarhaddon*. London: British School of Archaeology in Iraq, 1958.

Yadin, Yigael. *The Art of Warfare in Biblical Lands*. Vol. 2. New York: McGraw-Hill, 1963.

Young, E. J. *Studies in Genesis One*. Philadelphia: P&R, 1964.

Index of Modern Authors

Index of Ancient Sources

Exodus

Leviticus

Numbers

Deuteronomy

Proverbs

Ecclesiastes

Isaiah

NEW TESTAMENT

Matthew

Mark

Luke

John

DEAD SEA SCROLLS

Hodayot (1QH)

OTHER

Alalakh Tablets

Atrahasis

Descent of Ishtar to the Netherword

El Amarna Tablets

Gilgamesh Epic

Midrash Rabbah

Sefire

Ugaritic Textbook